THE BRAZILIAN SOUND

CHRIS MCGOWAN *and* **RICARDO PESSANHA**

The Brazilian Sound

REVISED AND EXPANDED EDITION

*Samba, Bossa Nova, and the
Popular Music of Brazil*

Temple University Press
Philadelphia

Temple University Press
1601 North Broad Street
Philadelphia, Pennsylvania 19122
www.temple.edu/tempress

Text design by Kate Nichols

♾ The paper used in this publication meets the requirements of the American National
Standard for Information Sciences—Permanence of Paper for Printed Library Materials,
ANSI Z39.48-1992

Library of Congress Cataloging-in-Publication Data

McGowan, Chris,
The Brazilian sound : samba, bossa nova, and the popular music of Brazil / Chris
McGowan and Ricardo Pessanha. — Rev. and expanded ed.
p.   cm.
Includes bibliographical references, discography, and index.
ISBN 978-1-59213-928-6 (cloth : alk. paper) — ISBN 978-1-59213-929-3 (pbk. : alk.
paper)
1. Popular music—Brazil—History and criticism.   I. Pessanha, Ricardo.   II. Title.
ML3487.B7M4 2008
781.640981—dc22   2008012515

040109P

CONTENTS

PREFACE TO THE REVISED AND EXPANDED EDITION

Not so long ago, it was hard for those outside Brazil to find a wide variety of that country's music in record stores or on the radio. How things have changed! Temple University Press published its first edition of our book in 1998, as the Internet was beginning to reach a mass audience. It is remarkable to look back over the years since and realize how much Brazilian music aficionados have benefited. On-line stores such as Amazon.com and iTunes offer thousands of samba, bossa nova, choro, and forró CDs and downloads, vastly more than were ever available previously in "brick-and-mortar" music stores. Audio and video available on MySpace, YouTube, blogs, and other Web sites enable musicians, popular or obscure, to find an audience anywhere in the world there is Internet access. What all this means is that Brazilian music is vastly more accessible now to everyone, whether you live in Scotland or South Africa, Iceland or Iowa. You can access music and videos of Zeca Pagodinho in Rio, maracatu groups in Recife, or the Banda de Pífanos de Caruaru, as long as you have a computer. Things have gotten better indeed.

Whereas once it was hard to find much information about Brazilian music in libraries or music stores, now there is an overwhelming amount of data available on the Internet. Yet it still helps to have a starting point to better understand samba, choro, bossa nova, and forró. With this second Temple University Press edition, as with our first, our intent is to provide an interesting and reliable introduction to Brazil's popular music, with an emphasis on major genres and artists. We have tried to present the most accurate information possible, and to make the music and artists come alive through anecdotes, descriptions, quotes, and biographical details.

Of course, Brazil is a huge country and its music is a vast subject. Trying to cover it all would be like trying to encompass all of the music of the United States in one book. Therefore, there are some areas—such as indigenous music from the Amazon, regional music from southern Brazil, and children's music—that we touch on only briefly.

We hope *The Brazilian Sound* will inspire the reader to listen to more artists from the Southern Hemisphere and that it will serve as a useful guidebook for new musical journeys.

ACKNOWLEDGMENTS

Monica Ferreira offered invaluable help on this new edition with her proofreading and by coordinating photos and interviews for the book. We want to thank Carla Cintia Conteiro for her insights, ideas, and criticism; Bruce Gilman for his suggestions; Ana Cecília Brignol, Adryana BB, Cristina Portella, José Emilio Rondeau, and Alda Baltazar for their help in Brazil; Janet Francendese, Charles Ault, Kate Nichols, and Gary Kramer of Temple University Press; our copyeditor, Suzanne Wolk; and Andrew Fisher, Linda Yudin, and Joe Robinson for assistance in the Northern Hemisphere. We are much obliged to João Parahyba (of Trio Mocotó) for his participation in our photo shoot of samba instruments.

Our thanks also go out to Criss Requate (Putumayo), Bruce McIntosh (Universal Music Latino), Cem Kurosman (Blue Note), Daniela Gebaile (Trama), Jodie Thomas (Decca Label Group), Priscila Stille (Biscoito Fino), Christina Campos (EMI Brazil), Bebel Prates, Eric Taller, David McLoughlin, José Dantas, and Lou Mounic.

And we greatly appreciate help given along the way by Tad Lathrop (the editor for our book's first edition, published by Billboard Books in 1991), Paul Winter (who wrote the preface to that version), Mario Aretana (Kuarup Discos), John Ii, Dexter Dwight, Sérgio Mielniczenko, photographer David Glat, Bahiatursa, Embratur, Lígia Campos, Charles Perrone, Terri Hinte, Lisa Urgo, Viola Galloway, Francisco Rodrigues, photographer Cláudio Vianna, and Carlos de Andrade.

We are greatly indebted to our interviewees, most especially Adryana BB, Antonio Adolfo, Alcione, the late Laurindo Almeida, Carlos de Andrade, Leny Andrade, Mario de Aretana, Geraldo Azevedo, Ana Maria Bahiana, João Bosco, Carlinhos Brown, Kirk Brundage, the late Charlie Byrd, Oscar Castro-Neves, Dori Caymmi, Gal Costa, Cravo Carbono, Hermínio Marques Dias Filho, Djavan, George Duke, Dexter Dwight, Engenheiros do Hawaii, Gilberto Gil, Don Grusin, Tim Hauser, Rildo Hora, the late Tom Jobim, Josias of Salgueiro, Jovino Santos Neto, Rita Lee, Téo Lima, Ivan Lins, Lobão, the late Herbie Mann, Lyle Mays, Mazzola, Zuza Homem de Mello, Sérgio Mendes, Margareth Menezes, Andre Midani, Sérgio Mielniczenko, Airto Moreira, Milton Nascimento, Paulo Cordeiro de Oliveira Neto, João Parahyba, Fernanda Porto, Flora Purim, Paulo Ricardo, João Jorge Rodrigues, J. Emilio Rondeau, Lulu Santos, Jovino Santos Neto, Bezerra da Silva, Simone, Toquinho, Alceu Valença, Herbert Vianna, Paulinho da Viola, Paul Winter, and Linda Yudin.

THE BRAZILIAN SOUND

MARABAIXO

CARIMBÓ
GUITARRADA
LAMBADA
SIRIÁ
TECHNOBREGA

BUMBA-MEU-BOI

(Northern Brazil)
BOI-BUMBÁ

(Northeast Brazil)
BAIÃO   FORRÓ
COCO   XOTE
EMBOLADA   XAXADO

RORAIMA

AMAPÁ

São Luis

Belém

Fortaleza

AMAZONAS

PARÁ

MARANHÃO

CEARÁ

RIO GRANDE
DO NORTE

• Manaus

PIAUÍ

PARAÍBA

PERNAMBUCO • Recife

ACRE

ALAGOAS

RONDÔNIA

TOCANTINS

BAHIA

SERGIPE

Salvador

MATO GROSSO

GOIÁS

Brasília

MINAS GERAIS

(Central Brazil)
MÚSICA SERTANEJA
CATERETÊ

Belo Horizonte

ESPÍRITO
SANTO

(Southeast Brazil)
JONGO
CALANGO
CAXAMBU
TOADA
MÚSICA SERTANEJA

MATO GROSSO
DO SUL

SÃO PAULO

• Três
Pontas

RIO DE JANEIRO

São Paulo

Rio de Janeiro

PARANÁ

AXÉ MUSIC
SAMBA-REGGAE
AFOXÉ
SAMBA DE RODA
CAPOEIRA

SANTA CATARINA

(Southern Brazil)
MÚSICA SERTANEJA
CHULA
BOI-DE-MAMÃO
VANERÃO

Porto Alegre

RIO GRANDE
DO SUL

SAMBA
CHORO
MAXIXE
MARCHA
BOSSA NOVA

FREVO
MARACATU
MANGUE

BRAZIL

Important Brazilian musical
genres and categories, and the
areas in which they first arose
or with which they are most
associated.

In Brazil, music is everywhere. You can find it in a complex rhythmic pattern beaten out by an old man with his fingers on a café table, in the thundering samba that echoes in the streets of Rio in the months prior to Carnaval, and in the bars where a guitar passes from hand to hand and everyone knows all the lyrics to all the classic Brazilian songs played late into the night. Music is part of the Brazilian soul, and rhythm is in the way people speak, in the way they walk, and even in the way they play soccer.

In Rio de Janeiro, after the national team has won an important soccer game, fireworks explode in the sky and samba detonates in the streets. On sidewalks and in city squares, the celebration begins. Impromptu percussion sections appear, made up of all types of Brazilians, rich and poor, black and brown and white. As participants pick up instruments—a drum, a scraper, a shaker—an intricate, ebullient samba *batucada* (percussion jam) builds. Each amateur music maker kicks in an interlocking rhythmic part to create a groove that would be the envy of most professional bands in other parts of the world. The singing and dancing inevitably go on for hours.

Music is a passport to happiness for Brazilians, an escape from everyday frustrations and (for most) a hard and difficult material life. "There's an amazing magical, mystical quality to Brazilian music. Their music is paradise," said jazz flutist Herbie Mann.[1]

▲ Rio de Janeiro. *(Courtesy of Embratur.)*

In the twentieth century more than a little of this paradise reached the outside world, and Brazil arguably had more of an impact on international popular music than any country other than the United States. It was successful abroad for as many reasons as there are types of Brazilian music. Just as the United States has exported a wide variety of musical genres, so too has Brazil, even though very few countries speak its national language, Portuguese.

Most Brazilian music shares three outstanding qualities. It has an intense lyricism tied to its Portuguese heritage that often makes for beautiful, highly expressive melodies, enhanced by the fact that Portuguese is one of the most musical tongues on the earth and no small gift to the bal-

◄ Musical notes in a sidewalk in Vila Isabel, a neighborhood in Rio known as the home of many great samba composers and musicians. *(Photo by Ricardo Pessanha.)*

lad singer. Second, a high level of poetry is present in the lyrics of much Brazilian popular music. And last, vibrant Afro-Brazilian rhythms energize most Brazilian songs, from samba to *baião*.

Brazilian music first grabbed international attention with the success of the dance-hall style *maxixe* in Europe between 1914 and 1922. The public was captivated by this vivacious and provocative song and dance, much as Europeans were taken with *lambada* in the summer of 1989. The 1940s saw the first exportation of samba, as songs like Ary Barroso's marvelous "Aquarela do Brasil" (known to most of the world as simply "Brazil") reached North America. Barroso's tunes were featured in Walt Disney films and covered in other Hollywood productions by a playful, exotic young woman who wore colorful lace skirts, heaps of jewelry, and a veritable orchard atop her head. Her name was Carmen Miranda, and she sang catchy sambas and *marchas* by many great Brazilian composers in a string of Hollywood feature films. For better or worse, she would symbolize Brazil to the world for decades and become a cultural icon in North America and Europe, a symbol of fun and extravagance.

Samba became a fundamental part of the world's musical vocabulary. Since it was first recorded early in the last century, samba has branched into a rich variety of styles. It has underpinned Rio's annual Carnaval celebrations and inspired the formation of "samba schools" around the world, full of non-Brazilians devoted to the batucada.

One of samba's subgenres, a cool modern variety called *bossa nova*, entered the world spotlight after the songs of Antonio Carlos Jobim and Luiz Bonfá were heard on the soundtrack of the 1959 movie *Black Orpheus*, which won the Cannes Film Festival Grand Prize and the Academy Award for Best Foreign Film. In North America, a bossa craze was ignited by the 1962 smash hit album *Jazz Samba*, recorded by guitarist Charlie Byrd and saxophonist Stan Getz. Jazz artists helped globally popularize the new sound, which had a breezy syncopation, progressive harmony, and a deceptive simplicity. Bossa nova was the big

▲ Two youngsters in Rio playing the tamborim. *(Photo by Ricardo Pessanha.)*

pop-music trend of the early 1960s, until it was supplanted by the English rock invasion led by the Beatles.

Bossa, like samba, is now a solid part of the international repertoire, especially in the jazz realm. Bossa's leading figure, Antonio Carlos Jobim, was one of the most popular songwriters of the twentieth century, and his stature rivals that of George Gershwin, Duke Ellington, and other great composers of Western popular music. Bossa nova initiated a widespread infiltration of Brazilian music and musicians into North American music.

Beginning in the late 1960s, Brazilian percussion became an essential element of many international jazz and pop recordings, and a new generation of talented Brazilian musicians began a long-term interchange with jazz artists. Percussionist Airto Moreira and vocalist Flora Purim were two of these musicians, and they performed

on groundbreaking albums that helped establish the new subgenre called "jazz fusion."

At the same time that Brazilian music was influencing jazz in the Northern Hemisphere, a remarkable new generation of singers and songwriters was coming to the forefront in Brazil in the late 1960s and 1970s. They fashioned original sounds from an eclectic variety of sources in and outside of Brazil. Milton Nascimento, Gilberto Gil, Caetano Veloso, Ivan Lins, João Bosco, Djavan, Gal Costa, Maria Bethânia, Alceu Valença, Chico Buarque, and others created and performed songs that came to be referred to as *MPB* (an acronym for *música popular brasileira*), a new catch-all category. Their superb integration of rhythm, melody, harmony, and lyrics resulted in one of the richest bodies of popular music ever to come from one country. In the '80s, a new musical movement swept Salvador: *axé music* became the name for new Afro-Bahian pop styles, including *samba-reggae*. Olodum, Carlinhos Brown, Timbalada, Daniela Mercury, Ara Ketu, Margareth Menezes, and Ivete Sangalo were artists who popularized axé music throughout Brazil in the '90s. In Recife, that decade saw the rise of the *mangue beat* movement, as Chico Science, Nação Zumbi, and

▲ Gilberto Gil. *(Courtesy of Tropical Storm/WEA.)*

▼ Elba Ramalho. *(Photo by Livio Campos. Courtesy of BMG.)*

Mundo Livre S/A fused *maracatu* and *embolada* with rock and hip-hop. In recent years Belém has become another important musical center, with the rise of *guitarrada* and *technobrega*. And, throughout Brazil, the last two decades have seen musicians reworking bossa nova and samba, mixing them with funk, rap, techno, drum 'n' bass, lounge, and international pop to create new cosmopolitan hybrids.

Today, as in past decades, Brazil's popular music can lay claim to a dazzling variety of song forms and musical traditions. There are the troubadours who strum *violas* and trade improvised stanzas back and forth, each trying to top the other, in traditional *desafio* song duels. There are accordion virtuosos who lead their bands in rollicking syncopated *forró* music. There are ritualistic *afoxés*, festive marchas, frenetic *frevos*, and the leaping instrumental improvisations of *choro*. And there are the walls of sound and waves of color that are the *escola de samba* (samba school) parades during Rio's Carnaval. Each escola's rhythm section, made up of some three hundred drummers and percussionists, works in perfect coordination with thousands of singers and dancers to create an awe-inspiring musical spectacle, the greatest live show on the planet.

Whether manifested in these or other forms, Brazilian music above all has a profound ability to move the soul. In its sounds and lyrics, it reflects the Brazilian people—their joy or despair, their remarkable capacity to celebrate, and the all-important concept of *saudade* (a deep longing or yearning).

To best understand Brazil's rich musical heritage, we must first journey back several hundred years, to where Brazil and its music both began.

CARTE DU BRÉSIL.

FIVE CENTURIES OF MUSIC

In Brazil, the first world and the third world exist side by side. Brazil is highly industrialized in some areas and absolutely medieval in others. It is wealthy and miserable, chic Ipanema and mud-and-stick hut, high-tech engineer and Stone Age Indian, computers and bananas. As a common joke goes: if there were no Brazil, someone would have to invent one.

Another argument for Brazil's singularity is that nowhere else on earth do different races, cultures, and religions coexist as peacefully as they do there. That is partly because intermarriage has been common in Brazil for centuries, creating a truly mixed society: most everyone has ancestors from two or three continents. There is prejudice among Brazilians (more on this later), but it is rare to encounter overt racial or religious hatred of the kind that is common in many other countries. A good example of Brazilian tolerance can be seen in the commercial district in downtown Rio called *Saara* (Sahara). There, Brazilians of Jewish, Lebanese, and Syrian descent all go to the same *botequins* (bars) at the end of the workday for a beer, a chat, and, on Fridays, a little samba. Brazil has been a real melting pot for centuries, not a mixed salad like the United States. As such, a person in Brazil of Lebanese or Yoruba or Japanese ancestry usually identifies himself or herself first and foremost as *Brazilian*.

THE FIRST BRAZILIANS

Brazil's national character and its rich musical tradition both derive from the profound mingling of races that has been going on since April 1500, when the Portuguese explorer Pedro Álvares Cabral stepped onto the lush tropical coast of what would later be southern Bahia.

Of course, Cabral was not the first human to arrive in Brazil, and long before his foot touched Bahian sand, a long musical tradition had been at play for thousands of years. The ancestors of today's Brazilian Indians migrated from Asia to the Western Hemisphere somewhere between twelve thousand and forty thousand years ago and eventually made their way down to South America. When Cabral first came to Brazil, the indigenous population probably exceeded two million. In their music, they sang songs solo and in chorus, accompanying themselves with flutes and whis-

▼ A simple house in Maranguape, Ceará, in the Northeast of Brazil. *(Photo by Chris McGowan.)*

tles. They beat out rhythms with hand-clapping, foot-stamping, rattles, sticks, and drums.

Their music did not, however, play a major role in the development of Brazilian popular music. In part, this is because so many tribes were devastated by Portuguese invaders, and the Indians that survived often lost their cultural traditions when they left their native homes and went to live in cities and towns. There is Indian influence in some Brazilian popular music, as seen in songs by musicians like Egberto Gismonti and Marlui Miranda, instruments like the *reco-reco* scraper, and traditions such as the *caboclinho* Carnaval groups. But generally one must journey to the remote homelands of the Yanomâmi, Bororo, Kayapó, and other indigenous groups to hear their music.

THE PORTUGUESE CONQUEST

Cabral encountered a land of great geographical diversity that is now the world's fifth-largest nation in terms of land mass. Brazil is a tropical country, situated largely between the equator and the Tropic

▲ Ângelo Agostinho's depiction of entrudo in Rio in 1880, a rude celebration that was one of the elements of nineteenth-century Carnaval in Brazil. *(Courtesy of Agência JB.)*

of Capricorn. It possesses some forty-six hundred miles of coastline, as well as the vast Amazon River basin, home to the largest rainforest on the planet. While parts of that humid region can receive up to 150 inches of rain a year, Brazil's arid, drought-stricken Northeast has areas that may go years with almost no rain at all. Other regions include a savannah-covered plateau in central Brazil, grassy plains in the South, and a lush coastal belt that was once covered by Atlantic rainforest.

Cabral sailed back to Portugal and the court of King Manuel I, bearing monkeys and parrots but—to everyone's disappointment—carrying no jewels, silks, or spices. However, royal expeditions that returned to the new continent shortly thereafter discovered something quite valuable: plentiful stands of brazilwood, a tree that yielded a useful red dye and that gave the country its name. Handsome profits from the brazilwood trade soon increased the number of visiting Portuguese and French traders; naturally, the Portuguese Crown

decided to expand its exploitation of Brazil and get rid of the French interlopers. In 1532 the first settlement, São Vicente, was established near present-day Santos in São Paulo state.

Some respectable Portuguese settlers came with their families to Brazil. But for the most part, writes E. Bradford Burns in *A History of Brazil*, "Portuguese monarchs customarily sent out on their global expeditions a combination of soldiers, adventurers, and petty criminals condemned to exile. Women were excluded. The Portuguese female was noticeably rare during the first century of Brazilian history. Her scarcity conferred a sexual license on the conquerors, already well acquainted with Moorish, African, and Asian women and seemingly attracted to dark-skinned beauty."[1] A colony of mixed races was soon in the making, quite different from the civilization that would be created in North America by English Protestants and their families, who came to settle permanently, kept more of a distance from the natives, and maintained an air of superiority with regard to other races.

Whether they were adventurers or settlers, the Portuguese brought their culture to the new land. In the realm of music, this included the European tonal system, as well as Moorish scales and medieval European modes. They also brought numerous festivals related to the Roman Catholic liturgical calendar and a wealth of dramatic pageants such as the *reisado* and *bumba-meu-boi,* which are still performed seasonally in the streets. The reisado celebrates the Epiphany, and the processional bumba-meu-boi dance enacts the death and resurrection of a mythical ox. Both are *autos*, a dramatic genre from medieval times that includes dances, songs, and allegorical characters. Jesuit priests introduced many religious autos that eventually took on local themes and musical elements.

In addition, the Portuguese brought many musical instruments to Brazil: the flute, piano, violin, guitar, viola, clarinet, triangle, accordion, *cavaquinho*, violoncello, Jew's harp, and tambourine. The Portuguese used a lot of syncopation and brisk, complex rhythms—traits that would help their music mesh well with the music the Africans brought to Brazil—and they had a fondness for lyric ballads, often melancholy and suffused with saudade.

Portuguese song forms included *moda*, a sentimental song that became the *modinha* in Brazil in the eighteenth century; *acalanto*, a form of lullaby; *fofa*, a dance of the eighteenth century; and (later) *fado*, a melancholy, guitar-accompanied Portuguese ballad. And along with their music, the Portuguese brought the *entrudo*, a rude celebration that was the beginning of Brazil's Carnaval tradition.

As they settled the new land, planted tobacco and cotton, and built sugar mills, the Portuguese looked on the native peoples as prime candidates for forced labor on the sugarcane plantations being developed in northeastern Brazil. But the Indians were unsuitable—they either escaped to the forest or died from the brutal work. So the colonizers of Brazil looked east, to Africa.

THE AFRICANS IN BRAZIL

The first recorded importation of Africans into Brazil occurred in 1538. From that year until the slave trade ended in 1850, historians estimate that four to five million Africans survived the crossing of the Atlantic to Brazil (hundreds of thousands died en route). This was many times more than were taken to North America.[2] The institution of slavery continued in Brazil until its abolition in 1888.

Three main ethnic and cultural groups made the journey. The *Sudanese* groups (Yoruba, Fon, Ewe, and Ashanti peoples) were brought from what are now Nigeria, the Republic of Benin (formerly Dahomey), and Ghana. *Bantu* groups came from Angola, the Democratic Republic of the Congo (called Zaire for many years), and Mozambique. And the *Moslem Guinea-Sudanese* groups (Tapas, Mandingos, Fulahs, and Hausa) were taken from Ghana, Nigeria, and neighboring areas.[3]

The African peoples brought their music, dance, languages, and religions, much of which survived in a purer form in Brazil than in North America. In part this was due to the sheer numbers of Africans arriving in Brazil, and the large concentrations of slaves and free blacks in coastal cities such as Rio, Salvador, and Recife. It was also affected by Portuguese attitudes toward their slaves, the influence of the Catholic Church, and the existence of *quilombos* (colonies formed by runaway slaves).

The Mediterranean world had already experienced great religious and linguistic diversity by the time Cabral first came to Brazil. On the Iberian Peninsula, Christians and Moors had been enslaving one another for hundreds of years. African influence in Portugal, in fact, predated the settlement of Brazil by several centuries and was quite apparent long after Moorish rule ended in A.D. 1249. Thus, compared with northern Europeans, the Portuguese were relatively tolerant of, or indifferent to, the native culture of their captives.

The formation of Catholic lay brotherhoods called *irmandades*, beginning in the seventeenth century, also helped perpetuate African traditions. These voluntary organizations functioned as social clubs and mutual aid societies and were organized along social, racial, and ethnic lines. Thus, because many slaves from particular cultural groups in Africa belonged to the same irmandades after they arrived in Brazil, they were

▲ An outdoor candomblé ceremony in Salvador.
(Courtesy of Bahiatursa.)

able to continue their homeland traditions. In many cases, they syncretized elements of their own festivals and ceremonies with those of the Catholic Church.

Many irmandades were located in large cities, which were centers of slave importation and in general provided opportunities for enslaved and free blacks to gather together. "Until 1850," writes Diana Brown in *Umbanda: Religion and Politics in Urban Brazil,* "thousands of Africans per year were still arriving in Brazil, bringing with them fresh infusions of the cultures of their African homelands." "The numbers and density of Afro-Brazilian populations," she continues, "provided favorable conditions for the maintenance of their cultural traditions; in addition, these large cities offered to these groups a relatively greater degree of free time and movement than was true, for example, of rural plantation life. Not surprisingly, it was these cities in which the various regional Afro-Brazilian religions first developed."[4]

In addition, the Portuguese intermarried extensively, partly because most of the early settlers came without wives. A racially mixed population was soon formed by the offspring of the Portuguese, Indians, and Africans, who intermingled at all levels of society. And many wealthy white officials and planters were exposed to African culture as children by playmates and nannies, and as adults by mistresses and wives.

Quilombos formed by runaway slaves in the interior of Brazil also helped preserve African culture. The largest and most famous of these was Palmares, established in the rugged interior of northeastern Alagoas state in the seventeenth century. The inhabitants of Palmares made an effort to organize a society based in African traditions. The quilombo lasted for several decades and had a population in the thousands (some say as high as twenty thousand). To the Portuguese, Palmares was a threat to the established order, not to mention the institution of slavery. Numerous armed expeditions were mounted against the quilombo by the Portuguese Crown beginning in 1654. All were unsuccessful until the last major campaign, waged in 1694, which overwhelmed and destroyed Palmares.[5] Zumbi, the quilombo's famed war commander, was captured and killed the following year. The legendary warrior is still celebrated in

Brazilian music today, and his birthday (November 20) has been a holiday in Rio since 1995.

African heritage survives in modern Brazil in a variety of manifestations. Brazilian Portuguese has incorporated many Yoruba and other African words. The cuisine in Bahia is quite similar to that of West Africa. And Brazilian music, dance, and culture in general are heavily rooted in Africa. In fact, Brazil has the largest African-descended population outside of Africa itself. In 1980, Brazil's population was 44.5 percent black or mulatto, according to the government census, and more than half of all Brazilians have at least one ancestor from the mother continent.

ISSUES OF RACE IN BRAZIL

Yet, despite generations of racial intermarriage in Brazil, racism persisted in an overt form for many years after the abolition of slavery, and the government persistently repressed public displays of Afro-Brazilian culture. By the late twentieth century, racial attitudes had changed for the better, yet inequalities and prejudice still persist.

It is certainly true that Brazil is one of the most tolerant countries in the world in terms of interracial dating and marriage, which are commonplace. And it is perfectly ordinary to find people of all colors interacting amiably in the bars, at the beaches, and on the streets of cities like Rio. People of different ethnicities are at ease with one another socially, especially among the working class—where racial conflict has often been extreme in other countries. Most Brazilians believe that discrimination in their homeland today is more often tied to one's wealth and perceived social standing than it is to one's skin color.

In speaking of Brazil, it is important to remember how different it is from countries like the United States, which follows a "bipolar" model in which anyone with any degree of African ancestry is considered "black." Brazilians, on the other hand, see racial identity as a fluid continuum. They distinguish between *preto* (black) and *mulato* (mulatto) and have words for a wide variety of skin colors resulting from varying degrees of Afri-

▲ Naná Vasconcelos parading with Olodum during Carnaval in Salvador. *(Photo by Artur Ikishima. Courtesy of Bahiatursa.)*

can, European, or Amerindian heritage. Another difference between the two countries is that African Americans are in the minority in the United States, while people with at least some degree of African ancestry are in the majority in Brazil.

Beginning in the 1930s, influenced by the sociologist Gilberto Freyre and others, "Brazil nurtured the notions that its multiethnic heritage was a source of strength, and that any social inequality that did exist was based not on ethnicity but on class. The national identity of 'Brazilian' was promoted and ethnic identity as 'black' was discouraged," observes G. Reginald Daniel.[6]

Yet there persists in Brazil an association, sometimes openly acknowledged and other times subtly implied, of lighter skin with higher status. Magazine and television advertisements regularly feature models who look as if they are from northern Europe. Black Brazilians are conspicuous by their overwhelming presence in many *favelas* (slums) and in their marked absence from the elite levels of business, politics, and society. Mulattos and blacks, especially the latter, suffer disproportionately more from poverty and lack of opportunity than do lighter-skinned Brazilians.

Daniel and other social critics argue that Brazil's "racial democracy" is a myth, and that racism is a serious problem about which most Brazilians are in perpetual denial. Yet contemporary music is an arena in which racial topics have been openly addressed. Since the 1980s, Afro-Brazilian pride has been more frequently asserted—and racial injustices protested—in lyrics by artists like Gilberto Gil, Nei Lopes, Martinho da Vila, and Bezerra da Silva; in Carnaval songs written for Rio's escolas de samba; and in the lyrics of Bahia's *blocos afro*. Brazil's hip-hop culture has intensified the debate: some Brazilian rappers publicly and aggressively focus on racial issues in their music, to an unprecedented extent that many consider "un-Brazilian."[7]

This is a significant change from previous decades, when racial commentary in music usually consisted of jokes at the expense of blacks and mulattos. For example, one of the most popular Carnaval songs of all time is Lamartine Babo's 1932 *marcha* "Teu Cabelo Não Nega" (Your Hair Doesn't Deny It), in which he sings, "Your hair doesn't deny it, mulata / Your color is mulata / But as color isn't contagious / Mulata, I want your love."

The subject of racial slurs in pop songs came to the forefront in 1996 because of lyrics considered offensive to blacks in the single "Veja os Cabelos Dela" (Look at Her Hair) by Tiririca (Francisco Everardo Oliveira), who is himself a mulatto. An activist group filed a lawsuit against the song and a judge in Rio ordered Tiririca's record removed from stores, an unprecedented move that provoked as much controversy as the tune itself. About the situation *Veja* magazine wrote, "The principal improvement is that it is no longer possible to keep the black in his condition of invisible citizen, without rights—including that of complaining."[8]

Whether one believes or does not believe that racial prejudice is a major problem in Brazil, the debate is now fully open.

AFRO-BRAZILIAN RELIGION

While a combination of racism and the Roman Catholic Church resulted in a long-standing suppression of Afro-Brazilian religions, they nevertheless became firmly rooted in the national culture and also had a tremendous influence on the development of Brazil's popular music.

The enslaved Yoruba, Ewe, and other peoples brought their animist beliefs from Africa to the New World. These religions are probably thousands of years old, predating Christianity, Islam, and Buddhism. Their belief systems were maintained for millennia as living oral traditions in ritual and music handed down from generation to generation. The Yoruba, who had the greatest influence on Afro-Brazilian religion, came primarily from what is now Nigeria.

▼ An umbanda supply store called Bazar Oxalá in Rio. *(Photo by Chris McGowan.)*

▲ Ceremonial umbanda drums and figurines in the Bazar Oxalá. *(Photo by Chris McGowan.)*

Their *òrìṣà* tradition, carried across the Atlantic Ocean, was transformed in Brazil into *candomblé*. It became *santería* in Cuba and *Shango* in Trinidad. The Yoruba deities, the òrìṣàs are called *orixás* in Brazil and *orishas* in Cuba. Anthropologist Migene González-Wippler estimated that by 1989 there were more one hundred million practitioners of Yoruba-based religions in Latin America and the United States.[9] Most of them are in Brazil.

In Haiti, the òrìṣà religion also played a role in the formation of *vodun*, which incorporates many traditions but is especially dominated by those of the Fon from Dahomey (which became the Republic of Benin in 1975). In the American South, especially Louisiana, vodun became known as *voodoo*, the subject of a great deal of outrageous legend and misunderstanding.

In Brazil, *macumba* is a common generic name—used mostly by outsiders—for all orixá religions. Candomblé is the closest to the old West African practices, while *umbanda* is a twentieth-century variation with considerable influence from spiritist beliefs. *Xangô*, *catimbó*, *caboclo*, and *batuque* are regional variations, with different sects reflecting influences from particular African ethnic or cultural groups—*nações* (nations).

The Afro-Brazilian religions began to take an organized form in the nineteenth century, and *terreiros* (centers of worship) were first reported around 1830 in Salvador and 1850 in Recife.[10] The religions were syncretized in Brazil into new forms by their followers because of government and Roman Catholic repression that persisted into the twentieth century. Devotees secretly worshipped their West African gods during Catholic ceremonies. Blacks who prayed to a statue of the Virgin Mary often were actually thinking of Iemanjá, the goddess of the sea. Saint George might represent Ogun, god of warriors; Saint Jerome could stand in for Xangô, god of fire, thunder, and justice; and Jesus Christ might really signify Oxalá, the god of the sky and universe. Catholicism, with its abundance of saints, meshed well with the orixá tradition and inadvertently sheltered it.

If you are a follower of an Afro-Brazilian religion, you always have two different orixás, a male and a female, that "rule your head" and are seen as your spiritual parents. For example, you might have Xangô and Iemanjá as the "masters of your head." The head priestess, the *mãe-de-santo* (mother of the saints), typically discovers this and asserts that these two orixás, because of their specific personalities and powers, are the natural guides for you and your life. During the ceremonies, the drums and singing call down the orixás, and they or their intermediary spirits "possess" the bodies of the initiated sons and daughters.

While the traditional sect of candomblé focuses solely on the orixás, umbanda has incorporated many influences from *espiritismo* (spiritism), a religion that formed in the nineteenth century around the ideas and writings of Allan Kardec, the pseudonym of the French philosopher Léon Hipolyte D. Rivail. Today, candomblé and umbanda are an accepted and integral part of Brazilian culture, with many leading cultural figures counted among their adherents. One notable example was the novelist Jorge Amado (1912–2001), who was a son of Xangô. Many Brazilian musi-

cians praise or refer to Afro-Brazilian deities in their song lyrics, and some have included invocation songs for the orixás on their albums.

About 90 percent of Brazilians currently identify themselves as Christians (roughly 75 percent Catholic and 15 percent Protestant), yet a large percentage of the country's population also follows Afro-Brazilian religions. Rio, for example, has hundreds of umbanda supply shops that sell beads, candles, dried herbs, and plaster-cast figures of spirits and saints. Offerings of food for an orixá can often be found beside flickering candles late at night alongside a road. Each orixá is called by a particular rhythm and song, and these rituals have kept alive many African songs, musical scales, musical instruments, and rhythms.

The wide assortment of African-derived instruments still played in Brazil today includes the *agogô* (a double bell struck by a wooden stick), *cuíca* (a small friction drum), and *atabaque* (a conical single-headed drum). The African influence also reveals itself in Brazil's traditional and folk music (as

▼ Carnaval in Salvador. *(Courtesy of Bahiatursa.)*

it does in the rest of the Americas) through the use of syncopation and complex rhythmic figures, the importance of drums and percussion instruments, certain flattened or "falling" notes, the so-called metronome sense of West Africa, the use of call-and-response patterns, short motifs, improvisation, and—perhaps most important—the tendency of music to play a central role in life.

Religious, ceremonial, and festive African music form the basis of Afro-Brazilian songs and dances that eventually developed into various musical forms: afoxé, *jongo*, *lundu*, samba, maracatu, and more.

THE DEVELOPMENT OF BRAZIL

Brazil's mixed population today reflects its Portuguese, Amerindian, and African ancestors, and the arrival of numerous German, Italian, Japanese, and Lebanese immigrants since the nineteenth century. Tragically, the number of Brazil's indigenous Indian peoples has declined drastically over the centuries. Many were slain early on by the Portuguese conquerors or decimated by European diseases. Others were absorbed into colonial settlements, voluntarily or against their will. And a great many intermarried with the Portu-

▼ An amateur musician playing pagode samba in a bar in the Salgueiro neighborhood of Rio. *(Photo by Ricardo Pessanha.)*

guese, adding to Brazil's miscegenation. Today there are only a few hundred thousand full-blooded Indians in Brazil, and their population has continued to decline in recent decades as agri-business, timber companies, and new settlers push farther into the Amazon Basin.[11]

After the colonization began, Portugal ruled Brazil until 1822, when Dom Pedro, heir to the Portuguese throne, declared Brazil's independence and became its first emperor. His successor, Dom Pedro II, was overthrown in 1889 and a republic was established. Since the nineteenth century, Brazil has had both authoritarian and democratic governments. It was ruled by a military regime between 1964 and 1985, but since then has been a democracy.

Brazil's economic development was powered initially by trade in brazilwood; then sugar, gold, diamonds, coffee, and rubber fueled the country's growth. Industrialization came largely in the twentieth century, accelerating especially during the Getúlio Vargas regimes (1930–1945, 1950–1954). By the late twentieth century Brazil had diversified and become an important exporter of soybeans, orange juice, beef, iron ore, and steel, and manufactured goods such as military weapons, airplanes, automobiles, textiles, and footwear. After the turn of the millennium, it also became a leader in biofuels. Brazil now has one of the largest economies in the world, and a population of more than 180 million people.[12] While Brazil is a country that possesses great wealth, it also suffers from pervasive corruption, a bloated bureaucracy, high crime rates, and an extremely unequal distribution of income. Perhaps it is true, as Brazilians often say, that soccer, beer, *cachaça* (sugarcane liquor), and Carnaval are the only things that keep the poor from staging a revolution.

A MUSICAL MELTING POT

Over the course of the last five centuries, Portuguese, African, and—to a lesser extent—Amerindian rhythms, dances, and harmonies have been mixing together, altering old styles and creating new forms of music. One of the most important early Brazilian

▲ Sambista Paulinho da Viola (*left*) and rocker Lobão (*right*). (*Photo by Cristina Granato. Courtesy of BMG.*)

genres was the lundu song form and circle dance, brought by Bantu slaves from what is now Angola to Brazil, where it shocked the upper class.

The first recorded reference to lundu in Brazil was in 1780. The dance was considered lascivious and indecent in its original form, which included the *umbigada* navel-touching movement, an invitation to participate that was characteristic of many African circle dances. By the end of the eighteenth century, lundu had made an appearance in the Portuguese court, transformed into a refined style sung with guitar or piano accompaniment and embellished with European harmonies. By the mid-nineteenth century lundu was performed in Brazil both in salons and in the streets. As a popular style, it featured sung refrains and an energetic 2/4 rhythm carried by hand-clapping. Both types of lundu would remain popular in Brazil until the early twentieth century.

Another important song and dance, maxixe, was created in Rio around 1880 by Afro-Brazilian

musicians who were performing at parties in lower-middle-class homes. The first genuinely Brazilian dance, maxixe was a synthesis of lundu, polka, and Cuban *habanera* with additional voluptuous moves performed by the closely dancing couple (influences from Argentinian tango came later). Maxixe gave as erotic and scandalous an impression as lundu had one hundred years earlier and as lambada would one hundred years later.

Maxixe and other Brazilian styles would be popularized by a native music industry that dates to 1902, with the release of Brazil's first record: the lundu "Isto É Bom" (This Is Good), written by Xisto Bahia and performed by the singer Baiano for the Casa Edison record company.[13] Later in the twentieth century, Brazil developed a large domestic music industry and began to export its songs all over the world.

Musically, Brazil has continued to reflect the great racial and cultural miscegenation of its history, and to continually absorb and modify new ideas and styles. A good example of this is the long and rich tradition of Brazil's most famous musical form: samba.

SAMBA: THE HEARTBEAT OF RIO 2

He who doesn't like samba isn't a good guy
He's rotten in the head or sick in the feet

Dorival Caymmi, "Samba da Minha
Terra" (Samba of My Land)

On a hot and humid summer night in Rio de Janeiro, a small stage is
packed with dozens of musicians holding assorted drums and percussion instruments, engaged in an escola de samba (samba school) rehearsal. They are inside a
colorful, decorated pavilion crowded with people—black, white, brown—who all
have one thing in common: the samba.

Surdos (bass drums) pound out a booming beat, and their incessant drive provides the foundation for the rest of the *bateria*, the drum-and-percussion section
that will later parade triumphantly during Carnaval. Snare drums called *caixas*
rattle away in a hypnotic frenzy, and above them tamborins—small cymbal-less
tambourines that are hit with sticks—carry a high-pitched rhythmic phrase like
popcorn in an overheated pot. Enter the sad cries and humorous moans of the
cuíca (friction drum), the crisp rhythmic accents of the reco-reco (scraper), and
the hollow metallic tones of the agogô (double bell). Other percussion instruments
add more colors; the ukulele-like cavaquinho offers its high-register plaintive harmonies, and the *puxador* (lead singer) belts out the melody.

Dense polyrhythms dance and cross, reinforce and contrast with one another.
By now the sound is deafening and it's impossible to talk to the person next to you.
Sweat flows, your head spins with the dense sound, and the festive atmosphere

carries you away in euphoria. Cares are tossed to the wind. There's no doubt in anyone's mind: samba is what it's all about.

A cold technical definition would never express what samba, and the whole universe that revolves around it, is. For one thing, in a musical sense, there are many varieties of samba—from dense, thundering *samba de enredo* played by the escolas de samba during Carnaval, to melodious, sophisticated *samba-canção*, to earthy, exuberant *pagode samba*. And if we ask an average Brazilian (especially a carioca) what samba is, the answer is generally subjective and doesn't always refer to music. "It's something that runs in my veins, it's in my blood," say many samba musicians and devotees.

It is common for cariocas to say, rather ironically, that everything ends up in samba. If things go wrong, there's always samba to lift one's spirits. Samba is solace, celebration, escape and abandon, and it is culture, philosophy, and tradition. Samba is a musical form that was largely created and sustained by the black and mulatto working classes in Rio, but today all types of Brazilians make samba and draw vitality from it, and most of the country dances to it during Carnaval. Almost every Brazilian musician—whether from the areas of MPB, jazz, or even rock—records a samba at some point in his or her career.

SAMBA'S ROOTS

Samba coalesced into a distinct musical genre in Rio de Janeiro in the early twentieth century. The exact course of samba's early evolution is unknown, but there is no shortage of theories about its origins. The word *samba* appears to have come from Angola, where the Kimbundu word *semba* refers to the umbigada, the "invitation to the dance." Some scholars believe that samba and the other Afro-Brazilian circle dances that feature or once featured the umbigada are all variants of the same theme.

There are those who argue that lundu, in Brazil since the eighteenth century, was the true musical parent of samba. Others theorize that a primitive

▲ A member of a samba school pounding out the rhythm on a surdo during Carnaval in Rio. *(Photo by Lidio Parente. Courtesy of Embratur.)*

type of samba, or at least its essential elements, was brought to Rio from Bahia more than one hundred years ago. Some scholars cite "Moqueca Sinhá" (a lundu), "Laranjas da Sabina" (Sabina's Oranges), and "A Morte do Marechal" (Marechal's Death), from 1870, 1888, and 1893, respectively, as early examples of songs that "tended rhythmically towards samba."[1]

The mystery of samba's roots is complicated further by the fact that the word *samba* was used in the late nineteenth century both as a synonym for various Afro-Brazilian dances and to designate parties held by slaves and former slaves. But it was certainly in Rio that samba was developed, embellished, and transformed into a distinct genre.

Many slaves and former slaves emigrated to Rio, the nation's capital, in the late nineteenth century because of a decline in the fortunes of tobacco and cocoa plantations in Bahia state, and because of two important acts: the Law of the Free Womb in 1871 (which declared free all children born to slaves), and the abolition of slavery in 1888. The immigrants worked at the docks, as street vendors, and as domestic servants, struggling to make a living any way they could. They brought with them African and Afro-Brazilian batucadas (percussion jams) and dances, both usually referred to by the generic name of *batuque* prior to the twentieth century. Many of the new arrivals settled in a central area of Rio called Praça Onze.

Praça Onze and the Birth of Carioca Samba

Such was the influx of Bahian—and hence Afro-Brazilian—culture, that by 1915 Praça Onze (Plaza Eleven) was called "a true Africa in miniature." Here, many of these immigrants and their children gathered together in their leisure time to make music, dance, and worship the *orixás* (Afro-Brazilian deities) at the homes of old Bahian matriarchs, re-

▼ Praça Onze, a seminal site in the history of samba. *(Courtesy of Agência JB.)*

spectfully called *tias* (aunts). Neo-African culture had survived to a greater extent in Bahia than in other parts of Brazil, in part because of the large black population in Salvador and the ongoing trade between that city and ports in Nigeria and Dahomey. And it was kept alive in Rio by the tias, once they had immigrated from Bahia.

Near Praça Onze, an important site in samba's evolution was Rua Visconde de Inhaúma, number 177, the home of a woman nicknamed Tia Ciata (Hilária Batista de Almeida, 1854–1924). Born in Salvador, Tia Ciata was renowned in Rio as a maker of sweets and as a party hostess. Her house was a point of encounter and a party site for expatriate Bahians and members of Carnaval groups, and bohemians, journalists, laborers, and middle-class professionals. Tia Ciata was a daughter of Oxum, and devotees worshipped the orixás in her backyard. The parties at her house were enlivened by the inspired music making of several gifted young men who would alter the course of Brazilian popular music.

In the early years of the twentieth century, the now legendary Pixinguinha, Donga, João da Baiana, Heitor dos Prazeres, and Sinhô gathered at Tia Ciata's house. There they played lundus,

marchas, choros, maxixes, and batuques in jam sessions that must have been incredible to hear. These men were talented instrumentalists and part of Rio's first generation of professional songwriters. Together they discussed music, created songs, and began to shape the urban carioca form of samba that we know today.

The emerging style of samba gained influences from polka, habanera, and the lively genres of marcha and maxixe. From this rich matrix emerged a vibrant musical form distinguished by its responsorial singing and percussive interplay and a less formal sound than either maxixe or marcha. Technically, samba has a 2/4 meter, an emphasis on the second beat, a stanza-and-refrain structure, and interlocking, syncopated lines in the melody and accompaniment. The main rhythm and abundant cross-rhythms can be carried by hand-clapping or drums and percussion (the batucada), which may include more than a dozen different instruments. Samba is commonly accompanied by guitar and four-string cavaquinho and—less frequently—brass.

Although there is some dispute as to what was the first true samba ever recorded, the consensus among the majority of Brazilian music historians is that "Pelo Telefone" (On the Telephone) was the first *officially registered* samba. It was also the first case of stolen authorship in the style. The melody was a collective creation at Tia Ciata's house and the words were Mauro de Almeida's, but Donga registered it as his alone in December 1916, under the designation of "samba." The song was released in 1917, performed by Banda de Odeon.[2]

The commandant of fun
Told me on the phone
To dance with joy

At the time, the differences between maxixe, samba, and marcha had not yet completely crystallized. Thus Ismael Silva, one of the founders of the first escola de samba, complained to Donga that "Pelo Telefone" was not a samba but a maxixe.

▲ Pixinguinha and the Batutas in 1919. Top row (*left to right*): José Alves, Pixinguinha, Luis Silva, Jacó Palmieri. Seated (*left to right*): Otávio Viana, Nelson Alves, João Pernambuco, Raul Palmieri, Donga.

"What's samba then?" asked Donga rather angrily.

"'Se Você Jurar,'" answered Ismael, citing one of his own successes.

"'Se Você Jurar' is not a samba. It's a marcha," replied Donga.[3]

The debate went on for years, and in fact some musicologists today refer to "Pelo Telefone" as a samba-maxixe. But it was a hit Carnaval song that year, and samba took its place alongside marcha as a preferred Carnaval musical style in Rio and much of Brazil.

Pixinguinha (Alfredo da Rocha Vianna Jr., 1898–1973) stood out as one of the most important of samba's founding fathers and was also renowned in the choro and maxixe genres (see Chapter Eight). He was a virtuoso flutist with superb technique and improvisational creativity (later he added saxophone). Pixinguinha was also an original arranger who enriched the harmony of samba, and the leader of Os Oito Batutas (The Eight Masters), an all-star band that included Donga and performed Brazilian music before European audiences in 1922. Besides this, Pixinguinha composed more than six hundred tunes. Some of his more famous sambas are "Teus Ciúmes" (Your Jealousies), "Ai Eu Queria" (How I Wanted It), and "Samba de Negro" (Black's Samba).

Pixinguinha's contemporary Sinhô (José Barbosa da Silva, 1888–1930) was a dance-hall pianist

◄ Os Batutas and Duque in 1922. Standing (*left to right*): Pixinguinha, José Alves de Lima, José Monteiro, Sizenando Santos "Feniano," and Duque. Seated (*left to right*): China, Nelson dos Santos Alves, and Donga. (*Public domain photo.*)

and fellow habitué of the musical sessions at Tia Ciata's. His many Carnaval hits earned him the title "king of samba" in the '20s and made him the most popular of the first *sambistas.* Accusations of plagiarism against Sinhô by Heitor dos Prazeres triggered a long-standing feud between the two, with former friends Pixinguinha and Donga taking Heitor's side.

Sinhô was a regular in every bohemian spot in town, and he wrote sambas, marchas, and love songs that were chronicles of nocturnal city life. Sinhô gained attention in 1918 with "Quem São Eles?" (Who Are They?) and achieved his greatest popularity in the 1920s with marchas like "Pé de Anjo" (Angel's Foot) and sambas such as "Jura" (Swear It) and "Gosto Que Me Enrosco" (I Like It Bad). The last song was co-written with Heitor dos Prazeres and explored the consequences of late-night carousing.

> One shouldn't love someone if he's not loved
> It would be better if he were crucified
> May God keep me away from today's women
> They despise a man just because of the
>   nightlife

Together and apart, these former visitors to Tia Ciata's home—Sinhô, Pixinguinha, Donga, Heitor dos Prazeres, and João da Baiana—popularized samba, started developing its structure, and set it on its course toward becoming one of the world's great musical genres.

Estácio

Nearby Praça Onze was the Estácio neighborhood, now known as "the cradle of samba." Today its narrow streets are lined with two-story houses from the turn of the century that were once elegant but are now run down. Despite the urban decline, locals there still spend hours drinking, talking, and singing at the small simple bars called botequins, much as they did in the 1920s.[4]

From Estácio came such now-legendary sambistas as Bide, Ismael Silva, Nilton Bastos, and Armando Marçal. They took the fledgling samba genre and clearly differentiated it from maxixe and marcha, introducing longer notes and two-bar phrasing, and making the tempo slower, in contrast to the maxixe-like sambas composed by Sinhô and Donga. The form they codified became the standard reference of samba, to which sambistas always return. The other major historical contribution of these pioneers was that in 1928 they created the first escola de samba: Deixa Falar (Let Them Talk).

Ismael Silva (1905–1978) was the most important of the Estácio composers because of his melodic creativity and sophisticated modulations. His often ironic lyrics created strong poetic images out of simple common themes. In "Meu Único Desejo" (My Only Desire), Silva's sly verse speaks of unrequited love.

You've returned the photographs
My letters and my presents
I didn't accept them

There's only one thing I really want
To have you return
All the kisses I gave you

His many famous sambas include "Se Você Jurar" (If You Were to Swear), "Nem É Bom Falar" (It's No Good Talking About It), and "Antonico." He also co-wrote many songs with Nilton Bastos, Noel Rosa, and Lamartine Babo and had a pro-

---

Early Sambistas

Donga (Ernesto Joaquim Maria dos Santos, 1891–1974), the son of Tia Amélia, started playing music with Pixinguinha and others at Tia Ciata's house in 1916. He was the registered composer of "Pelo Telefone" and wrote the hits "Passarinho Bateu Asas" (The Little Bird Beat Its Wings), "Cantiga de Festa" (Party Song), and "Macumba de Oxossi." Adept with cavaquinho and guitar, he played with the rancho Dois de Ouro, the Grupo de Caxangá, and the Oito Batutas.

▲ Donga (*left*) and Pixinguinha (*right*) at the bust of Heitor Villa-Lobos in 1968. *(Photo by Jacob. Courtesy of Agência JB.)*

João da Baiana (João Machado Guedes, 1887–1974) was the grandson of slaves and the son of the baiana Tia Prisciliana. At the age of ten he paraded with Dois de Ouro and with the rancho Pedra de Sal. He is credited with introducing the *pandeiro* as a samba instrument. When the police were cracking down on batucadas in 1908, they confiscated João's pandeiro, and he was unable to perform at a party at the house of Senator Pinheiro Machado. The senator, a fan of the young musician, presented him with a new pandeiro the very next day. João was invited to tour Europe with Pixinguinha and Os Batutas but never made the trip. He composed the tunes "Mulher Cruel" (Cruel Woman), "Pedindo Vingança" (Asking for Vengeance), and "O Futuro É Uma Caveira" (The Future Is a Skull).

Heitor dos Prazeres (1898–1966), a cavaquinho player, composed famed sambas like "A Tristeza Me Persegue" (Sadness Follows Me) and "Mulher de Malandro" (The Malandro's Woman), was active in the formation of the Portela and Mangueira samba schools, and was a well-regarded painter.

Caninha (Oscar José Luis de Morais, 1883–1961) was one of Sinhô's principal competitors for the title "king of Carnaval" in the 1920s. Caninha is famous for writing such songs as "Me Leve, Me Leve" (Take Me, Take Me), "Seu Rafael" (Mr. Rafael), and—with Heitor dos Prazeres—"É Batucada" (It's Batucada).

▲ Ismael Silva. *(Photo by Antonio Teixeira. Courtesy of Agência JB.)*

found influence on later Brazilian composers like Chico Buarque.

Two other Estácio stalwarts were Bide (Alcebiades Barcelos, 1902–1975) and Armando Marçal (1902–1947), a powerful songwriting team in the 1930s and 1940s who co-wrote warm, flowing samba masterpieces including "A Malandragem," "Sorrir" (To Smile), and "Agora É Cinzas" (Now It's Ashes).

When Armando died, his family kept the music alive. His son, Nilton Marçal, was a famous percussionist and a *mestre de bateria* (percussion conductor) for Portela. Nilton's son, also named Armando, is a superb percussionist as well, highly respected in Brazil and known to North American jazz fans for his work with the Pat Metheny Group.

The musical language elaborated by the Estácio masters was an important form of expression for the carioca lower classes in the early twentieth century. Samba became a voice for those who had been silenced by their socioeconomic status, and a source of self-affirmation in society.

Crooners, Composers, and Malandros

At the height of the radio era in the 1930s, many of the great songs of the Estácio songwriters reached a wide audience through the interpretations of vocalists Mario Reis, Francisco Alves, and Carmen Miranda, among others. It was a time when samba was becoming identified as the national music of Brazil.[5] An especially successful crooner from this era was the singer-songwriter Orlando Silva (1915–1978), who became known as "the singer of the multitudes." Silva made his debut on Radio Cajuti in 1934 and initially recorded under the pseudonym Orlando Navarro. He was the first vocalist to record Pixinguinha's "Carinhoso" (Affectionate) and the first singer to have his own show on Radio Nacional. He also appeared in movies such as 1938's *Banana da Terra*. His many hits included "A Jardineira" (The Gardener) and "Lábios Que Beijei" (Lips That I Kissed). In the late '30s and early '40s he was the most popular singer in Brazil.

Two important samba composers who supplied hit songs for these vocalists were Ataulfo Alves and Assis Valente. Alves (1909–1969) married lyrical

▼ Ataulfo Alves. *(Courtesy of EMI.)*

laments with long, slow musical phrases, a songwriting style that may have been influenced by his youth in slow-paced, bucolic Minas Gerais. Some of his most popular songs were "Ai, Que Saudade de Amelia" (Oh, How I Miss Amelia), "Pois É" (So It Is), and "Mulata Assanhada" (Restless Mulata).

Assis Valente (1911–1958), one of the most popular songwriters of the 1930s and 1940s, wrote lyrics that were witty snapshots of the times in which he lived. He also had an almost naive preoccupation with glorifying what he considered authentically Brazilian, as shown in the song "Brasil Pandeiro" (Brazil Tambourine).

> Uncle Sam wants
> To know our batucada
> He's been saying Bahian spices
> Improved his dishes

Carmen Miranda recorded many Valente compositions, including the samba-choro "Camisa Listrada" (Striped Shirt), "Recenseamento" (Census), and "Fez Bobagem" (You Were Foolish).

An important samba singer from this era was Moreira da Silva (1902–2000), who sang sambas when not strolling the boulevards. He invented an original way of performing sambas: he would stop the song, use dialogue to dramatize the situation described in the lyrics, then continue. It was called *samba de breque* (break samba). His most famous song in this style is "Acertei no Milhar," written by noted samba composers Wilson Batista and Geraldo Pereira and recorded by Moreira da Silva in 1938. It tells the story of a man who dreams he won a fortune in a lottery and tells his wife all that they will do with the cash windfall. Moreira da Silva was a colorful figure who personified the lifestyle of the *malandro*, a type of hustler or layabout that was a romantic bohemian ideal for some in Rio in the 1930s and 1940s. Malandros did not work. They made their living exploiting women, playing small confidence tricks, and gambling. They liked to dress well, typically in a white suit and white hat, and were proud of their lifestyle. A great cinematic portrait of these characters may be seen in Ruy Guerra's *Ópera do Malandro*, a 1987 film musical based on Chico Buarque's stage play.

Samba-Canção

In more upscale neighborhoods in Rio in the 1930s, a brilliant new generation of middle-class samba and marcha composers also came of age. The most famous among them were Noel Rosa, Braguinha, Lamartine Babo, Ary Barroso, and Dorival Caymmi, and they composed sambas that emphasized the melody more than the rhythm, added more complex harmonies, and had more sophisticated lyrics—usually tied to sentimental themes. It was a kind of cool, softened samba, later labeled samba-canção, and it popularized the genre with the middle class. These songwriters wrote both Carnaval songs and "middle-of-the-year" songs (as the non-Carnaval compositions were known), and set the trend for Brazilian popular music until the advent of bossa nova in the late 1950s.

Noel Rosa and Braguinha

Noel Rosa (1910–1937) was born in Rio and is so popular today that he has a statue on the main street of Vila Isabel, the carioca neighborhood where he lived. Rosa was known for Carnaval

▼ Noel Rosa as pictured on one of his albums.

songs like his first big success, "Com Que Roupa?" (With Which Clothes?), released in 1931. He composed melodies that were harmonically rich and pioneered the use of colloquial language and social criticism in samba lyrics. Rosa died at an early age from tuberculosis but left more than two hundred songs for posterity. Some of his tunes were collaborations with others, including many fine sambas co-written with the pianist Vadico (Osvaldo Gogliano, 1912–1962). Rosa's masterpieces include "Conversa de Botequim" (Bar Talk), "Três Apitos" (Three Whistles), "Palpite Infeliz" (Unfortunate Suggestion), and "Onde Está a Honestidade" (Where's the Honesty?). His song "Último Desejo" (Last Desire) demonstrates the raw emotional power of Rosa's lyrics. It is a melancholy coda to a romance that has ended.

> Our love that I can't forget
> Began at the festival of St. John
> And died today without fireworks
> Without a photograph and without a
>   message
> Without moonlight, without guitar
> Near you I'm silent
> Thinking everything, saying nothing
> I'm afraid of crying
> I never again want your kisses
> But you can't deny me
> My last desire
> If some friend of yours asks
> You to tell her
> Whether or not you want me
> Tell her you adore me
> That you cry and lament our separation
> The people that I detest
> Always say I'm worth nothing
> That my home is a saloon
> That I ruined your life
> That I don't deserve the food
> That you bought for me

Noel's short but rich life was portrayed in *Noel, o Poeta da Vila*, a 2007 movie directed by Ricardo van Steen.

For some time Rosa played guitar and sang with a group called Os Tangarás. One of the members of this group was Carlos Braga (1907–2006), who was also from Vila Isabel. Since Braga was the son of a rich man and in those times being a popular musician was not considered honorable, he invented another name for himself: João de Barro. Also called Braguinha, he became one of the greatest Carnaval hit makers, writing lighthearted and lively sambas and marchas with lyrics that featured good-humored and apt social criticism.

Braguinha composed classic songs such as "Touradas em Madrid," a hit in the Carnaval of 1938 and known in the United States through the recordings of Carmen Miranda, Dinah Shore, and Xavier Cugat. Like Noel Rosa, Braguinha was an intuitive musician who never studied music. He played a little guitar but composed his songs by whistling. Besides samba, he also excelled in children's songs, celebration songs for Festas Juninas (festivities honoring Saints John, Peter, and Anthony), and even *repentes* (a northeastern style with improvised verses). Other successes include "Chiquita Bacana," "Balancê," "Yes! Nós Temos Bananas" (Yes, We Have Bananas), and "Copacabana" (recorded by Dick Farney and considered a precursor of the bossa nova style), all composed with partner Alberto Ribeiro (1902–1971). A life-size bronze statue of Braguinha has greeted visitors to Copacabana's Princess Isabel Avenue since 2004.

Another important figure from that era was Lamartine Babo (1904–1963), who composed the standards "Teu Cabelo Não Nega" (Your Hair Doesn't Deny It), "Eu Sonhei Que Tu Estavas Tão Linda" (I Dreamed You Were So Beautiful), and "Moleque Indigesto" (Indigestible Urchin).

Ary Barroso

Ary Barroso (1903–1964), a legendary composer of Carnaval marchas and samba-canção tunes, wrote one of the most famous Brazilian songs of all time, "Aquarela do Brasil" (Watercolor of Brazil), internationally known as "Brazil." Born in

▶ Ary Barroso. *(Photo by Campanella Neto. Courtesy of Agência JB.)*

Ubá, Minas Gerais, Barroso studied classical piano as a youth and played for dance-hall orchestras after moving to Rio in 1920.

Barroso only decided to write Carnaval songs because he wanted to get married, and the only way he could think of to make enough money for his wedding was to have a Carnaval hit. So he wrote "Dá Nela" for the 1930 Carnaval. It won Casa Edison's annual Carnaval song contest and was the most popular marcha that year. From then on he was a successful composer whose many beautiful sambas were known for their elaborate harmonies. For many years he was also the host of a radio show that showcased new singing talent.

In 1934 Ary took a trip to Bahia and was deeply inspired by the beauty and atmosphere of Salvador. As a result, he composed several of his most popular tunes, all of them recorded by Carmen Miranda: "Na Baixa do Sapateiro," "No Tabuleiro da Baiana" (On the Baiana's Tray), "Quando Penso na Bahia" (When I Think of Bahia), "Boneca de Piche" (Tar Doll), with Luis Iglesias, and "Como Vaes Você?" (How Are You?).

In 1939 Ary wrote his famous "Aquarela do Brasil," which popularized a new subgenre, *samba-exaltação*: songs that praise the beauty and richness of Brazil.

Brazil, Brazil
For me, for me
Oh! These murmuring fountains
Where I quench my thirst
And where the moon comes to play
Oh! This brown and beautiful Brazil
You are my Brazilian Brazil
Land of samba and tambourines
Brazil, Brazil, for me, for me

"Aquarela do Brasil" received international exposure in the 1940s. Walt Disney heard the song on a trip to Brazil in 1941 and chose to include it in his 1942 animated film *Saludos Amigos* (called *Alô Amigos* in Brazil), which starred Zé Carioca, a Rio malandro in cartoon parrot form.

Ary also contributed the song "Rio de Janeiro" to Disney's 1944 film *Brazil*, and he received an Academy Award nomination for it. Another Disney animated movie, *The Three Caballeros* (1945), included Barroso's "Na Baixa do Sapateiro" (renamed "Baia" [*sic*] in the film) and "Os Quindins de Iaiá" (Iaiá's Yolk-and-Coconut Sweets), sung by Aurora Miranda, Carmen Miranda's sister.

"Aquarela do Brasil" would be remembered for years to come and be recorded a few hundred times by musicians within and outside Brazil. And decades after its first film appearance, "Aquarela" would be used as the theme song for Terry Gilliam's 1985 black comedy *Brazil*, the music representing a vision of beauty and freedom to the protagonist, trapped in a futuristic totalitarian society.

Dorival Caymmi

Another key figure in the history of samba is Dorival Caymmi, (1914–2008), born in Salvador. He contributed many samba-canção standards as well as *toadas*, modinhas, *canções praieiras* (fishermen's songs), and *pontos de candomblé* (invocation songs for orixás). His tunes "Samba da Minha Terra" (Samba of My Land), "Modinha para Gabriela," "É Doce Morrer no Mar," "Marina," "Saudade de Itapoã," "Das Rosas" (English title: "Roses and Roses"), "João Valentão," "Requebre Que Eu Dou um Doce," "Rosa Morena," and "Oração da Mãe Menininha" have become part of Brazil's musical heritage.

Caymmi was the son of a civil servant who played guitar and mandolin. At the age of twenty-four he decided to seek his fortune in Rio and left for the big city aboard a ship that traveled slowly down the Brazilian coast. The young man had inherited his father's musical ability, and at night a group of passengers would gather on the deck to listen to Caymmi play guitar and sing in his deep, smooth, often dolorous voice.

Once in Rio, he found work as a graphic artist with the magazine *O Cruzeiro* and began studying for the law school entrance exam. But soon he switched his efforts to his music and rose to the top with astonishing speed. Composers Assis Valente and Lamartine Babo took him to the Radio Nacional station, where he was given a chance to sing his composition "Noite de Temporal" (Stormy Night), a canção praieira that mixed elements of samba and the *capoeira* rhythm. He was a success and was contracted by Radio Tupi station, where he first performed his samba "O Que É Que a Baiana Tem?" (What Is It That the Bahian Woman Has?). That same year, 1938, the producer Wallace Downey was arranging songs for the movie *Banana da Terra*, which would star, among others, Carmen Mi-

▲ A Dorival Caymmi album cover. *(Courtesy of EMI.)*

randa. One scene was to feature Miranda wearing—for the first time—what would become her trademark: the turban, skirt, and ornaments of a *baiana* (a Bahian woman).

Downey planned to use Ary Barroso's "Na Baixa do Sapateiro" for the scene, but Barroso wanted more money than Downey was willing to pay and the song was dropped. It was then that Miranda remembered a young composer at a radio station who had once shown her a song about Bahia. Downey tracked him down, and Caymmi was on his way. The film debuted in 1939. "O Que É Que a Baiana Tem?" was a huge success and introduced into the national vocabulary the Bahian word *balangandã* (an ornamental silver buckle with amulets and trinkets attached). It also set the style for Miranda's costumes. She would steadily exaggerate and embellish her Bahian outfit, often to the point of absurdity, in the years to come.

Miranda recorded that song and "A Preta do Acarajé" in duet with Caymmi on an Odeon single. Next came Miranda's recording of Caymmi's "Roda Pião" and his own solo recording debut with "Rainha do Mar" (Queen of the Sea) and "Promessa de Pescador" (Promise of a Fisherman). Caymmi's more urban material was perfect for the radio era, and he subsequently wrote numerous hit songs. Many were harmonically progressive, with altered chords and other innovations. "I arrived here [in Rio] with an unusual way of playing guitar for that time," he said. "I always had the tendency of altering the perfect chords. There were two soloists who did approximately the same thing as me, but with a difference: they were studious musicians and I wasn't. They were Anibal Sardinha [Garoto] and Laurindo de Almeida."[6]

Along with using unusual harmonic touches, Caymmi had an important influence on Brazilian lyric writing with his poetic use of colloquial language from Bahia and natural simplicity in storytelling. His urban sambas and evocative folkloric songs have been recorded by Miranda, Angela Maria, Dick Farney, João Gilberto, Gilberto Gil, Caetano Veloso, Gal Costa, Paul Winter, Andy Williams, Richard Stoltzman, and Caymmi himself. Many credit his guitar playing and compositions as being an important influence on the bossa nova generation. And beyond that is another legacy: his children—singer Nana, guitarist-composer-arranger Dori, and flutist-composer Danilo—have made important marks on Brazilian music as well.

Carmen Miranda

In the 1940s Carmen Miranda was the personification of Brazil for many people in other countries. She was a beautiful woman who wore bangles on her arms, heaps of jewelry elsewhere on her body, and tropical fruits atop a turban. She danced in clogs with outrageously high heels, sang with enthusiasm and playfulness, and illustrated each stanza with expressive hand gestures and eye movements. Although few outside of Brazil are aware of it, Miranda (1909–1955) was a samba star at home in the 1930s before journeying to the United States to capture Hollywood's imagination.

Miranda was not entirely Brazilian. She was born in Marco de Canavezes, Portugal, but at the age of one moved with her family to Rio de Janeiro. A charming singer and exuberant performer, she conquered Brazil in 1930 with "T'aí,"

a marcha written by Joubert de Carvalho. A string of hit records followed, as she interpreted sambas and marchas by Dorival Caymmi, Ary Barroso, Assis Valente, Lamartine Babo, and other leading songwriters.

In 1939, thanks to help from her friend Sonja Henie, the Olympic ice-skater, and her American agent, Lee Shubert, Miranda made her Broadway debut, wearing an exaggerated, embellished version of the colorful Bahian dress that she had worn in *Banana da Terra*, and singing catchy songs like "South American Way" and "Mamãe Eu Quero." Exotic, merry, and vivacious, Carmen took Manhattan by storm. Soon her face was everywhere, on magazine covers and billboards. Saks Fifth Avenue sold her exclusive line of tur-

▼ Carmen Miranda with no fruit atop her head, from the 1944 movie *The Gang's All Here. (Courtesy of Museu Carmen Miranda.)*

bans and costume jewelry, and she appeared in advertisements pitching Rheingold beer.

During concerts Miranda was backed by the Bando da Lua (the Moon Gang), a superb group led by Aloysio de Oliveira, who would later play a major role in helping launch bossa nova. Miranda soon got a call from Hollywood, and she acted and performed musical numbers in many films in the 1940s, including *Down Argentine Way, That Night in Rio, Weekend in Havana, The Gang's All Here, Greenwich Village*, and *Copacabana*. She also recorded numerous singles, including the now famous choro "Tico Tico no Fubá" in 1945.

Along the way, her outfits became steadily wilder and more colorful, inspiring many Carmen Miranda impersonators. One of the first was Mickey Rooney, in the 1941 film *Babes on Broad-*

way, and decades later Miranda continues to be a popular character for costume parties. She is still seen by many as the personification of fun and extravagance.

SAMBA FROM THE MORRO

In the 1930s, as Carmen Miranda was crooning radio hits and the samba-canção songwriters were hitting their stride, the central area of Rio de Janeiro underwent great changes. Hundreds of houses were razed to make way for new streets and avenues. Suddenly the area where the poor blacks who had created samba lived became too expensive for them, and they had to move. Some relocated to the outskirts of town, but most preferred to make new homes in the *morros*, the hills

---

The Radio Era

The first radio broadcast in Brazil took place on September 7, 1922, during the celebrations of the centennial of Brazilian independence. In 1931 radio advertising was officially permitted, and radio stations sprouted all over the country. Mainly because of drama and musicals, radio soon became the most popular form of entertainment in Brazil. Radio helped develop popular music, giving singers, songwriters, musicians, and arrangers a secure professional environment for work, since they were signed by Brazilian stations much as Hollywood stars were signed by the big American studios. The medium's heyday in Brazil was the mid-1930s through the 1950s.[7]

Carmen Miranda, Aurora Miranda, Linda Batista, Marlene, Emilinha Borba, Araci de Almeida, Dolores Duran, Dalva de Oliveira, Orlando Silva, Ary Barroso, Lamartine Babo, Francisco Alves, Silvio Caldas, Nelson Gonçalves, Cauby Peixoto, Luis Gonzaga, Dorival Caymmi, Elizete Cardoso, and Angela Maria were some of the artists who boasted legions of fans and celebrity status, as the stations gave airplay to samba, samba-canção, bolero, and baião. Radio was the dream factory that stirred people's imaginations and set trends. "Cantoras do Rádio," recorded by the Miranda sisters, shows the importance of radio in those days:

> We're radio singers
> We sing our life away
> We send you to sleep at night
> We wake you up in the morning
> Our songs cross the blue space
> And join hearts from north to south
> In a big embrace

Braguinha, Lamartine Babo, and Alberto Ribeiro

---

that surround Rio. Samba may have been born in Praça Onze, but within a few decades it was performed there only once a year, during Carnaval.

By the 1950s the commercially popular samba-canção style had been diluted by contact with boleros, fox-trots, and cha-cha-cha. The musical quality declined, and some dissatisfied young musicians, mostly middle class, made their own revolution: bossa nova. But up on the morros, in the favelas where many of the poor people now lived, the samba pioneered in Estácio had survived and continued its own evolution, while sticking to the traditional instruments of cavaquinho, pandeiro, and tamborim. At the time, the media labeled this classic style of samba *samba de morro* (to distinguish it from samba-canção and offshoots such as *sambolero* and *sambalada*). In its almost purely percussive form it was sometimes called *samba de batucada*.

By the late 1950s, samba de morro was too strong a cultural manifestation to stay in Rio's ghettos. It invaded the city and then the entire country. Cartola, Nelson Cavaquinho, Clementina de Jesus, Monsueto, Silas de Oliveira, Mano Décio da Viola, Zé Keti, and others led the charge.

Zé Keti (José Flores de Jesus, 1921–1999) was an important composer who wrote "A Voz do Morro" (Voice of the Hill) and "Opinião" (Opinion). Along with romantic songs, he wrote outspoken sambas with melancholy and fatalistic lyrics. They denounced the sad poverty in which the majority of Brazilians seemed doomed to live and lamented the fact that so many died needlessly. One such song was "Acender as Velas" (Light the Candles).

> *When there's no samba*
> *There's disillusion*
> *It's one more heart*
> *That stopped beating*
> *One more angel that goes to heaven*
> *May God forgive me*
> *But I'll say it*
> *The doctor arrived too late*
> *Because on the hill*

▲ Cartola. *(Photo by Paulo Moreira. Courtesy of Agência Globo.)*

> *There are no cars to drive*
> *No telephones to call*
> *No beauty to be seen*
> *And we die without wanting to die*

When Cartola (Angenor de Oliveira, 1908–1980) became identified with samba de morro, he was already a veteran sambista who in 1929 had helped found the most traditional escola de samba in Rio: Estação Primeira de Mangueira. In the 1930s he composed many hit sambas, including—with frequent partner Carlos Cachaça—"O Destino Não Quis" (Destiny Didn't Want It). Cartola's songs were acclaimed for their artful melodies and poignant lyrics.

In the early 1960s he and his wife, Zica, ran Zicartola, a restaurant that became a point of encounter between the bossa nova crowd of the Zona Sul (southern Rio) and the samba de morro artists of the Zona Norte (northern Rio). There it was easy to find, in the audience or on stage, names like Tom Jobim, Ismael Silva, Paulinho da Viola, João do Vale, Zé Keti, Dorival Caymmi, Clementina de Jesus, and Nara Leão.

Cartola's career was revived in the early 1970s, when many well-known singers covered his songs and popularized them throughout Brazil. Nara Leão recorded "O Sol Nascerá" (The Sun Will Rise), whose lines included "I intend to lead my life smiling / Because I lost my youth crying"; Gal Costa covered "Acontece" (It Happens); and Beth Carvalho released "As Rosas Não Falam" (The Roses Don't Talk), perhaps his most revered composition. In 1973, at age sixty-five, Cartola finally got a chance to record his first album, on the Marcus Pereira label.

Two other noted sambistas also had late-blooming commercial success: Clementina de Jesus and Nelson Cavaquinho (Nelson Antonio da Silva, 1910–1980). The latter was nicknamed for his facility with the cavaquinho during his early days of playing choro music. Later he switched to guitar, on which he created original chords and developed his own distinctive technique of playing with only the thumb and index finger of his right hand, pinching the strings. That, together with his harsh, weary voice, made commercial acceptance of his music even more difficult than it had been for Cartola. Alone or with his frequent partner Guilherme de Brito, Nelson Cavaquinho wrote more than two hundred songs. But his lyrical sambas had to wait until 1965 to achieve public acclaim, when singers like Nara Leão, Elizeth Cardoso, and Elis Regina started recording them. That opened the door for Nelson to release his own record in 1970. Among his classics are "Rugas" (Wrinkles), "Luz Negra" (Black Light), and "A Flor e o Espinho" (The Flower and the Thorn).

Clementina de Jesus (1902–1987) had to wait even longer to achieve mass acclaim. When she was sixty, Clementina was "discovered" by the writer and impresario Hermínio Bello de Carvalho, who arranged concert appearances for her. Clementina was something of a living musical archive, singing old lundus, jongos, and *sambas de partido alto* that had fallen into obscurity. She recorded her first album when she was sixty-eight: *Clementina, Cadê Você?* (Clementina, Where Are You?).

While samba-canção ruled the carioca airwaves, many great sambistas from the morros had composed and performed in relative obscurity. But by the late 1950s, the tide had turned. The escolas de samba were expanding into large and formidable institutions. They gave samba de

◄ João Bosco and Clementina de Jesus. *(Photo by Ricardo Pessanha.)*

More Late Bloomers and Old Timers

Clementina de Jesus and Cartola were followed decades later by another wave of late bloomers at the end of the 1990s and in the early years of the twenty-first century. All were talented samba singers and songwriters who had enjoyed long careers and unanimous recognition by their peers yet had suffered a total lack of interest on the part of music companies. Several were associated with the Velha Guarda da Portela, a group of veteran singers and songwriters connected to Portela escola de samba. Opportunity knocked when singer Marisa Monte produced the collective album *Tudo Azul* in 1999. "I like a lot of things in music, but just a few really move me. One of them is the Velha Guarda da Portela," said Marisa Monte.[8] Following that album, the Portela elders Casquinha (Otto Trepte, born in 1922), Jair do Cavaquinho (1922–2006), Argemiro (1923–2003), and Tia Surica (Iranette Barcelos, born in 1940) each recorded CDs. Their solo albums preserved the voices of a whole generation of Portela artists that otherwise would have been lost.

Another Portela Veteran, Monarco (Hildemar Diniz, born in 1933), also gained more visibility with *Tudo Azul*. Monarco is a singer-songwriter with a deep, full voice whose elegant sambas have been recorded by Zeca Pagodinho ("Coração em Desalinho," "Vai Vadiar") and Beth Carvalho ("Dor da Saudade").

The album also indirectly benefited Wilson Moreira (born in 1936), associated with Portela for several decades. Moreira is a versatile composer who feels comfortable writing sambas, lundus, jongos, and *calangos*. "He can put music to any group of words, even the phone directory," commented Delcio Carvalho.[9] Along with the Portela sambistas, Walter Alfaiate (Walter de Abreu, born in 1930) was another late bloomer who launched his first solo album, *Olha Aí*, in 1998, and followed it with *Samba na Medida* (2003) and *Tributo a Mauro Duarte* (2005). A refined crooner with a rich, grave voice who likes to use vibrato in the lower notes, Alfaiate is a professional tailor, and his interpretations are as precise and stylish as a well-cut suit.

Guilherme de Brito (1922–2006) wrote the masterpieces "A Flor e o Espinho" and "Folhas Secas" with Nelson Cavaquinho, but only recorded his first album in 2001. It featured a mere sampling of the collection of sambas he had kept in a suitcase for decades. Guilherme de Brito and Nelson Cavaquinho were connected with Mangueira, and so is Nelson Sargento (Nelson Mattos, born in 1924). Sargento is the author of classics such as "Agoniza Mas Não Morre." Nelson released few solo albums in his career, but in 2005 a box set brought together his *Flores em Vida* (2001), *Só Cartola* (1998), *Encanto da Paisagem* (1986), and *Sonho de um Sambista* (1978), and helped fill the gap.

Dona Edith do Prato was born in 1916 in Santo Amaro da Purificação, Bahia, the same city as Caetano Veloso and Maria Bethânia. She is the guardian of an almost lost tradition: as she sings her *sambas de roda* with a husky voice, she accompanies herself, scratching a plate with a knife. Dona Edith released her first album, *Vozes da Purificação*, in 2003, at eighty-seven years of age.

These musicians are "talented artists that struggled for the preservation of samba as a model of culture, entertainment, and discussion of social issues," in the words of Luis Carlos da Vila, a samba composer (born in 1949) from the next generation.[10]

morro a stronger and more elaborate rhythmic force and presented it in a new, grandiose form, with thousands of singers and dancers and hundreds of drummers and percussionists.

From the days of "Pelo Telefone" and ever after, samba would be intimately tied to Carnaval. It would transform Rio's Carnaval into one of the greatest popular festivals in the world. And the annual need for Carnaval songs to sing and parade to would in turn accelerate the development of samba.

CARNAVAL

A poor man's happiness resembles
The grand illusion of Carnaval

> Tom Jobim and Vinicius de Moraes,
> "A Felicidade" (Happiness)

Carnaval, disillusion
I left pain waiting for me at home
And I sang and danced
Dressed up as a king
But on Wednesday the curtains always fall

> Chico Buarque de Hollanda, "Sonho
> de Carnaval" (Carnaval Dream)

Every year, seven weeks before Easter, Brazil stops. It is Carnaval time. For four days, from Saturday through Tuesday, as a climax to summer in the Southern Hemisphere, the country sings and dances in dance halls and clubs, on the streets and beaches, or wherever there are people and music. In cities like Salvador, the celebration may go on for seven or eight days.

The music may be provided by a three-hundred-piece escola-de-samba drum section, a horn-and-percussion band, or a spontaneous group of people beating cans and bottles. Some wear special outfits for the occasion, some don't. You'll see clowns, pirates, sheiks, Indians, and lots of men dressed up as women. On display are as many dif-

▼ Good times at a Salgueiro escola de samba rehearsal in 2007. *(Photo by Chris McGowan.)*

ferent costumes as the imagination can conjure. Every part of Brazil celebrates the holiday in its own way. The intense street Carnaval of Salvador features the Afro-Brazilian rhythms of afoxés and blocos afro, and lively axé music (see Chapter Six), while Recife is renowned for its maracatu groups and frevo music (Chapter Seven). In this chapter we focus on Rio de Janeiro's Carnaval, the most famous celebration in Brazil.

Not every city in Brazil has a bustling street Carnaval. In some, you'll only find relatively well behaved indoor balls. People with less "carnavalesco" souls use the holidays to travel to places where they can relax far from the drums during the day and, if they feel like it, go dancing at night. But between New Year's Eve and Carnaval nothing really important is decided in Brazil. Quoting a popular Chico Buarque song, most people will say, "I'm saving myself for when Carnaval comes." The weather is hot, people become more outgoing, and sensuality is in the air. But amid all the craziness and frivolity, Carnaval serves the important purpose for Brazilians of maintaining cultural traditions—encoded in the music, dance, and costumes of the celebrations across the country.

Carnaval is a pre-Lent celebration (like Mardi Gras in New Orleans and Carnival in many Spanish-speaking countries) that has its roots in pre-Christian festivities held by the ancient Greeks, Romans, and others. Around the sixth century B.C., the Greeks held spring festivals in honor of Dionysus, the god of wine, and the power of wild nature. Merrymakers would often parade down the streets of their towns, sometimes with floats. The Romans carried on the seasonal celebration, expanding it into *saturnalia*, wherein slaves and masters would exchange clothes and engage in orgiastic behavior, and *bacchanalia*, drunken feasts in honor of Bacchus, the Roman version of Dionysus. It was, and is, a time to make merry, to drink, dance, and be crazy. The normal social order is turned upside down and mocked, and anything goes.

Despite their pagan origins, these festivities were assimilated into the traditions of Roman Catholic countries in Europe. There, as Carnaval evolved, it retained some of the characteristics of the ancient celebrations, such as the use of masks, and the general time of year (Carnaval takes place in late February or early March, just before spring in the Northern Hemisphere), but started losing its orgiastic features. It remained an important societal safety valve, a time to vent pent-up frustrations.

Entrudo, Zé Pereiras, Cordões, and Ranchos

Carnaval arrived in Brazil in the form of the chaotic Portuguese entrudo, in which celebrants would go to the streets and throw mud, dirty water, flour balls, and suspect liquids at one another, often triggering violent riots. The first masked Carnaval ball in Rio took place in 1840 at the Hotel Itália, with waltzes and polkas as the music of choice. Out in the streets, a young Portuguese shoemaker named José Nogueira Paredes had the idea in 1848 of entering a Carnaval parade and beating a big bass drum. In the following years many Zé Pereiras (a name that possibly was a distortion of José Paredes) filled the city with their songs and drums. The first European-style parades appeared in 1850, and these would become competitive events, with horses, military bands, and adorned floats, often sponsored by aristocratic groups called *sociedades*.

Around this time, Rio's poor people, who could not afford tickets to the expensive masked balls and were bored by the orderly parades, formed *cordões*, all-male groups that celebrated violently in the streets and paraded to African-based rhythms. This Afro-Brazilian influence increased after 1870, when the decline of the coffee plantations in northern Rio de Janeiro state forced a great number of slaves and former slaves to emigrate. Many came to Rio, the capital, looking for work.

From cordões came *ranchos*, a more civilized type of *cordão* that includes women. They made their first organized Carnaval appearance in 1873 and were important in the history of Carnaval for their introduction of themes to their parades. Like moving theater pieces, ranchos told their stories until their space in Carnaval was taken by the escolas

▲ A cartoon by Ângelo Agostinho depicting the death of the entrudo tradition during Carnaval. *(Courtesy of Agência JB.)*

de samba. Ranchos paraded as a category for the last time on Fat Tuesday of 1990, attracting little attention from merrymakers. In 2001 a group of artists led by Elton Medeiros founded Flor do Sereno, a rancho that since then has paraded in Copacabana, preserving the elegance of historical ranchos and dancing to *marcha-ranchos*, slow and more melodically developed variations of the marcha.

The Marcha

In 1899 the cordão Rosa de Ouro asked composer Chiquinha Gonzaga (1847–1935) to write a song for their parade. She composed a tune that incorporated a boisterous rhythm that she had heard cordões parading to as they passed by her house. The result was "Ô Abre Alas" (Make Way), the first registered marcha as well as the first song to be written specifically for Carnaval. It was also an enormous popular success, having just what it takes to be a successful Carnaval song: a contagious rhythm and simple, easy-to-memorize lyrics.

Hey, make way
I want to pass
I like parties
I can't deny that

In the 1920s, the marcha (or *marchinha*) began taking over Carnaval celebrations, especially the indoor ones. It was based on the song form developed by Gonzaga but gradually added influences from ragtime and the North American one-step. Today, marcha is a happy, festive style. It has a strong accent on the downbeat, lots of horns and drum rolls on the snares, and simple, humorous lyrics that often contain some kind of social criticism.

The 1930s were the golden decade of Carnaval songwriting. Innumerable marchas and sambas written then are classics today. The generation of composers that became popular around that decade—Noel Rosa, Ary Barroso, Lamartine Babo, Braguinha, and others—are legendary, and their songs are still sung during Carnaval and frequently recorded by contemporary artists. Other famous

◄ Chiquinha Gonzaga. *(Public domain image.)*

▼ The bloco Cacique de Ramos parading in 1970. *(Photo by Antonio Teixeira. Courtesy of Agência JB.)*

Carnaval songwriters of the 1930s and 1940s include Caninha, Eduardo Souto, Haroldo Lobo, Joubert de Carvalho, Benedito Lacerda, Antônio Nássara, Romeu Gentil, and Wilson Batista.

Samba has been the most popular Carnaval music in Rio since the early 1960s. But even though marchas have taken second billing ever since, the old standards from decades ago are still performed every year during Carnaval time. And *bandas*, which pass through Rio's streets with crowds trailing behind, primarily play marchas. Bandas have drums and a brass section and are informal in their structure, with some people wearing costumes or T-shirts with the banda's name and others dressing as they wish. In many ways bandas have brought back the spontaneity of Rio's old street Carnaval. Almost every neighborhood and suburb of the city has its own such group now, following the example of the pioneering Banda de Ipanema, founded in the '60s.

Another type of celebration in Rio's Carnaval comes from *blocos de empolgação*, great masses of people wearing the same costume that parade in one solid block, dancing very enthusiastically. To see a big bloco like Cacique de Ramos, whose members always dress up like Indians, or Bafo da Onça (Jaguar's Breath), with their six to seven thousand members coming down the street, is an unforgettable sight as they dance to thundering *samba de bloco*, played by the bateria that closes the parade. Samba, of course, is also the mainstay of Rio's most important Carnaval institution, the escolas de samba.

THE ESCOLAS DE SAMBA

Since their beginning in 1928, the escolas de samba have been an integral part of Rio's Carnaval and have evolved into a grand spectacle, an overwhelming experience for both participants and observers. The parade of the escolas encompasses dazzling floats, outlandish costumes, thousands of dancers, and veritable symphony orchestras of rhythm. It is like a giant popular opera, with so much happening, musically and visually, that you can't possibly take it all in at once.

The first escola de samba, Deixa Falar (Let Them Talk), was founded on August 12, 1928, in Estácio by Ismael Silva, Bide, Armando Marçal, Nilton Bastos, and others. Apparently the name "samba school" was an ironic reference to a grade school across the street from where the group met. Deixa Falar was more like a club or a fraternity, dedicated to making music and parading during Carnaval.

At the time, however, the police discouraged the blocos (Carnaval groups) of blacks and mulattos from celebrating downtown. This wasn't unusual, because the police were still repressing many manifestations of Afro-Brazilian culture at the time. In defiance, Deixa Falar went out for a small parade during the Carnaval of 1929 in Estácio and Praça Onze, where blocos from Mangueira, Oswaldo Cruz, and other neighborhoods also appeared. Deixa Falar was short-lived: by 1933 it was defunct. But a seed had been planted, and other samba schools were soon created.

On April 30, 1929, the members of several blocos formed an escola that ultimately proved to be the most traditional and longest-lived of them all: Estação Primeira de Mangueira (Number-One Station of Mangueira), whose founders included famed composers Cartola and Carlos Cachaça. Mangueira made its debut as a samba school in the Carnaval of 1930.

Another milestone came in 1935, when Paulo da Portela (Paulo Benjamim de Oliveira), Heitor dos Prazeres, and others created Portela. The new escola had its roots in the bloco Baianinhas de Oswaldo Cruz, which was founded in 1923 and later turned into Vai Como Pode. Portela was the most innovative of the escolas for many decades.

Also in 1935, the Getúlio Vargas federal administration stopped discouraging Rio's escolas and officially recognized their parades. Consequently, the festivities moved from Praça Onze to the wide avenues of downtown Rio. Every year grandstands were assembled, drawing large audiences, generating big expenses, and creating terrible traffic hazards. This problem was solved in 1984 when the city built the Passarela do Samba (Samba Path) on Rua Marquês de Sapucaí. Cariocas call it the Sam-

▲ A samba school parade in Rio. *(Photo by Lidio Parente. Courtesy of Embratur.)*

bódromo. Designed by the famous architect Oscar Niemeyer, it is a seven-hundred-meter-long pathway flanked by concrete stands that seat ninety thousand people. At its end is the huge, aptly named Praça da Apoteose (Apotheosis Square).

Over the past few decades the escolas have grown to become vital cultural institutions, and their importance stretches far beyond just staging parades. In 2007 there were seventy-one officially registered escolas de samba in Rio de Janeiro and dozens more in other Brazilian cities. Today there are also several dozen informal samba schools and blocos located in countries such as Germany, Japan, Great Britain, the United States, and Finland.

Although some escolas in Rio are located in middle-class neighborhoods, many are in favelas or working-class areas, with mostly low-income people as their members. For them, the escolas are a source of pride and in some cases the center of the community in which they are located. They are often social and recreational clubs, and some sponsor schools and nurseries and provide medical assistance and other services to their members. The money for all this comes from members' donations and income from dances, record sales, open rehearsals, and performances all over the world. The escolas are also supported by the rich, including many engaged in criminal activities such as illegal lotteries, casinos, and even drug dealing.

The parade during Carnaval is an eighty-minute climax around which life in an escola revolves the whole year. "The parade is the realization of people. They feel like kings for a day," says Hermínio Marquês Dias Filho, director of the Arranco do Engenho de Dentro escola de samba.

Much of the passion cariocas display toward their escola's presentation is generated by the event's competitive nature. Parade presentations are judged on music, theme, costumes, and other criteria. Those parading at the Sambódromo vie to remain or become one of the twelve samba schools showcased in the select "Special Group," which is the focus of the media's attention. Each year the two lowest-scoring escolas are demoted to

"Access Group," while the two highest-ranked "Access" units are promoted and parade with the top group at the next Carnaval.

The Parade

Mounting an escola-de-samba parade is a vast undertaking that involves tens of thousands of people, including musicians, dancers, craftsmen, costume makers, and other contributors, but its basic format is always the same. To begin with, every parade must have a theme, the *enredo*, which might be political or historical or a tribute to a particular person. Some aspect of the enredo has to be related to Brazil. It is chosen by the *carnavalesco*, a type of art director who is responsible for the visual aspect of the escola. Once the board of directors approves the enredo, the carnavalesco writes a synopsis of it, describing the message he wants to convey visually in the parade. Then, around June, this synopsis is distributed among the escola's composers so that they can begin writing sambas on the theme. Such a samba is called a *samba-enredo*.

When the composers have their sambas ready, they submit them to the directors, who choose the best ones. Around September rehearsals begin in the escola's headquarters, where musicians play old sambas and the contending sambas-enredo. The reaction of the members to the new sambas is decisive in the picking of the samba-enredo for the parade. On a certain night, usually at the end of October, the escola chooses the winner from the finalists.

It is a very special night. The escola-de-samba headquarters are noisy and crowded, and the composers organize groups of rooters who dance and sing loudly, carrying flags adorned with the name of their favorite samba. The competing sambas are sung in sequence, and at the end of the night the escola's president announces the winning song. The result is not always welcome, and fights can break out. The tension is understandable: the samba-enredo is crucial for a good parade and also generates money for the winning songwriters. The sambas-enredo from the escolas in the spe-

cial group are included in an annual album that usually is a best-seller.

For Carnaval in 1988, Mangueira's samba-enredo was "100 Anos de Liberdade: Realidade ou Ilusão" (100 Years of Freedom: Reality or Illusion), commemorating the centennial of Brazil's abolition of slavery in 1888 and protesting the poverty of many blacks in the country. The lyrics, written by Hélio Turco, Jurandir, and Alvinho, include an allusion to Ary Barroso's "Aquarela do Brasil."

> *Today, in reality, where is freedom*
> *Where is that which nobody has seen*
> *Little boy, don't forget that the Negro also*
>   *built*
> *The riches of Brazil*
> *Ask the Creator who painted this watercolor*
> *Free of the plantation's whip*
> *Imprisoned in the misery of the favela*

The winner that year was Vila Isabel, whose samba-enredo also explored Afro-Brazilian history. "Kizomba, Festa da Raça" (Kizomba, Festival of the Race) sang of Zumbi, the famous leader of the Palmares quilombo, samba singer Clementina de Jesus, and numerous aspects of African-based culture. Themes related to Afro-Brazilian heritage are commonplace. In 2007 Salgueiro presented the story of Candaces, a dynasty of African queens that included the queen of Sabah and Nefertiti. Here's an excerpt of the lyrics, by Dudu Botelho, Marcelo Motta, Zé Paulo, and Luiz Pião:

> *Majestic Africa*
> *Cradle of my ancestors*
> *Reflects the saga of black women and their*
>   *ideals*
> *In the mirror of life*

In contrast, other escolas in 2007 took themes such as gambling (Viradouro), the Portuguese language (Mangueira), the art of photography (Tijuca), and the fight against racial discrimination (Porto da Pedra). In any year some sambas-enredo are celebratory, while others are serious protests. And by the time Carnaval comes around, most people in Rio know many of that year's sambas-enredo by heart, having purchased the annual album (recorded and released before the parades), or having heard the most popular enredos played over and over on the radio.

After an escola's samba-enredo is chosen, all energy is focused on preparations and rehearsals for the parade. By this time the carnavalesco has already designed and ordered the costumes for the *alas*—the parade units into which escolas de samba are divided. Each ala wears a different costume and plays a specific part in the development of the theme. The number of alas varies from escola to escola. Beija-flor, for instance, has more than forty-five alas, whereas Imperio Serrano has fewer than thirty. But the total number of participants is usually the same—around four thousand participants in each big escola. Most have to buy their costumes from the escola, and many do so by making small monthly payments. Some costumes are inexpensive; others are quite elaborate and costly. Wealthy contributors sometimes pay for the outfits of poor but loyal members.

Two alas are mandatory. The *ala das baianas*, introduced by Mangueira in 1943, includes older women dressed Bahian-style who wear turbans

and broad, long-laced dresses. The other obligatory ala is the *comissão de frente* (front commission), a group that usually wears sophisticated costumes related to the enredo. They open the parade performing a carefully choreographed dance.

Practically every Brazilian can dance to samba, but few master its specific steps. Those men and women who do are called *passistas*. The *mestre-sala* (master of ceremonies) is a key passista who performs intricate, energetic samba steps as he escorts the *porta-bandeira* (flag-bearer), a woman who swirls and floats as she carries the escola's flag. These characters made their first appearances with the nineteenth-century sociedades. Dancing elegantly, the porta-bandeira carries the escola flag, while the mestre-sala dances around her, providing symbolic protection.

In between alas come the *carros alegóricos*—huge decorated floats that depict important aspects of the enredo. These floats are true pieces of art, mixtures of sculpture, architecture, and engineering. On top of them stand the *destaques*—men and women wearing either luxurious, expensive costumes or almost nothing at all. The making of the floats employs hundreds of people for at least six months. Seamstresses, sculptors, carpenters, and painters work busily together like

◄ The ala das baianas. *(Photo by Lidio Parente. Courtesy of Embratur.)*

▲ Surdos (biggest drums), repiques, and caixa played during a rehearsal for the bloco afro Orunmilá (a Carnaval alternative to the samba schools). *(Photo by Ricardo Pessanha.)*

a colony of ants up to the last minute, so that everything is ready for the February parade.

Organizing the thousands of people who will parade in an escola is extremely complicated. That is what the *diretores de harmonia* (harmony directors) are for. They do not have fun. They just work. Hours before the escola enters the Sambódromo, the harmony director begins organizing the parade in an outside area, the *concentração* (concentration), putting the arriving ala members in their proper places and setting the alas in the right order.

Some time before the parade, the puxador (main singer) beside the sound float begins to sing the samba-enredo. He is responsible for keeping thousands of voices in time with the drum section, the bateria. He will sing the same song for more than one hour and must make no mistakes. Slowly the members start singing with him, stimulated by the harmony director, who also takes care of keeping the energy high during the parade. After the whole escola has sung the samba two or three times without accompaniment, the most exciting moment in the parade preparation occurs: the musical entrance of the bateria. No one who has witnessed this moment will ever forget it. Some three hundred percussionists under the command of the mestre de bateria (percussion conductor) start playing perfectly in synch with the singing, coordinated by the mestre's whistle— which serves as his baton.

The Bateria

The number and type of percussion instruments used varies from escola to escola. Paulo Cordeiro de Oliveira Neto wrote an in-depth study of the Unidos da Tijuca bateria that was published in *Habitus*, an online social studies journal of Rio de Janeiro Federal University. He told us that in 2002 the escola's bateria paraded with the following lineup (by instrument and number of musicians playing that instrument): *surdo de primeira* (12),

▲ João Parahyba, member of Trio Mocotó, with a cuíca. *(Photo by Ricardo Pessanha.)*

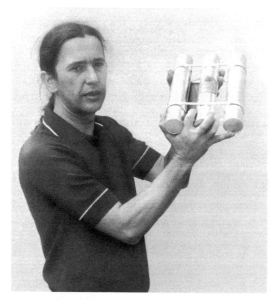

▲ João Parahyba playing a ganzá. *(Photo by Ricardo Pessanha.)*

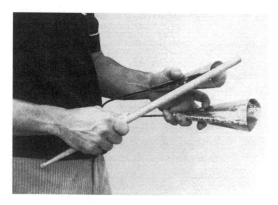

▲ João Parahyba with an agogô. *(Photo by Ricardo Pessanha.)*

surdo de resposta (12), *surdo cortador* (12), caixa (120), cymbal (1), cuíca (12), *chocalho* (23), *repique* (36), and tamborim (48).[11] But each escola has its own mix. Mangueira, for example, uses only one kind of surdo and has agogôs in its bateria. Some add *ganzás*, *reco-recos*, or *frigideiras* (percussion instruments shaped like frying pans) to their mix.

There are three types of surdos usually used by the baterias. The most important is the *surdo de marcação* (marking surdo), also called the *surdão* or surdo de primeira. It is the heaviest surdo, the one that plays on the second beat of the samba's 2/4 meter. The surdo de marcação holds the rhythm and is the base for the whole bateria.

The second-largest surdo is the *surdo de resposta* (answering surdo). As its name suggests, it answers the surdo de marcação by playing on the first beat, though less forcefully than the latter. The surdo cortador (cutting surdo) is the smallest surdo, and it plays on the beats and offbeats, "cutting" the rhythm and adding syncopation. In small samba groups the percussionist uses one surdo to play all three parts by himself—Airto Moreira provides an example of this technique on the samba-based song "Dreamland" on Joni Mitchell's album *Don Juan's Reckless Daughter*.

The conductor has a truly educated ear: during rehearsals he is able to spot one percussionist making a mistake among thirty playing the same instrument and a hundred playing others. He goes up to the erring musician and shouts instructions or tells him to stop and listen. And he must be able to keep all the percussionists synchronized in complicated *viradas* (changes in percussion patterns) and *paradinhas* (full stops), in which a bateria ceases playing during the parade so that everyone can hear other members carrying the song with only their voices. Then the playing resumes. This operation is the musical equivalent of stopping a jumbo jet's takeoff at the end of the runway and then getting it to take off again, but they do it.

A bateria percussionist is, together with the composers, passistas, destaques, baianas, and directors, part of the elite in an escola de samba. It's challenging to be one of them. Lobão, a rock drummer and singer who used to play tamborim for Mangueira, says, "I took a test to enter, a very hard one. The technique is very sophisticated. You've got to be very precise with a tamborim. You play together with seventy others, but everybody's got to play at the same time. You've got to hear only one beat. If not, the effect is lost."[12]

In the concentração, when the bateria starts playing, the energy level rises incredibly. As Lobão puts it, "The sound is twice as loud as a heavy metal band." Excitement takes over. Everything is ready for the parade.

Right before the gates open and the clock starts running, fireworks explode in the air. Then the comissão de frente steps into the Sambódromo, greeting people and asking permission to pass. One more parade has begun.

The bateria follows the first half of the escola into the *passarela*. They pass in front of thousands of spectators and along the way come to a space set off to the side for the bateria to play in front of the jury. There the drummers and percussionists play before the judges, while the second half of the escola passes. Then the bateria, following the last ala, closes the parade. By this time, the next escola is preparing to enter the Sambódromo.

The jury awards grades from one to ten for theme, samba-enredo, harmony, comissão de frente, mestre-sala and porta-bandeira, costumes, *evolução* (dance performance of the escola), bateria, baianas, and floats. The results are announced on Ash Wednesday. The winning escola celebrates in its headquarters, stretching Carnaval for one more night.

One big escola parade can cost more than a million dollars. It may seem absurd for poor people to spend so much money on something that lasts just eighty minutes. But what moves them is passion. Just as they are crazy about soccer, people in Rio love their escolas de samba. People do not say, "My favorite escola is Mangueira," or "I like Vila Isabel." They say, "I am Salgueiro," or "I am Portela." It's part of them. It's in their blood. It's in their souls.

Although today's escolas are made up of people from all races and social classes, they remain vital

▲ Chocalho. *(Photo by Ricardo Pessanha.)*

▲ João Parahyba with a metal reco-reco. *(Photo by Ricardo Pessanha.)*

▲ João Parahyba playing a tamborim. *(Photo by Ricardo Pessanha.)*

strongholds of Afro-Brazilian culture. As a standard-bearer from a São Paulo escola told us, "Candomblé and escolas de samba are the twentieth century's quilombos."

Television Coverage and Growth

In the early 1960s the escola Acadêmicos de Salgueiro hired Fernando Pamplona (born in 1926), who became the first outside professional designer to be a carnavalesco and design an escola's float and costumes. When Salgueiro, with Pamplona in charge, won the samba school parade in 1963, it was indicative of how both the role of carnavalesco and the ambition of each escola's presentation had expanded greatly. From that point on the parades became increasingly theatrical and grandiose. This trend coincided with the growth of the Brazilian television industry, and since the 1960s the parades have been televised live every year, from start to finish.

The parades were generating huge amounts of money, but at first the samba schools received very little of it. Riotur, the state tourism agency, had a lock on the ticket sales and broadcast rights income and handed out only a small percentage of the profits to the escolas. Then, in 1988, the major samba schools formed an association and demanded a new deal. They got it: 40 percent of Sambódromo ticket sales and a million-dollar contract with TV Globo (of which Riotur received 10 percent). The escolas also formed their own record company to release the lucrative annual compilation album of sambas-enredo.

The samba parades are now of an enormous scale and technical sophistication that would have been inconceivable to the founders of Deixa Falar in 1928. They are also vital to Rio's tourist business and generate huge sums through broadcast, music, and video rights. Not everyone has been happy about the transformation of the escolas into giant artistic and commercial enterprises. They have become highly organized productions, quite different from spontaneous street Carnaval celebrations elsewhere in Rio and the rest of Brazil. Some alas are well rehearsed in their movements,

▲ The 1990 version of the annual Sambas de Enredo album, a compilation of the year's Carnaval songs from the samba schools in the special group. *(Courtesy of BMG.)*

and the natural eroticism of Carnaval is often transformed into show business. The *rainhas da bateria* (drum-section queens) and other female destaques can resemble showgirls in a lavish floor show. Veteran singer-songwriter Caetano Veloso writes that the escolas have become "the street version of the Folies Bergère," although he praises the baterias as being "the most impressive manifestation of originality and musical competence to be found anywhere in Brazilian popular culture."[13]

Paulinho da Viola, a major samba figure of the last four decades, left Portela for many years because he felt that the escolas had become overly commercial and bureaucratic, a common complaint at the end of the twentieth century. He mourned that something got lost along the way. "Nowadays commercial interests are more important than cultural ones," he told us. "What was spontaneous has become official. An escola de samba now has an average of four thousand members. You can imagine the fights there are to choose the suppliers for all these people who will need shoes, costumes. That has attracted people to the escolas who don't belong to that cultural environment."[14] And, what is worse, the funding needs of the samba schools have made many dependent on the financial largesse of gangsters who run the *jogo de bicho* (animal game) lottery and illegal casinos. Some samba school directors and board members have been assassinated by criminal rivals. Yet the show must go on, and people from all levels of Brazilian society seek to participate in the annual parades. Portela, Mangueira, and the other big escolas continue to mount ever more ambitious and lavish parades each year.

The Major Escolas de Samba

Mangueira, the oldest active escola, has attracted many illustrious songwriters and singers during its long history, including Nelson Sargento, Elza Soares, Beth Carvalho, Alcione, Leci Brandão, Jamelão, and Guilherme de Brito. Portela, the second-oldest, has been responsible for setting most of the patterns that the others have followed. Its founder, Paulo da Portela, and his associates introduced into the parade such now-obligatory items as the enredo (theme), the comissão de frente (front commission), and the carros alegóricos (decorated floats). In addition, many famed composers and singers have been associated with Portela, including Zé Keti, Paulinho da Viola, Candeia, João Nogueira, Paulo César Pinheiro, Marquinhos de Oswaldo Cruz, Monarco, Marisa Monte, and Zeca Pagodinho.

Portela is located in the neighborhood of Madureira, as is another historically important escola, Império Serrano. Composers Silas de Oliveira (1916–1972) and Mano Décio da Viola (1908–1984), singers Jorginho do Império (Mano's son), Roberto Ribeiro, and Dona Ivone Lara (the first woman to have one of her compositions sung by an escola) are among those who have been associated with Império during its history.

While Salgueiro set the precedent for ever more ostentatious parades, Beija-Flor has taken this tendency to its extreme and is now famous, though occasionally criticized, for its visually glittering and luxurious presentations. Fittingly, Joãozinho Trinta—who worked under Pamplona at Salgueiro—was Beija-Flor's carnavalesco in the

1970s and 1980s; he later moved to Unidos do Viradouro, which was champion in 1997. Aside from its audacious floats and costumes, Beija-Flor has had talented singers such as Neguinho da Beija-Flor, a puxador who has recorded several best-selling samba albums. The escola has been quite successful, winning the Sambódromo competition five out of the six years between 2003 and 2008.

Mocidade Independente, another major force, is traditionally famed for the perfection of its bateria, generally conceded to be the most synchronized and precise of any escola. One of its past conductors, Mestre André, was the inventor of the immensely difficult aforementioned paradinha maneuver.

Today's escolas have a faster, more uniform percussion pattern than in years past, in large part because of time constraints. If a samba school takes longer than eighty minutes for its parade, it loses precious points in the final judging. Before the events were so organized, the samba schools played slower, mellower, and more melodic sambas-enredo. Nowadays they are faster, jumpier, and less musically differentiated. Still, there are clear differences between the escolas. For example, Mangueira sounds different because traditionally all of its surdos are surdos de primeira, played only on the second beat of each bar. Salgueiro displays a heavier use of cuícas, which adds more flavor to the general sound and lessens its percussive impact. And Império Serrano's extensive employment of agogôs gives its sound a more metallic texture.

Escolas de samba have many talented members, old and young, traditionalists and revolutionaries. They exemplify the creative power of a carioca population that in general lives in poor socioeconomic conditions. The escolas are often their community center, and samba a source of spiritual sustenance.

Other important samba schools include Porto da Pedra, Unidos da Tijuca, São Clemente, Estácio de Sá, Vila Isabel, Imperatriz Leopoldinense, Viradouro, Caprichosos de Pilares, Grande Rio, and União da Ilha.

The Rebirth of Rio's Street Carnaval

The opening of the Sambódromo in 1984 caused a temporary decline in the free Carnaval manifestations in the streets of Rio. Cariocas who weren't directly involved with the official parade preferred to leave town or stay away from the streets, and the number of bandas and blocos diminished considerably. But that didn't last too long. From 2000 on, new Carnaval groups appeared, and others that had gone through hard times began to grow considerably. In 2006, for instance, Suvaco do Cristo (Christ's Armpit), a bloco from the Jardim Botânico neighborhood, gathered more than fifty thousand merrymakers. That scared its directors. The following year they didn't inform the press about what time the parade would start, hoping that only the more loyal and traditional fans would appear, having gotten the information by word of mouth. It should be added that all one has to do to participate in a bloco parade is show up, in contrast to the discipline and requirements imposed on participants by the escolas. The structure of a bloco is very simple, requiring only basic organization, and it leaves a lot of space for creativity and improvisation.

Besides the Suvaco de Cristo, some of the largest blocos and bandas that paraded in 2008 were Simpatia é Quase Amor, Banda de Ipanema, Monobloco (created by singer-songwriter Pedro Luís), Bloco do Cordão do Bola Preta (founded in 1918), and Carmelitas. These groups dragged huge crowds of up to a hundred thousand people at a time through the streets of Rio.

According to *Programa* magazine, in 2006 more than five hundred blocos and bandas paraded in Rio during the four days of Carnaval.[15] There are also celebrants who follow traditions from other parts of Brazil. The blocos afro Orunmilá, Agbara Dudu, and Lemi Ayo, for instance, and the Rio Maracatu group represent the Carnaval cultures of Salvador and Recife, respectively, in Rio de Janeiro.

THE MODERN SAMBA ERA

Paulinho da Viola, whom we mentioned above, is someone whom music critic Sérgio Cabral considers "a legitimate heir of the Estácio sambistas,"[16] meaning that he follows in the footsteps of such innovative composers as Ismael Silva, Bide, and Marçal from the Estácio neighborhood, the "cradle of samba." Paulinho is a defender of samba in its traditional form, as it was created by the Estácio composers. He does not accept samba mixed with bolero or diluted with other pop currents, and he likes playing it with the traditional instruments: guitar, cavaquinho, pandeiro, tamborim. Paulinho has commented, "It seems absurd that I have attached myself to these formulas that are considered of the past, but I like them very much. To me the most important thing is the feeling, and this form of music moves me more."[17]

Paulinho combines modern arrangements with a subdued, elegant vocal style. His lyrics, known for their clarity, are full of feeling but avoid sentimentality. Born in Rio in 1942, Paulinho (Paulo César Batista de Farias) had a guitar-playing father, César Farias, who was a respected choro musician. Every week during Paulinho's childhood, Jacó do Bandolim and his choro group, Época de Ouro, got together at César's place to make some music. That made little Paulo decide to learn how to play the guitar and instilled in him a love for traditional samba.

His first contact with escolas de samba was with a small one—Unidos de Jacarepaguá—but in 1963 he was admitted to the *ala dos compositores* (group of composers) from Portela. The samba that opened the door for him was "Recado" (Message), written with Casquinha. Today it is a classic.

Take this message
To her who only did me wrong
Tell her I'm better the way I am
In the past I was a sufferer

▲ Paulinho da Viola, with his cavaquinho. *(Photo by Walter Firmo. Courtesy of BMG.)*

He also composed Portela's unofficial hymn, "Foi Um Rio Que Passou em Minha Vida" (There Was a River That Passed Through My Life). Paulinho joined Zé Keti's group, A Voz do Morro, and the group's two albums in 1965 included five of Paulinho's sambas and were critically acclaimed. The following year he recorded an album with his partner and friend, Elton Medeiros, *Na Madrugada* (Late at Night). Choro-master Henrique Cazes considers Medeiros "a very special melodist who knows how to make a perfect mix of intuition and technical sophistication."[18] The collaboration resulted in excellent sambas like "Arvoredo," "Quatorze Anos" (Fourteen Years), and "Momento de Fraqueza" (Moment of Weakness). In 1969 came Paulinho's first big hit, "Sinal Fechado" (Red Light), with which he won TV Record's music festival.

The tune is considered a perfect metaphor for that closed, dark dictatorship era. It is a dialogue between two friends who have not seen each other for a long time, as by chance they stop side by side at a traffic light.

I had so much to say
But it vanished in the dust of the streets . . .
I also have something to say
But I have just forgotten it

Paulinho also frequently explored the choro genre, recording compositions in that style such as "Abraçando Chico Soares" (Hugging Chico Soares). After "Prisma Luminoso" (Luminous Prism) in 1983 came a six-year silence from Paulinho in terms of recording. "I wouldn't get strong promotion from the record companies. It was a time when they had decided that only rock would sell," he commented. Paulinho's comeback record was called *Eu Canto Samba* (I Sing Samba), a clear statement of his musical beliefs and of the purity of his art. His album *Bebadosamba* (1996) reaffirmed that statement. Its title is a pun that can be translated either as "Drunk Samba" or "Drink from Samba." Paulinho is now a master who inspires new generations of samba and MPB musicians; his 2007 *Acústico MTV* album featured some of his classic tunes with new arrangements and was chosen as the best album of the year by *Rolling Stone Brasil*.[19]

Clara, Beth, Alcione, and Elza

Four names stand out among female samba singers who achieved popular success during the late twentieth century: Clara Nunes, Beth Carvalho, Alcione, and Elza Soares. The four fully explored all the stylistic evolutions and permutations undergone by samba, carrying the genre's history in their collective albums.

▼ A Clara Nunes album cover. *(Courtesy of EMI.)*

Clara Nunes (1943–1983) was the best-selling samba vocalist of the 1970s, her success propelled by an impassioned, sensual voice and a generally strong choice of material. Her big breakthrough came in 1974 with her *Alvorecer* (Dawn) record, the first album by a female singer in Brazil to sell more than five hundred thousand units.

From then on, all of Nunes's releases went gold or platinum. She was also an international success, and toured Europe and Japan. Her innumerable hit songs covered not only contemporary pop and samba tunes but also old-guard compositions (by Ataulfo Alves, for example) and songs that explored her Afro-Brazilian heritage. "A Deusa dos Orixás" delved into candomblé mythology, while "Ijexá (Filhos de Gandhy)" used the Bahian *ijexá* rhythm.

Singer Beth Carvalho (born in 1946), who helped launch the pagode movement in the early 1980s, has had a knack for picking the best work of Brazil's samba songwriters. She has also helped preserve Brazil's musical heritage by recording songs in a variety of genres. For example, her 1987 release *Ao Vivo—Montreux Festival* (Live at the Montreux Festival) included renditions of *partido alto* ("Carro de Boi"), samba de bloco ("Cacique de Ramos"),

▲ An Alcione album cover. *(Courtesy of BMG.)*

pagode samba ("Da Melhor Qualidade," "Pé de Vento"), a folkloric jongo ("A Vovó Chica"), a pagode sendup of Jobim's bossa nova "Samba do Avião," and an Edil Pacheco and Moraes Moreira afoxé ("O Encanto do Gantois"). "O Encanto" is a tribute to Mãe Menininha, a mãe-de-santo (head priestess) of the venerable Gantois candomblé terreiro (worship ground) in Salvador. Carvalho interprets her selections with a powerful, smoky voice and richly rhythmic arrangements.

Like Clara and Beth, vocalist Alcione (born in 1947) covers a wide range of regional styles on her albums. She can switch effortlessly from romantic ballads perfect for a dark nightclub to regional pop styles and folkloric excursions. For example, her 1986 album *Fruto e Raiz* (Fruit and Root) had pop sambas and ballads, a bumba-meu-boi ("Mimoso"), and a forró ("Eu Quero Chamegar"). With her robust, commanding voice, Alcione has had numerous hit albums ever since her first smash, 1975's *A Voz do Samba* (The Voice of Samba). "Samba is the principal music of this country," she told us. "It's capable of miracles, it has a power that is magical even for those who don't listen to it throughout the year. When the month of Carnaval arrives, samba can unite all types of persons, from every religion, race, color, musical background, and economic class."

▲ Beth Carvalho. *(Courtesy of BMG.)*

Born in São Luis de Maranhão in 1947, Alcione came to Rio when she was only twenty. But she adapted quickly, joining the Mangueira escola de samba by the early 1970s and later becoming a member of its board of directors. "I don't sing with Mangueira, I *am* Mangueira. My blood is pink and green [Mangueira's colors]."

Elza Soares (born in Rio in 1937) has had a long career full of ups and downs, alternating periods of popularity with others of ostracism. Her coarse, powerful voice and jazz-influenced interpretations gained her both admiration and rejection. A recording artist since 1959, Soares made her latest comeback with *Do Cóccix até o Pescoço* (2002), an album that featured new compositions by Chico Buarque, Caetano Veloso, and Jorge Benjor written especially for her.

Martinho da Vila

In the Vila Isabel neighborhood, once the haunt of Noel Rosa, another famous name is Martinho da Vila (real name Martinho José Ferreira), a singer-songwriter who was born during Carnaval in 1938 in Duas Barras, a small town in Rio de Janeiro state. His first escola was Aprendizes da Boca do Mato, of which he was the musical director; he was serving in the army at the time. In 1965 Ferreira switched his allegiance to Vila Isabel and identified so much with his new escola (and vice versa) that he became Martinho da "Vila."

Martinho's songwriting would play a role in the lyrics of sambas-enredo becoming shorter and more colloquial. "Carnaval de Ilusões" (Carnival of Illusions), his first effort for Vila Isabel, was revolutionary. At that time sambas-enredo had extremely long narrative lyrics and a subdued, mellow tempo. Martinho's 1967 composition, written with Gemeu, was based on partido alto, an old type of samba featuring short, light refrains that the singers must follow with improvised verses. "What I did was to add a story to the partido alto structure," Martinho explains in *Nova História*.

At that point Martinho didn't think he could make a living making music. Then in 1968 came his first big success, "Pra Que Dinheiro?" (Money,

What For?). The next few years brought many more hits, among them "O Pequeno Burguês" (The Little Bourgeois); "Iaiá do Cais Dourado" (Iaiá of the Golden Pier), the samba-enredo for Vila Isabel in 1969; "Segure Tudo" (Hang on to Everything); and "Batuque na Cozinha" (Batuque in the Kitchen). Sergeant Ferreira retired from the military in 1971. He enjoyed enormous commercial success in the '70s, commonly selling more than half a million copies of each album (big numbers for the Brazilian record market at the time).

Martinho's songs feature his relaxed, subtle, husky voice, which softly and confidently works in and around the intricate, compelling rhythms played by his band. It is a rich sound, one that allows listeners to savor all the rhythmic and textural subtleties of his material. And his songs range across many genres: in albums like *Batuqueiro* (Drummer), *Coração Malandro* (Malandro Heart), and *Festa da Raça* (Party of the Race), he explores partido alto, *congada*, bossa, afoxé, and *pontos de umbanda*. He returned to the top of the charts in

▼ Martinho da Vila. *(Courtesy of Sony.)*

◀ Mart'nália (*center, on pandeiro*), performing samba. *(Photo by Ricardo Pessanha.)*

1995 with *Tá Delícia, Tá Gostoso* (It's Delightful, It's Delicious), which sold more than one million copies. He has attempted to expand his international audience with *Conexões* (2003), which had French versions of some of his hits, and the Latin Grammy–nominated *Brasilatinidade* (2005), which offered Italian, Romanian, and Spanish songs spiced with samba.

Besides being an innovative sambista, Martinho has a special devotion to black culture. He has been to Angola many times to learn about other aspects of African music, and during the 1980s he organized Kizomba, a festival of black culture in Rio. But he wants to share his cultural blessings and Afro-Brazilian axé (a Yoruba word for "positive energy," "life force," or "peace") with all, as he sings in "Axé Pra Todo Mundo" (Axé for All the World).

> I, *a black Brazilian,*
> *Desire this for all Brazil*
> *For all races, all creeds . . .*
> *Axé for all the world*

Martinho also has a daughter, Mart'nália, who has become a star in her own right, singing sam-

bas, pop ballads, and compositions in other genres (see Chapter Four).

Pagode Samba

The 1970s were good years for samba, commercially and artistically. Record sales for the category soared, and deserving artists like Martinho da Vila and Clara Nunes thrived. So did João Nogueira (1941–2000), whose singing style featured a personal phrasing filled with surprising pauses and a typically carioca irreverence. Also included in the success were many singers without strong cultural roots who pleased the public with samba-based songs with romantic lyrics. Using this formula, Benito de Paula, Luis Airão, Agepê, and Wando cumulatively sold millions of albums. But, more important, a new generation of samba musicians emerged in that decade who would update the genre while also bringing it back to its roots. Their style of samba would gain the commercial label of pagode, and it soon became a major musical movement.

It all started in the mid-1970s, when a group of musicians associated with the Carnaval bloco Cacique de Ramos started getting together for a pagode, a party where people played samba. Every Wednesday night, Bira, Ubirany, Sereno, Almir Guineto, Neoci, Jorge Aragão, and various other talented musicians united for beer, appetizers, and samba in the bloco's rehearsal space. The atmosphere was informal, the mood collective. The music, often based in the old partido alto style, featured improvising by the singer and the singing of the refrain by everyone else. It was more like being back at Tia Ciata's house, a musical gathering of friends. There was no distinction between players and audience.

In addition, the samba being made in Ramos added some new instrumental twists. Sereno introduced the *tan-tan*, a type of atabaque, which replaced the larger and heavier surdo. This was more practical for spontaneous samba get-togethers, as the tan-tan could be carried more easily on buses, the mode of transportation for Rio's working class. Almir Guineto added a banjo, which was louder than a cavaquinho and better for open-air gatherings. Ubirany started playing a hand-held repique, called a *repique de mão*, and dispensed with the customary use of drum sticks. And Bira played the pandeiro in unusual ways. The sound was intimate and earthy, with new percussive textures. Their lyrics were unpretentious, focusing on situations from their daily life.

"They changed the sonority of samba, they brought back the 'batuque,' the instrument played with the hands," said Beth Carvalho.[20] She also pointed out the innovation of Almir Guineto, who "created a different banjo, with a shorter arm, tuned like a cavaquinho." Carvalho recalled, "So I got there and saw those harmonies, that swing . . . drums played with the hands! A tribal sound, closer to Africa."[21]

Brazil's top samba record producer, Rildo Hora, told us, "Beth invited me to go to Cacique to listen to the songs and the different percussion that they were playing there. I liked what I saw and heard so much that I talked to Beth and we decided to do something that changed the way people sang and played samba in Rio: we invited those Cacique percussionists to play on Beth's next album."[22]

▲ Grupo Fundo de Quintal's Bira playing a pandeiro. *(Photo by Armando Gonçalves. Courtesy of RGE.)*

▲ Grupo Fundo de Quintal's Sereno playing a tan-tan. *(Photo by Armando Gonçalves. Courtesy of RGE.)*

▲ Zeca Pagodinho early in his career. *(Courtesy of RGE.)*

▲ Zeca Pagodinho. *(Courtesy of Universal Music Brazil.)*

The album, *De Pé no Chão* (Feet on the Ground, 1978), and *Beth Carvalho no Pagode* (1979) brought the compositions and playing of the Ramos musicians to the Brazilian public for the first time. Several of those musicians formed the Grupo Fundo de Quintal (Backyard Group), which—with Carvalho's help—secured a recording contract with RGE and released their debut album, *Samba é no Fundo de Quintal,* in 1980. Someone who noticed that Fundo de Quintal was creating something new was Nei Lopes, a singer, songwriter, and scholar who dedicates his time to music, literature, and the study of Afro-Brazilian urban culture. He wrote several songs with Sereno and from the beginning gave the group his total support.

The Ramos composers helped to revitalize the partido alto style of samba, as Lopes notes in his book *Partido-Alto: Samba de bamba.*[23] Hora told us that in the pagode get-togethers, "everyone sings a lot of partido alto because it's a samba that has a repeated refrain. In between the refrains, there is musical play, improvised verses. It's inviting."[24] The style, also employed by Martinho da Vila, became closely identified with the *pagodeiros,* although they explored other types of samba as well.

Many big names started recording songs by the Fundo de Quintal composers, whose sambas had catchy melodies and strong rhythms, and the record companies and press started calling their music pagode. Carvalho popularized their compositions on her albums, and the Grupo Fundo de Quintal's sales increased with each new release. Guineto secured a record deal with RGE and a compilation album called *Raça Negra* (Black Race) introduced Jovelina Pérola Negra (1944–1998), Mauro Diniz (Monarco's son), Pedrinho da Flor, and a young Zeca Pagodinho to the public. Around 1985 their careers took off, and they started selling millions of records. Within a few years the commercial success of pagode had peaked, but it had popularized worthy new artists, added some great songs (like Guineto's "Caxambu") to the list of samba standards, and breathed new life into Brazil's most notable genre.

Zeca Pagodinho

Among the artists of the pagode movement, singer-songwriter Zeca Pagodinho has become the most celebrated. Zeca blossomed into Brazil's most charismatic samba performer and one of the nation's most popular musicians. "He is the people, he's samba in power," we were told by Rildo Hora, Zeca's longtime producer and arranger, explaining the popular appeal of Jessé Gomes da Silva Filho, born in Rio in 1959. His unassuming manner and very personal style of composing and singing have made Zeca "the spokesman of those who have a simple way of life and appreciate samba," observed Hora, who added that Brazilians identify with Zeca because he's informal and funny, and "his interviews show he's modest, a good father, a good son, a good friend." Aside from his personality, "the artistic and technical quality of his music is undeniable," noted Hora. His singing style possesses an "interesting rhythmic division [that] pleases sophisticated musicians, jazz musicians. Even João Gilberto praised him for the way he divides the samba nuances."[25]

Since 1986 Zeca has enjoyed a long string of hit songs and albums. He has recorded many of his own compositions, which are accurate reports about life in Rio drawn from real experience. And he is also "the major interpreter of a group of songwriters who come from the working classes and have followed him since the beginning of his career," commented Hora. "Coração em Desalinho," "Samba pras Moças," "Faixa Amarela," "Não Sou Mais Disso Não," "Deixa a Vida me Levar," and "Vai Vadiar" are a few of the songs he has made famous.

Pagodinho has made multiple gold and platinum records but has stayed true to his early inspirations. He still listens to the same favorite artists at home: Velha Guarda da Portela, Paulinho da Viola, João Nogueira, Silvio Caldas, and Jackson do Pandeiro, among others. And he doesn't dodge his responsibility as a keeper of the best samba traditions in these commercial times. Yet he is unpretentious and doesn't want to be a hero. As he told *Jornal do Brasil*, "I'm a human being. I can't

be always perfect. I can get hoarse, I can get ill, I can drink too much."[26]

Zeca Pagodinho's philosophy can be summarized by the lyrics Serginho Meriti wrote for "Deixa a Vida me Levar," a song Zeca made famous:

> *Let life take me*
> *Life, take me*
> *I'm happy and thankful*
> *for everything God gave me*

Jorge Aragão and Dudu Nobre

Jorge Aragão, born in Rio in 1949, is another member of the Cacique de Ramos group who has achieved great popularity. An eclectic singer-songwriter who has written hits for many interpreters ("Coisinha do Pai" and "Vou Festejar" for Beth Carvalho, "Enredo do Meu Samba" for Sandra de Sá, and "Não Sou Mais Disso" for Zeca Pagodinho, for instance), Aragão defined his musical persona with his 2004 album *Da Noite Pro Dia*, which augmented his samba with a rap song, lots of romantic lyrics, and some lavish arrangements. "Where I come from, it's not a sin to use keyboards and strings. I'm from Padre Miguel but I don't come from any escola de samba. I was a member of Fundo de Quintal, but my arrangements were never limited to cavaquinho, banjo, and tan-tan. I learned a lot listening to seresta and dance orchestras. If you want to talk about stereotypes, I'm the anti-sambista," he commented. In 1999 Aragão recorded an instrumental version of Charles Gounoud's "Hail Mary," with Jorge playing cavaquinho in a samba rhythm. In 2002 he interpreted the "Ária (Cantilena)" from the "Bachianas Brasileiras no. 5" of Villa-Lobos. In *Da Noite Pro Dia* he decided to record a Portuguese version of "Can't Take My Eyes Off of You" entitled "O Céu nas Mãos." He observed, "Samba is my root, but I'm not rootsy."[27]

Dudu Nobre (born in Rio in 1974) is a legitimate samba heir. His parents organized pagodes in downtown Rio in the '80s and for six years he played cavaquinho in Zeca Pagodinho's band. In 1999 he left to record his first album, *Chega Mais*, which was the starting point of a solid career. Dudu pays tribute to the samba ancestors and he sometimes includes maxixes and candomblé songs in his albums, but he's also capable of starting a song with scratches and distorted guitars before slipping into his customary infectious samba groove, as he did on "Blitz Funk," from his second CD, *Moleque Dudu* (2001). Renowned music critic Tárik de Souza considers Dudu a renovative force in samba.[28]

Bezerra and Dicró

Also important in the 1980s and 1990s was singer Bezerra da Silva (1927–2005), who interpreted sambas that he called "heavy partido alto," which painted a vivid picture of life in Rio's favelas. Bezerra was born in Recife and later moved to Rio, where he established his career. He told us, "The authors of the songs are humble people who live on the morros. They write about the day-to-day reality of the morro,"[29] including the prejudice and victimization suffered by residents there.

The lyrics of Bezerra's sambas feature so much slang from the morro that they are sometimes

▼ Bezerra da Silva singing a samba. *(Photo by Ricardo Pessanha.)*

barely intelligible to the Brazilian middle class. They generally talk about drug dealing, murder, crime, police repression, racism against blacks, and other situations experienced by favela residents. The lyrics of "Bicho Feroz" (Wild Animal), written by Tonho and Claudio Inspiração and recorded by Bezerra, are not far afield from those of American gangster rap.

> *When you have a gun*
> *You are real mean*
> *Without it, your walk changes*
> *So does your voice*

Dicró, another singer, runs on the same track as Bezerra, singing lyrics that are a window into favela life. Critics have labeled their music *sambandido* (bandit samba).

Pop Samba

In 1992 a group from São Paulo called Raça Negra that had been performing on the road for ten years finally achieved commercial success, invading the airwaves with its own material and covers of rock and *sertaneja* tunes sung in samba rhythm. What

Raça Negra created was also labeled pagode by the industry and the press, but in fact it was a new variation of samba that most traditional sambistas do not like. They replaced pagode's tan-tans, cavaquinho, and banjo with keyboards, saxophone, and bass guitar, included corny lyrics, and gave their songs what Luiz Carlos da Silva, the band leader, calls "a funky swing," heavily influenced by the soul music of Tim Maia and the rhythms of Jorge Benjor. It is a pop samba that is quite different from the pagode made by Pagodinho and his peers.

In the following years, many new groups followed Raça Negra's lead. And in spite of Beth Carvalho's opinion ("the romantic pop stream is a corruption of the real pagode"),[30] acts like Só Prá Contrariar, Molejo, Grupo Raça, Negritude Junior, Art Popular, Exaltasamba, Soweto, Kiloucura, Swing e Simpatia, Grupo Revelação, Sorriso Maroto, and singers Gustavo Lins and Belo were extremely popular in the 1990s and 2000s.

Other groups achieved great commercial success with a pop variation of samba de roda. Two of the most successful bands were Companhia do Pagode and Gera Samba, which scored the respective hits "Na Boquinha da Garrafa" and "É o Tchan" in the mid-1990s. Both groups were from Bahia and featured a bouncy pop samba sound that included simple lyrics loaded with sexual double entendres. Their songs are on a completely different track from the other offspring of the music created in Praça Onze and Estácio, but they are another variation of the vast genre that is samba. Samba has also been mixed with electronic music (see Chapter Ten), as in Fernanda Porto's international dance-floor hit "Sambassim."[31]

The Lapa Renaissance

At the end of the '90s, college students, intellectuals, and musicians started to get together in the streets and bars of Lapa, Rio's old decaying bohemian neighborhood. There they played, sang, danced, or just listened to choro and rootsy samba. Talented young artists appeared, and the bar owners began to cater to a new public. That phenomenon soon crystallized into a preservation movement of Rio's dearest musical traditions and a vital urban transformation. Antique shops and run-down two-story houses were renovated and turned into theaters, music venues, restaurants, and nightclubs. Those places came back to life as new customers came to listen to performances of songs by old samba masters mixed with more recent material by Paulinho da Viola, Chico Buarque, Zeca Pagodinho, and Djavan, among others. Some artists who came of age in Lapa after the start of the new millennium had already been on the road for quite a while, but singing and playing there gave them the boost they needed to reach larger audiences.

Such was the case of Teresa Cristina, whom Hora calls the "queen of Lapa."[32] A Rio native born in 1968, Teresa sings traditional sambas with a suave, captivating voice and intimate style. Ana Costa, also born in 1968, comes from Vila Isabel, the land of Noel Rosa and Martinho da Vila. She has been singing pagode samba accompanied by her cavaquinho since her days with O Roda, one of the first all-women samba bands. Nilze Carvalho (born in Nova Iguaçu in 1969) spent seven years playing in Japan and all over the world, and then returned to Lapa, playing her cavaquinho and singing samba with a powerful voice. Dorina (born in Rio in 1959) is a singer with a Portela heritage and also hosts a radio show dedicated to the best samba. Mariana Baltar, with her fine repertoire of rare traditional sambas, singer Diogo Nogueira (the son of samba master João Nogueira), singer/producer Leandro Sapucahy, and Casuarina, an excellent samba and choro band, were also regulars in the scene. Those are just a few of the rising artists who displayed their talent on busy Lapa nights, creating the samba and choro of a new generation.

The Samba Resolution

In Brazil millions of people sing, dance to, or just listen to samba. Its importance in the maintenance of relative social peace is hard to measure, but it is evident. One doesn't need to wait for Carnaval to see how samba brings people from all social classes and races together and keeps them in harmony. All you have to do is go to downtown Rio on Friday during "happy hour" after work. The bars and sidewalks in the center of the city are full of secretaries, executives, office boys, bankers—various levels of professionals celebrating the oncoming weekend. They all drink, sing, and dance together. And the party music is always samba.

After all, in Brazil everything sooner or later ends up in samba.

BOSSA NOVA: THE NEW WAY

"Desafinado" (Off-Key), sung by João Gilberto in his very personal, intimate, whispering style, was an ironic reply to critics who mockingly said that bossa nova was "music for off-key singers."

This negative reaction had been occasioned by Gilberto's previous record, a landmark 78-RPM single with "Chega de Saudade" (written by Antonio Carlos "Tom" Jobim and Vinícius de Moraes) and "Bim-Bom" (by Gilberto himself), which came out in July 1958. Much of the Brazilian public was intrigued by the two songs, but others were offended by their unconventional harmonies, the apparently strong influence of American jazz, and Gilberto's unusual vocals.

The prevailing singing style at that time was operatic. Great loud voices were a must for successful crooners. Although singers like Johnny Alf, Dick Farney, and Lúcio Alves had already developed more introspective singing styles, it was only with João Gilberto, the young man from Bahia, that people started noticing that something new was happening in the Brazilian music scene.

As for the criticism surrounding "Desafinado," Tom Jobim told us, "Actually, it's not an off-key song. It's crooked on purpose. It's tilted. It could be a very square song, except for the endings of the musical phrases that go down unexpectedly. It criticizes experts. The guy next door, he's off-key but he's in love with this girl, and he can say that to her because loving is more important than being in tune. Some

▲ João Gilberto's 1959 album that launched bossa nova in Brazil. (Courtesy of EMI.)

Brazilian and international pop music of the time. It had a harmonic richness previously heard only in classical music and modern jazz. For example, the unexpected melodic alterations of "Desafinado" included the use of the "tritone interval" (an augmented fourth), which many listeners found hard to accept in a pop song.

"He managed for the first time to popularize songs with a harmonic form that was strange for people to hear," keyboardist-arranger Eumir Deodato told music critic Zuza Homem de Mello.[2] He cited "Chega de Saudade" and "Desafinado" as examples, noting that the latter was "harmonically very elaborate."

Bossa achieved great success in North America in 1962 following the release of Stan Getz and Charlie Byrd's *Jazz Samba* album (which included tunes by Jobim, Bonfá, and Baden Powell). Other bossa-themed albums were recorded that year by Herbie Mann, Paul Winter, and Coleman Hawkins, among others.

Pop and jazz listeners alike were entranced by the cool Brazilian swing and warm lyrical beauty of the "new way." In the decades to follow, bossa nova had a significant impact on jazz and international music, as well as on the next generation of Brazilian composers. The genre provided many enduring tunes of remarkable lyricism, musical economy, and harmonic sophistication. One of its most famous hits was "Garota de Ipanema" (The Girl from Ipanema), which has endured as one of the best-known songs in the world.

people are always in tune, but they don't love anybody."[1]

"Desafinado" was released in November, four months after "Chega de Saudade." It became a defiant but good-humored anthem for the emerging Brazilian musical style of bossa nova, which was casual, subtle, and imbued with an infectious swing.

Bossa would explode in popularity in 1959—in Brazil with the success of Gilberto's album *Chega de Saudade*, and internationally with the release of Marcel Camus's award-winning film *Orfeu Negro* (Black Orpheus), the soundtrack of which featured songs by Tom Jobim, Vinícius de Moraes, and Luiz Bonfá.

Bossa nova was a new type of samba in which the genre's rhythmic complexity had been pared down to its bare essentials, transformed into a different kind of beat. It was full of unusual harmonies and syncopations, all expressed with a sophisticated simplicity. Sometimes small combos performed bossa; but it was ideally suited to a lone singer and a guitar. This "new fashion" or "new way" (the approximate translation of "bossa nova") of singing, playing, and arranging songs was born in Rio de Janeiro in the mid-1950s.

Developed by Jobim, Gilberto, and their peers, bossa nova was "off key" only in relation to the

BOSSA'S BEGINNINGS

Derived from samba, bossa nova had many musical antecedents, especially in progressive samba-canção tunes written by Noel Rosa, Ary Barroso, and Braguinha. Braguinha's tune "Copacabana," recorded in 1946 by Dick Farney (with arrangements by Radamés Gnatalli), was a suave and sophisticated piece that foreshadowed the bossa sound. And the guitarist Garoto (Anibal Sardinha, 1915–1955), who added altered and extended chords to sambas and choros, would be a strong influence on all bossa nova guitarists.

Johnny Alf, who was on the periphery of the bossa movement, had a large impact on many of its composers. Alf (Alfredo José da Silva) was born in 1929 in Rio's Vila Isabel neighborhood. Heavily influenced by George Gershwin, Cole Porter, Debussy, and bebop jazz, Alf could be heard by the early 1950s in clubs around town such as the Plaza, where many future bossa musicians were often in attendance. By then he was already using his sharp harmonic and melodic senses to shape Brazilian songs, such as Dorival Caymmi tunes, in a way that sounded avant-garde to Brazilian audiences used to bolero and samba-canção. His singing was jazzy, with scatting and mannerisms typical of bebop, and his piano attack was heavily syncopated. In 1953 Alf cut his debut single, "Falsete" (Falsetto), and in 1955 scored his first hit with the single "Rapaz de Bem" (Nice Guy), which featured new harmonic conceptions and casual lyrics. It wasn't bossa, but it was approaching it.

As the musicians that would form the new movement were getting together in the late 1950s, Alf received an invitation to work in São Paulo. Bad timing, but the money was good, and Alf left town for several years. He cut his first album, *Rapaz de Bem*, an instrumental work with a trio, in 1961. By the time he moved back to Rio the following year, bossa had already peaked commercially. He had a big hit song, "Eu e a Brisa" (Me and the Breeze), in 1967, but his career never really took off, hindered in part by his introspective and melancholic personality.

Guitarist Luiz Bonfá (1922–2001) wrote several songs that presaged the bossa style. Examples include "Perdido de Amor" (Lost in Love), a hit for Dick Farney in 1951, and the tunes he wrote in the mid-1950s with Jobim: "Engano" (Mistake), "Domingo Sincopado" (Syncopated Sunday), "Samba Não é Brinquedo" (Samba Isn't a Toy), "A Chuva Caiu" (The Rain Fell), and others. João Gilberto, who would one day be called the "pope" of bossa nova, credited both João Donato and Bonfá as important influences on his innovative guitar sound.

Pianist João Donato (born in 1934) developed a percussive, harmonically adventurous playing style that struck many listeners as weird. His chords seemed crooked and dissonant, but his rhythmic sense was secure and precise. Donato's sound had points in common with Thelonius Monk's piano playing, and he took a decidedly jazz-influenced approach to Brazilian tunes. He and João Gilberto became good friends and wrote a song together: "Minha Saudade" (My Saudade). But Donato was ahead of his time, and his oblique piano playing was not welcome in nightclubs. People complained that he disorganized the rhythm. So Donato decided to try his luck elsewhere and took off in 1959, the year Gilberto released his first album, to tour Mexico with vocalist Elizeth Cardoso (1920–1990).

Newton Mendonça's songwriting in the 1950s helped establish the bossa nova sound. In 1953 his and Tom's "Incerteza" (Uncertainty) debuted, and in 1954 he composed the initial theme of "Samba de uma Nota Só," a collaboration with Jobim recorded by João Gilberto in 1960. It became a bossa standard, as did "Desafinado" and "Meditação," two other songs on which Jobim and Mendonça shared the music and lyric writing. Mendonça (1927–1960) died prematurely at age thirty-three, before gaining the recognition due him. The 2001 biography *Caminhos cruzados: A vida e a música de Newton Mendonça* reaffirmed the importance of his contributions.[3]

Tom Jobim (1927–1994), the most accomplished songwriter of the group, would cite modern classical music, including Brazil's twentieth-century composer Heitor Villa-Lobos, as the major influence on his work. Other bossa composers drew their inspiration more from the harmonic elements, tone colors, and performance style of "West Coast" cool jazz, a smooth, light, and relaxed jazz style of the 1950s.

In 1956 Carlos Lyra and Roberto Menescal formed a guitar academy in Copacabana, and the two spent a lot of time experimenting with chords influenced by the music of cool-jazz players Gerry Mulligan, Chet Baker, and Shorty Rogers. The academy became a meeting point for future bossa musicians, as did the home of one of their students—Nara Leão. There could be found Lyra,

Menescal, and other up-and-coming musicians like Marcos Valle and Ronaldo Bôscoli.

These musicians, along with Jobim, Gilberto, and others, absorbed the rich musical currents flowing through Brazil at the time (samba-canção, jazz, Villa-Lobos) and drew from them to create an economical and colloquial new style of popular music. The rhythm usually came from samba, but on occasion baião, bolero, and marcha were used and transformed by the bossa sensibility. Harmonically, bossa nova tunes included altered chords, inverted chords, and unusual harmonic progressions, as well as unexpected melodic leaps and tonal shifts. Yet, as the bossa songwriters applied complex chords, they were also taking out extraneous notes. The effect was elegant and precise, deceptively simple, and low key.

This new musical vanguard would find a spiritual and professional center in Rio de Janeiro's most famous neighborhood: Copacabana.

A Cozy Corner and a Guitar

In Copacabana in the mid- to late 1950s lived the more sophisticated carioca middle class, which had a taste for jazz, American movies, and other forms of culture from abroad. They often frequented three hip little nightclubs on a narrow side street off Rua Duvivier nicknamed the Beco das Garrafas (Bottles Lane).

Why was it called Bottles Lane? Because Copacabana is a long, narrow strip of tall buildings squeezed between the ocean and the mountains, and sound has only one way to go: up. And a lot of sound did drift up from the Beco das Garrafas, especially since there were often more people milling around outside the small clubs than there were inside. So tenants from the adjacent buildings, fed up with the late-night carousing and frequent fighting going on in the lane, would sometimes throw bottles down on the noisemakers.

In these three clubs—Bottles Bar, Little Club, and Baccarat—met the musicians who would make up the core of the bossa movement. They had their own slang and code of behavior, and a way of making music that was unknown outside

▲ Nighttime view of Rio de Janeiro's Copacabana Beach, where nearby nightclubs and homes were the headquarters of bossa nova musicians. *(Photo by Lidio Parente. Courtesy of Embratur.)*

Copacabana. Their informal shows sparkled with creativity and lots of improvisation. "We did the music because we liked to; nobody was trying to create a movement," recalled guitarist-composer Oscar Castro-Neves. "We just made music and showed it to our friends. We used to go to Jobim's house and we'd leave the place with a fever, because we'd get so excited by the harmonies and everything else."[4]

Often they would end up at the home of Nara Leão, who hosted guitar sessions that lasted until dawn at her parents' apartment on Avenida Atlantica, the avenue that runs along Copacabana Beach. Leão (1942–1989) was a muse to the movement as a teenager and developed into a singer with a cool, gentle style. She would later record many of her friends' songs.

Among those performing and communing in the Beco das Garrafas were Carlos Lyra, Tom Jobim, Roberto Menescal, Durval Ferreira, Luis Eça, Baden Powell, and Sérgio Mendes. One of the most dedicated participants was the poet Vinícius de Moraes, who would become the most prolific and important bossa lyricist. He and his friend Antonio Maria, a journalist and lyricist, would stay in these bars until the very last song and then, after many doses of what de Moraes called "bottled dog" (whisky—man's best friend), they would go to the beach and watch the sunrise.

The mood of the bossa musicians reflected that of the Brazilian middle class in the 1950s, especially those who lived in Rio. The future was bright. The country had a popular and democratically elected president, Juscelino Kubitschek, and he was building the new federal capital, the daring and futuristic city of Brasília, on the high plains of Goiás state. Kubitschek's motto was "fifty years of development in five."

Everyone thought Brazil would finally shed its role as the eternal country of the future and become a developed nation. Everything pointed in this direction in the late 1950s and early 1960s. The national soccer team won the World Cup for the first time in 1958, a great source of pride to a soccer-crazed country. Oscar Niemeyer was creating his most famous buildings, including those in Brasília. The movie industry's progressive Cinema Novo movement was emerging. In all of the arts, it was a time of effervescence.

Bossa's lyrics reflected this optimism. Most bossa musicians lived in Rio's Zona Sul (South Zone) and they sang casually of simple things and their daily environment: the beautiful beaches, waves, sailboats, flowers, blue skies, and, most of all, women. Music making itself was also celebrated, as in Jobim's "Corcovado": "A cozy corner and a guitar / This is a song to make the one you love happy."

Lyrics in bossa nova were used not only for their meanings but also for their musical sounds. Ronaldo Bôscoli wrote the words for a Roberto Menescal song called "Rio" in which short words with similar sonorities are used to evoke Rio de Janeiro on a hot summer day: "É sal, é sol, é sul" (It's salt, it's sun, it's south). In many bossa songs,

especially in the music of João Gilberto, such elemental lyrics were not meant to stand out. Rather, they were intended to blend into the music and contribute to the whole. Harmony was essential, and few understood this as well as Tom Jobim.

Jobim

Antonio Carlos (Tom) Jobim was born on January 25, 1927, in a Rio de Janeiro neighborhood called Tijuca. When he was one year old his family moved to Ipanema. There he grew up running in the dunes, swimming in the unpolluted sea, playing soccer on sandy unpaved streets, and contemplating the birds, trees, dolphins, and other aspects of nature that were abundant in Rio in the 1930s. When Tom was fourteen his stepfather bought a piano for Tom's sister Helena; it wasn't long before young Tom himself was playing it. So his stepfather found him a piano teacher, Hans Joachim Koellreutter.

Koellreutter (1915–2005) was a German who settled in Brazil in 1938. He had studied at the Berlin State Academy of Music and in Brazil was a leader of the *música viva* (living music) group, which organized concerts of modern European

▼ A re-release edition of a 1965 album by Tom Jobim. *(Courtesy of Discovery Records.)*

The wonderful world of
Antonio Carlos Jobim
-WITH THE NELSON RIDDLE ORCHESTRA-

A Sampler of Jobim Standards

Tom Jobim: "Triste" (Sad), "Luiza," "Ela É Carioca" (She's a Carioca), "Samba do Avião" (Samba of the Plane), "Corcovado" (English title: "Quiet Nights of Quiet Stars"), "Vivo Sonhando" (I Live Dreaming; English title: "Dreamer"), "Gabriela," "Wave," "Surfboard," "Águas de Março" (Waters of March).

Tom and Vinícius de Moraes: "Garota de Ipanema" (The Girl from Ipanema), "Por Toda Minha Vida" (For All My Life), "Água de Beber" (Water to Drink), "Só Danço Samba" (I Only Dance Samba; English title: "Jazz Samba"), "Insensatez" (Foolishness; English title: "How Insensitive"), "O Grande Amor" (The Great Love), "Modinha," "Amor em Paz" (Love in Peace; English title: "Once I Loved"), "Chega de Saudade" (Enough Saudade; English title: "No More Blues"), "Se Todos Fossem Iguais a Você" (If Everyone Were Like You), "A Felicidade" (Happiness).

Tom and Aloysio de Oliveira: "Dindi," "Inútil Paisagem" (Useless Landscape), "Demais" (Too Much), "Só Tinha Que Ser com Você" (It Could Only Have Been with You).

Tom and Newton Mendonça: "Desafinado" (Off-Key; English title: "Slightly Out of Tune"), "Samba de Uma Nota Só" (One-Note Samba), "Meditação" (Meditation), "Discussão" (Discussion), "Caminhos Cruzados" (Crossed Paths), and "Tristeza" (Sadness).

Tom and Chico Buarque: "Sabiá," "Retrato Em Branco e Preto" (Portrait in Black and White), "Anos Dourados" (Golden Years).

---

composers, beginning in 1939. Koellreutter was an enthusiastic advocate of Arnold Schoenberg's twelve-tone system and an excellent music professor who influenced a whole generation of avant-garde Brazilian pianists.

Tom absorbed a great deal of knowledge about harmony and composition from Koellreutter, but his love for music became a passion when he discovered the works of the Brazilian composer Heitor Villa-Lobos, who had written such masterpieces as the "Bachianas Brasileiras," which merged baroque forms with Brazilian folk music elements.

As a young man, Jobim at first chose architecture as his occupation. He found a job in an architect's office but soon became disappointed in it. Tom came home every day with the sensation of time lost. So he decided instead to dedicate his life to music.

Jobim studied theory and harmony intensively and drew inspiration from the classical composers

he had studied, but he never forgot popular music. "I could write a piece using the twelve-tone scale, but Brazil, with all its rhythms, was more important. I liked Pixinguinha, Donga, Vadico, and Ary Barroso," he said.[5]

Tom started playing in nightclubs around 1950, but he was married already and money was short. Things started to get better only when he found a job at the Continental record company in 1952, where he transcribed songs for composers who could not write music. The next year he landed a job as the artistic director for the Odeon label.

Meanwhile, he began writing songs with Newton Mendonça, an old beach friend and very good pianist. In 1954 Tom began his career as an arranger and worked on records by Dick Farney, Os Cariocas, and Elizeth Cardoso. He also started collaborating with another partner, Billy Blanco. The pair composed "Teresa da Praia" (Teresa of the Beach) and the ten-inch album *Sinfonia do Rio de Janeiro: Sinfonia Popular em Tempo de*

Samba. The latter included vocals by Farney, Cardoso, Os Cariocas, Lúcio Alves, Doris Monteiro, and others in tune with the nascent bossa nova style.

Tom was developing his own innovations in regard to Brazilian popular music, adding new twists to the venerable samba and creating a sound that was all his own. He told us, "I had those new harmonies coming from me only. I was always revolting against the establishment, against normal harmonies. It was a very personal thing. Sure, I heard Debussy and Ravel, but they didn't have this African beat we have here."[6]

Jobim was not a great instrumentalist, like Bonfá or Powell, or a charismatic singer, like Lyra or Gilberto. But his compositions would make him the most famous Brazilian musical figure of his time.

By the mid-1950s Tom had garnered a great deal of prestige in the Brazilian music scene. He had a television show in São Paulo called "Bom Tom" (a pun that means both "nice Tom" and "good taste"). He was writing songs with Mendonça, Blanco, and—by this time—Bonfá, revitalizing the samba-canção. Then, in 1956, Tom

began working with a brilliant and fast-living poet who would be his most important songwriting partner.

Vinícius de Moraes

Vinícius de Moraes (1913–1980) applied his considerable poetic gifts to writing lyrics for more than two hundred songs. His words demonstrated a powerful sense of rhythm, sound, economy, and metaphor. Vinícius's lyrics, like those of his bossa contemporaries, often centered on elemental themes, especially love, with a subtlety and profundity that usually defy translation.

Before gaining fame as a bossa lyricist, Vinícius had already established a respected place for himself in Brazilian literature as the author of several books of acclaimed poetry. His poems had evolved from an early formalism—his first book was published in 1933—to a very personal approach in which he brought the eternal, the cosmic, the inexplicable into the reality of daily life.

He wrote his first song lyrics in 1932 for a foxtrot called "Loura ou Morena" (Blonde or Brunette), co-written with Haroldo Tapajós. But that

▶ Foreground: Vinícius de Moraes (*left*) with Toquinho (*right*), a frequent musical partner, in concert in the 1970s. (*Courtesy of BMG.*)

didn't start a musical career. After penning two more songs in 1933 that were recorded by artists at RCA, Vinícius moved on to other things, not returning to lyric writing until 1952.

During those intervening years, he graduated from law school, studied English poetry at Oxford, and became a diplomat. He was posted in Los Angeles between 1946 and 1950 and became vice consul at the Brazilian consulate there. Once he returned to Rio, Vinícius worked as a journalist and plunged into the nightlife again. He resumed songwriting and composed his first samba, "Quando Tu Passas por Mim" (When You Pass by Me).

Vinícius, barely scraping by financially, asked for another diplomatic position abroad. He was lucky: in 1953 he was assigned to Paris. There he met Sacha Gordine, to whom he sold a story for a film: *Orfeu da Conceição*. But the French producer had problems raising the money for the film. So, back in Brazil, Vinícius decided to stage the story as a play and started looking for a composer to write the music. Then he remembered a young musician he had once seen perform in a nightclub called Club da Chave: Tom Jobim.

Bossa nova was arguably born in 1956, the year that Jobim and Vinícius collaborated on music for the play *Orfeu da Conceição*, as well as the song "Chega de Saudade." Several years later Vinícius recalled, "I did not know I was giving this young composer from Ipanema a signal to begin a new movement in Brazilian music. About the same time, by a kind of telepathy, other young Brazilian composers like Carlos Lyra, Roberto Menescal, and Oscar Castro-Neves were beginning to compose in a similar style."[7]

The play transplanted the Greek myth of Orpheus and Eurydice into the favelas and Carnaval of modern-day Rio. *Orfeu da Conceição*, with sets by Oscar Niemeyer, opened at Rio's Teatro Municipal on September 25, 1956. It was a big hit, and so too was an accompanying record of the score, which included songs by Jobim and de Moraes like "Se Todos Fossem Iguais a Você" (If Everyone Were Like You) and "Eu e o Amor" (Me and Love). *Orfeu da Conceição* was re-released on CD by EMI Brazil in 2006.

In 1957 Sacha Gordine, finally with financial backing, came to Rio with director Marcel Camus to make the *Orfeu da Conceição* movie. Gordine wanted original music for the French-Brazilian production, to be retitled *Orfeu Negro* (Black Orpheus). The new score included Luiz Bonfá's "Samba de Orfeu" (Samba of Orpheus) and the lovely "Manhã de Carnaval" (Morning of Carnaval), with lyrics by Antonio Maria. Jobim and Moraes composed new tunes, including the sweetly melancholy "A Felicidade" (Happiness).

Sadness has no end, but happiness does
Happiness is like a feather the wind carries
    into the air
It flies so lightly, yet has such a brief life

João Gilberto

Vocalist Elizeth Cardoso's 1958 album *Canção do Amor Demais* (Song for an Excessive Love) features João Gilberto's new style of guitar playing, Jobim and Moraes's songs, and Jobim's arrangements. Tom recalled, "We were developing our style. You can see it very clearly in this album."[8]

▼ João Gilberto in concert in 1977. *(Photo by Karl Garabedian.)*

Gilberto's arrival on the scene opened new perspectives with "the rhythm that he brought," according to Jobim. "The harmonic and melodic part of the bossa equation was already established, but "the beat of bossa nova appeared for the first time on the guitar played by João on Elizeth Cardoso's album. That album constituted a boundary mark, a fission point, a break with the past."[9]

João Gilberto was born in 1932 in Juazeiro, a small city in the interior of Bahia state. Jobim's description of bossa in the *Chega de Saudade* album liner notes also aptly characterizes Gilberto's artistic personality. Tom writes, "Bossa nova is serene, it has love and romance, but it is restless." Gilberto's singing and playing seem natural now that they have been incorporated into the repertoire of international music, but back in the 1950s they were extremely unusual.

Gilberto's highly syncopated style of plucking acoustic guitar chords— nicknamed *violão gago* (stammering guitar) by some—introduced a type of rhythm that resembled a cooled and slowed samba but was very difficult to play. "He was the only one who could do that beat at first," said Brazilian music critic Zuza Homem de Mello. "After time others could, too."[10]

According to Oscar Castro-Neves, Gilberto's guitar style was "a decantation of the main elements of what samba was, which made bossa nova more palatable for foreigners and the rhythm more easily perceived. He imitated a whole samba ensemble, with his thumb doing the bass drum and his fingers doing the *tamborins* and *ganzás* and *agogôs*. The rhythm was right there with his voice and guitar alone. You didn't feel anything was missing."[11]

João's singing was new as well. Both voice and guitar were simultaneously melodic and highly rhythmic, as he syncopated sung notes against guitar motifs. "The way he phrases is incredible," said Castro-Neves. "The guitar would keep the tempo going and he would phrase in a way that was completely free, atop that pulsating rhythm. The way his phrases would fall—he would delay a chord here, put a note there—was very hypnotic."

"And he had a blend between the volume of his voice and the volume of the guitar. He could emphasize a note in the vocal and it would be like completing a chord on the guitar. Suddenly the voice really complemented the harmonic structure of the chord."[12]

Gilberto sang quietly, subtly, with a low-pitched, smooth, precise voice without vibrato, as if whispering an extremely intimate secret to the listener alone (Miles Davis was quoted as saying that Gilberto "would sound good reading a newspaper").[13] Tom Jobim recalled taking João Gilberto one day to a studio so that some recording industry bosses could hear him sing. After João finished singing, there was complete silence. Nobody knew what to say. After some time, one of the guys murmured to the one next to him, "Tom said he'd bring us a singer but ended up bringing a ventriloquist."[14]

Gilberto's style was anti–show business, cozy and conversational, and the music business executives didn't understand it—yet.

THE BOSSA BOOM

Fortunately, Jobim had connections at the Odeon label, where he had once worked. He was friends with the artistic director there, Aloysio de Oliveira, the ex-leader of the Bando da Lua, which had backed Carmen Miranda in the United States in the 1940s. Through Oliveira's efforts, Odeon agreed in 1958 to release Gilberto's first single, "Chega de Saudade" (the Jobim-de Moraes song written two years earlier), which most historians consider the first recorded bossa nova song. The arrangements were Tom's, and the critical reaction was to a large extent highly negative. But the single sold well enough that Odeon decided to let João record an album.

In 1959 came the *Chega de Saudade* album, arranged by Jobim and produced by de Oliveira. The record put the movement on track and is considered the first bossa nova album. Besides the title song, it included "Desafinado" and other tunes by Tom and Vinícius, three Carlos Lyra compositions, and two Ary Barroso classics.

Another major event of 1959 was the premiere

◄ A still from the film *Black Orpheus,* with the stars Bruno Mello (Orpheus) and Marpessa Dawn (Eurydice). *(Courtesy of the Voyager Company.)*

of the movie *Orfeu Negro*, which placed bossa nova on the world musical map. Shot in Rio the previous year, mostly in the hills overlooking the city, it was beautifully photographed and filled with the vivid colors, sounds, and excitement of Rio and Carnaval. The extraordinary Jobim-de Moraes-Bonfá soundtrack featured vocals by Agostinho dos Santos and Elizeth Cardoso, guitar work by Bonfá, and heavily percussive samba and candomblé ritual music.

The movie won the Grand Prize at the Cannes Film Festival that year (and an Academy Award for Best Foreign Film). Its theme song, Bonfá's "Manhã de Carnaval," a worldwide smash hit, was covered by countless musicians, and its various renditions sold millions of copies. The film's music inspired critical adjectives such as "joyous," "rapturous," "unforgettable." Bonfá and Jobim became internationally famous.

This radical and romantic new sound was a huge success, and during the next four years its beat took over the country. Bossa artists Lyra, Nara Leão, Roberto Menescal, Ronaldo Bôscoli, Marcos Valle, Baden Powell, and many others came into the spotlight. After *Chega de Saudade*, Gilberto recorded two more very successful albums: *O Amor, o Sorriso e a Flor* (Love, a Smile, and a Flower) in

1960 and *João Gilberto* in 1961. These albums included both new bossa tunes and bossa interpretations of old standards by composers like Dorival Caymmi and the sambistas Bide and Marçal.

The new sound was also popularized by many talented groups that played at the Beco das Garrafas clubs and at other Brazilian hot spots (including venues in São Paulo like the Paramount) in the late 1950s and 1960s. Among them were the Tamba Trio (Luis Eça, Bebeto, and Hélcio Milito), the Zimbo Trio (which included Luis Chaves and Amilton Godoy), the Sambalanço Trio (with César Camargo Mariano and Airto Moreira), the Bossa Jazz Trio (with Amilson Godoy, younger brother of Almilton), Bossa Três (with Edison Machado), 3-D (with Antonio Adolfo), the Jongo Trio, and the Sexteto Bossa Rio (led by young keyboardist Sérgio Mendes). Other vocalists who performed bossa nova songs during this era included Leny Andrade (who often sang with the Sexteto Bossa Rio), Pery Ribeiro, Maysa, Sylvia Telles, and Alayde Costa.

Baden Powell

Another Brazilian guitarist who gained fame during the bossa nova era was Baden Powell de

Aquino (1937–2000), called simply Baden Powell. Born in Varre-e-Sai, a small town in Rio de Janeiro state, Baden had a technical mastery of the guitar and a singular capacity to mix Afro-Brazilian influences with jazz and classical elements. When he performed, Powell wove a hypnotic spell with his guitar, producing sounds as soft and melodious as a mother singing a lullaby and as swinging and percussive as any drummer.

Castro-Neves described Baden Powell as "a marriage of a great performer and player. Very charismatic on stage. Baden was influenced by jazz but filtered it through his Brazilian soul. His solos are very Brazilian, with definitely Brazilian phrasing. And he has fast fingers, the chops, to go with it. The way he does rhythm is very personal, such as the way he plucks the strings in fast succession. He was extremely influential."[15]

Baden entered the bossa nova scene at an early age. He was twenty-two when he co-wrote "Samba Triste" (Sad Samba) with Billy Blanco in 1959, and over the next two years he appeared as a session guitarist on many bossa albums. In 1962 he began collaborating with Vinícius de Moraes. On many occasions, often for days on end, the two would hole up in Vinícius's apartment in Copacabana to drink whiskey and make music.

Baden and Vinícius composed more than fifty songs together, most with beautiful melodic themes that Powell would elaborate imaginatively on the acoustic guitar. Some were bossas and some were what they termed *afro-sambas*. While Baden was mulatto, Vinícius was white but identified strongly with Afro-Brazilian culture. He was a son of Xangô in the candomblé religion and jokingly referred to himself as "the blackest white man in Brazil." The pair researched Afro-Brazilian music from Bahia and incorporated it into their compositions. The song "Berimbau," for example, was named after the Bahian musical bow used to accompany capoeira. In the recording, Baden plays the *berimbau*'s rhythmic part on the guitar. "Canto de Ossanha," a song for the orixá Ossanha, begins with a simple brooding base-note riff on the guitar that is accompanied by muted plucked guitar patterns and soft percussion. It

A Sampler of Bossa Standards

Carlos Lyra: "Lobo Bobo" (Foolish Wolf), "Saudade Fez um Samba" (Saudade Made a Samba), both co-written with Ronaldo Bôscoli; "Maria Ninguém" (Maria Nobody). All three appear on the *Chega de Saudade album.*

Carlos Lyra and Vinícius de Moraes: "Primavera" (Springtime), "Minha Namorada" (My Girlfriend), "Pau de Arara," "Sabe Você" (You Know), "Samba do Carioca," "Você e Eu" (You and Me), "Coisa Mais Linda" (Most Beautiful Thing), "Maria Moita," "Marcha da Quarta-Feira de Cinzas" (Ash Wednesday Marcha).

Ronald Bôscoli and Roberto Menescal: "O Barquinho" (Little Boat), "Rio," "Você" (You), "Nós e o Mar" (Us and the Sea), "Telefone" (Telephone), "Vagamente" (Slightly), "A Volta" (The Return).

Marcos Valle and Paulo Sérgio Valle: "Samba de Verão" (Summer Samba), "Lágrima Flor" (Flower Tear), "Preciso Aprender a Ser Só" (I Need to Learn to Be Alone), "Viola Enluarada" (Moonlit Guitar).

Durval Ferreira: "Sambop," "Chuva" (Rain), "Batida Diferente" (Different Beat).

Oscar Castro-Neves: "Patinho Feio" (Ugly Duckling), "Onde Está Você?" (Where Are You?).

builds steadily until the song explodes into a joyful, upbeat guitar-percussion celebration. Many of their best numbers in this vein were gathered together for their 1966 album *Os Afro-Sambas*.

One of their most famous songs, "Samba da Benção" (Blessing Samba), was included in the 1966 Claude Lelouch movie *Un Homme et une Femme* (A Man and a Woman). They also composed tunes such as "Consolação" (Consolation), "Apelo" (Appeal), "Tempo Feliz" (Happy Time), "Deve Ser Amor" (It Must Be Love), and "Deixa" (Leave It).

Once the two split up, Baden moved to Europe and spent the next two decades there. In the years that followed he recorded numerous albums, including *Uma Viola na Madrugada* (A Guitar Late at Night), *Baden Powell Swings with Jimmy Pratt*, *La Grande Reunion* (with jazz violinist Stephane Grappelli), and *Baden à Vontade* (Baden at Ease). In 1994, back in Brazil, he had the pleasure of recording a live album with his sons Philippe (piano) and Louis Marcel (guitar).

Bossa Nova Criticism

Of course, musicians and singers who had nothing to do with the movement also wanted to sing or write bossa nova songs. "Bossa nova" turned into an adjective for everything modern, surprising. There were bossa nova girls, a bossa nova president (as Kubitschek was called), and even bossa nova cars. There was also a lot of bossa nova criticism.

Many Brazilian music critics, including the well-respected José Ramos Tinhorão, blasted bossa nova as being little more than an imitation of cool jazz. Yet that was far from the truth, and classifications of bossa as a mixture of jazz and samba are oversimplified. Jazz certainly influenced most bossa musicians, but the genre's greatest songwriter, Jobim, was most heavily inspired by samba-canção and classical music. In any event, it is clear that bossa nova put together many musical elements in an original way and was definitely Brazilian.

Jobim commented, "Many people said that bossa nova was an Americanized phenomenon. I think this is entirely false. Much to the contrary, I think what influenced [North] American music was the bossa nova. I received letters and telegrams from various illustrious composers . . . saying that bossa nova had been the biggest influence on American music in the last thirty years."[16]

THE NORTH AMERICAN INVASION

In 1958 John Coltrane had cut a jazz-samba cover of Ary Barroso's "Baia" [*sic*], known in Brazil as "Na Baixa do Sapateiro," and Capitol had released *Brazil's Brilliant João Gilberto* in 1961, but the American public was not yet ready for bossa nova.

More seeds were being sown at the start of the 1960s, when American jazz musicians Charlie Byrd, Herbie Mann, Kenny Dorham, Roy Eldridge, Coleman Hawkins, Zoot Sims, and Paul Winter toured Brazil, some of them in connection with a State Department–sponsored visit, and were exposed to the new sound.

When Charlie Byrd returned from Brazil, he brought back with him a Gilberto record and played it for a friend, the saxophonist Stan Getz. Charlie had a natural affinity for the style, in part, he said, because "I had been studying the classical guitar for about ten years and playing with my fingers, which is the way the Brazilians play it. And it's the way you can play those rhythms much more authentically than you can with a pick." At that time, recalled Byrd, "there were no jazz guitarists but me who played that way."[17]

Byrd (1925–1999) loved the melodies of bossa nova. In the ingredients of what became bossa, he noted, "you can't discount the strength of the tunes by Jobim, Gilberto, and Menescal. It was very strong material, a key factor in making things happen. And I've said it before—I think Jobim is the most significant writer of popular music in the second half of the twentieth century. He is one hell of a songwriter, and he has written in all kinds of styles. His songs have beautiful lyrical lines, and he has rhythmically and harmonically constructed them like a fine watchmaker."[18]

▲ Musicians Stan Getz and João Gilberto, whose earlier collaboration *Getz/Gilberto* marked the climax of the bossa invasion of North America, pictured with vocalist Miúcha, João's second wife, on their 1976 album. *(Courtesy of Sony.)*

When Getz (1927–1991) listened to the Gilberto album, he was so impressed with it that he and Byrd decided to record an album together that would feature songs in the new style. They chose songs by Jobim (including "Desafinado" and "Samba de Uma Nota Só"), Bonfá, Baden Powell, Billy Blanco, and Ary Barroso. Getz and Byrd's *Jazz Samba* was produced by Creed Taylor and released by Verve in April 1962.

"Desafinado" made the *Billboard* Top 20 for pop singles and won a Best Instrumental Jazz Performance (Soloist or Small Group) Grammy Award for Getz. The album did even better: it received a five-star review in *Downbeat* magazine and shot to the number 1 position on the *Billboard* pop chart. It sold hundreds of thousands of copies, remarkable for a jazz record (especially an instrumental one), and stayed on the charts for seventy weeks. It was really jazz-bossa rather than bossa nova, but the new sound had struck a nerve. Byrd quipped, "I knew it was something that would have a lot of public appeal. I didn't know it would inspire bossa nova neckties."[19]

Before the release of *Jazz Samba*, a young saxophonist named Paul Winter had also checked out a Gilberto album (played for him by critic and lyricist Gene Lees), loved it, and then toured Brazil and heard more of the new style. "It was such a breath of fresh air," recalled Winter. "We were hearing a very gentle voice that had the kind of soul and harmonic beauty that we loved in jazz. But as opposed to the very hard-driving bebop that we were playing then, it was astounding to find a very quiet, gentle music that had an equal amount of magic. It was a whole new possibility for us.

"Guitar wasn't something that was part of our universe, and here was someone doing all this subtle magic on the classical guitar. João Gilberto was sort of a new prophet. Following that tour, guitar became an integral part of my musical world," Winter added.[20] In that year, 1962, Paul's sextet recorded *Jazz Meets the Bossa Nova* in Rio and New York, interpreting tunes by Jobim, Lyra, Menescal, and Dorival Caymmi. It also fell into the area of jazz-bossa but was more "Brazilian" than *Jazz Samba* in that it included Brazilian percussionists who added instruments like the *afoxê*, *reco-reco*, and *cuíca* to the sound. It marked the beginning of Winter's long relationship with Brazilian music.

Do the Bossa Nova with Herbie Mann was another album released in 1962. Flutist Herbie Mann (1930–2003) recalled his trip to Brazil the previous year: "I was so totally mesmerized by the country and the music that I realized it was going to save my musical life. Up till that point my success had come from having an Afro-Cuban-type jazz band with four percussionists. But Afro-Cuban and African music were so simplistic melody-wise that it really got boring. When I went to Brazil I saw that their music could be as rhythmically involved as other ethnic musics were, but with it they had these melodic masterpieces. So, as a jazz person, it was the best of both worlds—to have great melodies to improvise with, combined with these rhythms."[21]

Mann and trumpeter Kenny Dorham flew to Brazil in September 1962 and recorded an album there with Baden Powell, Jobim, Durval Ferreira, the Tamba Trio's Bebeto and Hélcio Milito, and the Sérgio Mendes Bossa Sextet, which Mann described as "like Horace Silver or Cannonball Adderley with a samba beat."[22] *Do the Bossa Nova* was an important meeting of American and Brazilian musicians, as was an album recorded in December of that year: *Cannonball's Bossa Nova.* That album, released on Riverside Records in 1963, teamed the jazz saxophonist Cannonball Adderley with the Sexteto Bossa Rio. Mann and Adderley, like Byrd and Winter, would record and play extensively with Brazilians for years to come.

On November 21, 1962, at Carnegie Hall in New York, a concert that would become legendary was staged by impresario Sidney Frey (owner of Audio Fidelity Records). The show presented the Brazilian artists Gilberto, Bonfá, Castro-Neves, and others with American jazzmen enamored of the new style, including Getz, Byrd, Gary Burton, Gary McFarland, and Lalo Schifrin. Despite inclement weather, it was a sellout, with some twenty-eight hundred spectators inside and more than a thousand turned away. The show was disorganized and the sound was terrible, but the concert got recording contracts for many Brazilian artists and marked the growing affinity of American jazz musicians for bossa nova.

Bossa conquered the United States with its fresh sophistication, bridging popular music and "art" music. After the huge success of *Jazz Samba,* magazines and newspapers were full of articles about bossa nova, and dozens more jazz-bossa albums were released that year and the next. In the early 1960s, Ella Fitzgerald, Al Hirt, Zoot Sims, Vince Guaraldi, Coleman Hawkins, Curtis Fuller, Ray Charles, and Lalo Schifrin all recorded bossa-inspired tunes or albums, as did an abundance of pop musicians. Elvis Presley sang "Bossa Nova Baby," and Eydie Gormé recorded "Blame It on the Bossa Nova." And Quincy Jones's *Big Band Bossa Nova* (1962) yielded a tune called "Soul Bossa Nova" enlivened by an irresistible cuíca; many years later it would resurface as the theme for the *Austin Powers* comedy films.

Getz and Byrd went their separate ways after the *Jazz Samba* success. Byrd would record many Brazilian-flavored albums in succeeding decades, delv-ing deeply into the works of venerable Brazilian composers like Pixinguinha and Ernesto Nazaré.

GETZ, GILBERTO, AND THE GIRL FROM IPANEMA

Getz grabbed the lion's share of fame from the bossa boom with his next few releases. His second jazz-bossa effort was *Big Band Bossa Nova,* which hit number 13 on the pop charts. He teamed with Bonfá for *Jazz Samba Encore* in 1963, and then—just as the bossa craze seemed to be dying out—he joined Gilberto and Jobim for the album *Getz/Gilberto,* released in 1964. On it João added guitar and vocals, Tom played piano, Milton Banana was on drums, and Tommy Williams played bass. Two of the tunes featured the cool, light, gentle vocals of João's wife, Astrud Gilberto.

According to Brazilian journalist Ruy Castro, it was Astrud who suggested that she sing on "The Girl from Ipanema," an idea backed up by producer Creed Taylor.[23] The song was a new version of the song "Garota de Ipanema," composed by Jobim and Vinícius de Moraes in 1962, with English lyrics added by Norman Gimbel. Getz, how-

▼ Astrud Gilberto, whose vocals on "The Girl from Ipanema" helped begin a Brazilian music boom in the United States in the early 1960s, pictured here on her 1987 Verve release. *(Courtesy of Verve.)*

▲ Tom Jobim, Helô Pinheiro (the real-life inspiration for "The Girl from Ipanema"), and Pinheiro's daughter, in the late 1980s. *(Photo by Lidio Parente. Courtesy of Embratur.)*

▶ The former Veloso bar, now renamed for the song that made it famous. The street, also renamed as shown on the sign, bears tribute to Vinícius de Moraes. *(Photo by Ricardo Pessanha.)*

ever, remembered it differently and said that Astrud had participated at his insistence.[24] Either way, the result was one of the most popular songs of all time.

> *Tall and tan and young and lovely*
> *The girl from Ipanema goes walking*
> *When she walks she's like a samba*
> *That swings so cool and sways so gently*

"The Girl from Ipanema" was a duet between João (in Portuguese) and Astrud (in English), and it bridged the language gap with the U.S. audience. The breezy song won the Grammy Award for Record of the Year in 1964 and went to number 5 on the *Billboard* singles chart. More important, it opened the minds of many Americans to the richness of Brazilian music. Its smooth syncopation and graceful lyricism made it into a standard, one of the most recorded and performed songs of its time. Unfortunately, in the 1960s and 1970s it was so overplayed and covered by so many musicians (some great, some good, many bad) that in the United States "The Girl from Ipanema" began to epitomize cocktail-lounge music. Happily, time has dissipated the excesses of commercialization, and a replaying of the song's definitive version (with João, Astrud, Jobim, and Getz) is again a delight to hear: cool, seductive, and wistful.

The inspiration for the song was a beautiful, tan teenage girl named Heloisa Eneida Pinto (now Pinheiro) who used to "sway so gently" past a bar called Veloso on her way to Ipanema beach. Two regulars at Veloso were Tom and Vinícius, who turned their appreciation of Helô's sexy gracefulness into a song, and an unknowing muse into a pop icon of youth and beauty. The first recordings of the song came in 1963 in Brazil, where it was interpreted by Jobim, the Tamba Trio, and singer Pery Ribeiro. Only after the song became famous was Helô introduced to Tom on the beach. Today the Veloso bar is named Garota de Ipanema after the song. The street it faces, Rua Montenegro, is now called Rua Vinícius de Moraes.

The album *Getz/Gilberto* garnered three other Grammys (Best Album, Best Instrumental Jazz Performance [Small Group], and Best Engineered Recording [Non-Classical]) as well and went to number 2 on the pop charts. It failed to reach number 1 only because the Beatles were making pop-music history that year. *Getz/Gilberto* spent an extraordinary ninety-six weeks on the charts, fifty of them in the Top 40. Interestingly, just a few years later, the Beatles and bossa nova would both be strong influences on a new Brazilian musical movement: *Tropicália*.

Also in 1964 came another excellent jazz-bossa album, when Paul Winter and Carlos Lyra teamed up for *The Sound of Ipanema*. Recorded in Rio, it featured Lyra's compositions and included the playing of Sérgio Mendes (piano), Sebastião Neto (bass), and Milton Banana (drums). Winter, in fact, was the only American on it, and he fit very well with the bossa spirit because of his lyrical and open-minded musical sensibility. The album was a smooth and engaging American-Brazilian fusion. Winter then cut the also superb *Rio* in 1965, featuring Bonfá, Roberto Menescal, and Luis Eça.

AFTER THE BOSSA BOOM

While bossa nova was enjoying its heyday in North America, the bright, optimistic era that had begun with Kubitschek and helped create bossa nova was fading. A few years earlier, in 1961, Janio Quadros, the next president of Brazil, had resigned for reasons that are still obscure. His cryptic letter of resignation mentioned "foreign" and "terrible" forces that opposed him. The vice president, João (Jango) Goulart, took over. He had a more leftist orientation and faced great opposition from the conservative sectors of society. Artists in general supported the new president, who courted Cuba, reestablished relations with Eastern Europe, condemned foreign economic imperialism, and promised to carry out basic reforms. He also further limited the profits that foreign corporations could extract from Brazil, in response to those who felt that multinational firms were exploiting the country.

Politically, Brazil was torn in two. In 1964 a military coup toppled the Brazilian government and replaced it with a repressive authoritarian regime. This accelerated the movement of bossa nova's songwriters in different directions. Some bossa artists became more involved in politics.

Carlos Lyra, Sérgio Ricardo, Marcos Valle, and Paulo Sérgio Valle began to use their song lyrics to protest poverty and social injustice in Brazil.

Nara Leão became a voice of protest when she participated in the didactic *Opinião* (Opinion), a piece of musical theater directed by Augusto Boal of Teatro de Arena. The show opened in December 1964 and matched the white Leão, from the wealthy Zona Sul, with two black performers of humble origins: sambista Zé Keti, from a Rio favela, and songwriter João do Vale, from rural Maranhão. *Opinião* protested social injustice in Brazil, alternating music and passages read aloud. The show combined the "charm of nightclub bossa nova shows with the excitement of politically engaged art," in the opinion of Caetano Veloso.[25]

Elis Regina, along with singer Jair Rodrigues, hosted a television show in 1965 called *O Fino da Bossa* (The Best of Bossa), which often featured the more socially oriented bossa tunes, which the government was not yet censoring to any great degree.

In 1965 began the era of the Brazilian musical festivals, which would launch a new generation of Brazilian singers and songwriters whose eclectic music came to be known as MPB (música popular brasileira). Many bossa figures were absorbed by MPB, a few continued the bossa line, others moved into jazz and instrumental music, and some traveled to the United States and Europe to establish careers abroad.

Guitarist Luiz Bonfá moved to the United States in the 1960s and frequently performed there and in Europe in succeeding decades. A vital bossa musician and accomplished classical guitarist, he played an important role in the evolution of Brazilian guitar playing. "He is an incredible soloist with a lot of technique and a very beautiful and personal quality of sound," noted Oscar Castro-Neves. "You can hear two notes and know this is Bonfá."[26] Musicians continue to cover his "Manhã de Carnaval."

Carlos Lyra (born in 1936) led bossa into its activist phase, adding social commentary and northeastern folk elements to his music in albums

▲ A 1970 RCA release by Luiz Bonfá. *(Courtesy of BMG.)*

such as *Pobre Menina Rica* (Poor Little Rich Girl), from the play he co-wrote with Vinícius. Then, because of the political atmosphere, he left for Mexico. He stayed there from 1966 to 1971, writing music for film and the theater. Meanwhile, the Brazilian dictatorship in 1968 began its heaviest phase of censorship and repression. When Lyra returned to his homeland, he found a different country from the one he had left. He made a record in 1973, but only two of its songs passed the government censorship; it was released with old material substituted instead. He did not record again in Brazil until 1996.

Ronaldo Bôscoli (1929–1995) and Roberto Menescal (born in 1937) wrote many bossa successes together, and both worked as producers in later years. One of Menescal's production efforts was Leila Pinheiro's beautiful 1989 collection of bossa classics, *Benção, Bossa Nova* (Blessing, Bossa Nova), and he helped his son Marcio update the genre on Bossacucanova's *Brasilidade* album in 2001.

Singer Nara Leão (1942–1989) had made her professional debut in *Pobre Menina Rica* in 1963. The next year she starred in the didactic play *Opinião* and released her first album, *Nara*, which featured both bossa tunes and songs by samba composers Zé Keti, Nelson Cavaquinho, and Car-

tola. She was political and nationalistic for a time, then in the late 1960s made another artistic switch and participated in the brief yet influential Tropicália movement with Gilberto Gil, Caetano Veloso, and others. By moving beyond bossa in the mid-1960s into a more eclectic repertoire, Nara was at the forefront of the emergence of what came to be known as MPB. She recorded a wide variety of music in the years that followed, and also returned to bossa nova from time to time.

Vocalist Leny Andrade was a "Beco das Garrafas" veteran and recorded her first album, *A Sensação Leny Andrade*, in 1960. She went on to a long and varied career performing jazz, bossa, samba, bolero, and other styles.

Composer-guitarist-arranger Oscar Castro-Neves (born in Rio in 1940) settled in the 1960s in Los Angeles. He served as music director for Sérgio Mendes's band for ten years, then worked extensively with the Paul Winter Consort in the 1970s and 1980s as a songwriter, guitarist, and co-producer. Oscar's many other credits include scoring films and television shows and working as a guitarist, arranger, or producer for Jobim, Quincy Jones, Lee Ritenour, Flora Purim, and Hubert Laws. One of his songs, "Kurski Funk," gained wide exposure as the theme song of the U.S. television show *Survivor*, which premiered in 2001; it was a traditional Russian folk song featuring the Dimitri Pokrovsky Singers that incorporated a funk-samba rhythm section and other embellishments by Castro-Neves, Paul Winter, and Paul Halley for the 1987 Paul Winter Consort album *Earthbeat*.

Johnny Alf, a big influence on many bossa musicians, enjoyed enduring respect from his peers and cult status as an artist long after the bossa nova era ended. Based in São Paulo, he has continued to play clubs there, to tour overseas, and to be much in demand as a guest artist.

João Donato left Rio just as bossa was being launched and resided in California for three years, performing with Latin jazz artists Mongo Santamaria, Cal Tjader, and Tito Puente. In 1962 he missed the historic Carnegie Hall concert that helped launch bossa in the United States, but afterward toured Italy with João Gilberto for several weeks. Back in Brazil, he recorded *Muito à Vontade* (1963), was an arranger-conductor on two Astrud Gilberto albums in the mid-1960s, and moved back to California for another ten years. There he recorded solo albums, teamed with Eumir Deodato for *Donato/Deodato* (1969), a fusion of Latin jazz and bossa, and composed "A Rã" (The Frog, written with Caetano Veloso) and "Caranguejo" (Crab), recorded by Sérgio Mendes, and "Amazonas." In 1975 he wrote another signature tune, "Bananeira," and returned to Brazil for good. He was much in demand as a composer and musical director after that, although his recording career slumped until the late '90s, when it enjoyed a major resurgence. Donato released a flurry of albums after that in Brazil and abroad, winning many musical prizes and accolades. He always stayed up to date: his 2002 *Managarroba* album featured hip-hop artist Marcelo D2, along with Joyce, Marisa Monte, and João Bosco.

As for Vinícius, his final important collaborator was Antonio Petti Filho, known as Toquinho, whom he met in 1970. Toquinho (born in São Paulo in 1946) is a singer-songwriter and accomplished guitarist who mixes bossa nova with classical-guitar technique and has absorbed influences from Baden Powell, Paulinho Nogueira, and Oscar Castro-Neves.

With Toquinho, Vinícius rediscovered the joy of making music. They worked a lot together, co-writing dozens of memorable tunes in the bossa nova and afro-samba veins, with Toquinho providing the strong melodies and Vinícius adding his inimitable poetic flair. Sharing vocals and often singing in unison, Toquinho and Vinícius performed in concert and recorded sixteen albums together (some in Italy and Argentina). They were remarkably popular as a duo. Such Toquinho-de Moraes tunes as "As Cores de Abril" (The Colors of April) and "Como É Duro Trabalhar" (How Hard It Is to Work) have become standards, heard wherever Brazilians pick up acoustic guitars to sing together. Another of their standards is "Aquarela" (Watercolor), in which they sing:

And the future is a spaceship
That we try to pilot
It doesn't have time or pity
Nor an hour of arrival

Their collaboration lasted until Vinícius's death in 1980. After that, Toquinho recorded many solo albums. One of the best was 1985's *A Luz do Solo* (Solo Light), an excellent retrospective of his career up to that point, featuring songs he had written with Vinícius and other artists.

João Gilberto lived in the United States from 1966 to 1980, when he moved back to Rio. Once back home, the shy and reclusive legend rarely gave concerts or interviews. But he continued to be an inspiration for guitarists and singers around the world, and many are the Brazilian musicians who remember the day, hour, and place where they first heard that strange new song "Chega de Saudade" coming over the radio.

João and Astrud divorced soon after their success, and he was married for a time afterward to the singer Miúcha, the sister of Chico Buarque. Astrud Gilberto (born in Bahia in 1940) continued the career that grew out of her serendipitous appearance on "The Girl from Ipanema" and was a popular solo artist internationally in following decades. João and Miúcha's daughter Bebel established her own international career in 2000 with the release of *Tanto Tempo* (see Chapter Four).

After the success of *Getz/Gilberto* and "The Girl from Ipanema," Jobim became a famous name in North America. He was a guest on American television specials, recorded solo albums like *Wave* (1967) and *Tide* (1970), and appeared on two albums with Frank Sinatra, *Francis Albert Sinatra & Antonio Carlos Jobim* (1967) and *Sinatra and Company* (1973). Tom's music had a profound effect on fans all over the world. Jobim recalled, "I got so many letters from people saying things like, 'I was going to commit suicide, but I heard your music and decided that life was worth living.'"[27]

Jobim didn't stop developing artistically during the heady days of the 1960s, creating music that ranged from samba and bossa to MPB and orches-

Sérgio Mendes

Sérgio Mendes (born in Niterói in 1941) was a fixture at a very young age in the Beco das Garrafas, where he added his jazz-influenced piano to the ongoing sessions. Early on he recorded albums such as *Sérgio Mendes & Bossa Rio* and was a participant on jazz-bossa albums with Cannonball Adderley, Herbie Mann, and Paul Winter. In 1964 he moved to the United States and cut an album called *Sérgio Mendes and Brasil 1965*. His sound mixed bossa, American pop, and MPB in a light, upbeat blend, usually with two female vocalists singing in unison, while a drummer—João Palma and Dom Um Romão were two—laid down a trademark crisp, catchy beat.

▲ Sérgio Mendes in the 1970s. *(Courtesy of A&M.)*

The Mendes formula was a huge success, starting with his A&M album *Sérgio Mendes & Brasil '66,* which hit number 7 on the pop charts. It went gold, as did his next three records (*Equinox, Look Around,* and *Fool on the Hill*). Mendes's band scored two Top 10 singles at that time, as well as a lesser hit with Jorge Benjor's "Mas Que Nada," sung in Portuguese. Sérgio is a bandleader who has been able to surround himself with top-flight musical talent and translate Brazilian sounds for international ears. His albums marked the first time that many foreigners had heard material by Jobim, Benjor (formerly known as Ben), Ivan Lins, Milton Nascimento, Gilberto Gil, and other leading Brazilian songwriters. Mendes stepped out of his usual mold with *Primal Roots* (1972), which included folkloric styles in the mix; the Grammy-winning *Brasileiro* (1992), which showcased rising Bahian songwriter Carlinhos Brown and fused MPB and Rio samba with axé music and funk; and the hip-hop-flavored *Timeless* (2006) produced by Will.i.am (William James Adams Jr.) of the American group the Black Eyed Peas.

tral. One of his greatest songs was "Águas de Março" (Waters of March), first recorded in 1972. "Águas de Março" is lively and wistful, a melodic-rhythmic-poetic masterpiece with beautifully crafted lyrics. Its alliterative images wind on and on, vivid and concrete, full of life and death, evoking the deep mystery of existence. It is a samba that feels like a bossa yet has an unusual minimalist, spiraling structure. Chico Buarque called it "the most beautiful samba in the world," while jazz critic Leonard Feather went further, terming it one of the ten most beautiful songs of the century.[28]

"Águas de Março" is one of three Jobim songs that are the subject of *Três canções de Tom Jobim* (the others being "Sabiá" and "Gabriela"). In the book, Arthur Nestrovski, a music critic and litera-ture professor, writes, "Tom Jobim wrote happy and sad songs, nostalgic and utopian, introspective, seductive, exaltative. 'Águas de Março' seems all of this at the same time." He describes the music as labyrinthine, a controlled "form without form" that generates tension with harmonic refinements worthy of Schumann, Schubert, and Chopin. Trying to explain the song's remarkable melding of word with sound, Nestrovski concludes, "What the poem expresses with the contrast between sunny and gloomy, between life and death . . . has a musical parallel in the counterpoint of the diatonic theme with the tragic chromatic line."[29]

German producer-arranger Claus Ogerman, after hearing "Águas de Março," was so impressed that he told Tom, "Your walking in the streets of New York with this music under your arm makes me think of what it must have been like in 1910 when Stravinsky was walking in Geneva carrying *The Rite of Spring*."[30]

While most Jobim songs suffered from their English-language adaptations, he handled "Águas de Março" himself, translating some lines directly but also making significant changes to the lyrics when certain Brazilian references wouldn't make sense to North Americans. Here is an excerpt of the English version (the first three lines below are the same as in the Portuguese):

A stick, a stone, it's the end of the road
It's the rest of a stump, it's a little alone
It's a sliver of glass, it is life, it's the sun
It is the night, it is death, it's a trap, it's a
  gun
And the riverbank talks of the waters of
  March
It's the promise of life, it's the joy in your
  heart

Jobim recorded "Águas de Março" a second time for the album *Matita Perê*, which also featured rich symphonic pieces by Tom orchestrated by Ogerman. In the January 1973 sessions, Jobim sang and played guitar and piano, Dori Caymmi helped with the arrangements, and Airto Moreira and João Palma added drums and percussion. But the most popular version of "Águas de Março" is a Jobim and Elis Regina duet recorded for the *Elis & Tom* album at MGM Studios in Los Angeles in 1974.

The project brought together Brazil's greatest female singer and its most renowned composer, but it wasn't smooth sailing, as Tom and Elis were hardly the best of friends at the time. Regina's near breaking into laughter at the end of the song was rehearsed and not the result of camaraderie between the two, according to music journalist Sérgio Cabral.[31] The project got off to a rocky start when Jobim objected to Regina's husband, Cesar Camargo Mariano, handling the arrangements (Jobim wanted Ogerman), and to Mariano's elec-

▲ The legendary composer Jobim in the late 1980s. *(Photo by Ana Lontra Jobim.)*

tric piano being used on some cuts. Despite the tension, Mariano stayed, as did his piano, and the album was completed with Hélio Delmiro and Oscar Castro-Neves on guitar, Luizão Maia on bass, Paulo Braga on drums, and Aloysio de Oliveira producing. The result has consistently ranked in polls as one of the top ten Brazilian albums of all time, and the Jobim-Regina rendition of "Águas de Março" is the definitive version of the song. The album also features memorable interpretations of "Triste," "Corcovado," "Retrato em Branco e Preto" (Portrait in Black and White, by Jobim and Chico Buarque), and "Chovendo Na Roseira" (Raining on the Rosebush).

From the 1970s on, Tom's lyrics often reflected his love of nature and concern for ecological problems. Songs like "Boto" (Amazonian Porpoise) celebrated nature, while "Borzeguim" called for the protection of all Amazonian life, including its indigenous peoples.

Leave the jaguar alive in the forest
Leave the fish in the water . . .
Leave the Indian alive
Leave the Indian alone

Jobim's music defied classification. One of his greatest works, the 1976 album *Urubu* (named for the Brazilian black vulture) was a meeting of MPB, bossa nova, Brazilian regional music (such as the capoeira rhythm), sounds of nature (including simulated bird calls), and classical music. The instrumental compositions on side two (three by Tom and one by his son, Paulo Jobim) were performed by an orchestra and were essentially modern impressionistic tone poems. Produced by Claus Ogerman, the recording featured Miúcha on vocals, João Palma on drums, Ray Armando on percussion, and Ron Carter on bass. Jobim's compositions on *Urubu* are part of a rich body of work that rivals, in sophistication and originality, the music of twentieth-century composers such as George Gershwin, Duke Ellington, and Jobim's idol, Heitor Villa-Lobos.

NOVA BOSSA NOVA

Bossa went from hip to kitsch in many countries after rock and roll took over the global market. There were too many crooners and lounge singers doing awful, overblown bossa nova renditions. Yet that very association with corny cocktail music helped spark a bossa revival when "lounge music" came to the forefront in the 1990s, and artists like Sérgio Mendes, Wanda Sá, Marcos Valle, and Walter Wanderley found a new popularity. At the same time, hip DJs and producers were mixing bossa and samba with drum loops and electronic music in a musical movement some called "nova bossa nova." DJ-producers Gilles Peterson, Nicola Conte, Joe Davis (Far Out Records), and Thievery Corporation's Rob Garza and Eric Hilton were among those employing bossa and Brazilian sounds in their remixes.

The popular drum 'n' bass sound in particular brought bossa nova, as well as samba, to a new generation. A type of electronic dance music that emerged in the early '90s in the U.K., drum 'n' bass features fast-tempo *breakbeats* (beats with a gap in the continuity) over bass lines at a slower tempo. The kinetic style meshed well with bossa and samba, which were incorporated in many dance hits. Singer-songwriter Fernanda Porto recalls, "Drum 'n' bass motivated me to compose. I was in love with the rhythm and thus a musical synchronism occurred."[32] She mixed samba with drum 'n' bass in "Sambassim" and showed it to a fellow Brazilian, DJ Patife. His 2000 remix was a hit on London dance floors and became one of the top-selling international drum 'n' bass singles the next year. Porto, Patife, and DJ Marky also collaborated on a hit remake of Jobim's "Só Tinha Que Ser com Você" (It Could Only Have Been with You). Porto comments, "After shows, many teenagers sought me out to say that they first discovered Jobim dancing to the electronic version of 'Só Tinha Que Ser com Você.'"[33] That song and "Sambassim" are both included on Porto's 2002 self-titled debut album.

▼ Celso Fonseca. *(Photo by Klaus Mitteldorf. Courtesy of Six Degrees.)*

The European group Zuco 103, with Brazilian lead singer Lilian Vieira, mixed bossa and samba with electro-jazz and drum 'n' bass, while Rosalia de Souza's 2003 album *Garota Moderna* (Modern Girl), produced by Conte, updated bossa nova songs like Carlos Lyra's "Maria Moita." Patrícia Marx has also added electronica and other contemporary touches to bossa. Bossacucanova (with keyboardist Alexandre Moreira and bassist Marcio Menescal, Roberto's son) applied dance-floor beats to bossa classics in the playful *Revisited Classics* (1999), with the elder Menescal joining them in *Brasilidade* in 2001 (see Chapter Ten). And Suba (Mitar Subotić, 1961–1999), a Serbian composer-producer who resided in Brazil, produced a sublime mixture of Brazilian music with electronica on his 1999 album *São Paulo Confessions*, with João Parahyba providing percussion.

Bossa nova was also reinvigorated as many notable musicians interpreted the genre in a more traditional manner. Guitarist and singer-songwriter Celso Fonseca released a trio of albums—*Juventude/Slow Motion Bossa Nova* (2001), *Natural* (2003), and *Rive Gauche Rio* (2005)—that lent subtle electronic touches to his soft vocals and sensual, unhurried explorations of the idiom. Marcos Valle added easy-listening jazz to bossa (sometimes reminiscent of fusion group Azymuth) in *Jet Samba* (2005). Paula Morelenbaum, the Quarteto Jobim-Morelenbaum (of which Paula is a part), and Morelenbaum2/Sakamoto (Paula and husband Jacques, plus Ryuichi Sakamoto) all recorded excellent albums devoted to bossa nova, especially Jobim's compositions.

Singer Leila Pinheiro covered bossa standards on several albums, as did jazz pianist and vocalist Eliane Elias. Rosa Passos paid tribute to Joao Gilberto in *Amoroso* (2004), teamed up with jazz bassist Ron Carter to interpret bossa classics in *Entre Amigos* (Between Friends, 2003), and sang "Chega de Saudade" on classical cellist Yo-Yo Ma's 2003 *Obrigado Brasil* (Thank You, Brazil). These were just a few of the many bossa-themed albums released by a wide variety of Brazilian and international artists in the 1990s and 2000s.

THE BOSSA LEGACY

As Jobim argued, bossa nova had a huge impact on American music. In fact, it became a permanent subset of jazz, and countless jazz and pop composers would incorporate bossa melodies, harmonies, rhythms, and textures into their songs in succeeding decades. In addition, arguably, the guitar would be reinvigorated as a jazz instrument in part because of the inspired playing of João Gilberto, Baden Powell, Luiz Bonfá, Bola Sete, Laurindo Almeida, Oscar Castro-Neves, and the bossa-influenced Charlie Byrd. Globally, bossa nova helped popularize the nation's music as a whole; it engendered the first large-scale international exposure of Brazilian music and musicians.

The importance of bossa nova in the evolution of Brazilian music itself was also immense. After its golden days, 1958 to 1964, the bossa nova movement lost momentum, but every musician who came after it fed on its sophisticated harmonies. Young musicians who before bossa nova would look for novelties abroad started looking for them inside Brazil, inside themselves. In the years to follow, many artists, when asked about the beginning of their serious interest in music, would answer, "Well, it all started with bossa nova."

MPB: A MUSICAL RAINBOW

It could be a fox-trot or even rock
Because on my part there was never any
Prejudice, resentment, or intolerance
I want to be far from those who think like that . . .
I prefer Portela with Paulinho's mind
I prefer Elis, Aldir, and João Bosco forever
Forever Nazareth, Radamés, and Jobim
I prefer the night with Leni and Luis Eça
After a cold beer, without much hurry

Ivan Lins and Vitor Martins,
"Bonito" (Beautiful)

In the late 1960s and early 1970s, a new group of composers and musicians came into prominence in Brazil. Their music was dubbed MPB, an acronym for música popular brasileira. It referred to a whole generation of artists such as Edu Lobo, Geraldo Vandré, Elis Regina, Chico Buarque, Milton Nascimento, Dori Caymmi, Simone, Caetano Veloso, Gilberto Gil, Maria Bethânia, Gal Costa, Alceu Valença, Geraldo Azevedo, João Bosco, Ivan Lins, and Djavan.

MPB can be used for Brazilian popular music in general, but it has become a common label for these performers, and those who followed in their footsteps, whose music defies easy categorization. It is eclectic, varying greatly in style from artist to artist, and developed from a collision of bossa nova, regional folk music, protest songs, samba, rock and roll, the Tropicália movement, and other influences. These elements were mixed together in such a way that the final result cannot be placed into any particular genre such as bossa, samba, forró, or rock. Instead, it is a new category, and MPB has proved to be a convenient name for it.

An especially important characteristic of MPB songwriters is their keen ability to combine compelling melodies, rich harmonies, varied rhythms, and poetic lyrics. The popular music that they created from the 1960s through the 1980s is among the best ever produced by one generation in any country in the world. Most

▲ Clockwise from bottom left: Maria Bethânia, Gilberto Gil, Gal Costa, and Caetano Veloso on the cover of their collective LP.

of the leading MPB musicians gained national fame in a series of music festivals that began in the mid-1960s and coincided with the early years of a brutal military dictatorship that would rule Brazil for twenty-one years.

THE DARK TIMES

The up-and-coming MPB artists were shaped by the political tumult of the era, which stifled some artists and inspired others. In fact, most MPB stars hit their stride during a time of heavy government repression, and many were exiled, jailed, censored, or otherwise harassed during this time. Theirs was an art sometimes created under great duress.

On March 31, 1964, the right-wing Brazilian military overthrew the government of João (Jango) Goulart. The generals who commanded the takeover said they would stay in charge only for a year, while they "reorganized the country," and then would hold new elections for president. But they ended up retaining power for two decades, until they allowed the Brazilian Congress to elect a civilian president in 1985.

For a few years after the coup there was still some peaceful resistance. However, because most union leaders and opposing politicians had been stripped of their political rights, artists, students, and journalists became the spearhead of opposition. Students held demonstrations in the streets, demanding better universities and democratic elections. The biggest one took place in Rio in 1968 and had more than one hundred thousand participants. Such protests generated a strong and violent reaction from the military, including the invasion of universities and the killing of students.

By the end of 1968 the political scene was radicalized to its limit. Fights between rightist and leftist students were frequent. Right-wing terrorist groups like MAC (the Anti-Communist Movement) and CCC (the Communist Hunter Command) had appeared as a counterpoint to leftist demonstrators.

In Brasília, Congressman Márcio Moreira Alves gave a speech in which he proposed a boycott against the September 7 Independence Day celebrations. The senior officers of the military considered his words offensive to the armed forces and wanted to put him in jail. Congress, however, denied permission for Alves to be tried. That was the excuse the generals needed for a second and deeper coup. On December 13, 1968, the military implemented Institutional Act No. 5, and Brazil was plunged into the fiercest dictatorship of its history. Congress was closed, all civil rights were withdrawn (anybody could be kept in jail without a trial), and all forms of press and the arts had to be censored before they reached the public. Acting president General Costa e Silva wielded dictatorial powers.

Politicians, students, artists, and intellectuals were arrested and tortured. Many dissidents "disappeared" and were never found; hundreds or even thousands of citizens were killed—nobody knows the total. Others were forced to leave the country. Many small guerrilla groups rose up to fight the government, but they weren't successful. By 1972 the military had the country firmly in its hands.

Act No. 5 was not revoked until 1978. The following year political prisoners were granted amnesty, marking the beginning of the Brazilian *glasnost* that would only be complete ten years later, with direct elections for president in 1989.

THE FESTIVALS BEGIN: VOICES OF PROTEST

Amid the climate of growing fear and repression, the televised music festivals were a vital cultural outlet for many Brazilians. Not only did many musical careers begin there, but for a time (until Act No. 5 in 1968) they were a forum for political dissent—as expressed in song.

The festival era opened in 1965. The first important one was sponsored by the TV Excelsior channel and took place in Guarujá, a beach town in São Paulo state. Generally, at these and later festivals, the television station organized a jury formed of musicians, journalists, and other music industry people. They sorted through tapes sent by applicants and classified those songs that would compete. With the television cameras transmitting, the nominees then performed live before large audiences at arenas and theaters.

Audiences participated boisterously, cheering for their favorites and booing the others. The public responded to songs according to both musical merit and how they related to issues of Brazilian nationalism and politics. The juries picked the winning compositions, and the victorious singers and songwriters were rewarded with trophies, money, and national exposure. First prize at the TV Excelsior Festival went to "Arrastão" (Fishing Net), interpreted by a talented young singer named Elis Regina and written by Edu Lobo and Vinícius de Moraes.

Edu Lobo

The young co-author of "Arrastão" was a singer, guitarist, and songwriter. Edu Lobo wrote beautiful, stirring songs that combined regional folk music with bossa nova harmonies. His lyrics protested the injustice and misery of Brazil's Northeast, an area that has suffered more than the rest

of the country from poverty and neofeudalism.

Lobo's song "Borandá" (Let's Go), written in 1964 and released on his first album in 1965, was a bossa with a slight northeastern flavor and poignant lyrics bemoaning the terrible droughts in the region.

Let's go, the land is dry already
Let's go, the rain won't come

His 1967 song "Ponteio" (Strumming), written with Capinam, was also a protest song, with words that were a subtle comment on the political repression of the time. "Ponteio," performed by Lobo and Marília Medalha, took first place at the TV Record Festival that year.

Running in the middle of the world
I never leave my guitar
I'll see new times coming
And a new place to sing

Born in Rio in 1943, Lobo was proficient in both samba-canção and bossa when he met Carlos Lyra in the mid-1960s. Lobo was impressed by Lyra's new bossa style, which used northeastern musical elements and socially conscious lyrics. Edu began to follow a similar line and—together with singer Elis Regina and the composers Geraldo Vandré and Sérgio Ricardo, among others— he would expand bossa nova's intimate sound into extroverted, epic protest songs that the new military government did not like one bit.

At this time, bossa nova split between the old guard and the new protest singers, and the Brazilian audience became sharply divided in its preferences. Nationalistic music with a clearly Brazilian flavor was set against "foreign" music, such as the rock songs heard on the *Jovem Guarda* (Young Guard) television show in the mid-1960s.

Edu composed many standards: with moviemaker and lyricist Ruy Guerra, Edu wrote "Canção da Terra" (Song of the Earth) and "Reza e Aleluia" (Pray and Say Hallelujah), and with Gianfranceso Guarnieri he composed "Upa Neguinho." Edu's aforementioned "Ponteio," which took first place in the 1967 TV Record Festival, was the last protest song to win a festival. From then on, censorship and the general hopelessness of the country dramatically reduced the number of such tunes performed at these events.

The political climate in Brazil convinced Edu that he should leave. In 1969 he moved to the United States, where he appeared on Paul Desmond's album *From the Hot Afternoon* (which included four Lobo songs). He returned to Brazil in 1971 and since then has concentrated on writing music for plays, movies, and ballets. After many years he began to record again, releasing fine albums like *Meia-Noite* (Midnight) in 1995.

Geraldo Vandré

Singer-songwriter Geraldo Vandré, as mentioned above, was another musician who was shaking and stirring the bossa in a radical way. Vandré was the artistic last name of Geraldo Pedrosa de Araújo Dias, born in 1935 in João Pessoa, Paraíba. Geraldo, whose first guitar teacher was João Gilberto, incorporated many folkloric genres into his music, among them toada, moda, baião, and *aboio*. He said he interpreted these styles in a "more ideologic than formal way," meaning he used them to create protest songs that had strong, angry lyrics.

Vandré's "ideological" adaptations had a distinctly progressive edge, in part because of the creative virtuosity of his backup bands. In 1966 and 1967 he worked with Quarteto Novo (New Quartet), a now-legendary group that included Hermeto Pascoal on flute, Airto Moreira on percussion, and Heraldo do Monte and Théo de Barros on guitar. Then, in 1968, he was backed by Quarteto Livre (Free Quartet), which included percussionist Naná Vasconcelos and guitarist Geraldo Azevedo. Most of the musicians in Vandré's groups went on to become stars in their own right.

Vandré's songs, performed by others, took first place in two festivals in 1966. "Porta-Estandarte" (Standard-Bearer), written with Fernando Lona, captured the TV Excelsior event, where it was performed by Tuca and Airto. And Vandré and Barros's "Disparada" (Stampede), sung by Jair Rodrigues, tied for first place in the TV Record contest. "Disparada" was a toada that told the story of a northeastern *vaqueiro* (cowboy) who is enraged that he and the other vaqueiros are treated like cattle.

We mark, drive, brand
Fatten and kill the herd
But with people it's different

For his fiery protest songs Vandré became a national hero, more famous even than Lobo. Armed only with his guitar, he was perceived as a serious threat by the military government.

Vandré's masterpiece, "Prá Não Dizer Que Não Falei de Flores" (Not to Say I Didn't Speak of Flowers), also known by the shorter name of "Caminhando" (Walking), was considered by Brazilian journalist Millôr Fernandes a "Brazilian 'Marseillaise,' the true national anthem."

There are armed soldiers, they may be loved
*   or not*
Almost all of them lost, with guns in their
*   hands*
In the barracks they are taught an old lesson
To die for their country
And to live a meaningless life

"Caminhando" took second place in Rio's third annual FIC, Festival Internacional da Canção (International Song Festival), in 1968. Vandré's provocative song was subsequently banned by the censors for ten years. In the October 10, 1968, issue of the newspaper *Correio da Manhã*, General Luis de Franca Oliveira presented his reasons for the prohibition of "Caminhando." He cited its "subversive lyrics, its offensiveness to the armed forces, and the fact that it would serve as a slogan for student demonstrations."

He was right. Even after it was banned, "Caminhando" never ceased to be sung wherever there were people who resisted the dictatorship. It was still heard at protests at the end of the 1970s, when

Brazilian society started to challenge the government, demanding a return to democracy.

Once Act No. 5 was invoked, Geraldo had to leave Brazil to ensure his personal safety. From 1969 to 1973 he wandered through Chile, Algeria, Greece, Austria, Bulgaria, and finally France—where he made his only record during this time, *Das Terras do Benvirá*. When he returned to Brazil in 1973, he was arrested upon arrival. A month later he was released from jail and appeared on a national news program saying, among other things, that he hoped he could integrate his latest songs with the new Brazilian reality and that the connection between his music and certain political groups had been made against his will.

This public statement was probably the price he had to pay to be allowed to remain in the country. After that, Geraldo recorded no more new songs and got rid of his stage name, Vandré. After seven albums, Geraldo's short but incandescent career was over. Eventually there was only Geraldo Dias, the lawyer. Nevertheless, he'll always be remembered as the author of songs that make one want to stand and fight for what is right.

Chico Buarque the Poet

The 1966 TV Record Festival ended in a tie for first place between "Disparada" by Vandré and "A Banda" (The Band), performed by bossa nova muse Nara Leão and a newcomer, singer-songwriter Chico Buarque de Hollanda. With his melancholy nasal voice, Chico sang beautifully crafted, extremely literate sambas and marchas. He soon became very popular and would ultimately be considered one of the greatest lyricists of all time in Brazilian popular music.

Born in Rio in 1944 but raised in São Paulo and Italy, Chico achieved national acclaim when he released his first three albums in the mid-1960s. He was considered an heir apparent to the great samba-canção composers of the 1930s, like Noel Rosa, and his popularity was the only thing that almost all of polarized Brazil agreed about: Chico was the man every woman wanted to marry and every man admired. To many he seemed the true defender of

▲ An early album from Chico Buarque, one of Brazil's greatest songwriters. *(Courtesy of RGE.)*

traditional Brazilian music against the furious attack of protest songs, the aesthetic revolution proposed by Tropicália (the musical movement led by Gilberto Gil and Caetano Veloso), and the alien electric guitars in the music of Jovem Guarda rockers Roberto Carlos and Erasmo Carlos.

Chico found his path composing traditional sambas like "A Rita," "Olê Olá," and "Pedro Pedreiro" (Pedro the Bricklayer), and marchas like "A Banda." In "A Banda," Buarque depicts music as a force that rejuvenates and spreads happiness, but only temporarily, while the band plays on.

> *But to my disenchantment, what was sweet*
> * ran out*
> *Everything back in its place, after the band*
> * had passed*
> *And each back in his corner, and in each*
> * corner sorrow*
> *After the band had passed, singing songs of*
> * love*

Chico's early lyrics were subtle yet powerful, and often strongly nostalgic. Short excerpts do them little justice because they were intricately constructed, building themes and ideas over many verses. They almost always told of good things that had already gone by. Maybe that explains his enormous success: the present was so insecure that listening to a talented young musician who praised the past and reverently revived old Brazilian musical genres gave people hope that soon things would return to the good old days. Such songs were very popular. Old or young, rich or poor, communist or capitalist, everybody loved Chico, the nice green-eyed young singer . . . until around 1968.

Chico didn't like being idolized. He felt used and abused, and his answer to his fans' blind devotion came in 1968 in the form of a play: *Roda Viva* (an expression that means "rat race"). The drama tells the story of a young pop star who is devoured by the public. Literally. During the performance of the play, actors offered pieces of the star's "liver" to the audience. This caused a scandal and an extreme backlash from conservatives. In São Paulo, CCC right-wing extremists invaded the theater and beat the actors. In Porto Alegre, after the first night, members of the cast were told to leave the city or they would be killed. Government censors immediately prohibited any further performances. *Roda Viva* marked the death of "nice guy" Chico Buarque.

While Buarque was angering the government with his play, Gilberto Gil and Caetano Veloso were attacking him for the formal conservatism of his music. Chico was no longer the national choice. After the *Roda Viva* debacle, Chico went to Italy, where he spent more than a year, playing on European stages with such disparate performers as Josephine Baker and Toquinho.

In 1970 Chico was the first of the exiled MPB musicians to return to Brazil. Although he wasn't arrested, he was a favorite target of the censors; in 1971 they approved only one out of every three songs he wrote. Some passed and then were censored later. For example, "Apesar de Você" (In Spite of You) was banned after it became a hit. The censors must have missed the irony in the lyrics that were obviously directed toward the government.

In spite of you
Tomorrow is going to be another day

I ask you where you are going
To hide from the immense euphoria

In 1971 Chico recorded his fifth album, *Construção* (Construction). It was a dramatic record that represented a break in his career. Nostalgic subjects give way to an almost hallucinatory treatment of the disappointments and tragedies of everyday life. Buarque vividly evokes the dehumanization caused by work, marriage, routine, the system.

In the album's title song, blaring, edgy horns build tension, and the percussion keeps a steady, ominous "tick-tock" beat. The lyrics describe the last day of a bricklayer who dies in the middle of the road after falling from a window.

He tripped over the sky as if he heard music
And floated in the air as if it might be
Sunday
And ended up on the ground like a timid
bundle
Agonized, shipwrecked in the middle of the
sidewalk
Died on the wrong side of the street
disturbing the public

When they returned from exile in the early 1970s, Veloso and Gil patched up their friendship with Buarque, which had been badly shaken for a time because of aesthetic differences. Soon after, Chico recorded a live album with Veloso and then in 1973 wrote "Cálice" (Chalice) with Gil. Using powerful Catholic religious imagery, the song is a metaphorical comment on the repressive times and the silencing of an entire nation.

How to drink this bitter drink
Gulp down the pain, swallow the drudgery
Though my mouth is quiet, my breast
remains
No one hears the silence in the city . . .
Father, take this cup away from me

The song's title carries two meanings: "Cálice" translates as "chalice" yet is also a homophone of the phrase *cale-se*, which means "shut up."[1] And that is exactly what the authorities did to Buarque and Gil when they first attempted to perform "Cálice" in public. The police came on stage and turned off the microphones as they were singing. The song was banned, but it became yet another anthem of protest against the dictatorship.

The censors continued to hound Buarque for the next several years, and in 1974 and 1975 almost none of the songs that he wrote met with their approval and made it on record. Brazilians came to regard Chico as a symbol of cultural resistance, although little of his work actually reached the public. At one point Buarque apparently gave up trying to get his own material through and instead recorded only covers on his 1974 album *Sinal Fechado* (Red Light). The record included the title song by Paulinho da Viola (which actually was a clever, coded protest) and tunes by Veloso, Gil, Noel Rosa, Toquinho, and an unknown newcomer, Julinho da Adelaide. The press material for the album included a biography for Julinho and described him as a sambista from the morro. His song "Acorda Amor" (Wake Up, Love) had a theme of fear of the police. Trouble was, Julinho didn't exist—he was an alter ego for Chico, and the truth was soon discovered. From then on, any composer sending a song to the censors had to include a copy of his or her identification card.

In the 1980s the government censors became more lenient. Buarque began including formerly banned songs along with new ones on albums like 1981's *Almanaque* (Almanac). By this time Chico had turned into an eclectic composer, writing marchas, fados, waltzes, and even rock tunes, but his main style was still samba. Throughout the decade his songwriting partners varied greatly; he worked with Francis Hime, Gil, Sivuca, Milton Nascimento, Toquinho, and Jobim, among others. Buarque's lyrics continued to use subtle irony and evocative imagery, contrast dreams with reality, and artfully blend the comic with the tragic. Often, he reflected on existential matters, as in "Vida" (Life), from 1980.

> Look what I've done
> I left life's sweetest slice

> On the table of men with empty lives
> But life, at that time
> Who knows, I was happy

Chico also devoted many songs to romantic matters, giving love an ironic, knowing treatment, as in "Deixa a Menina" (Let the Girl Go).

> Behind a sad man there's always a happy
>   woman
> And behind that woman a thousand men,
>   always so genteel

Vinícius de Moraes, one of Buarque's greatest fans, said that Chico "is a phenomenon who accomplished the perfect union of both cultivated and popular culture."

Beginning in the '90s, Buarque devoted a lot of his time to literature and published the novels *Estorvo, Benjamim,* and *Budapest,* and the children's book *Chapeuzinho Amarelo. Estorvo* was turned into a movie by director Ruy Guerra. Yet his musical charisma remained untouched. In 2006 Chico embarked on his first tour in seven years to promote his new album, *Carioca,* and concerts were sold out everywhere he performed.

Elis Regina

Not all of the artists who gained prominence at the music festivals were highly politicized singer-songwriters. Many were simply talented musicians who delved into controversial material only on occasion, or never at all. An example of the latter was Elis Regina, who sang "Arrastão," the winning entry at the TV Excelsior event.

Born in 1945 in Porto Alegre, Elis Regina Carvalho da Costa was only twenty years old when she took first place at the festival. Yet by this time she had already gained some recognition for her appearances on various television programs, where her impassioned singing style was the opposite of subdued bossa nova behavior. The TV Excelsior victory helped propel her to the top, and her contagious energy, superb intonation, and strongly emotional interpretations soon made Elis a big star in Brazil.

▲ Elis Regina performing at the Montreux Jazz Festival. *(Courtesy of Tropical Storm/WEA.)*

Nana Caymmi and Dori Caymmi

The 1966 International Song Festival (FIC) in Rio was won by Nana Caymmi, a young vocalist who was the daughter of the legendary Bahian composer Dorival Caymmi. She triumphed with the tune "Saveiros" (Fishing Boats), written by Nelson Motta and Nana's younger brother, Dori Caymmi. Nana (born in 1941) is a sophisticated, jazz-influenced singer who has long been a favorite of Brazilian musicians. Nana has a deep, soulful voice that is wonderful for interpretations. A good example of her expressiveness is her vocal on "Velho Piano" (Old Piano) on her brother's album *Dori Caymmi*, in which she marvelously captures the shifting tensions, complex modulations, and intricate rhythms in the composition. She has recorded many fine solo albums as well as recordings with the rest of the Caymmi family.

Dori Caymmi (born in 1943) is one of the most accomplished arrangers, composers, and guitarists of his generation. Don Grusin, a composer and producer who has often collaborated with

She recorded bossa, samba, and the new eclectic songs of the emerging MPB composers. She co-hosted the television show *O Fino da Bossa* (The Best of Bossa) with singer Jair Rodrigues from 1965 to 1967 and the MPB television show *Som Livre Exportação* (Free Sound Export) with Ivan Lins in 1971 and 1972. She also staged ingenious live shows that blended music and theater harmoniously.

Elis had a remarkable ability to find talented new composers. She was the first to record songs by Ivan Lins, Milton Nascimento, João Bosco, and Belchior, all of whom would later achieve great renown. During her very successful career, some of Regina's biggest hits were Lins's "Madalena," Renato Teixeira's "Romaria" (Pilgrimage), Lobo's "Upa Neguinho" (Hey Black Boy), Belchior's "Como Nossos Pais" (Like Our Parents), Bosco and Blanc's "O Bêbado e a Equilibrista" (The Drunkard and the Acrobat), and Jobim's "Águas de Março" (Waters of March).

But the charismatic singer's life was cut tragically short by a cocaine overdose in 1982, just when her artistic abilities were in full flower. Most critics and MPB fans in Brazil considered her the most important Brazilian singer of all time. For many years after her death, one could find the words *Elis vive* (Elis lives) in graffiti on the walls of Brazilian cities.

▼ Dori Caymmi. *(Photo by Diego Uchitel. Courtesy of Qwest/WEA.)*

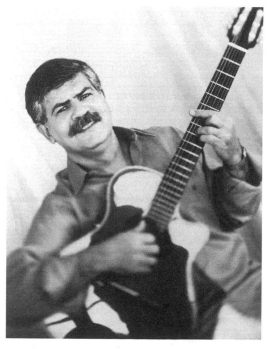

Brazilian musicians, said of Dori that "his melodies are my favorite melodies in the world, and some of his chords are too." Grusin noted that, on his guitar, Dori often "tunes the top E down to a B, so that he has a double B. Then he makes these cluster chords by putting one finger on the top string and the second finger just one fret off, and he gets minor-second clusters." Grusin observed that such tonal effects were also favored by Ravel and Debussy. "It's a way to make the harmonic basis a lot more interesting."[2]

Caymmi's musical arrangements in the late 1960s reveal his many talents. He arranged the debut albums of Caetano Veloso and Gilberto Gil, had his songs recorded by Nascimento, Jobim, Djavan, Regina, and Maria Bethânia, and wrote scores for movies and plays. Dori's music is a collection of impressionistic images, mixing Brazilian rhythms with influences from Bill Evans, Villa-Lobos, Debussy, and Ravel. "I'm pretty much the guy who looks at nature and makes my portraits. I use my music like a painter," he said.[3]

In 1987 he arranged jazz singer Sarah Vaughan's album *Brazilian Romance*, which featured five of Dori's compositions and was nominated for a Grammy award. With the release in 1988 of the lyrical, richly textured *Dori Caymmi*, on which he sang and played guitar, Dori earned a wider audience outside Brazil. Later albums have included *Kicking Cans, If Ever . . .* , and *Rio Bahia* with singer-songwriter Joyce.

Tropicália

As the music festivals entered their third year, they continued to launch new artists. In 1967 it was the time of Gilberto Gil and Caetano Veloso, who used this forum to kick off a radical new musical movement: Tropicália.

By this time, these events had become a national craze. The streets of Brazil would be deserted on festival nights because everybody would be home watching them on television, just as they did when big soccer games took place. The audience behavior at the concerts was also similar to that of soccer fans at stadiums like Maracanã.

Those attending the festivals would go to the theater to support their favorites with banners and applause and try to disturb the "enemies."

When Veloso performed his Tropicália anthem "Alegria Alegria" (Joy Joy) at the TV Record event that year, he was booed. Much of the audience was intensely nationalistic. They revered "authentically" Brazilian music and detested what symbolized U.S. colonialism. To them, "Alegria Alegria" was Americanized because it was a rock song and Veloso was backed by a rock group, Os Beat Boys. Many also didn't respond to its strange, fragmented imagery.

Walking against the wind
Without handkerchief, without documents
In the almost December sun, I go
The sun scatters into spaceships, guerrillas
 . . .
Teeth, legs, flags, the bomb, and Brigitte
 Bardot

Gil's entry, "Domingo no Parque" (Sunday in the Park), received a much warmer response, in part because it wasn't rock and roll. But it was something markedly different. It included a Bahian capoeira rhythm, electric instrumentation, and cinematic lyrics. The song was arranged by Rogério Duprat, a Paulista who had a solid background in both classical and experimental electronic music. He was willing to add his experience as an avant-garde musician to the popular music being made by the Tropicalistas.

The arrangement was influenced by the Beatles' "A Day in the Life" from their 1967 *Sgt. Pepper's* album. When Gil wrote "Domingo," he was listening over and over to the Beatles' song, which he calls "my myth of the time."[4] Gil then created an equally fascinating song, in which Bahia met George Martin and Rogério Duprat.

At the TV Record Festival, the winning song was Edu Lobo's "Ponteio." The jury put "Domingo no Parque" and "Alegria Alegria" into second and fourth place, respectively. But those tunes had an enormous impact and introduced Tropicália music to the public. Music critic Tárik de

Souza wrote about Veloso's performance: "The introduction of electric instruments to Brazilian popular music, until then unplugged, the new costumes, made of plastic, the bristling hair of the performers and the aggressive stage performances, making a stark contrast with the acoustic guitar and the quietude of bossa nova, were elements that changed definitely the course of Brazilian popular music."[5]

"It was as if the Beatles had pollinated Brazilian pop music. It was sophisticated, thrilling, imaginative, surprising, sometimes breathtaking pop music and it rocked, even if sometimes in a totally un-rock and roll way," commented music critic José Emilio Rondeau. "It was music of the younger generation and so fresh that at that point bossa nova, initially considered a revolution, immediately became square in comparison, even though it was an inspiration for Tropicália."[6]

Gilberto Gil and Caetano Veloso—both from Bahia—had moved to São Paulo two years earlier and were exposed to the burgeoning, heady arts scene there and in Rio de Janeiro. They developed the idea of creating an iconoclastic mixture of music in which everything would have its space. Luiz Gonzaga, the Beatles, João Gilberto, Chuck Berry, film director Jean-Luc Godard: everything would be cannibalized and put into the stew. Their lyrics would be sometimes poignant, other times surreal, always provocative.

In Tropicália, anything went: rock and samba, berimbaus and electronic instruments, folk music and urban noise, the erudite and the kitsch. There had been rock and roll in Brazil since the late 1950s, but this was the first time it was being mixed with native styles (and much else). On one level, Tropicália could be understood as a "rereading of the tradition of Brazilian popular song in light of international pop music and vanguard experimentation."[7]

Tropicália was an art movement that lasted roughly from 1967 to 1969. It manifested itself in music, theater, poetry, and the plastic arts. The word *Tropicália* came from a 1967 ambient-art piece by Hélio Oiticica. Some of the Tropicalistas' ideas had precedents in the works of the Paulista

▲ Tom Zé. *(Courtesy of Luaka Bop.)*

poet Oswald de Andrade, who four decades earlier had created the concept of artistic cannibalism, which he discussed in his 1928 "Manifesto Antropofágico" (Cannibalistic Manifesto). Gil and Veloso took Andrade's ideas to heart, devouring everything—national music and themes and imported cultural elements—and then re-elaborating it all "with autonomy," as Andrade had urged. "Power to the imagination" and "down with [aesthetic] prejudice" were slogans that inspired Tropicália. Other musicians who participated in the movement included Júlio Medaglia (another classical conductor), Gal Costa, Torquato Neto, Os Mutantes, Capinam, Nara Leão, and Tom Zé.

Tom Zé (Antonio José Santana Martins) had studied classical music with the renowned professors Ernst Widmer (a follower of Igor Stravinsky and Béla Bartòk), Walter Smetak (who later tutored Uakti in the construction of strange, original instruments), and Hans Joachim Koellreutter (who had taught Jobim). In his own quirky experimental music, Tom Zé used everyday objects (typewriters, blenders, floor polishers) in his orchestrations and combined avant-garde music with northeastern styles. Years later, Tom Zé described his music as "a mixture of Schoenberg, Beethoven, and Jackson do Pandeiro."[8]

Tom Zé and the others collaborated on the concept album *Tropicália, ou Panis et Circensis*, in 1968. Christopher Dunn, who wrote *Brutality Garden: Tropicália and the Emergence of a Brazilian Counterculture*, describes the group shot on the cover: "Costa and Neto appear as a conventional, well-mannered couple; Gil sits on the floor in a bathrobe printed with tropical motifs holding a graduation portrait of Capinan; Duprat daintily holds a chamber pot as if it were a tea cup; Tom Zé plays the northeastern migrant, holding a leather satchel; Os Mutantes ostentatiously show off their guitars; and Veloso is seated in the middle holding a large portrait of Nara Leão."[9] Musically and lyrically, Tropicalista songs were usually intelligent and ironic montages, and the album included one of the movement's most representative songs: Gil and Neto's "Geléia Geral" (General Jelly).

"Geléia Geral" mixed bumba-meu-boi, a folkloric style from the Northeast, with electric rock instrumentation. In the song's lyrics, the traditional ("sweet mulata," "Mangueira where samba is purer," and "saintly Bahian baroque") was juxtaposed with the modern ("TV," "Formiplac and the azure sky," and "I get a jet, travel, explode").

Rogério Duprat's arrangements punctuated and stressed the contemporary and traditional references. For example, he added caixa percussion when the samba school Portela was mentioned. To further add to the mix, the term *bumba-meu-boi* was juxtaposed ironically with *iê-iê-iê* (yeah-yeah-yeah), the pejorative name given by Brazilian critics to 1960s rock and roll.

In the general jelly
That Jornal do Brasil announces
It's bumba-iê-iê-boi
Next year, last month
It's bumba-iê-iê-iê
It's the same dance, meu-boi

Not all the public understood what Gil and Veloso were doing. Many of them hated it. They didn't like the rock and roll part of it; they didn't like the electric guitars. When Veloso presented his latest outrage in 1968 in São Paulo, during the International Song Festival, he was booed even more loudly than he had been for "Alegria Alegria." He appeared with the rock group Os Mutantes (the Mutants) and performed "É Proibido Proibir" (Forbidding Is Forbidden), the title inspired by a popular slogan of the May 1968 student protests in Paris.[10] The Mutantes dressed in odd plastic clothes that seemed straight out of an early *Star Trek* episode. Rogério Duprat conducted a long atonal introduction to kick off the song, and Veloso interrupted his singing to recite an old poem by Fernando Pessoa. To top it all off, a tall American named Johnny Dandurand appeared on stage, howling and grunting unintelligibly. Veloso's "happening" was not appreciated by the audience, mostly pro-left nationalist students, and they responded with booing and swearing.[11] The festival jury was more open-minded and the song was approved for another round.

During the next performance, the majority of those in attendance turned their backs to the stage during the opening of the song, and the Mutantes wittily turned their backs in kind.[12] Instead of reciting the Pessoa poem, Veloso gave a now-famous extemporaneous speech castigating his intolerant audience, saying, "You are the youth who will always kill tomorrow the old enemy that died yesterday! You can't understand anything."[13]

Tropicália opened a temporary gap between the political avant-garde and cultural avant-garde, but by the early 1970s its ideas would be quite acceptable. Tropicália songs were aesthetically daring and sporadically brilliant and included a few masterpieces, such as "Domingo no Parque." Ironically, the most controversial Tropicália tunes—the ones with the strongest rock and roll influence—were generally the weakest of the bunch. The movement had a brief life (it was over by 1969), but it greatly accelerated MPB's musical experimentation and hybridization, and gave all Brazilian musicians who came after it a greater sense of creative

◀ Chico Buarque and Caetano Veloso, in concert on their television show *Chico & Caetano*. *(Courtesy of Som Livre.)*

freedom. Tropicália has inspired a growing number of critical essays and academic papers, and also enjoyed an international revival starting in the '90s, after the U.K. and North American re-release of Tropicalist recordings. Singer-songwriter Beck was a notable example of a foreign artist who was influenced, and in 1998 he released the album *Mutations*, which included his own tribute song, "Tropicália."

Gilberto Gil

The creativity of Gilberto Gil by no means ended once the Tropicália years were over; in the years afterward he continued to experiment with new musical styles, blending international pop music (rock, funk, reggae) with Brazilian urban and rural music in his own singular extroverted, upbeat style.

Born in 1942 in Salvador, Gil spent his childhood and adolescence in the small town of Ituaçu, in the interior of Bahia state. There he absorbed a wide variety of influences: Luiz Gonzaga, classical music, polka, Italian music, fado, Celia Cruz, mambo, samba, bolero, Yma Sumac, Duke Ellington, Miles Davis, and Chet Baker. Gil's first instrument was the accordion; he switched to guitar after hearing a startling new song on the radio: João Gilberto's "Chega de Saudade."

After studying business administration at the federal university in Salvador (where he met Veloso and Bethânia) and working a brief stint for a multinational corporation in São Paulo, Gil became a full-time professional musician. His recording career kicked off in 1965 with a single containing the folkish protest tunes "Roda" (Wheel) and "Procissão" (Procession). In 1966 Elis Regina and Jair Rodrigues recorded the Gil–Torquato Neto tune "Louvação" (Praise), and it was a big success. Gil began to appear regularly on the *O Fino da Bossa* television show and soon proved that he was a charismatic performer with a lilting voice.

As the Tropicália movement took off in 1967, Gil released his first album, *Louvação*. Gil, Veloso, and the other Tropicalistas succeeded in irritating the military dictatorship, who feared that the movement might sway Brazilian youth toward an alternate lifestyle involving drugs, chaos, and hippiedom. Gil was jailed in 1969 but was never charged with a specific crime. "Just for being different," recalled Gil, "unexpected, daring, bold, adventurous, unknown, and dangerous." He laughed. "I never considered my lyrics and everything as really heavy. Never. My attitude, okay. But my words . . ."[14]

In prison Gil took up yoga, meditation, and a

macrobiotic diet. Once out, he left for England, as did Veloso, and lived there in self-imposed exile until 1972. When he returned to Brazil, both the government and nationalist-minded Brazilians were less critical of Gil and his Tropicalista peers. Their rock-and-roll-flavored music was no longer seen as subversive by the Right or as culturally imperialistic by the Left. It was instead viewed as healthy experimentation.

The world was changing, and Gil set his sights on the future. In "Expresso 2222" he sang of a train traveling from a Rio suburb to modernity.

The 2222 Express started running
From the central station of Brazil
It goes directly from Bonsucesso
To beyond the year 2000

From that point on, Gil began to delve heavily into his Afro-Brazilian roots and to incorporate them into his global pop fusions. In 1977 he attended the Festival of Black Art and Culture in Lagos, Nigeria; it was an experience that affected him profoundly. In Lagos Gil met Fela Kuti, Stevie Wonder, and other African descendents from all over the world. "That caused something shaking, emotional, very intuitive, telluric. Like being replanted in the soil of Africa and then being able to flourish as a new tree," he said.[15]

Gil expanded his exploration of African culture. *Refavela* (Re-Favela) in 1977 included "Baba Alapalá" (an homage to the orixá Xangô), the marvelous afoxé "Patuscada de Gandhi" (Revelry of the Filhos de Gandhi), the use of Yoruba words in several songs, and the marked influence of Nigerian musical forms like *highlife* and *ju-ju*. Gil's self-immersion at this time in his African roots paralleled the rise in Salvador of blocos afro (Afro-Brazilian Carnaval groups). His participation in Bahia's "re-Africanization" helped propel the whole process.

Gil's following albums experimented with a variety of song styles. He blended funk and afoxé in "Toda Menina Baiana" (Every Bahian Girl) in 1978. Numerous tunes were based on reggae, including "Vamos Fugir" (Let's Escape), recorded with the Wailers in 1984. Many songs added Brazilian touches to rock and technopop. Gil's acute lyrics critiqued society, while his rhythmic blends continued to break new ground. Indeed, Gil was creating what was later labeled "world music," beginning with "Domingo no Parque."

In the late 1980s Gil became involved in politics, taking time off from music to serve as the secretary of culture and on the city council for the city of Salvador. After returning to the recording studio he hit another artistic peak with *Parabolicamará* (1991), a rootsy yet high-tech effort that

◄ Gilberto Gil in the 1980s. *(Photo by Livio Campos. Courtesy of Braziloid.)*

blends samba-reggae, samba de roda, capoeira, and funk. It yielded the joyful tune "Madalena," a hit that year in Carnaval.

Politics called him again when Inácio Lula da Silva was elected president of Brazil in 2002 and asked Gil to be his minister of culture; he continued in that position after Lula's re-election until mid 2008. Along the way, he was awarded the Légion d'Honneur by the French government in 2005.

Caetano Veloso

Caetano Veloso (Caetano Emanuel Vianna Telles Veloso) was born in 1942 in Santo Amaro da Purificação, Bahia. As a singer, he was heavily influenced by his idol, João Gilberto. As a composer, Caetano has an extraordinary ability to weave poetry and melody together so seamlessly that it is difficult to imagine them separately. He is always ready to try new musical paths; for example, he was the first Brazilian artist to incorporate reggae elements into a song, which he did in 1972 in a rock tune called "Nine Out of Ten." Yet in his own way Veloso has been quite nationalistic with regard to music. He is famous for his knowledge of old Brazilian songs and aided in the comebacks of venerable figures like Luiz Gonzaga, the king of baião, who had been forgotten during the '60s.

Throughout that decade and those that followed, Caetano would embrace old styles and create new ones. *Domingo* (Sunday), his 1967 debut album with Gal Costa, was mostly bossa nova, with Veloso obviously following the path of João Gilberto. The collaborative montage of the *Tropicália* album came the next year. In 1969 he recorded "Atrás do Trio Elétrico" (After the Electric Trio), which captured the sound of the musicians who played kinetic frevos atop sound trucks called *trios elétricos* during Carnaval in Salvador.

But the government did not view him as nationalistic in an acceptable sense. Caetano—like Gilberto Gil—disturbed the authorities with his Tropicalista "chaos." He was imprisoned by the regime for four months in 1969, before a two-year exile in London. After he returned home, leftists who had neither understood nor liked Caetano during Tropicália tried to adopt him as a symbol of resistance to the government, as they had with Chico Buarque. Caetano destroyed this idea in his first show by dancing on stage like Carmen Miranda, shocking both the Left and the Right. Brazil was not ready for such androgynous behavior. The military kept Gil and Veloso under surveillance. But in the recording studio Caetano was equally unconventional. His 1972 album *Araçá Azul* combined static, folkloric music and incidental noise (it was one of the worst-selling albums of all time by a big-name MPB artist). Since then, Veloso's work has ranged freely from iconoclastic compositions to romantic, lyrical ballads.

◄ Caetano Veloso and Paulinho da Viola.

His songs frequently focus on themes of self-renewal and expanded possibilities. The song "O Querires" (What You Want) from 1984 is quintessential Veloso.

> Where you want the act, I am spirit . . .
> Where you want romance, [I am] rock'n'roll
> Where you want the moon, I am the sun
> Where you want pure nature, [I am]
>   insecticide

"My role is to change people's minds," he has said, and his lyrics are often provocative and discursive, as in "Ele Me Deu um Beijo na Boca" (He Gave Me a Kiss on the Mouth), a 1982 song of many verses that Caetano conceived as an imaginary dialogue with a friend covering life, politics, music, art, spirituality.

> He gave me a kiss on the mouth and told me
> Life is empty like the bonnet of a headless
>   baby
> Like the burrow of a drunken fox
> And I laughed like crazy
> And said enough of this talk, this bottomless
>   well

Caetano has explored rock, bossa, afoxé, frevo, reggae, and other genres, counterpointing his inquisitive words and delicate, Gilberto-influenced vocals. Mass popular acceptance came in the 1980s, when Caetano went from cult figure to full-fledged star in Brazil. He co-hosted a television musical show with Chico Buarque (*Chico & Caetano*) and had his songs covered extensively by other artists. Near the end of the decade he recorded albums such as *Caetano* and *Estrangeiro* (Foreigner) that found him still on his searching, wondering path.

Estrangeiro illustrates Caetano's "turbulent poetry"[16] with the harsh electric guitar of Arto Lindsay and a biting, rock-oriented production by Lindsay and Peter Sherer that often evokes a cold, unsettling mood. One of the songs, "Os Outros Românticos" (The Other Romantics), conveys a sense of impending apocalypse.

> They were the other romantics, in darkness
> They made a cult of another middle age
> Located in the future, not in the past
> Being incapable of following
> The blah blah blah of economics recited on
>   television
> These irreducible atheists simulated a
>   religion
> And the Spirit was the sex of Pixote
> In the voice of some German rock singer
> With hatred for those who killed Pixote by
>   hand
> They nurtured rebellion and revolution

The song contains references to the Hector Babenco film *Pixote* (1980), which is about a homeless boy in São Paulo and his tragic and violent life. Fernando Ramos da Silva, who played the protagonist, Pixote, was himself living on the streets before becoming an actor; he followed his character's fate when he was killed by police in São Paulo in 1987. *Estrangeiro* won high praise from foreign critics: Stephen Holden and Jon Pareles of the *New York Times* both picked it as one of the top albums of 1989.[17] An in-depth analysis of Veloso's lyrics is provided by Charles Perrone's academic study *Masters of Contemporary Brazilian Song*, which looks at the song texts of several major MPB composers.

Veloso's career was busy over the next twenty years, as he scored films (*O Quatrilho, Tieta do Agreste, Orfeu*), and was heard on the soundtracks of Salma Hayek's *Frida* and Pedro Almodóvar's *Hable con Ella* (Talk to Her). He also sang a duet with Lila Downs at the 2003 Academy Awards, published a musical memoir (*Tropical Truth*), and released new works such as *Livro* and *Prenda Minha* and interpretations of Spanish-language classics (*Fina Estampa*) and English-language standards (*A Foreign Sound*).

Gal Costa

Another participant in Tropicália was singer Gal Costa (Maria da Graça Costa Penna Burgos), born in 1945 in Salvador. Wearing beads, necklaces, and colorful blouses, Gal was the female singer most involved with the movement, which she later termed "political" because of its emphasis on transforming behavior. Indeed, in the years afterward, Gal's artistic career and lifestyle were symbols, in a way, of the openness and freedom that Tropicália sought: she was a hippie, a sophisticated torch singer, a Carnaval celebrant, and an audacious sex symbol.

From the Tropicália days through the 1980s, Gal worked in close collaboration on many albums with Gil and Veloso, her friends from Bahia. In 1967 she made her recording debut with the *Domingo* album with Veloso. In 1968 she appeared on the *Tropicália* collective album and also released her first solo album, *Gal Costa*.

While Gil and Veloso were living in exile, Gal was their spokesperson and would record their songs in Brazil. She also interpreted tunes by Roberto Carlos and Erasmo Carlos, Luis Melodia, and Jorge Benjor. In the early years of her career, Gal's naturally beautiful voice could sometimes be raucous and uncontrolled, especially on rock or blues-based numbers. But she worked hard to improve her technique and developed a well-tuned voice that can be poignant or aggressive, gentle or piercing.

Throughout her career she has recorded in a variety of styles, including samba, baião, frevo, blues, and rock. She has released thematic albums like 1976's *Gal Canta Caymmi* (all Dorival Caymmi songs), 1988's *Aquarela do Brasil* (Ary Barroso tunes), and 1995's *Mina D'Água do Meu Canto* (material by Veloso and Buarque). One of Gal's most popular recordings was her version of the Moraes Moreira–Abel Silva frevo "Festa do Interior" (Party in the Interior), the signature dance song of the 1982 Carnaval season and part of the double-platinum album *Fantasia* (which can be translated "costume" or "fantasy"). Later albums saw Gal continue to expand her repertoire, recording tunes by everyone from Cole Porter to Carlinhos Brown.

Maria Bethânia

It should not be surprising that, like Gal Costa, vocalist Maria Bethânia has also been closely linked with Gil and Veloso throughout her career, since she is Caetano's sister. Bethânia was the first of the foursome to gain fame. With her eloquent, sensuous contralto voice, she quickly attracted attention as a singer. In 1965 she replaced Nara Leão in the musical theater show *Opinião* and took over the singing of what had become every night's highlight, the performance of João do Vale's hard-hitting protest song "Carcará," which took its name from a bird of prey from the northeastern backlands and focused attention on the starvation and misery there. The refrain "pega, mata e come" ("catch, kill, and eat") evoked the ferocity of the bird and gained fervor with each repetition. The song's phrase "Carcará, mais coragem do que homem" (Carcará, more courageous than man) seemed a vague cry for insurrection, according to Veloso.[18] Nara's version had been the climax of the show, yet Bethânia made it even more powerful with her dramatic flair. Her recording of the song brought her recognition as an intense, passionate vocalist.

▼ Gal Costa. *(Courtesy of BMG.)*

▲ Maria Bethânia. *(Courtesy of BMG.)*

Born in 1946 in the town of Santo Amaro da Purificação, Bethânia was largely a cult figure—like Caetano—until 1978. A small but faithful group of fans would attend her shows, in which she would perform barefoot, walking and running around the stage, reciting poetry and singing theatrically, capturing the hearts and minds of the audience with her magnetism. She did not seem to want stardom and did not even take part in Tropicália. Keeping away from groups, she was nicknamed "Rio's Greta Garbo." But Maria's 1978 album *Álibi* marked a turning point in her career. Her interpretations of romantic ballads by Chico Buarque, Gonzaguinha, and others so pleased the public that the album eventually sold more than one million copies, the first time an album by a female recording artist had done that in Brazil.

The album's success started a trend wherein female singers became the biggest record sellers: Bethânia, Gal Costa, Simone, Clara Nunes, Beth Carvalho, and others sold millions of records in the late 1970s and early 1980s. After that, Maria became the female counterpoint to Roberto Carlos; she was the queen and he was the king of Brazilian romantic music. Appropriately, her 1993 album *As Canções Que Você Fez Pra Mim* (The Songs You Made for Me) was dedicated entirely to the compositions of Robert Carlos and Erasmo Carlos.

An artist who started by singing for small, elite audiences, Maria became an idol who sang sentimental songs for legions of fans and provided the background music for many a Brazilian romantic rendezvous. Yet her albums have consistently ventured into interesting new territory, including guest artists such as Carlinhos Brown, French actress Jeanne Moreau, and South African vocal group Ladysmith Black Mambazo.

Jorge Benjor: Rhythm and Samba

Jorge Benjor is another Brazilian artist who has helped bring cultural walls tumbling down, although without being shocking like the Tropicalistas or overtly political like Edu Lobo and Geraldo Vandré. Benjor has simply fused the styles of different countries in his music in a smooth, nonabrasive way that few listeners can resist. One of Brazil's most rhythmically creative musicians, Benjor creates music with a contagious swing, a transcontinental Afro-groove. The singer-guitarist-composer has been mixing rhythmic elements from North America, Brazil, and Africa since the 1960s, and some have termed his music "rhythm and samba."

Jorge (Jorge Duílio Menezes) was born in Rio in 1940. He adopted the stage name "Jorge Ben" (Ben was his Ethiopian mother's maiden name), which he used for almost thirty years. In 1989 he took a new pseudonym: Jorge Benjor. He started performing during the bossa boom years but hit his stride during the MPB era. His career was helped by appearances in the festivals, notably the 1969 International Song Festival (FIC) in Rio.

Critics who give more importance to harmony and melody than to rhythm have accused Jorge's music of being repetitive. But with Jorge it is

▲ Jorge Benjor. *(Courtesy of Tropical Storm/WEA.)*

rhythm that is most important, and that is where his creativity runs free. His songs fuse samba with blues and funk, and sometimes incorporate elements of rock, maracatu, candomblé, and baião. His blends always carry Jorge's unique musical signature and ever-present swing.

Jorge's best concerts are like tribal celebrations in which the entire audience dances almost to the point of a trance, propelled by his funky, infectious guitar strumming and the dense rhythms of his band, Zé Pretinho. The band often features two drum sets and three or more percussionists. Colorful and energetic, Benjor's music creates a festive atmosphere.

Like many musicians of his generation, Benjor started to take his guitar playing seriously only after he heard João Gilberto. He developed his own style, using "mostly the bass strings of the guitar, resolving the song in the minor tones. That made bass and guitar clash all the time," explained bassist Roberto Colossi,[19] who sometimes accompa-

nied Jorge when he was playing bossa nova in the early 1960s.

Back then it was so hard for bassists to play with Jorge that, on some cuts of his first album, the producer decided not to have a bass, leaving it all for Jorge's guitar. Jorge also began ignoring the normal relation of syllables to notes, singing the lyrics in a way that many conservative musicians thought was wrong. Often his words were longer than the musical phrases, which made him stretch the melody to fit his verses. And many times those verses pursued unusual themes, such as alchemy, soccer, spaceships, and bandits, as well as love and daily life.

As Jorge Ben, he achieved success in 1963 with the kinetic, irresistible "Mas Que Nada" (Oh, Come On), a light pop mix of bossa and samba that dropped references to macumba and had a soaring chorus. The latter element would be well exploited by Sérgio Mendes, who scored a hit in the United States with "Mas Que Nada" in 1966, with Lani Hall and Karen Philip singing the tune in Portuguese. Herb Alpert, Dizzy Gillespie, and José Feliciano would also record Benjor's tunes.

In the years to come, many of Jorge's songs became standards in Brazil. Examples include "Chove Chuva," "Bicho do Mato," "País Tropical," "Que Maravilha" (with Toquinho), "Charles Anjo 45," "Fio Maravilha," "Xica da Silva," and "Taj Mahal." His repertoire has been recorded by a wide variety of Brazilian artists, including the Paralamas do Sucesso, Biquini Cavadão, Leila Pinheiro, Marisa Monte, Fernanda Abreu, and Skank.

Music fans outside Brazil heard a little of "Taj Mahal," released by Jorge in 1972, a few years later without realizing it. Rod Stewart copied portions of the song in his 1979 hit "Do Ya Think I'm Sexy?" The British rock performer acknowledged the similarity shortly afterward and donated his royalties to the United Nations Children's Fund.

In 1989 Jorge said goodbye to the name Ben and released *Benjor*, which featured Nigeria's King Sunny Ade and Brazil's rock band Paralamas do Sucesso. He has been known as Jorge Benjor ever since, and his songs continue to be covered by other performers. "Mas Que Nada" was a hit again in 2006, thanks to a hip-hop infused version recorded by Sérgio Mendes and the Black Eyed Peas.

The Decline of the Festivals

Since political themes were never part of Jorge's songs, he did not have problems staying in Brazil during the dictatorship. But by the time the 1970 FIC was staged, Act No. 5 was in full swing and many musicians had already left. The festivals began to lose their vitality, with many stars absent and the shadow of the dictatorship looming ominously. At that year's event, government censors prohibited twenty-five of the thirty-six finalists from performing their songs. Tom Jobim, Chico Buarque, and many other leading musicians signed a petition against censorship. They were arrested.

Benjor's song "Eu Também Quero Mocotó" did go on stage, performed by the singer-conductor Erlon Chaves and three female backup vocalists. They were arrested too, because the censors decided the dancing of the women was too lascivious.

By 1972, when Benjor won the FIC with "Fio Maravilha," the festival era was essentially over. There would be other, smaller musical contests held later in the decade, but that year's festival would be the last major event of its kind.

Ivan Lins and Vitor Martins

During the prime of the big televised festivals, many young musicians felt shut out of the FIC, TV Record, and similar contests. In 1968 a festival called Universitário became an alternative. It was directed toward college students and sponsored initially by Rio's TV Tupi channel. One of those who attracted a lot of attention at the Universitário events was a singer-songwriter who played the piano: Ivan Lins.

American jazz flutist Herbie Mann stated, "Ivan Lins is the genius of lyrical music in Brazil, a magician with harmony. I've recorded fifteen to twenty of his songs, and for me he's on the same par as Gershwin, Kern, and Rodgers and Hart, as well as Ravel and Debussy."[20] Pianist George Duke said, "He reminds me of a modern-day Michel Legrand, the way his chords move, the way the circle of fifths move around. His chords are complicated, but the melody is so strong it's undeniable."[21]

Born in Rio in 1945, Ivan grew up in its Tijuca neighborhood. As a pianist, he was influenced by Luis Eça and João Donato and performed in a jazz-bossa trio while in college. Ivan also loved the singing of David Clayton-Thomas, the lead vocalist for the American jazz-rock band Blood, Sweat and Tears, and in trying to sing like him developed a hoarse, soulful style. It didn't really sound like Clayton-Thomas, but it intrigued TV Globo executives, who were looking for artists to fill the shoes of exiled stars like Buarque, Gil, Veloso, Lobo, and Vandré. Globo created a show, *Som Livre Exportação* (Free Sound Export), and invited Lins and others from the university festivals to host and perform on it. The program was a great success, and Ivan became a pop star. Unfortunately, he was massively overexposed, and when the network canceled the show, the young artist went through hard times for several years.

▼ Ivan Lins. *(Courtesy of PolyGram.)*

Gonzaguinha

Singer-songwriter Gonzaguinha (Luiz Gonzaga Jr., 1945–1991), son of the famed northeastern musician Luiz Gonzaga, also gained visibility through the university music festivals. From 1973 on, with aggressive and ironic lyrics sung atop a mixture of urban and rural Brazilian music, he protested the country's situation and battled government censors (they blacklisted fifteen songs from his debut album). In many ways, Gonzaguinha filled the vacuum that had been created by Geraldo Vandré's departure from the spotlight. In time, after the censorship waned, Gonzaguinha's romantic and good-humored side came to the fore with songs like "Feijão Maravilha" (Marvelous Beans). But he never forgot his desire for a more just society, as expressed in his 1988 samba "É" (Is).

> We want to make our love valid
> We want affection and attention
> We want the best of everything

▲ Gonzaguinha and Fagner. *(Courtesy of BMG.)*

Commercial success returned in 1977 with Lins's record *Somos Todos Iguais Nesta Noite* (We Are All the Same Tonight). By then he was already working with his most important lyricist, Vítor Martins, and had developed his instrumental skills after studying with Wilma Graça, who had also taught Lobo, Nascimento, Francis Hime (another notable MPB composer), and Gonzaguinha. For the album's title song, Martins protested the military regime with symbolic lyrics.

> We are all the same tonight
> In the coldness of a painted smile
> In the certainty of a dream that is over

Ivan's harmonies had begun to incorporate difficult chords and make frequent use of minor seconds. He noted, "There was a lot of jazz influence, bossa nova, Milton Nascimento, Dori Caymmi, Debussy, and Ravel."[22] Ivan's singing gradually became more natural and less strained. He scored hits like "Nos Dias de Hoje" (In the Days of Today), "Começar de Novo" (Start Again, known as "The Island" in its English-language version), "Vitoriosa" (Victorious), and "Dinorah, Dinorah."

Vítor Martins's eloquent lyrics, which ranged from romantic verses to anthems, contributed greatly to Ivan's comeback. Martins continued to battle political repression through metaphors, as did many of his MPB peers. In the xaxado "Formigueiro" (Ant Hill), Martins mentions the *repinique* (also called *repique*) and caixa drums, the *xique-xique* rattle, and batuque (Afro-Brazilian drumming) to stand for the mind control exerted by the dictatorship.

> Repinique and xique-xique, so many caixas
>   with repiques
> To block our eardrums, to mask our groans
> When the batuque ends, another trick
>   appears
> As does another miracle of the type we're
>   used to

"Formigueiro" was released on Ivan's 1979 album A Noite (The Night), as was "Antes Que Seja Tarde" (Before It Is Too Late), which included some of Vítor's most stirring words.

> We must liberate the dreams of our youth
>   before it is too late
> Men must be changed before the call is
>   extinguished
> Before faith dies out, before it is too late

At the end of the '70s, Ivan was gaining recognition as a composer outside his country. Paul Winter recorded Lins and Ronaldo Monteiro's "Velho Sertão" (Old Sertão) in 1978, renaming it and using it as the title track for his album Common Ground. Jazz guitarist and vocalist George Benson's Give Me the Night, produced by Quincy Jones, included Lins's "Love Dance" (English lyrics by Paul Williams) and "Dinorah, Dinorah." In 1981, for his album The Dude, Jones recorded Ivan's "Velas" (Sails), which won a Grammy for best jazz instrumental performance.

After this, some of America's greatest jazz artists scrambled to record Lins's compositions, which were coveted for their strong melodies, Brazilian rhythms, and interesting chords. Patti Austin, Herbie Mann, Sarah Vaughan, Joe Pass, Diane Schuur, the Manhattan Transfer, and Ella Fitzgerald covered Ivan's songs, although unfortunately they were usually fitted with new English lyrics that were far inferior to Martins's poetic words.

Ivan sang two of his tunes on Dave Grusin and Lee Ritenour's 1986 Grammy-winning Harlequin album, and two others on the 1988 Crusaders album Life in the Modern World. Jazz singer Mark Murphy and trumpeter Terrence Blanchard devoted entire albums to Lins tunes, with Night Mood (1987) and The Heart Speaks (1996), respectively, and a variety of jazz artists covering his songs in the tribute album A Love Affair: The Music of Ivan Lins (2000). After Jobim, Ivan Lins and fellow MPB artist Milton Nascimento are the most recorded Brazilian composers outside Brazil in recent times.

João Bosco and Aldir Blanc

João Bosco, one of MPB's most eclectic and imaginative musicians, also gained attention after successful appearances at university song festivals. Bosco often performs solo in concert, with just an acoustic guitar to accompany his singing. That's more than enough: he is the most self-sufficient of musicians, a band unto himself. He sits on a stool in a venue like Rio's Canecão, wearing a red bow tie and a white silk shirt, easily inspiring the audience to sing along to a beautiful melody. Then he is apt to throw out a funny

▶ João Bosco. (Photo by Ricardo Pessanha.)

improvised line to make them laugh uproariously. Plucking the guitar strings with an infectious samba swing or in intricate flamenco patterns, Bosco moves across the musical spectrum from merengue to jazz, Jackson do Pandeiro to Ary Barroso. He'll add a few bars of Gershwin or scat a rendition of Ravel's *Bolero*. He is like a post-modern troubadour, alternating the sublime with the ironic in songs that flow freely through key and idiom and tone.

Born in 1946 in Ponte Nova, Minas Gerais, Bosco has recorded many successful albums and has had his songs covered by many of Brazil's leading singers. Until the mid-1980s, almost all of his compositions were written with Aldir Blanc, a psychiatrist who gave up his profession to pen lyrics for Bosco's sambas and boleros. Blanc's lyrics were, in Elis Regina's words, "the most sincere narration of their time."[23]

Blanc (born in Rio in 1946) writes stanzas that can be serious, ironic, surreal, ludicrous, simple, and full of multiple meanings—all in the same song. They are packed with Brazilian cultural references and frequently comment on social manners and life among the working class. In "Bandalhismo" (Good-for-Nothing-ism) in 1980, Blanc wittily updated a 1902 poem by Augusto dos Anjos ("Vandalismo"), bringing it into a setting of the modern underclass.

> *My heart has squalid taverns . . .*
> *Where trembling vagabond hands*
> *Beat out sambas-enredo on a matchbox*

"Escadas da Penha" (The Steps of Penha) found a killer reflecting on a crime of passion in front of Rio's Penha church.

> *On the steps of Penha*
> *He grieved over the candle stub*
> *He watched the craziness of the flame*
> *And called his guardian angel*
> *He put his remorse in a song*
> *Sang the lie of the black girl*
> *Denied the jealousy that murders*
> *That murdered his samba-school friend*

In more playful lyrics, Blanc may use Portuguese, Yoruba, Tupi, French, English, and Spanish words, polylingual combinations, and imaginative puns. Working together, Blanc and Bosco created some of MPB's greatest standards, including "O Mestre-Sala dos Mares," "Bala com Bala" (Bullet with Bullet), "De Frente pro Crime" (Facing the Crime), and "Kid Cavaquinho." Many of their modern sambas are important contributions to that genre. Bosco's 1984 album *Gagabirô* was a creative tour de force that fused Brazilian, African, and Cuban styles and showed off Bosco and Blanc's multifaceted, virtuosic talents.

By the end of the 1980s Bosco and Blanc were no longer writing songs together and had gone their separate ways. Bosco worked with lyricist Antônio Cícero on 1991's *Zona de Fronteira* (Border Zone), while Blanc teamed with singer-songwriter Guinga on 1994's *Delírio Carioca* (Carioca Delirium).

Luis Melodia

In 1975 the TV Globo network tried to revive the by then nearly defunct festivals. It promoted an event called Abertura (Opening) that on the whole was unsuccessful but had the merit of giving larger exposure to a musician who was a cult artist at the time: Luis Melodia.

Samba, rock, blues, funk, and baião—Melodia's musical language uses all these vocabularies. *Bluesamba* might be a good label for his work. His inventive tunes, full of original rhythmic divisions, are intricate and oblique. His lyrics are surprising, somewhat surrealistic, sung in an anguished, very personal voice. But despite being a subtle and moving singer, Melodia is not a big name in Brazil. He is more of a cult figure.

Luis Carlos dos Santos (his real name) is from Rio's Estácio neighborhood, the cradle of samba. Born in 1951, he had his first taste of popularity at the age of twenty, when Gal Costa and Maria Bethânia recorded his songs. Gal sang "Pérola Negra" (Black Pearl), which is now a classic. In the song, soothing trombone, piano, and bass guitar notes build a bluesy atmosphere in which the

▶ Luiz Melodia in concert in 1988. *(Photo by Luis Bettencourt. Courtesy of Agência JB.)*

instruments tenderly work as a counterpoint to Melodia's calm voice tinged with sadness. The melody is slow, recitative, seductive.

Pérola Negra, Melodia's first album, was released in 1973 to critical acclaim and featured a mix of soul music, choro, rock, and samba-canção. In 1975 Luis appeared at the Abertura festival and recorded his biggest hit, "Juventude Transviada" (Youth Led Astray). The following year he released a second album, *Maravilhas Contemporâneas* (Contemporary Marvels), then left his native Rio to live on Itaparica, an island near Salvador. He spent two years there, fishing, playing the guitar, and writing new songs. When he thought he was ready, he came back to make a new album. Such periodic cycles of stardom and withdrawal have formed the routine of his career. He has not been prolific as a recording artist, but his works have always had a loyal audience that includes many of Brazil's top musicians. In 2007 he reaffirmed his traditional samba chops with *Estação Melodia*, interpretations of classics from the 1930s, '40s, and '50s.

Djavan

The song "Fato Consumado" (Consummated Fact) by Djavan took second place at the same 1975 Abertura Festival at which Melodia per-

formed his big hit. Djavan was the last big MPB star to be introduced by the waning festival system.

One of Brazil's most popular musicians in the 1980s, Djavan Caetano Viana is also one of its best-known performers outside the country. His songs, with their radiant melodies and funky, jazzy Brazilian swing, have been covered by many international artists. He is also known for his bright, clear, highly expressive voice, heard by many North Americans on his U.S. albums *Bird of Paradise* and *Puzzle of Hearts*.

Born in 1949 in Maceió (the capital of the northeastern state of Alagoas), Djavan came to Rio at sixteen to try a musical career. He brought with him a guitar and a bag of mixed influences, including Bahian and northeastern music, bossa nova and jazz. Comparing himself to his famous peers from the Northeast such as Fagner, Alceu Valença, and Geraldo Azevedo, Djavan said, "They make a music that is more regional; mine is more cosmopolitan." With these musical elements, Djavan forged a sophisticated, rhythmically vibrant, pan-American style that is his alone. He has viewed his music as a demonstration of affection toward people. "When I started my career, Brazil was a different country already. I don't write protest songs like those that appeared after 1964. I write love songs, and expressing love is a way of

▲ Djavan. *(Courtesy of Sony Brazil.)*

protesting against this violent world."[24] Djavan's lyrics might be called minimalist-symbolist. He sparingly uses exact words to convey his messages—sometimes clear, sometimes cryptic—as he explores love, emotion, nature, and mysticism in songs like "Sina" (Destiny):

Father and Mother
Gold from the mine
Heart, desire, destiny
All the rest, sheer routine

Or "Faltando um Pedaço" (Missing a Piece):

Love is a big lasso, a step into a trap
A wolf running in circles, to feed the pack

After Djavan's third album, *Djavan*, singers like Nana Caymmi, Gal Costa, Caetano Veloso, and Maria Bethânia began to record his songs. His 1982 album *Luz* (Light), which included Stevie Wonder, Hubert Laws, and Ernie Watts as guest artists, made Djavan a superstar. Small theaters were not

big enough for his concerts anymore; he filled arenas all over the country. *Lilás* (Lilac) in 1984 was also recorded in the United States and has a jazzy American accent in the arrangements and instrumentation. Djavan went back to his roots on *Meu Lado* (My Side), recorded in Rio with drummer Téo Lima, bassist Sizão Machado, and keyboardists Hugo Fattoruso and Jota Moraes. It fuses Brazilian and Hispano-American rhythms and includes a beautiful rendition of South African Enoch Sontonga's "Hymn of the African National Congress." Then as now, Djavan has aptly balanced the sounds of three continents in his music, and his popularity has continued with such releases as the double-volume album *Djavan: Ao Vivo* (1999).

Simone

The singer Simone, one of Brazil's most popular vocalists, was another great MPB artist who was not introduced by the festivals. Her deep, mellifluous voice has a special quality: it can seduce like a mistress, comfort like a mother, and beckon like a siren. Simone has a stage presence that is elegant,

▼ Simone. *(Courtesy of Sony Brazil.)*

sexy, commanding. Don Grusin has said of her, "She has a kind of phrasing that I think no one else has. She really is a master of phraseology, as they used to say about Sinatra. When she lays out just a few notes and words and comes to the end of it and her voice turns just a little, it kills me."[25]

Tall, lean, and striking, Simone Bittencourt was born in Salvador in 1949 and was a member of the Brazilian national basketball team before becoming a professional singer. She recorded her first album, *Simone*, in 1973. Like Gal Costa and Bethânia, Simone has interpreted a wide variety of material on her albums, from sambas to romantic ballads, by Bosco and Blanc, Nascimento, Buarque, Tunai (João Bosco's brother), Francis Hime, Moraes Moreira, and Sueli Costa.

Simone has twice performed to more than one hundred thousand fans, in 1981 at São Paulo's Morumbi stadium and in 1982 in Rio's Quinta da Boa Vista park. She is one of Brazil's most outspoken musicians and on occasion she includes political anthems in her repertoire. In 1979 she gave a now-legendary concert at which she performed Geraldo Vandré's most famous protest song, "Caminhando." This was a courageous act, since the government's Abertura (Opening) policy had only recently curtailed heavy censorship and the military was still solidly in charge of Brazil. A great rustling and excitement could be heard in the audience when Simone began singing the song's first line, "Walking and singing, following the tune."

Guinga

Guinga (Carlos Althier de Souza Lemos Escobar, born in 1950) succeeded in placing a song in Rio's 1967 international song festival when he was just seventeen. The guitarist-composer, a dentist by day, accompanied many MPB greats in concert yet started his own recording career only in the '90s, long after the festival era had ended. He is considered one of Brazil's best songwriters, whose compositions feature intricate melodies and surprising harmonies and are rooted in an astonishing variety of styles: sambas, choros, boleros,

▲ Guinga. *(Photo by Adriano Scognamillo. Courtesy of Biscoito Fino.)*

frevos, modinhas, baiões, and jazz ballads, to name a few. His songs have been recorded by Elis Regina, Michel Legrand, Leila Pinheiro, Chico Buarque, Clara Nunes, and Ivan Lins. He has often collaborated with the lyricist Aldir Blanc (the former songwriting partner of João Bosco) as well as other notable composers. Leila Pinheiro devoted her album *Catavento Girassol* entirely to Guinga's music, and his songs added to the flavor of Sérgio Mendes's Grammy-winning *Brasileiro* album. He became a solo recording artist in the '90s with releases for the Velas label, and won acclaim for albums such as *Suíte Leopoldina* (1999), where he was joined by Toots Thielemans, Ed Motta, and Lenine.

João Parahyba

João Parahyba (born in 1950 in São Paulo) is an artist who bridges the gap between the MPB generation that gained fame with the festivals and the current crop of Brazilian artists who are heavily steeped in rock, funk, and electronica. Parahyba, a percussionist, composer, and arranger, has had a rich musical career that is a monument to persistence. He was part of Trio Mocotó, a rhythm-and-samba group (some also called what they played samba rock) that backed Jorge Ben in his 1969 festival appearance in Rio and in a 1970 concert at MIDEM in Cannes. João played drums, Fritz Es-

▲ Trio Mocotó. *(Courtesy of Trama Records.)*

covão cuíca, and Nereu Gargalo pandeiro. They appeared on three Ben albums, released their own album—*Muita Zorra!*—in 1971, and followed that with two more albums. Alas, their rhythm-and-samba sound fell out of favor, and the band had trouble finding gigs and stopped performing. Parahyba, meanwhile, worked for a time in his family's business, then in the early 1980s studied composition and arranging at the Berklee College of Music in Boston. He started performing again behind Ivan Lins and other MPB artists. In 1992 he met the Serbian producer Suba (Mitar Subotić), and the two became fast friends and musical soul mates, collaborating on the electronic-instrument album *Kyzumba*, recorded in 1993 and '94. Parahyba also added drums and percussion to Suba's *São Paulo Confessions*, a brilliant mix of Brazilian music and electronica. Around this time, Parahyba's old work found new fans. Toward the end of

the 1990s, São Paulo radio stations and European dance DJs rediscovered Trio Mocotó and their recordings of two decades earlier. Encouraged by this interest, the group re-formed and returned to the studio after twenty-six years away. The result was *Samba Rock* (2001), a festive, high-spirited romp that blends samba, rock, soul, funk, and ijexá in irresistible grooves.

MPB's New Generations

What if the military dictatorship and censorship had not affected the evolution of MPB? Gilberto Gil's answer was, "We don't know. We were just beginning to develop."[26] Singer-songwriter Geraldo Azevedo, who was imprisoned twice by the regime, felt the repression "interrupted a Brazilian cultural cycle."[27] André Midani, former president of WEA Brazil, disagreed. "It didn't kill a thing. On the contrary, I think it was a kind of catalyst. You had your big enemy, you wrote against him and tried to pass your message along in spite of him. But when censorship disappeared, many MPB composers lost their compass; suddenly you could say whatever you wanted."[28]

However one judges the effect of the political climate, MPB's composers and interpreters were a vital part of Brazil's cultural life during the dictatorship. They came of age under brutal repression as their country suffered through the dark years of a military regime, and they spoke for those who had been silenced by the government. MPB singers and songwriters took global popular music to new heights in the 1960s and 1970s, and the veter-

> ### More Noted MPB Musicians
>
> Some of the artists who fall into the broad category of MPB are discussed in other chapters. They include Milton Nascimento, Moraes Moreira, Baby Consuelo, Pepeu Gomes, Alceu Valença, Geraldo Azevedo, Elba Ramalho, Fagner, Fafá de Belém, Roberto Carlos, and Ney Matogrosso. Other prominent MPB singers, songwriters, and musicians not mentioned elsewhere include Jane Duboc, Tânia Alves, Zizi Possi, Jair Rodrigues, Emilio Santiago, Rita Ribeiro, Selma Reis, Luciana Mello, Francis Hime, Oswaldo Montenegro, Vander Lee, Paulinho Moska, Guilherme Arantes, Jorge Vercilo, the band Arranco de Varsóvia, and the vocal groups Boca Livre, Quarteto em Cy, and MPB-4.

ans of that era have continued to produce important work ever since.

Brazilian popular music went in many different directions after the passing of the dictatorship, and most of the new stars coming to the forefront fell into categories like rock, pagode, música sertaneja, and axé music. However, many talented new artists also appeared who followed in the footsteps of Gil, Veloso, Buarque, Bethânia, and others mentioned above. One of the most important was a singer-songwriter named Marisa Monte.

Marisa Monte: Birth of a Diva

Marisa Monte, who established her career at the end of the '80s, is a true heir of the MPB artists who preceded her. Monte (born in Rio in 1967) has a beautiful, versatile voice that can be tender and precise or slinky and sensuous. She is also an excellent songwriter. Monte's home environment helped shape her formidable musical abilities. Her father was on the board of directors of the Portela samba school, and on the weekends samba

▼ Marisa Monte. *(Photo by Marcia Ramalho. Courtesy of World Pacific.)*

musicians often jammed in the family's living room. Her mother loved bossa, jazz, and blues, and Marisa herself listened avidly to pop from Brazil, the United States, and the United Kingdom. She began studying music seriously at fourteen, then decided she wanted to be an opera singer; by eighteen Marisa was studying *bel canto* in Italy.

But opera wasn't her true calling, and she returned home intent on pursuing a musical path that came more naturally to her, one that would bring together all the styles that she loved. She started performing in bars and small clubs, building a following and attracting the attention of EMI-Odeon. In 1989, when she recorded her debut album, *Marisa Monte*, the record company backed her with a primetime television special and heavy promotion. The album deserved the push: it is a confident work that ranges adeptly through hard rock (from the Titãs), "South American Way" (a 1940 Carmen Miranda number), songs by George Gershwin and Kurt Weill, a reggae version of "I Heard It Through the Grapevine," and Luiz Gonzaga's old hit "O Xote das Meninas." A brilliant new vocalist had clearly arrived, revealing a voice that was both full of feeling and technically flawless.

Her next effort, *Mais* (More), in 1991, was less eclectic than her debut album but more coherent in its approach. Produced by Arto Lindsay (who had worked on Caetano Veloso's *Estrangeiro*), *Mais* features Japanese keyboardist Ryuichi Sakamoto, American saxophonist John Zorn, northeastern guitar wizard Robertinho de Recife, and standout percussionists Naná Vasconcelos and Armando Marçal. *Mais* ranges from folk-rock to choro to heavy samba (samba with hard rock), as Marisa interprets songs written mostly by herself and Titãs alumni Nando Reis and Arnaldo Antunes, plus Pixinguinha's venerable choro "Rosa," Cartola's samba "Ensaboa" (Soap It), and the Caetano Veloso ballad "De Noite na Cama" (At Night in Bed). *Mais* cemented Monte's stardom; fans showered the stage with roses at her concerts, and countless young women sought to emulate her elegant style.

In 1994 she recorded *Verde Anil Amarelo Cor de Rosa e Carvão* (released in the United States as *Rose and Charcoal*). It is a rich, lyrical work that has more songs written by Monte, Antunes, and Reis; the compositions and percussion of axé-music phenomenon Carlinhos Brown; an old samba by Jamelão and Bubu da Portela; the swinging Jorge Benjor samba "Balança Pema"; and Lou Reed's "Pale Blue Eyes." U.S. avant-garde musicians Philip Glass and Laurie Anderson also appear on the album, as do Paulinho da Viola and the Velha Guarda da Portela (Old Guard of Portela).

Two years later, Monte's *Barulhinho Bom* (English title, *A Great Noise*) offered both studio recordings and live versions of her songs and Brazilian standards. There is an intriguing reading by Monte of an Octavio Paz poem, "Blanco" (White); new tunes by Brown; and inspired covers of "Cérebro Eletrônico" (Electronic Brain) by Gilberto Gil, "Panis et Circensis" (Bread and Circus) by Gil and Veloso, George Harrison's "Give Me Love," Lulu Santos's "Tempos Modernos" (Modern Times), and Paulinho da Viola's "Dança da Solidão" (Solitude's Dance). It showcased Monte's impressive musical range and positioned her as arguably the greatest contemporary vocalist in Brazilian popular music.

In 2002 Marisa and her frequent songwriting collaborators Arnaldo Antunes and Carlinhos Brown released *Tribalistas*, an intimate, melodic album that blended the voices of the three and was a best-seller in Brazil. Another interesting effort was the simultaneous release of two albums in 2006: *Universo ao Meu Redor*, a sublime mix of old and new sambas, and *Infinito Particular*, which offers lovely introspective pop songs written by Monte and colleagues Antunes and Brown and intriguing arrangements by Philip Glass, Eumir Deodado, and João Donato.

FEMALE VOICES: GROUNDBREAKING SINGER-SONGWRITERS

At the start of the twenty-first century, MPB boasted many successful female singer-songwriters along

▲ Joyce. *(Courtesy of Verve.)*

with Marisa Monte, but it wasn't always that way. Prior to Joyce (Joyce Silveira Palhano de Jesus, born 1948), there had been few successful female composers in Brazil (Chiquinha Gonzaga and Dolores Duran being two notable exceptions). And there were fewer still who wrote lyrics in a first-person feminine voice.

Joyce, who started out with the first generation of MPB musicians, drew attention with her song "Me Disseram" (They Told Me), a finalist in the 1967 song festival in Rio, and the following year launched her debut album, *Joyce*, which was produced by Dori Caymmi and included an introductory text by Vinícius de Moraes. In the following decades she enjoyed one of MPB's more remarkable careers. In 1970–1971 she and heavyweights Nelson Ângelo, Novelli, Toninho Horta, and Naná Vasconcelos made up the group A Tribo. Joyce toured with bossa legend Vinícius de Moraes in 1975 and '76, and recorded noteworthy solo albums and collaborative works with Ângelo,

Horta, João Donato, Dori Caymmi, and others. Her song "Clareana" was a pop hit in 1980.

Milton Nascimento, Elis Regina, Maria Bethânia, Boca Livre, Nana Caymmi, Quarteto em Cy, Joanna, Fafá de Belém, and Ney Matogrosso recorded Joyce's compositions (Milton covered "Mistérios" on the landmark *Clube da Esquina* 2), and her urbane, jazz-inflected voice won praise from Jobim and other peers. She linked MPB and jazz on albums like *Language and Love* (1991), which featured Jon Hendricks. Joyce found a new international audience when her songs were "discovered" by English dance and acid-jazz DJs in the '90s. She released her twenty-fifth album, *Rio Bahia*, with Dori Caymmi in 2005.

Luhli and Sueli Costa were two other pioneering female songwriters in Brazilian music. Luhli (Heloisa Orosco Borges da Fonseca) was especially associated with Ney Matogrosso's Secos e Molhados band in the 1970s and was known for her songs "O Vira," "Fala," "Pedra de Rio," "Aqui e Agora," and "Bandolero." Sueli Costa's songs were first recorded in 1967, when Nara Leão sang "Por Exemplo Você." Her many other compositions recorded by MPB artists include "Aldebarã," "Assombrações," "Sombra Amiga," and "Vinte Anos Blues" (co-written with Vitor Martins).

Rosa Passos, who didn't hit her artistic stride until the 1990s, is one of the best Brazilian vocalists of her time, a songwriter who has collaborated with Guinga and Ivan Lins, and a formidable contemporary interpreter of bossa nova. Born in 1952 in Salvador, Rosa participated in '70s music festivals and made her recording debut in 1979 with *Recriação* but then took several years off to raise her children, returning to performing in 1985. She has recorded her own compositions (nine on *Morada do Samba*, 1999), devoted albums to the music of Tom Jobim and João Gilberto, and recorded with classical cellist Yo-Yo Ma and jazz bassist Ron Carter (*Entre Amigos* in 2003).

Sueli, Joyce, Luhli, and a few other women like Rita Lee and Dona Ivone Lara were in the definite minority in the '70s as far as songwriters were concerned, but they paved the way for a strong wave of talented female composers in succeeding decades.

FEMALE VOICES: THE NEXT GENERATION OF SINGER-SONGWRITERS

Among those who followed was Zélia Duncan, born in 1964, an accomplished MPB composer and a singer with a deep, full voice. She ranges freely between MPB and pop rock, and gained fame in the '90s as a performer and songwriter. She demonstrated versatility with *Eu me Transformo em Outras*, a 2004 tribute to venerable composers such as Ary Barroso, Dorival Caymmi, Cartola, and Jobim. Two years later Zelia was invited to sing with Os Mutantes on their reunion tour. She was up to the challenge, giving energetic performances on Mutantes standards such as "Baby" and "Caminhante Noturno."

Isabella Taviani (Isabella Maria Lopes Leite) debuted in 2003 with an eponymous solo album and immediately found a wide audience for her vocals and compositions. Simone Guimarães, with her distinctive nasal vocals, gained critical praise for her second album, *Cirandeiro* (1997), and won the allegiance of MPB musicians like

▼ Zélia Duncan. *(Courtesy of Universal Music Brazil.)*

Milton Nascimento. Her songs have been recorded by Leila Pinheiro and Ivan Lins.

Singer-songwriter Suely Mesquita has gained the attention of MPB musicians with her versatile, original compositions and poignant lyrics. Her music can be both sweet and harsh, mild and aggressive, and full of subtle and unexpected qualities. She elegantly interpreted her own work on her 2002 solo album *Sexo Puro*. Her songs have been covered by the likes of Ney Matogrosso, Fernanda Abreu, Pedro Luís, and Celso Fonseca.

Vanessa da Mata (born in 1975) is a prolific composer whose career got a boost when producer Nelson Motta, who helped launch Marisa Monte, heard her song "Case-se comigo" (Marry Me) and decided to record her. She also has striking looks that helped her win a contract with the Elite modeling agency. Vanessa's first two albums, *Vanessa da Mata* (2002) and *Essa Boneca Tem Manual* (This Doll Has a Manual, 2004) were top sellers. Her single "Ai, Ai, Ai" (co-written with Liminha), with its catchy simple chorus and strong bass line, reminiscent of George Harrison's "Taxman," became a radio hit in 2006, in part because of its inclusion in the soundtrack of the TV Globo novela *Belíssima*. Her next album, *Sim*, further established her as a rising MPB talent, with its

▲ Fernanda Porto. *(Courtesy of Trama Records.)*

broad scope, including a duet with Ben Harper on "Boa Sorte" (Good Luck) and guests João Donato and reggae legends Sly & Robbie.

Adriana Calcanhotto debuted with *Enguiço* in 1990 and has established herself as one of Brazil's most popular MPB singers and a writer of both serious, passionate songs and children's tunes (the latter recorded under the name Adriana Partimpim). Ana Carolina is a singer, songwriter, guitarist and arranger who got her start with *Ana Carolina* in 1999. She soon became one of Brazil's most popular recording artists with her deep, richly nuanced voice and intelligent songwriting.

Fernanda Porto (Maria Fernanda Dutra Clemente) is a singer, songwriter, and multi-instrumentalist who gained international attention with Brazilian drum 'n' bass songs that were hits on international dance floors, as described at the end of Chapter Three. Fernanda, who was born in 1965 and raised in São Paulo, studied musical composition with the renowned Hans Joaquim Koellreutter, as had Antonio Carlos Jobim and Tom Zé. She specialized in electro-acoustic music and was influenced by MPB figures and the avant-garde composers Karlheinz Stockhausen, Edgard Varèse, and John Cage. Fernanda sang operatic arias and played piano, guitar, drums, and saxophone. She began her professional career by composing soundtracks for independent films and documenta-

▼ Adriana Calcanhotto. *(Courtesy of Sony/BMG.)*

▲ Céu. *(Courtesy of Six Degrees.)*

ries in the 1990s, and then applied her experience in electronic music to her eponymous debut album in 2002, which was close to a one-woman effort.

She composed or co-composed all but one song, produced and arranged the tracks, sang, programmed the electronic parts, and played almost all the instruments. The album, which earned a Latin Grammy nomination, mixed drum 'n' bass with samba and bossa nova. It also had sonic explorations, like the modern maracatu, "Baque Virado," which balances Fernanda's urgent vocals and driving piano against *alfaia* and caixa drums played by the group Maracatu Leão Judá. Two years later Fernanda released *Giramundo,* a more collaborative effort that featured Chico Buarque, guitarist Ulisses Rocha, pianist Cesar Camargo Mariano, and Will Calhoun and Doug Wimbish of Living Colour. The album augmented Porto's Brazilian drum 'n' bass with ballads and MPB, elements of rock, jazz, and reggae, and the electronic ijexá of the title cut. With her nimble versatility, Fernanda is one of MPB's most interesting contemporary artists.

Singer-songwriters Céu and Cibelle began their careers with music tinged with electro-pop. Cibelle worked with the late Suba on the landmark *São Paulo Confessions* and then made her solo debut with a self-titled 2003 album, following that with *The Shine of Dried Electric Leaves.* Céu (Maria do Céu Whitaker Poças) received a Latin Grammy nomination for best new artist in 2006, following

the release of *Céu* in Brazil the previous year. The album married the singer's lightly jazzy, sensual vocals to samba, reggae, dub, and electronica, with the immersive production of Beto Villares. It featured the hit single "Malemolência," co-written with Alec Halat. In 2007 Céu became the first international artist to be featured in the Starbucks Hear Music Debut CD series, an important career boost in a rapidly changing music industry.

MORE OF MPB'S NEW GENERATIONS

Maria Rita (Maria Rita Mariano) is a genetic and aesthetic link between MPB's past and future. She has a clear, expressive voice that is strikingly familiar to those who hear it for the first time; the reason is that she is Elis Regina's daughter and shares some of her mother's dynamic vocal attributes (her father is pianist-arranger Cesar Camargo Mariano). She made her debut with *Maria Rita* in 2003, which included a powerful rendition of Milton Nascimento's "Encontros e Despedidas" (Greetings and Farewells), met with immediate national and international success, and garnered two Latin Grammy awards. Four years later *Samba Meu* brought her credibility with a wider Brazilian audience. On this album she interpreted sambas by Arlindo Cruz (part of Fundo de Quintal in the 1980s) and others, and was backed by the Velha Guarda da Mangueira on "O Homem Falou."

Singer Bebel Gilberto also possesses famous DNA: her father is bossa nova pope João Gilberto,

▼ Maria Rita. *(Courtesy of Warner Music Brazil.)*

▲ Bebel Gilberto. *(Courtesy of Six Degrees.)*

her mother is the singer Miucha, and her uncle is Chico Buarque. Her performing career followed an unusual trajectory: her solo debut was a 1986 EP that included songs she had co-written with rock star Cazuza. She moved to New York in 1991, appeared on a Kenny G album and on the *Red, Hot & Rio* compilation, and sang on stage with her famous father. Then, in 2000, she became famous with the album *Tanto Tempo*, which was produced by Suba and included five of Bebel's compositions, as well as Marcos Valle's "So Nice/Summer Samba" and João Donato's "Bananeira." Suba's production infused Bebel's sultry renditions of bossa and MPB with subtle electronica. The CD was a big hit in the international world music category. She showed further growth in her songwriting with her album *Bebel Gilberto* in 2004.

Mart'nália also has musical talent running in her veins: she's the daughter of samba great Martinho da Vila. But Mart'nália doesn't limit her singing to samba. She also uses her delicate, charming voice and her contagious swing to sing ballads and pop songs that she writes with partners like Zelia Duncan and Paulinho Moska. Her live DVD *Mart'nália em Berlim ao Vivo* captures one of her magnetic stage performances, recorded in Germany in 2006. Caetano Veloso thinks she's the perfect representation of the carioca spirit and wrote a song for her called "Pé do Meu Samba."

You're the Estácio square
The curve of Copacabana Beach
Everything Rio gave me

Composer André Abujamra is one of the great unsung musical talents in Brazil today. He has scored films (most notably *Carandiru*), written commercial jingles, and is the leader of the band Karnak, which has recorded few albums but made its mark with its eponymous 1995 debut album, an audacious work that featured audio sampling from Abujamra's global travels (from Egypt to Mongolia) and eccentric fusions of world music, rock, and Brazilian styles. Eclecticism is also evident in the music of Orquestra Imperial, an all-star big band with a modern sensibility. Orquestra Imperial's Thalma de Freitas and Nina Becker sing sambas; Moreno Veloso and Rodrigo Amarante (Los Hermanos) interpret boleros and salsa; and major MPB stars are frequent guests at live performances. Another new talent is singer-songwriter Glauco Lourenço. On his debut album, *Abalo Sísmico* (2008), he applies his wide vocal range to jazzy interpretations of the mellifluous songs he wrote with Suely Mesquita and Mathilda Kóvak.

Seu Jorge (Jorge Mário da Silva) is an heir apparent to the "rhythm-and-samba" style of Jorge Benjor. An actor, composer, and singer with a soulful voice, he was an integral part of the group Farofa Carioca on its 1998 album *Moro no Brasil*, an impudent mixture of samba, funk, jongo, rap, and reggae. He then went solo, releasing his first album, *Samba Esporte Fino*, in 2001 (English release title, *Carolina*), with a notable Benjor swing in his vocals and influences of Nelson Cavaquinho, Brazilian funk, and pagode samba. He gained exposure as an actor in the critically acclaimed *Cidade de Deus* (City of God). Seu Jorge also appeared in Wes Anderson's *The Life Aquatic with Steve Zissou*, with his renditions of David Bowie songs in Portuguese making up most of the soundtrack.

Monica Salmaso, one of Brazil's most distinctive female singers, won wide recognition for her first album, *Afro-Sambas*, a 1995 tribute to the songs of Baden Powell and Vinícius de Moraes, created with guitarist Paulo Bellinati. She won critical acclaim as well for her next three releases, *Trampolim*, *Voadeira*, and *Iaiá*. Carol Saboya, the daughter of composer-pianist Antonio Adolfo, has a bright, clear voice and offers sensitive interpretations of a diverse repertoire that touches on jazz and just about every sector of Brazilian music.

Roberta Sá is a singer from Rio Grande do Norte with an exceptionally pleasing voice, renowned for its beautiful timbre and intelligent phrasing. She explores samba and MPB and gained attention when her interpretation of Dorival Caymmi's "A Vizinha do Lado" (The Next-Door Neighbor) was included in the soundtrack of a TV Globo novela. She conquered the music press with her 2005 debut album, *Braseiro*, and its follow-up two years later, *Que Belo Estranho Dia Pra se Ter Alegria* (What a Beautiful Strange Day to Be Happy).

Mariana Aydar is another MPB vocal revelation with a lush, sensual voice. Her 2006 album *Kavita 1* ranged across samba, other Afro-Brazilian rhythms, and forró, and yielded the hit single "Deixa o Verão" (Let the Summer Go), written by Rodrigo Amarante, from rock band Los Hermanos. Vocalist Daniela Procópio brought together afoxé and ballads with an impressive jazzy range on a self-titled 2007 debut album that included a duet with Carlinhos Brown and the participation of Eumir Deodato, Paulo Moura, Toninho Horta, and other heavyweights.

LENINE

Guitarist-vocalist-composer Lenine (Osvaldo Lenine Macedo Pimentel), born in 1959 in Recife, established himself as a songwriter in the 1980s and then gained critical recognition with *Olho de Peixe* (with Marcos Suzano, 1993), as well as with his work on Chico Cesar's acclaimed *Aos Vivos*. In 1997 he broke through as a solo artist with *O Dia em que Faremos Contato*, an award-winning

▲ Lenine. *(Courtesy of BMG.)*

effort that also achieved the commercially enviable feat of having three songs picked for TV novelas. *Na Pressão* (1999) and *Falange Canibal* (2002) brought him further critical praise. Lenine has a husky, highly rhythmic voice that blends rock and embolada singing (the latter can resemble rap), and a characteristic hard, funky style on the rhythm guitar. His music reflects his native Recife, blending rhythms like maracatu with driving rock, hip-hop, samba drums, and electronic processing. Yet his songs can also be lyrical and have been recorded by Sérgio Mendes and Dionne Warwick. His albums garnered many honors at Brazilian awards shows in the 2000s and attracted collaborators such as Naná Vasconcelos, jazz trombonist Steve Turre, and Latin-funk band Yerba Buena.

With their rich work, which weaves together melody, harmony, rhythm, and poetry in strikingly original and powerful ways, Lenine and the other artists mentioned at the end of this chapter are able representatives of MPB, one of the planet's most eclectic, creative, and interesting musical realms.

MINAS GERAIS: MUSICAL TREASURES

I am from South America
I know you won't know
But now I'm a cowboy
I am of gold, I am you
I'm from the world, I am Minas Gerais

Lô Borges, Milton Nascimento, and
Fernando Brant, "Para Lennon e
McCartney" (To Lennon and
McCartney)

The rolling green hills of Minas Gerais hide many secrets. Some
of these are material, like the impressive deposits of gold and diamonds discovered
in the eighteenth century in this Brazilian state, whose name literally means "General Mines." These treasures built towns such as Ouro Preto, a masterpiece of colonial architecture. And they helped bankroll the industrial revolution, as Portugal
used gold from Minas to pay for English manufactured goods.

The region also holds secrets of a different kind: those of the heart. Political
conspiracies have been plotted here: the Inconfidência, an independence movement led by the dentist Tiradentes, was crushed in 1789 by the colonial government. Mineiros know how to keep their plans and real feelings to themselves. They
have a reputation in Brazil for being quiet, complex, mystical, and respectful of
tradition. Such a temperament befits their environment: Minas is mountainous,
landlocked, and located on a high plateau to the north of Rio de Janeiro and São
Paulo. It has a cooler climate than does the sultry, humid Atlantic coast. Accordingly, its inhabitants, the mineiros, are much less expansive than the extroverted
Brazilians one finds in Rio and Bahia.

The music of Milton Nascimento reflects this difference; in it one can hear the
pastoral, spiritual, and contemplative nature of the mineiros. Nascimento is one of
the most accomplished singers and composers that Brazil has ever produced, and

MILTON NASCIMENTO

Of all the members of the clube da esquina, Nascimento has achieved the greatest critical and commercial success. His music can be melancholy and haunting, or it can be upbeat, with catchy melodies and bouncy rhythms. Jazz musicians especially revere Nascimento's compositions for their beautiful melodies and unusual textures and harmonies. Milton's songs seamlessly weave together threads of mineiro toada, bossa nova, Gregorian chants, *nueva canción*, fado from Portugal, Spanish guitar, Andean flute music, jazz, rock, and classical music.

While Nascimento sometimes writes his own lyrics, more often they are penned by his longtime partners, an impressive group that includes Guedes, Brant, Márcio Borges, and Ronaldo Bastos (who, unlike the others, is a Fluminense, a native of Rio de Janeiro state). Usually the words are messages of compassion and friendship, expressions of loneliness and the need to love, or statements against oppression.

As a singer, Nascimento has a resonant and remarkably melodious voice that is rich in timbre and infused with emotional power. He has a wide vocal range that swings from a deep masculine sound to a high feminine falsetto, or soars in flights of wordless singing. "I think he's the best singer in the world now and one of the most original composers," Brazilian musicologist Zuza Homem de Mello told us. "Milton writes music that is apparently simple but in actuality is very difficult. It leaves musicians trying to decipher the secrets of the music when they attempt to play it. He has changes in rhythm in the middle of a song without your being able to perceive it."[1]

Milton says, "I use different divisions in my music: for example a 6/8 within a 4/4. I compose on the guitar and afterwards record. I always have difficulties writing my songs down on paper, because of rhythmic breaks, because of the design of the guitar." He adds that the type of music he makes is a toada—a short, stanza-and-refrain song, usually with a sentimental melody and narrative lyrics. "The toada is different according to the region," he

▲ A church in Ouro Preto, one of the oldest and most historic cities in Brazil. *(Photo by Chris McGowan.)*

many of his musical peers from Minas Gerais—such as Wagner Tiso, Toninho Horta, Lô Borges, Márcio Borges, Beto Guedes, and Fernando Brant—have also made important contributions to their nation's music. Collectively nicknamed the *clube da esquina* (corner club) by the Brazilian press, many of these musicians grew up in the same towns and first played together in cities like Três Pontas and Belo Horizonte, later establishing their careers on the larger stages of Rio and São Paulo.

Their music is generally highly lyrical, full of elaborate harmonies, a rich variety of styles, and a strong lyricism expressive of a yearning imagination. It carries influences from a wide variety of sources: the choir music sung in the baroque churches of Minas, the folk toadas heard in the countryside, and the melodic pop rock of the Beatles. Their songs reflect Minas Gerais yet have a universal appeal that crosses all boundaries.

▲ Milton Nascimento. *(Photo by Márcio Ferreira.)*

notes. "That of Dorival Caymmi is maritime. Mine has a connection with the region of Três Pontas. But I don't consider mine regional, as neither my harmonies nor melodies are regional. I was greatly influenced by having grown up in Minas, but I think jazz is also important in my music."[2]

From Três Pontas to Rio

Nascimento was born in 1942 in Rio de Janeiro, the son of Maria do Carmo Nascimento, who worked in the household of Lília Silva Campos, and Josino Brito de Campos. Maria died when Milton was an infant, and the de Campos family adopted him. When Milton was three, the family moved to the small rural Minas Gerais town of Três Pontas (Three Peaks). Surrounded by mountains, Três Pontas has narrow streets and one-story houses whose doors open directly onto the sidewalk. Life is slow-paced, and in the late afternoon families put chairs outside their front doors and have a chat before dinner.

Lília and Josino adopted two more children (Elizabeth and Luis Fernando) and had one daughter of their own (Joceline), but Milton was the only black member of the family and thus the target of malicious gossip. Though he felt mistreated and suffocated by the intolerant Três Pontas mentality of that era, at home he was accepted as a true son. "I'm fascinated by my family," Milton told us. "I couldn't have had more love, education, and freedom with any other family in the world. They shaped my life."[3]

His adoptive father, Josino, was a professor of mathematics at high schools in Três Pontas and also a bank clerk, a director of the local radio station, and an amateur astronomer. He spent many nights exploring Ursa Major, the Southern Cross, and the moons of Jupiter through his telescope, with his eldest son at his side, who came to know the heavens "like the palm of my hand."

Milton was singing and playing instruments from an early age. "My first instrument was a harmonica my godmother gave me. Then she gave me a button accordion, and when I got it, my musical life started." In the backyard, in the shade of mango, guava, and black currant trees, Milton began conceiving musical theater entertainments for a growing band of neighborhood pals. "It was very easy for me to make up stories, like Walt Disney ones, but my own. I would imitate voices, create songs, dialogues, everything on the spot. This was around age five or six."[4]

When he was fourteen, Nascimento played his first guitar. "It was then that I started looking for sounds, discovering chords, all by ear. This was a very fertile time here in Brazil. We used to listen to everything: samba, mambo, rock, bolero, rumba, fox-trots, classical music—influences from all over the world." Milton's favorite vocal artists included Yma Sumac of Peru, Ângela Maria of Brazil, and Ray Charles of the United States. At the same time, Nascimento was absorbing the various regional sounds of his state: its toadas, church music, and songs of the *folia de reis* folkloric groups[5] that performed their dramatic dances in the post-Christmas season.

As a teenager Milton became close friends

with Wagner Tiso, who lived on the same street. They formed a rock group that had many different names, including Luar de Prata (Silver Moonlight). Milton told us, "We played rock, ballads, fox-trots, Little Richard, every kind of music we knew. We didn't have any musical prejudices, because in small towns we liked what we liked and nobody cared what it was or where it came from. I only discovered that there was such a thing as prejudice in music when I moved to the big city."[6] Tiso would later serve as Nascimento's arranger and go on to become a renowned keyboardist and composer in his own right.

In 1958 Milton heard the João Gilberto single "Chega de Saudade." "I went nuts," he remembered. "This shock with bossa nova opened our minds. We started searching for bossa nova on the radio, changing stations all the time. We didn't have a TV set, and the radio broadcast we received was terrible, with lots of static. So we would listen to a song one day and only listen to it again two weeks or a month later.

▼ Wagner Tiso. (Courtesy of Verve.)

"So we had an agreement. Two of us would pick out the melody—usually Wagner and I—and somebody else would get the words. We'd invent our own harmony. Without perceiving it, we created our own style for accompanying those songs. Then, when we got to the big city and heard how [other musicians] played those same songs, we said to ourselves, 'Oh, we did it all wrong!' We decided to change everything, but people convinced us not to. They said nobody did it that way and that it was really great. So this was a great stimulus for our creativity."

Milton and Wagner and their band—now called W's Boys—began to play dances and travel throughout Minas Gerais, playing rock and bossa. Milton also worked as a disc jockey for the Três Pontas radio station managed by his father and was known for excessively spinning disks by Gilberto and Henry Mancini.

In 1963 Milton decided to move to the capital, Belo Horizonte, to take an accounting job in an office and, as he said, "to see what would happen." Once there, he met several like-minded musicians and wrote a letter to Wagner, urging him to come. The two began playing nightclubs like the Japanese bar Fujiama with new friends such as drummer Paulinho Braga and flutist-saxophonist Nivaldo Ornellas. Milton also met his future collaborators Lô and Márcio Borges.

In Belo Horizonte Milton had his first prolonged exposure to bossa and jazz musicians. The experience was overwhelming. "My first contact with jazz left me speechless. I had never seen anyone play drums that way. I had never seen anyone play bass that way. I simply felt sick. [Afterward] I couldn't sleep well, I couldn't eat. I said to myself, 'What's that? I'll never do anything like these people.'" But soon he found out that Belo Horizonte's jazz musicians felt the same way about his music. Thus began Milton's interest in jazz, and he listened intently to records by Miles Davis, John Coltrane, Charles Mingus, and Thelonious Monk.

Milton started out interpreting other people's songs. That all changed one day when he and his friend Márcio Borges went to the movie theater to see François Truffaut's *Jules and Jim*. The film's intense imagery and vivid characters had a strong effect on the two young musicians. They arrived in the afternoon and only left late that night, after the last show was over. Milton recalled, "We saw it maybe four times in a row, and Márcio Borges on that very same day became my first songwriting partner. When I left the movie theater I said to myself that I had to create something. So we went to Márcio's place and started writing songs. All my songs are like a movie—they're all very cinematographic."

Milton and Márcio continued to play together, sometimes performing in Márcio's group, Evolussamba. Milton also met Fernando Brant (he and Márcio would become Milton's most frequent songwriting partners), and he struck up a friendship with Márcio's little brother, Lô. It was with Lô that Milton discovered the Beatles, who made a deep impression. "In my youth my father had a lot of classical music and opera, so I was very given to classical music. And suddenly, with the development of the Beatles, I saw the fusion that George Martin had done with certain [classical] things and what had come with that generation."

Nascimento's singing and composing skills grew rapidly. In 1964 he appeared on a record with composer Pacífico Mascarenhas's quartet, Sambacana, and in 1965 he was invited by TV Excelsior in São Paulo to participate in its first Festival of Popular Music. Milton took fourth place for his interpretation of Baden Powell and Luis Fernando Freire's "Cidade Vazia" (Empty City), but, more important, he met a singer by the name of Elis Regina, who—as mentioned in the preceding chapter—won the event with Edu Lobo's "Arrastão."

Milton moved to São Paulo, seeking to establish a career. "I spent two years in São Paulo," he recalled, "but they were worth twenty. Some people liked me, like Elis and the Zimbo Trio, but it was very hard to get into the music scene. I played in nightclubs when I had the chance, but competition was fierce. There were fifty unemployed musicians for every opening." In 1966 Regina recorded Nascimento's "Canção do Sal" (Salt Song), but his struggles continued, and at times he returned to playing clubs in Belo Horizonte. Tiso, meanwhile, had moved to Rio to play in bossa nova groups and to study orchestration with saxophonist-arranger Paulo Moura.

Milton Discovered

Milton became famous in 1967, with a nudge from his friends and the bright spotlight of the second FIC (International Song Festival). His breakthrough almost didn't happen, because he was not inclined to enter his songs in the event, having hated the intense competition of the 1965 TV Excelsior contest. But singer Agostinho dos Santos, a popular singer who had sung on the *Black Orpheus* soundtrack, took the shy young musician under his wing. He submitted three of Milton's songs—"Travessia" (Cross), "Morro Velho" (Old Hill), and "Maria, Minha Fé" (Maria, My Faith)—to the FIC without Nascimento's knowledge. All three were accepted, a remarkable achievement that focused attention on the reticent Milton.

But Milton still didn't want to perform his tunes at the event. Enter Eumir Deodato, whom Milton had recently met and who was going to arrange the songs for the festival. Deodato insisted, Milton recalled, "that he'd write the arrangements only if I sang at least two. So I sang 'Travessia' and 'Morro Velho,' and Agostinho sang 'Maria, Minha Fé.'"

On the day of the competition, Milton walked out onto the stage, absolutely terrified, but by the end of the event he had won the award for best performer. "Travessia" was picked as the festival's second-best song and is now one of his standards, with its sad acoustic guitar chords, moving melody, and Milton's melodious voice soaring powerfully in the song's dramatic chorus. "Morro Velho" took seventh place, and "Maria, Minha Fé" also placed among the fifteen finalists.

All three of his songs from the FIC were included that year on Milton's first album, *Milton Nascimento*, arranged by Luis Eça (the record was later reissued with the title *Travessia*). His festival

▲ Keyboardist and producer Eumir Deodato, who helped persuade a shy Milton Nascimento to perform at the second International Song Festival in 1967. *(Courtesy of Atlantic Records.)*

performance and newly issued album drew both national and international attention. In 1968 he was invited to perform in Mexico and the United States, and he recorded the album *Courage* for American label A&M. Included were six songs from *Travessia*. Deodato (organ), Herbie Hancock (piano), and Airto Moreira (percussion) participated on the album, which was produced by Creed Taylor.

His career taking off, Milton returned to the studio in 1969 to cut two albums for EMI Brazil (*Milton Nascimento* and *Milton*), and contributed songs to director Ruy Guerra's film *Os Deuses e os Mortos* (The Gods and the Dead). Five of his tunes were included on jazz saxophonist Paul Desmond's *From the Hot Afternoon* album.

The following year Milton had a successful one-year run with his musical show *Milton Nascimento e o Som Imaginário*. One of Brazil's best progressive fusion (jazz-rock-Brazilian) groups ever, Som Imaginário (Imaginary Sound), was formed initially to accompany Milton and would back him on various albums. It went on to record three albums by itself, with a changing lineup that at different times included Tiso (piano), Zé Rodrix (organ and flutes), Toninho Horta, Tavito,

and Fredera (guitars), Luis Alves (bass), Robertinho Silva (drums), and Laudir de Oliveira and Naná Vasconcelos (percussion).

Clube da Esquina

In 1971 Milton and his "corner club" pals from Minas rented a house in Piratininga, a beach in Niterói, north of Rio. They stayed there for six months and composed the majority of the songs for Nascimento and Lô Borges's double album *Clube da Esquina*, which was orchestrated by Tiso and Deodato and recorded in 1972 at the EMI-Odeon studios in Rio.

The album primarily featured compositions by Milton and Lô, with lyrics contributed by Bastos, Brant, and Márcio Borges. Milton and Lô shared lead vocals and played guitar and were joined by Guedes (guitar and backing vocals), Som Imaginário's Horta, Tiso, Alves, Silva, Vasconcelos, and Tavito, and Danilo Caymmi (flute), Novelli (bass), Rubinho (drums), Nelson Ângelo (guitar), and Paulo Moura (several arrangements). It was a sprawling and ambitious work that mixed diverse styles fluently. Lô contributed the dreamy "mineiro rock" tunes such as "O Trem Azul" (The Blue

▼ Lô Borges. *(Photo by Cafi. Courtesy of Sire.)*

◄ Milton Nascimento and Wayne Shorter in concert a decade after their collaborative *Native Dancer* album, which introduced Milton to a large North American jazz audience for the first time. *(Photo by Márcio Ferreira.)*

Train), "Nuvem Cigana" (Gypsy Cloud), and "Tudo Que Você Podia Ser" (All You Could Be), with their strong hints of groups like the Beatles and Procol Harum. Milton's songs on the album are often more Iberian and South American in flavor, as on "San Vicente," in which MPB scholar Charles Perrone notes elements of the Chilean *tonada* style (in the guitar accompaniment) and Paraguayan *guarania* (in the bass lines).[7] Brant contributed its surreal lyrics.

American heart, I woke from a strange
    dream
A taste of glass and cut
A flavor of chocolate
In the body and in the city
A taste of life and death

There were many other memorable songs, including Nascimento's up-tempo "Cravo e Canela" (Clove and Cinnamon) and lively "Nada Será Como Antes" (Nothing Will Be Like Before). The album sold well, and Milton became commercially viable as a recording artist, as did Guedes, Horta, and Lô Borges. With this success to their credit, they all recorded albums individually or

together. The name "corner club" was used long afterward by the press to describe Milton and his collaborators, even those who weren't from Minas Gerais.

On 1973's *Milagre dos Peixes* (Miracle of the Fishes), Milton and the Som Imaginário delved into even more experimental territory, casting Milton's lonely voice against dense instrumental soundscapes, as the musicians went all out with electric, percussive, and vocal effects. They had to be especially expressive, since the government censors had banned almost all the lyrics on the album.

Minas to Geraes

Minas (1975) included Nascimento's two favorite songs: "Saudade dos Aviões da Panair" (Saudades for the Panair Planes) and "Ponta de Areia" (Sand Point). Also that year, Milton was the featured guest on the album *Native Dancer* by jazz saxophonist and composer Wayne Shorter, who had previously covered Milton's "Vera Cruz" on the 1970 album *Moto Grosso Feio* [*sic*] and in that decade was busy taking jazz into new realms with his group Weather Report.

Native Dancer featured five Nascimento songs—"Ponta de Areia," "Tarde" (Afternoon), "Miracle of the Fishes," "From the Lonely Afternoons," and "Lilia"—and the playing of Herbie Hancock, Airto Moreira, Tiso, Robertinho Silva, and David Amaro. The interplay between Nascimento's voice, Shorter's sax, and Hancock's piano created a moody, hauntingly beautiful work that profoundly affected many North American listeners, including a young American keyboardist named Lyle Mays.

"It was a watershed record, a classic, and I think it turned a lot of jazz musicians on to Milton," recalled Mays. "Even to this day it stands as one of the best blends of Brazilian music and American jazz. When I first heard it, I didn't know what to think. It was so different. I thought it was like magic, and I just couldn't imagine that music. I simply had to listen again, as I couldn't quite grasp it. I had never heard those kinds of tunes [that Milton had composed] before."[8]

On his next album, *Geraes*, in 1976, Milton journeyed far into his Brazilian roots and other Latin American folk styles. The album's title comes from an archaic spelling of Gerais, and many of its songs draw on research on regional music by Tavinho Moura—principally in the Jequitinhonha River valley, which winds through the backlands of northern Minas and southern Bahia. One example is "Calix Bento" (Blessed Chalice), which Moura had adapted from a folia de reis song. Milton also expanded his explorations of music from other parts of South America: "Volver a Los 17" (Return to 17) was written by Chilean songwriter Violeta Parra, and Milton interprets it in a duet with Argentinean singer Mercedes Sosa. Yet Milton did not forget Brazil's contemporary situation; he included the politically charged "O Que Será (À Flor da Pele)," penned by Chico Buarque, with whom Milton sang the moving duet.

Clube da Esquina 2

In 1978 Milton gathered together with the "clube" for a sequel, another double album. This time it would be more of a pan–South American fusion, with less rock and not as much North American influence. Nascimento, Lô Borges, Guedes, Tiso, Novelli, Horta, and Nelson Ângelo were joined this time by singer-songwriters Joyce and Flávio Venturini and guitarist Paulo Jobim (Tom's son). *Clube da Esquina 2* was even more ambitious than its predecessor, and aesthetically more successful. The dense album featured outstanding compositions, an astonishing variety of instrumentation and styles, consistently excellent arrangements, and a wealth of talented musicians participating in the production.

The album begins with "Credo," a song that opens and closes with beautiful a cappella singing and includes spirited Andean-style guitar, flute, and vocals backing up Fernando Brant's activist lyrics.

> *Let's go, walking hand in hand with the new soul*
> *To live planting liberty in each heart*
> *Have faith that our people will awake*
> *Have faith that our people will be shocked*

There follows one remarkable song after another. Venturini's beautiful "Nascente" features exquisite harmonizing between Venturini and Nascimento. "Paixão e Fé" (Passion and Faith) starts with a Mediterranean atmosphere evoked by Guedes's mandolin, which is soon overwhelmed by the angelic soaring vocals of Milton and the Canarinhos de Petrópolis choir, conducted by José Luiz. Another highlight is the moving "O Que Foi Feito Deverá," with Elis Regina's effusive singing set against the acoustic guitars of Nascimento and Natan Marques, and then joined by Milton's voice; this flows into "O Que Foi Feito de Vera" (What Happened to Vera), which continues an incomparable duet between two of Brazil's greatest singers. The celebratory "Maria Maria" has become yet another Nascimento standard.

Two memorable songs came from Milton's interpretations of compositions by musicians outside Brazil. In "Casamiento de Negros" (Marriage of

◄ Milton Nascimento and Pat Metheny in concert. *(Photo by Márcio Ferreira.)*

Blacks), adapted from Chilean folk music by Violeta Parra, the Uruguayan Grupo Tacuabé and a large chorus support Milton's lead vocals and guitar. And Nascimento and Chico Buarque together sing Cuban Pablo Milanés's "Canción por la Unidad de Latin America" (Song for Latin American Unity), adapted by Buarque.

Nelson Ângelo and Fernando Brant's "Canoa, Canoa" is a showcase for Milton's otherworldly voice, set against a sumptuous backing chorus provided by Nascimento, Novelli, Ângelo, and Lô Borges. Paulo Jobim's melancholy "Valse" (Waltz), recorded by his father on the 1976 *Urubu* album, here acquires lyrics by Ronaldo Bastos and becomes "Olho d'Água" (Water Spring). Joyce and Maurício Maestro contributed the beautiful song "Mistérios" (Mysteries), which received an affecting interpretation with Milton's voice. "Tanto" (So Much) is a classic Beto Guedes tune. And the rousing "Reis e Rainhas do Maracatu" (Kings and Queens of Maracatu) alternates exuberant samba with maracatu carried rhythmically by an agogô and triangle.

The *Clube da Esquina* albums affected American jazz artists Lyle Mays and Pat Metheny profoundly. Mays recalled the excitement he felt when he listened to them for the first time with Metheny: "It was an amazing, unpredictable combination of cultural influences of the Western classical har-monic sense and the African rhythmic sense, done in a completely different way from jazz. Listening to it gave me the same kind of excitement as when I first heard jazz. I don't think there's any parallel to those records in any music I've come across. The *Clube da Esquina* records have things in common with the Beatles and Miles Davis, a combination of hipness, accessibility, and exoticness."[9]

Sentinela to Anima

In 1980 *Sentinela* (Sentinel) further mixed contemporary sounds with traditional mineiro and Latin American influences, all filtered through Milton's transcendental sensibility. In the moving title song, the narrator is standing vigil at a deathbed of a brother or comrade, vowing to keep his spirit alive.

Death, candle, I am a sentinel
Of the body of my brother who's departing
In this hour I see again all that happened
Memory will not die

Milton's dirgelike singing and the haunting vocals of Nana Caymmi are given further emotional power by a full choir of Benedictine monks that backs them. Other songs on the album are livelier and less somber, such as Tavinho Moura's "Peixinhos do Mar" (Little Fishes of the Sea), an adaptation of a *marujada*, a dramatic dance with medieval roots. Nascimento's interpretation of Cuban poet Silvio Rodriguez's "Sueño com Serpientes" (Dream with Serpents) offers another excellent duet, between Milton and Mercedes Sosa. "Peixinhos," "Sueño," and three other tunes feature the classically trained avant-garde mineiro group Uakti, which adds richly resonant sound colors with instruments fashioned out of wood, glass, and PVC pipe. Other notable songs on the album include "Cantiga Caicó," an adaptation of a Villa-Lobos song, and "Canção da América" (America's Song), which features backing vocals by the group Boca Livre.

Next came Nascimento's most radical concept album to date: 1982's *Missa dos Quilombos* (Mass of the Quilombos), a choral work that combines Afro-Brazilian instruments and rhythms with Catholic hymns and chants. Originally performed before a huge audience in Recife, Pernambuco, and recorded in a colonial church in Caraça, Minas Gerais, this musical mass is an uplifting cry against oppression and servitude, with lyrics written by poet Pedro Tierra and Catholic bishop and liberation theologian Pedro Casaldáliga. At the end of the album, Hélder Câmara, the archbishop of Olinda and Recife, gives a rousing speech against hunger, injustice, and economic exploitation of the poor. It was all too unorthodox for the Vatican, which banned it.

The following year, a song from Milton's *Ao Vivo* (Live) album also provided political inspiration. "Coração de Estudante" (Student's Heart), written by Nascimento and Tiso, was adopted as the theme song for the Brazilian movement for democracy in 1984 and sung by thousands of student demonstrators in the streets.

The student's heart
Has to take care of life
Has to take care of the world

Nascimento's albums in the 1980s and '90s took several different musical and geographical directions. In *Anima* (1982), the percussion of Uakti and the jazz-rock guitar of Ricardo Silveira provide an interesting counterpoint to Nascimento's melodies and elaborate harmonies. *Miltons* (1989) is a serene work teaming Milton with percussionist Naná Vasconcelos and jazz pianist Herbie Hancock. That year, while Nascimento was on the tour

▶ Milton Nascimento and Mercedes Sosa.
(Photo by Paulo Ricardo. Courtesy of Sony.)

for *Miltons,* he became seriously interested in the plight of the inhabitants of the Amazon rainforest, whose livelihoods were being seriously threatened by deforestation and the illegal invasion of their lands by unscrupulous outsiders.

Nascimento was invited by the Union of Indigenous Nations (UNI) and National Council of Rubber Tappers (CNS) to take an eighteen-day journey by boat up the Juruá River, starting in the town of Cruzeiro do Sul, deep in the heart of the Amazon, meeting with local people along the way. Milton's manager, Márcio Ferreira, and sound engineers Roberto Marques and Demerval Filho were part of the trip, and the three made field recordings of the songs of the Yanomami, Kayapó, Waiãpi, and other inhabitants of the region. The fruit of this expedition was the 1990 album *Txai,* dedicated to the UNI, CNS, and the Alliance for the People of the Forest. Short excerpts of indigenous music are heard throughout the album, in which most of Nascimento's songs are inspired by people he met in the Amazon. Two of *Txai's* most interesting songs are the beautiful duet "Nozani Na," sung by Milton and Marlui Miranda, and "Curi Curi," in which Tsaqu Waiãpi plays flute and the actor River Phoenix reads text protesting the destruction of the Amazon and betrayal of its people.

Milton's songs during this period were widely recorded by international musicians, and his albums attracted legions of accomplished foreign musicians. *Encontros e Despedidas* (Encounters and Goodbyes) in 1985 included Pat Metheny and Hubert Laws; the 1987 album *Yauaretê* (Jaguar) featured Paul Simon, Herbie Hancock, and Quincy Jones; and the 1994 album *Angelus* included guests Wayne Shorter, Jon Anderson (of the rock group Yes), James Taylor, and Peter Gabriel. As a vocalist, Nascimento performed during this period on Paul Simon's *The Rhythm of the Saints,* the Manhattan Transfer's *Brasil,* and Sarah Vaughan's *Brazilian Romance.*

The title of Milton's 1997 album *Nascimento* signified both his last name and its literal meaning: "birth." *Nascimento* marries beautiful melodies and inspired poetry with surging drumming inspired by folk traditions from Minas, and won a Grammy in the World Music category. It is a deeply emotional work, dedicated to Milton's parents, paying tribute to two of Milton's friends who had recently passed away, and marking the singer's recovery from a bout of exceedingly poor health. The album opens stirringly with Milton's resonant voice set against a swelling chorus of drums, including the *caixas de folia*[10] typical of Minas folk music, in "Louva-a-Deus" (Praying Mantis). A wordless "Old Man River," with a vast choir, honors the actor River Phoenix, who had died not long after participating in the making of *Txai.* And Milton remembers another friend, the late Ana Maria Shorter, in "Ana Maria," written by Wayne Shorter for his wife and previously recorded on *Native Dancer,* an album that she had helped bring about. Another of the album's highlights was the exquisitely beautiful "Guardanapos de Papel" (Paper Napkins), a superb adaptation of a marvelous poem by Uruguay's Leo Masliah about the sweet, sad calling of poets. Nascimento performs the song twice, in Portuguese and in Spanish.

Carolina Jabor and Lula Buarque de Holanda directed a documentary tribute to Milton, *A Sede do Peixe* (The Fish's Thirst), released on DVD in 2003. An excellent introduction to his work, the film features conversations with Milton and most of the "corner club" gang, as well as musical performances of many of his well-known songs. Guest artists include Skank's Samuel Rosa, Zélia Duncan, Alcione, Carlinhos Brown, Gilberto Gil, and Nascimento's mineiro colleagues.

The power of Milton's vocals and the enduring appeal of his "world music"—forged in Minas—have made him one of Brazil's most popular performers and composers around the world.

MEMBERS OF THE CLUB

Milton's overall sound has been inextricably linked to the music of his mineiro friends and collaborators, Wagner Tiso, Beto Guedes, Toninho Horta, Tavinho Moura, Lô Borges, and others. Along with co-headlining *Clube da Esquina,* Borges (born in Belo Horizonte in 1952) released the solo albums *Lô Borges* in 1972, *A Via-Láctea* (The

▶ Milton with his longtime friend and noted keyboardist-arranger Wagner Tiso (*left*) and Manhattan Transfer leader Tim Hauser (*right*) at the Som Livre Studios in Rio, working on Nascimento's "Viola Violar" for the Transfer's 1987 Atlantic album *Brasil*. *(Photo by Chris McGowan.)*

Milky Way) in 1979, and *Nuvem Cigana* (Gypsy Cloud) in 1981, among other works.

Wagner Tiso, born in Três Pontas in 1945, has been an indispensable part of Nascimento's success. "The two of us together make the cross," said Milton.[11] Tiso played keyboards in the Som Imaginário group and has arranged and orchestrated many Nascimento albums. His solo releases, including *Assim Seja* (Thus It May Be), *Trem Mineiro* (Minas Train), *Branco e Preto* (Black and White), *Os Pássaros* (The Birds), and *Giselle*, have shown off Tiso's sophisticated compositions, as he alternates acoustic piano and electronic keyboards. The 1988 release *Manú Carué, uma Aventura Holística* is a phantasmagoric pop symphony that mixes rock, baroque, and Brazilian influences and demonstrates Tiso's composing, arranging, and playing skills. He has scored numerous Brazilian movies and collaborated on albums with Ney Matogrosso, Paulo Moura, Victor Biglione, and the Rio Cello Ensemble.

Another corner club standout is Beto Guedes, known for his original songwriting, his dexterity with various stringed instruments (guitar, mandolin, and others) and his distinctively high, astringent voice. He was born in 1951 in Montes Claros in northern Minas Gerais. As a young musician, Beto forged his own style by mixing Anglo-American 1960s pop styles with his boyhood influences: *música sertaneja* and the choros played by his father, Godofredo (a saxophonist and clarinetist).

▲ The cover of *Viagem das Mãos*, a 1985 album by Beto Guedes, who was a key member of the "corner club." *(Courtesy of EMI Music Brazil.)*

Beto followed his participation in *Clube da Esquina* by joining with three other alumni of that album to record *Beto Guedes, Danilo Caymmi, Novelli, Toninho Horta* in 1973. In that decade and the next he continued to contribute songs, vocals, and guitar playing to Nascimento's albums, while also releasing the excellent solo albums *Amor de Índio* (Indian's Love), *Sol de Primavera* (Spring Sun), *Contos da Lua Vaga* (Stories of the Vague Moon), *Viagem das Mãos* (Journey of the

Hands), and A *Página do Relâmpago Elétrico* (The Page of Electric Lightning).

New York Times critic Robert Palmer wrote of Guedes, "On the best of his albums, the remarkable *A Página do Relâmpago Elétrico*, he uses what sounds like four or five acoustic guitars, each playing a different rhythmic pattern, to weave richly detailed sonic tapestries; the disk contrasts rural string-band styles and jazzy electric music. On 'Novena,' a song from his excellent album *Amor de Índio*, he cushions a ballad's sinuously brooding melody with chord voicings built around minor seconds, creating an astonishing lyricism of dissonances."[12]

Another mineiro talent who has been an essential part of Milton's albums over the years is Toninho Horta, born in Belo Horizonte in 1948. Horta has participated in many of Nascimento's recordings, including both *Clube da Esquina* releases. In 1980 he cut his first solo album, *Terra dos Pássaros* (Land of the Birds). Toninho is a composer and guitarist who mixes influences from Minas modinha and religious music, the jazz guitar of Wes Montgomery, and the bossa nova of João Gilberto. Forged from such diverse sources, Horta's composing and playing have had a strong influence on many musicians outside Brazil.

▼ Toninho Horta. *(Photo by Buckmaster. Courtesy of Verve.)*

"Toninho has emerged as one of the most harmonically sophisticated and melodically satisfying Brazilian composers of recent times," wrote Pat Metheny in the liner notes of Horta's 1988 *Diamond Land* album. "He writes chord progressions that defy gravity, moving up when you think they're going down. His melodies stay with you for days; you're sure you've heard them before, but they're brand new." Metheny added that Horta, as a guitarist, plays "great voicings with such a cool time feel."

Toninho has appeared on jazz keyboardist George Duke's *Brazilian Love Affair* and released U.S. albums for Verve and other labels. *Diamond Land* and *Moonstone* were lyrical, imaginative, free-flying instrumental journeys characteristic of Toninho. He has performed around the world with a variety of jazz artists as well as with Joyce, Marisa Monte, Flávio Venturini, Flora Purim, and other prominent Brazilian musicians.

MORE MINEIROS

Other accomplished contemporary mineiro musicians include Uakti, keyboardist Túlio Mourão, and singer-songwriters Flávio Venturini, Tavito, Paulinho Pedra Azul, Sueli Costa, and João Bosco. Skank, Pato Fu, Jota Quest, and Sepultura are popular in the rock realm. The brothers Pena Branca (José Ramiro Sobrinho, born in 1939) and Xavantinho (Ranulfo Ramiro da Silva, 1942–1999) were an acclaimed duo that played rootsy música sertaneja and gained recognition in the 1980s with such albums as *Cio da Terra*, which was produced by Márcio Ferreira, with musical direction by Tavinho Moura. Their 1988 album *Canto Violeiro* was a showcase of folk music from Minas, with examples of toada, *seresta*, reisado, samba de roda, and *moda de viola*. Pena Branca has continued as a solo artist.

Minas, with its varied heritage and ties to tradition, has given birth to many remarkable musicians who have remained faithful to their roots even as they seek to transcend them. They have poured the mysticism and hidden emotion of the region into their music and fashioned a remarkably universal sound.

BAHIA OF ALL THE SAINTS 6

Sun, sun, and rain
Drops of water and light
Yes, we are so many songs
Sambas, ballads, and blues
And the mixture of so many nations
Frevo, choro, and happiness
Reggae, maracatus, and baião
Pernambuco, Jamaica, and Bahia

Moraes Moreira and Zeca
Barreto, "Pernambuco,
Jamaica e Bahia"

Salvador, the capital of Bahia state, is a port city that looks out across the Atlantic Ocean to West Africa—to Ghana, Nigeria, Angola. Its culture is so different from that of the Northeast's mestizo-populated interior that at times Salvador seems to be spiritually situated on the outskirts of Luanda or Lagos.

In its historical areas, Salvador (also often called "Bahia") is like many Portuguese colonial settlements, with its narrow cobblestone streets, baroque churches ornamented with gold, and old houses decorated with blue Portuguese tile. Yet it is culturally the most African of all Brazilian cities. It also has the highest concentration of African descendents of any major metropolis in Brazil: an estimated 80 percent of its nearly three million inhabitants are black or mulatto. Salvador has retained much of its African heritage, brought to Brazil by the enslaved peoples of past centuries. The white skirts and headdresses worn by many baianas (Bahian women) recall West Africa, as does the local food, often cooked in coconut milk or palm oil and spiced with red pepper.

NAGÔ NATION

Governor-General Tomé de Sousa established Portugal's colonial government for Brazil in Salvador in 1549. At that time, the city was called São Salvador da Bahia

◄ A Bahian man in Pelourinho, a historic square in Salvador, once a place where slaves were auctioned and punished but today a center of Afro-Brazilian culture and the headquarters for organizations like Olodum and the Filhos de Gandhi. *(Photo by Cláudio Vianna.)*

▲ An outdoor candomblé ceremony in Salvador. *(Courtesy of Bahiatursa.)*

de Todos os Santos (Savior Saint of the Bay of All the Saints). Over the next three hundred years, plantations of sugar and cocoa were established along the Atlantic coast, and slave traders sold hundreds of thousands of Africans to the Bahian plantation owners. The slaves were of many different ethnic and cultural groups, as discussed earlier, but those who came to dominate Bahia in number and culture were the Yoruba and Ewe peoples taken from what are now Nigeria and the Republic of Benin. In Brazil, the Yoruba were called *Nagô*, a term used by the Fon people; the Nagô included such subgroups as the Ketu and Ijexá. The Ewe were called *Gege* (also spelled *Jeje*), and the fusing of their culture with that of the Yoruba became known as *Gege-Nagô*.

The Nagô worshipped deities called orixás (òrìṣà in Yoruba) in the religion brought from their homeland that became known as candomblé in Brazil. Terreiros (centers of worship) were established in Salvador as early as 1830. The Bahian government, police, and press looked down on candomblé and persecuted public manifestations of African culture well into the 1940s.

Yet candomblé thrived in Bahia, with hundreds of terreiros established in Salvador in the nineteenth and twentieth centuries. There have been extremely Yoruba-centric temples (like Ilê Axé Opô Afonjá), Gege-Nagô terreiros, and centers representing other African nations. A particularly famous site is the Terreiro do Gantois, founded in 1849. One of its priestesses, Mãe Menininha (1894–1986), was known throughout Brazil and honored in songs by Caetano Veloso and

Dorival Caymmi. By the late twentieth century candomblé had become acknowledged as a mainstream institution in Salvador.

Candomblé has provided much of the foundation of Afro-Bahian culture, but important elements also came from outside the Gege-Nagô cultural complex, as is the case with capoeira.

CAPOEIRA

In the streets of Bahia you will often find a ring of spectators watching two young men—barefoot, shirtless, and wearing loose-fitting white pants—who execute spectacular spins and agile kicks to the astonishment of the crowd. This is done in harmony with an insistent buzzing rhythm played on the berimbau, a musical bow with a metal string and a gourd resonator. Berimbaus and additional percussion instruments are played by other participants (*capoeiristas*) who surround the two performers and urge them on by singing traditional songs. The two men perform cartwheels and handstands. They whirl about on their hands and spin their legs faster and faster as the tempo accelerates, coming ever closer with their kicks. Their movements grow increasingly daring, and it becomes obvious how capoeira—this spectacular martial art that resembles a dance—is an extremely effective fighting technique. In fact, capoeira is now taught all over Brazil, and in many other countries. And the music of capoeira has become a part of Brazil's musical vocabulary.

Capoeira was brought to Brazil by enslaved Bantu peoples from Angola. Many scholars find similarities between it and *n'golo*, an acrobatic dance performed by young males of the Mucope people of Angola.[1] The Angolan martial arts *njinga*, *basula*, and *gabetula* may also have influenced the creation of capoeira. The berimbau that accompanies capoeira during training and performances seems clearly derived from musical bows found in the Congo-Angola region. As it developed in Brazil, capoeira picked up West African elements, such as the use of the agogô and references to Yoruba orixás in the songs. Those who practice the art are called capoeiristas.

There are references to capoeira as early as 1770. During the slavery era, capoeira fighters sometimes attached knives or razors to their feet or shoes, using them to deadly effect when they

▼ Capoeira. *(Courtesy of Bahiatursa.)*

▲ Two men engaging in capoeira to the accompaniment of songs performed by the capoeiristas around them. *(Courtesy of Bahiatursa.)*

executed their whirling kicks. This was characteristic of the *maltas*, urban gangs of individual slaves and free men of the lower class. The Brazilian government took extreme measures to extinguish capoeira in the nineteenth century and made its practice an offense punishable by death. But on occasion they needed the aid of skilled capoeiristas, such as when they sent them to fight with the frontline troops in the war against Paraguay in the 1860s.

After abolition capoeira continued to be outlawed but soon became extremely widespread. Many in the lower classes used it for self-defense or intimidation, and for a long time it was identified with hustlers and hard criminals. In *Capoeira: A Brazilian Art Form*, Bira Almeida writes, "In 1920, the capoeiristas from Bahia felt the iron hand of police chief Pedro de Azevedo Gordilho, who placed the full power of his cavalry squadron

against outlaws, rodas de capoeira, terreiros de candomblé, and afoxés."[2]

This period saw the opening of the first public academies of capoeira. Manoel dos Reis Machado (1899–1979), known as Mestre Bimba, opened his establishment in 1927, and ten years later it became the first capoeira academy to be registered with the Brazilian government. He created a style called *capoeira regional* that mixed elements of capoeira and batuque (an African-based martial dance) and focused on the fighting elements of the martial art. Bimba wanted to de-marginalize capoeira and he encouraged middle- and upper-class Brazilians to study it. Ultimately, he was successful. Capoeira was legitimized and became popular throughout the country, partly because the repression of Afro-Brazilian culture declined after Getúlio Vargas assumed the presidency in 1930. By 1953 Vargas was calling capoeira "the only true national sport."

Vicente Ferreira Pastinha (1898–1981), known as Mestre Pastinha, was the other major teacher of that time. He advocated a more traditional form called *capoeira angola* that placed its emphasis on the ritualistic, philosophical, and stylistic aspects of capoeira. Musically, capoeira angola can be accompanied by orchestras that include three berimbaus, two pandeiros, one agogô, a reco-reco, and an atabaque.

The key instrument is the berimbau, made of a *verga* (wooden bow), an *arame* (steel wire), and a *cabaça* (hollowed-out gourd). A *dobrão* (large coin) changes the pitch of the wire, which is struck with a thin stick called a *baqueta*. The hand that holds the baqueta also holds a small wicker rattle called a *caxixi*. The berimbaus come in three sizes: the *berimbau gunga* (with the largest gourd and deepest tone), the *berimbau centro* (or *médio*, which maintains the rhythm along with the gunga), and the *berimbau viola* (with the smallest gourd).

In capoeira angola, the singing by the *roda* (the circle of capoeristas surrounding those performing the capoeira moves) has a traditional structure made up of three parts: the *ladainha*, the *chula*, and the *corrido*. According to musicologist Greg Downey, "The solo ladainha opens the musical sequence. The singer may tell a story, reflect philosophically, or pass messages to listeners paying close attention to the song. These solos are sometimes improvised. They are one of the most important vehicles for the transmission of oral history, political commentary, and traditional wisdom in capoeira angola." The chula follows the ladainha and consists of call-and-response between the soloist and the roda, in which the singer "delivers salutations and pays homage to those that merit such respect, leads prayers, and exhorts the players." Then comes the corrido, call-and-response singing that marks the beginning of the *jogo* (game). Downey adds, "A good lead singer will improvise calls which comment upon the game being played, address those present at the event, or advise the players."[3]

The roda's singing is an integral part of the art, "giving energy and feedback to the players and infusing the roda with spirituality and history." Downey adds, "While the supporting instruments move inexorably forward, the berimbaus push and pull on each other, stutter and challenge, and all the players turn to the roda. Different *toques* [rhythms] will call for different games—faster or slower, more aggressive perhaps."[4] Different capoeira schools may employ several dozen toques. A few of these are São Bento Grande, Iuna, Benguela, Santa Maria, Angola, Jogo de Dentro, and Cavalaria.

Capoeira rhythms have infiltrated Brazilian popular music in songs like Gilberto Gil's "Domingo no Parque" and Baden Powell and Vinícius de Moraes's "Berimbau." And Naná Vasconcelos and Airto Moreira have incorporated capoeira music into their jazz improvisations and developed the berimbau as a unique solo instrument.

While candomblé and capoeira exist year round, much of Bahia's musical heritage is tied to the annual festivity of Carnaval.

CARNAVAL IN BAHIA

Today, Salvador vies with Rio for which city has the most popular Carnaval in Brazil. Every year an estimated two million celebrants crowd Salvador's narrow streets to dance, sing, and party to the music of the blocos afro, afoxés, and trios elétricos. Hundreds of thousands of these revelers are from other parts of Brazil or foreign countries. They jam historic squares like the Praça Castro Alves and pack the cobblestone streets in a Carnaval that is chaotic, exhilarating, often violent, and probably pretty close in spirit to such ancient seasonal festivities in Rome as the Bacchanalia.

In the nineteenth century Salvador had a mixture of indoor and outdoor partying. As early as the 1840s, upper-class Bahians celebrated Carnaval with private aristocratic balls. Outside in the streets there was the entrudo, the same rough, dirty celebration of the common folk that took place in Rio and had been imported from Portugal. Entrudo was a source of concern in following decades for the press and the police, who had a difficult time trying to repress it. The authorities decided that in order to extinguish entrudo, it would be necessary to introduce another kind of celebration, Carnaval parades, to take its place.

In 1884 Salvador's first parade took place, when

▲ A bloco parading through the Campo Grande area during Salvador's Carnaval. *(Photo by Artur Ikishima. Courtesy of Bahiatursa.)*

songs, rhythms, dances, and percussion instruments—into the street in a secular context. Afoxés began in Salvador and have grown into massive groups that parade during Carnaval there and, to a lesser extent, in Fortaleza, Recife, and other cities. Earlier in the century, afoxé members were all candomblé devotees, and usually they would perform a ritual in the temple before heading out into the street. Traditional afoxés still do this today, but others have members who do not worship the orixás.

The slow, hypnotic ijexá rhythm of afoxé music comes from the rhythm and dance performed for the orixá Oxum in candomblé ceremonies (Ijexá, or Gexá, is also the name of a Yoruba subgroup in Nigeria). Ijexá is played on atabaques of three sizes (the *rum*, *rumpi*, and *lê*), with lots of syncopation on the *gonguê*, a deep-toned type of agogô. Other instruments sometimes used include the ganzá and the afoxê, a gourd with strung beads around it otherwise known as the *xequerê*. The sound of the afoxés is serene, not frenetic like frevo or thunderous like an escola de samba. Gilberto Gil described the most famous afoxé, the

▼ A member of the Filhos de Gandhi. *(Photo by Linda Yudin.)*

elegantly dressed members of the Clube Carnavalesco Cruz Vermelha (Red Cross Carnaval Club) took to the streets with a float. Over the next few years, the city's Carnaval emulated the pre-Lent celebrations of Venice and Nice. Floats paraded in the cobblestone streets, bands played polkas and opera overtures, and upper-class revelers dressed in luxurious European-style costumes.

At this time middle-class groups like the Clube Carnavalesco Cruz Vermelha, Cavalheiros da Malta, Clube dos Cacetes, Grupo dos Nenês, and Cavalheiros de Veneza were the leading participants, with onlookers awarding their favorites with loud applause. For ten more years the parades were basically an all-white festival, until Afro-Brazilians had their first organized participation with the arrival of the afoxés.

Afoxé

An afoxé is a procession that brings the ceremonial music of candomblé—with its corresponding

Filhos de Gandhi (Sons of Gandhi), as representing "the spiritual side of Carnaval."

The first afoxé to parade in Salvador was the Embaixada Africana (African Embassy), in 1895. The following year saw the debut of the Pândegos de África (African Merrymakers). Then others appeared, including the Chegada Africana (African Arrival), and Filhos da África (Sons of Africa).[5] They dressed in African-style clothes and celebrated African themes, honoring Oxalá or heroes like Zumbi, the leader of the Palmares quilombo. With their infectious beat, they were quite a contrast to the staid "floats of the great Societies with their French court themes," wrote novelist Jorge Amado in *Tenda dos milagres* (Tent of Miracles). "The *News Journal* called for radical measures: 'What will become of the Carnival of 1902 if the police do not take steps to keep our streets from becoming terreiros, fetishism rampant, with its procession of ogans [male initiates], and its native rattles, gourds, and tambourines?'"[6] There was "an epidemic of sambas and afoxés" in the streets and plazas.

Three years later the upper class was even more offended. Amado wrote, "Hadn't Dr. Francisco Antônio de Castro Loureiro, temporary Chief of Police, expressly forbidden the afoxés to parade anywhere in the city, under any pretext whatever . . . for 'ethnic and social reasons, for the sake of our families, decency, morality, and the public welfare and in order to combat crime, debauchery, and disorder'? Who had dared to disobey the law? The Sons of Bahia had dared. Never had such a majestic carnival pageant, such a constellation of grandeur and beauty, been seen or dreamed of: such rhythmic drumming, such marvelous colors."[7]

The afoxés were banished for nearly fifteen years, returning only in 1918. For the next three decades Carnaval in Bahia was celebrated in private clubs by the rich and in the streets by cordões (which survived much longer in Salvador than in Rio), blocos (Carnaval groups, often associated with neighborhoods), small escolas de samba, and a few afoxés, like the Filhos de Congo (Sons of Congo). Because of persistent police repression of

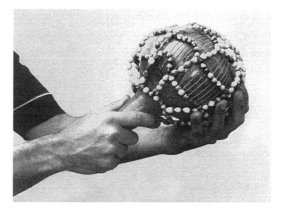

▲ João Parahyba playing an afoxê. *(Photo by Ricardo Pessanha.)*

Afro-Brazilian culture, which lasted until the late 1940s, it took much longer for Salvador to develop large Carnaval organizations like Rio's big escolas de samba. Blacks in Salvador had to force their way into the streets during Carnaval, fighting with the police. The situation started to change in 1948 with the founding of the Filhos de Gandhi, an afoxé that incorporated the pacifist, anticolonialist philosophy of Mahatma Gandhi.

The Filhos de Gandhi

"Antonio Curuzu, a founding member of the Filhos de Gandhi, was responsible for choosing Gandhi to be our patron," recalled one of the afoxé's founding members in an interview with dance ethnologist Linda Yudin. "The group realized that Gandhi had nothing to do with African or Afro-Brazilian culture, but he was a symbol of world peace. That was what was important to us. We wanted to demonstrate peacefully that our African heritage was positive for the community." He added, "After our participation, we hoped that the persecution of African manifestations in Bahia would stop occurring."[8]

Their nonviolent approach and use of the name Gandhi gave them respectability in the eyes of the authorities. The new afoxé applied for, and was granted, a permit from the Ministry of Justice to parade during Carnaval. It was thus protected from police interference and won the right to celebrate peacefully in the streets. The afoxé's roughly one hundred members, dressed in blue and white, made their debut in the Carnaval of 1949 and were warmly received by both the public and the authorities.

The Filhos de Gandhi have become one of the most highly respected institutions in Bahia and helped pave the way for the advent of the blocos afro in later decades. The group became an integral part of Bahian Carnaval, as did another new arrival to the festive Salvador streets the following year.

Dodô and Osmar: The Trio Elétrico

In the Carnaval of 1950, two musicians by the name of Dodô and Osmar appeared in the streets of Salvador in an old Ford pickup truck. Standing in the bed of the truck, they performed with an electrified guitar, electrified cavaquinho, and portable amps. Their style of music was frevo, a highly syncopated, fast-tempo marcha that originated earlier in the century in Recife, a large coastal city to the north in Pernambuco state.

▼ A trio elétrico keeping the crowds dancing. *(Photo by Artur Ikishima. Courtesy of Bahiatursa.)*

Dodô and Osmar created a sensation with their amplified frevo. In 1951 they added a third instrumentalist, and the term *trio elétrico* (electric trio) was born. Trio elétrico trucks soon became a common sight in Salvador during Carnaval, winding through the city's streets, inciting crowds to dance and sing. The trios grew in size, popularity, and ability to generate massive decibels. The sound trucks evolved into enormous custom-built rigs that served as mobile stages, weighed down by numerous musicians and banks of speakers. The sound they generate is deafening, overwhelming, as they lumber through the primary Carnaval areas of Campo Grande, Praça Castro Alves, and Barra. Behind the trios follow thousands of celebrants, dancing and leaping deliriously.

By the 1970s many Bahian blocos had begun to contract trios elétricos to provide the music for their parades. Some used heavy rope to cordon off a zone of protection around each sound truck. For the price of admission you received the bloco's costume and could parade in relative safety inside the cordão, separated from the often dangerous chaos in the streets. These days, sound trucks also carry the vocalists of blocos, like Timbalada, that do not identify themselves with the trios elétricos.

Many blocos feature well-known musicians atop the trucks, performing the latest Bahian hits. Daniela Mercury, Margareth Menezes, Ivete Sangalo, Claudia Leitte, Gilberto Gil, Caetano Veloso, and Chiclete com Banana are among those who have appeared atop the trios elétricos during Carnaval in Salvador.

In the 1960s and 1970s frevo developed into an important vehicle for instrumental improvisation. In Bahia it became inextricably mixed with the trio elétrico sound, which has come to mean frenetic guitar and cavaquinho soloing coupled with a voracious absorption of musical idioms. Trio elétrico musicians play everything from rock to Rimsky-Korsakov's "Flight of the Bumblebee." Anything that makes the listener jump and dance is incorporated, and this has helped create new musical styles. In addition, many notable Bahian musicians have gotten their start playing with the trios. But by the late 1970s the trios elétricos had to share space in the streets of Salvador with a new cultural manifestation: the blocos afro, short for *blocos afrobrasileiros* (Afro-Brazilian Carnaval groups).

Roots of the Afro-Bahian Renaissance

In the 1970s many Bahian blacks from the lower classes celebrated Carnaval in groups called *blocos de índio*—for example, the Apaches de Tororó, which were founded in 1968, and the Comanches, established in 1974. The members of the blocos de índio, dressed in Hollywood-style Indian costumes, danced to samba and were notoriously violent. As the rowdy blocos de índio grew in popularity, they were regularly met with harassment from the local military police. But in the 1970s and 1980s, with the formation of the blocos afro, poor Afro-Brazilians had a new outlet for their energy and creativity in Carnaval. Consequently, the blocos de índio declined in popularity, as many members joined the blocos afro.

The growth of the blocos afro was linked to a renewal of black consciousness then taking place in Salvador and the rest of the country. In the late 1960s and early 1970s, many young black Brazil-

ians were fascinated by the music of James Brown, the Jackson 5, and other African Americans. The wave of black pride that hit the United States (typified by the slogan "Black is Beautiful") also echoed in Brazil in the favelas of Rio and other large cities. The popularity of American soul music inspired a cultural movement nicknamed "black-rio" in Rio de Janeiro, "black-sampa" in São Paulo, and "black-mineiro" in Minas Gerais. It was panned by many critics as more "cultural imperialism" and "alienation" imposed by the United States. But among many blacks in Brazil, it inspired renewed pride in African roots, as did the wave of independence movements in Africa in the 1970s. Angola and Mozambique, former Portuguese colonies, were among the many African nations that achieved self-rule in that decade. In Bahia, Afro-Brazilian pride was further boosted by the popularity of reggae stars Bob Marley, Peter Tosh, and Jimmy Cliff, whose lyrics decried racism and government corruption while praising Mother Africa.

Ilê Aiyê

The surge of interest in black culture led Vovô and Apolônio—two men who lived in the Curuzu district of the Liberdade neighborhood of Salvador—to have the idea in 1974 of creating a bloco afro to parade during Carnaval. In their group, Ilê Aiyê, only very dark-skinned blacks could be members. Whites and mulattos were excluded. Their policy sparked controversy, which is rather ironic considering the unwritten but obvious boundaries of race and class that already existed in Salvador, a city whose governmental leaders and upper class were (and still are) almost entirely light-skinned, even though Afro-Brazilians make up the vast majority of the population.

There has long been segregation in Bahia's Carnaval both in indoor clubs and outside on the streets, according to Antonio Risério, who writes in *Carnaval Ijexá*, "Put on one side Badauê, Ilê Aiyê, Ara Ketu, etc. On the other side, those that are called 'Class A blocos,' like Barão, Traz-os-Montes, Internacionais, etc. And the conclusion is

▲ Drummers and dancers for Ilê Aiyê. *(Photo by Fernando Seixas. Courtesy of Eldorado Records.)*

obvious: there exists a relative, but evident, internal racial homogeneity in the blocos, dividing them into two species: those whose racial spectrum goes from black to light mulatto, and those whose spectrum goes from light mulatto to white. It's that simple. Moreover, some blocos of richer people, who don't want to mix with blacks, are contracting small (and lamentable) trios elétricos to play only for them, in the private space of the bloco, staked out by ropes."[9]

Recounting the origin of Ilê, Risério describes how Vovô and Apolônio were drinking and talking one night in Curuzu when the idea came up. Vovô recalled, "It was in that era of that business of black power, and so we thought about making a bloco just for blacks, with African themes."[10] They chose the name Ilê Aiyê (a Yoruba phrase that roughly translates as "house of life") and quickly attracted many musicians and members. Ilê Aiyê made its Carnaval debut in 1975, with about a hundred people in the bloco and assorted friends trailing after it, according to Vovô.

The local police tended to treat poor blacks as second-class citizens or potential criminals. This meant that an entirely black bloco defiantly affirming its *negritude* (blackness) would raise some eyebrows. Vovô told Risério, "There were blacks that didn't go with us because they were afraid of being arrested. In that era, we didn't know how it would go, we didn't have the least idea of what would happen. Everyone inexperienced, no big names, no political support. We went to the street just that way, with boldness and heart. It was a major polemic. There were people who asked us if it was a bloco or a protest."[11]

Parading down to the beach, pounding out Afro-Brazilian rhythms on surdos and repiques, Ilê performed raw, unadorned music with just vocals, drums, and percussion, which set the style for the blocos afro to follow. They created a lot of excitement in Salvador, singing the provocative lyrics of their theme song "Ilê Aiyê," written by Paulinho Camafeu.

What bloco is this, I want to know
It's the black world that we have come to
  show you
We're crazy blacks, we're really cool
We have kinky hair . . .

*White, if you knew the value that blacks
   have
You'd take a tar bath and become black too*

Gilberto Gil recorded the song on his 1977 *Re-favela* album, adding to Ilê's renown.

Ilê Aiyê developed into a Carnaval group with more than two thousand participants by the early 1990s. Each year they explored a different aspect of their African heritage, with costumes researched and woven to match the theme. Without compromise, Ilê Aiyê celebrated negritude, urged resistance against Brazil's dominant light-skinned elites, and provocatively used racist or condescend-ing terms against blacks (like *criolos doidos*—crazy blacks) in its lyrics. Within just a few years Ilê be-came a powerful organization that had a long-last-ing impact on Bahia's music and culture.

Muzenza, Malê Debalê, Badauê, and Ara Ketu

The success of Ilê Aiyê triggered the formation of many blocos afro in the late 1970s and 1980s. None of the other blocos imitated Ilê in its policy of excluding those with light skin, but they did follow Ilê's example in tying their identities and Car-naval themes to Africa and Afro-based culture.

Blocos Afro Outside Bahia

Blocos afro have also been founded outside Salvador. In Rio de Janeiro four blocos—Agbara Dudu (arguably the oldest in the city, founded in 1982), Dudu Èwe, Òrúnmìlá, and Lemi Ayò—recorded an album together in 1992 titled *Terreiros e Quilombos*. Raimundo Santa Rosa, who produced the album, applauded the overall importance of the blocos and said, "It's important to open space for new ideas related to blacks, allow for improvement of their living conditions, and stimulate greater awareness." Believing that such roles were no longer fulfilled by organizations like Rio's samba schools, he added, "The music performed by the escolas de samba today is sheer commerce."[12] Of course, the many venerable samba schools that serve as year-round community and cultural institutions might well take exception to that point.

▲ A practice session for Rio's bloco afro Orunmilá. *(Photo by Ricardo Pessanha.)*

Each of the larger blocos, with one thousand to three thousand members, has its own unique constellation of percussion, as is the case down south in Rio's samba schools.

Malê Debalê, founded in 1979, paraded one year with its thousands of members dressed as antiapartheid guerillas from Soweto. Badauê (1978) is an afoxé whose members wear costumes of golden yellow for the orixá Oxum and white for Oxalá. Ara Ketu (1980) is a bloco afro that usually celebrates Yoruba concepts in its parades. And Muzenza (1982) is a bloco with a special affinity for Jamaica that uses the green, yellow, and black colors of that country's flag.

Linda Yudin told us, "What is so profound about the blocos afro is that they have allowed the young black population of Salvador to identify themselves through the expressions of dance, song, and drumming, as opposed to outsiders telling them who they are or what their culture is about."[13]

The blocos afro carried forward the evolution of styles like afoxé and samba afro (samba mixed with candomblé rhythms), which is not to be confused with Vinícius de Moraes and Baden Powell's afro-sambas, played in the bossa nova style. Beginning in 1987 they began performing samba-reggae, a fusion of the two styles in which the repiques take the part of the rhythm guitar in reggae. Samba-reggae boosted the popularity of the blocos and became an essential element of Bahian axé music that decade and the next.

The drums and choruses of ten Bahian blocos afro and afoxés, along with the vocals of Luiz Caldas, Margareth Menezes, Gilberto Gil, and other local singers, were heard in 1988 on the album *Afros e Afoxés da Bahia*, organized by Durval Ferreira and Paulo César Pinheiro. Many blocos recorded solo albums in the late 1980s and '90s, and several—most notably Ara Ketu and Olodum—spun off small pop ensembles.

By 1983 there were sixteen blocos afro and twenty-three afoxés in Salvador, along with eight cordões, five blocos de índio, and two samba schools, according to anthropologist Daniel Crowley.[14] By the mid-1990s participation had shifted and the total number of blocos afro had dropped, with the most successful organizations—Ilê Aiyê, the Filhos de Gandhi, Olodum, Muzenza, and Malê Debalê—drawing members away from the smaller organizations. Cortejo Alto, founded in 1997, was a later addition to the group. Ten years later, those were still the main groups. Although their numbers were fewer, "their participation is strong, and they continue to have strong community participation," observed Yudin, adding, "I think that the blocos afro and afoxes permanently marked Salvador's culture."[15]

Return of the Filhos de Gandhi

Before the advent of Ilê Aiyê, one of the Carnaval groups doing the most to keep Afro-Brazilian identity alive in Bahia was the Filhos de Gandhi. Unfortunately, by the 1960s, the popularity of the afoxés was in sharp decline. The Filhos de Gandhi had paraded with roughly one hundred members during each Carnaval in their first two decades of existence, but by the 1970s they were struggling and in danger of dying out.

Three factors led to their revival. According to Yudin, one was that the Filhos de Gandhi began a concerted effort to recruit new members. Also, in the early 1970s the municipality of Salvador and Bahiatursa (the state's tourism arm) realized the value to tourism of groups like the afoxés and began to encourage the "re-Africanization" of Bahia's Carnaval, in sharp contrast to earlier government policies. A third impetus came when MPB star Gilberto Gil returned to Salvador from exile and went in search of the afoxé, hoping to involve himself in their music and culture. He told Risério, "I found about twenty of them, with their drums on the ground, in a corner of the Praça da Sé. They didn't have the resources, or the will to take a place in the Bahian Carnaval."[16] Gil joined and devoted himself to their music and cultural discipline.

His energy and celebrity helped revitalize the Filhos de Gandhi. In 1976's Carnaval, a year after Ilê Aiyê's debut, Gil paraded with his adopted afoxé, and the next year he recorded the afoxé

"Patuscada de Gandhi" (Revelry of Gandhi) on his *Refavela* album, along with "Ilê Aiyê." With the help of Gil and Bahiatursa, and the success of their recruitment efforts, the Filhos de Gandhi were thriving by the next decade, with more than a thousand members (all men) in 1980. The governor of Bahia, Antonio Carlos Magalhães, realizing the political potential of helping the venerable afoxé, gave them a renovated building in the historic Pelourinho to use as their headquarters.

The Filhos continued to grow and by 1996 had more than six thousand members, including children who participated in their parade. Visually, the Filhos de Gandhi are an awesome sight: a shimmering ocean of men dancing to the ijexá rhythm, dressed in costumes of white turbans, tunics, and sandals, royal blue socks, and blue-and-white sashes and beads. The Filhos de Gandhi and Ilê Aiyê had a major impact on Bahian music and culture, as did a bloco afro formed in 1979: Olodum.

Olodum

It is night in the Pelourinho, the famed historical square in the heart of old Salvador, in the late 1980s. A sultry breeze washes over the large, free-spirited crowd gathered here under a hazy moon.

Atop a makeshift stage stand singers, percussionists, and dancers from the group Olodum, their backs to the iron balconies, colorful façades, and tile roofs of centuries-old colonial buildings. Near the stage an unfurled banner reads, "África—Olodum—Bahia."

The surdo players begin to generate a solid beat and the caixas add a constant pattern of higher-pitched sixteenth notes, accenting the back beats. The repique kicks in a reggae cadence, other instruments like the African kalimba (thumb piano) join in, and rhythms build and interact. The music is mesmerizing, as samba meets reggae and creates a heavy, dense, ritualistic sound.

Women start to dance spontaneously in large groups, and athletic young men practice capoeira, throwing spinning kicks to the beat. Now the master percussionist appears behind his set of two timbales and adds sharp rhythmic bursts that contrast with the other instruments, leading and counterpointing them. The lead vocalist and chorus begin to sing of Egypt and Mozambique and South Africa. The thousands in the audience are carried off into a state of euphoria by the music and dancing.

Olodum (from Olódùmarè, the Yoruba supreme deity) has several thousand members and is headquartered in the Pelourinho, once the site of slave auctions and whippings, now a tourist attrac-

▶ Olodum. *(Courtesy of Sound Wave/WEA.)*

tion and center of Afro-Brazilian culture. Olodum is the most well known and commercially successful of the blocos afro. It is also a thriving community organization that sponsors courses and workshops for its members and for poor youths in Salvador. Its principal goals are to continue the struggle against racism and to seek the recovery and preservation of black culture.

Under the leadership of Neguinho do Samba (Luis Alves de Souza), Olodum has recorded many successful albums using ensembles composed of the top musicians of the bloco. Neguinho has been largely responsible for shaping Olodum's sound—which at first consisted exclusively of vocals and percussion—and developing its rhythmic innovations.

Olodum is generally credited with having created samba-reggae. According to musicologist Larry Crook, Olodum introduced the new style during rehearsals for the 1986 Carnaval.[17] In addition, the band augmented its repique-surdo sound with timbales (common in Cuba and Puerto Rico), which further distinguished its music from that of the other blocos. In 1987 Olodum recorded the new samba-reggae rhythm in "Faraó Divindade do Egito" (Pharaoh Egyptian Divinity), written by Luciano Gomes dos Santos. The song paid homage to ancient Egypt and proclaimed that some of the pharaohs were actually black. "Faraó," propelled by the catchy new beat, was the big hit of Carnaval that year and helped the band land a contract with Continental Records.

"Faraó" was featured on Olodum's first album, *Egito Madagascar* (Egypt Madagascar), which showcased the bloco's seismic drums and unveiled samba-reggae and other rhythmic experiments. Banda Mel also recorded "Faraó" in 1987 and achieved a commercial hit. Another tune on Olodum's album, Rey Zulu's "Madagascar Olodum," became a national success for Banda Reflexu's and was included in their best-selling *Da Mãe África* album that year.

"Girassol" (Sunflower), "Gira" (Spin), and "Revolta Olodum" (Olodum's Revolt) were popular tunes in the next few years for Olodum. Many of the bloco's songs protested Brazilian and global social injustices. Some tunes, like Pierre Onassis-Nego's hugely successful 1993 "Requebra" (Shake Your Hips), were just good party music and not political at all. In the '90s Olodum's sound expanded from a percussion-and-vocals base to include guitars and keyboards and mixed their trademark samba-reggae with forró and pop styles.

Olodum gained international fame from music videos, concerts in other countries, and appearances on the albums of famous global pop musicians. They participated in Paul Simon's song "The Obvious Child" from his *Rhythm of the Saints* album, and in the Bill Laswell–produced album *Bahia Black: Ritual Beating System*. Olodum's percussionists, pounding their trademark red-gold-green-black drums, performed in New York's Central Park for *Paul Simon's Concert in the Park*, in Michael Jackson's music video "They Don't Really Care About Us," directed by Spike Lee,[18] and during festivities for the 1994 World Cup soccer finals (which Brazil won).

BAHIAN POPULAR MUSIC

Along with the rich tradition of groups like the blocos and afoxés, many renowned individual artists have come from the city of Salvador or Bahia state, including Gilberto Gil, Caetano Veloso,

▼ Dorival Caymmi. *(Photo by Wilton Montenegro. Courtesy of EMI.)*

João Gilberto, Gal Costa, Raul Seixas, Maria Bethânia, and Simone. But one name comes up time and time again when contemporary musicians speak of their influences: Dorival Caymmi, one of the leading figures of the samba-canção era. Caymmi wrote songs marked by profound simplicity, picturesque lyrics, and unforgettable melodies. His music paints life on the Bahian coast: its fishermen and their *jangadas* (sail-rafts), the beauty and danger of the sea, lush palm-lined shores, and candomblé temples. It evokes the despair and courage of the poor, the charm and sensuality of the Baiana, and the easygoing tropical pace of Salvador.

Caymmi's samba "Acontece Que Sou Baiano" (It Happens That I'm Bahian) takes the listener into his culture with a reference to a *pai-de-santo* (a candomblé priest), whose help he seeks in regard to a woman with an alluring *requebrado*, a voluptuous movement of the hips.

> *I already put a hen's foot in my doorway*
> *I already called a pai-de-santo*
> *To bless that woman*
> *The one with the requebrado*

Caymmi co-wrote "É Doce Morrer no Mar" (It's Sweet to Die in the Sea) with his good friend the novelist Jorge Amado, also a famed chronicler of the region's folklore. In the sad and hypnotic toada, a woman mourns the loss of her mate—a fisherman who has gone to meet Yemanjá, the candomblé goddess of the sea.

> *In the green waves of the sea*
> *My beloved was drowned*
> *He made his bridegroom's bed*
> *In the lap of Yemanjá*

"Caymmi is timeless. He is specific, the vital force and the poetry of our region," stated the artist Carybé, adding, "He is the saudade of Bahia, the sadness of Bahia, the beaches, the sun."[19] (For more about Caymmi, see Chapter Two.)

The group Novos Baianos (New Bahians) played an important role in the evolution of Ba-

▲ Pepeu Gomes, former member of Os Novos Baianos. *(Courtesy of Pepeu Gomes.)*

hian music in the late 1960s and early 1970s. In their unique sound, Bahian Carnaval met Woodstock rock. One of their most successful albums was *Acabou Chorare* (No More Crying), which was released in 1973 and included the hit single "Preta Pretinha." Os Novos Baianos inspired the trios elétricos to mix rock with frevo—causing what Gilberto Gil later called the *rolling-stonização* of the trios. After the group split up in 1976, bassist Dadi formed the seminal instrumental group Cor de Som (Color of Sound), which played frevo, choro, and samba with jazz-fusion-like arrangements. Guitarist Pepeu Gomes and singer Baby Consuelo (who were then husband and wife) went on to establish solo careers in pop music.

The fourth principal member of Os Novo Baianos, singer-guitarist Moraes Moreira, was Brazil's foremost exponent of frevo in the 1980s. He displayed musical versatility in albums like *Mestiço É Isso* (Mestizo Is This), consistently keeping up with new musical developments such as the advent of the blocos afro. In 1979 he and Antonio Risério composed "Assim Pintou Moçambique" (Thus Arrived Mozambique), a song that

▲ Moraes Moreira. *(Photo by José Pederneiras. Courtesy of Sony.)*

fused the ijexá rhythm of the afoxé groups with the trio elétrico sound. The next year, Moreira dressed in the costume of the afoxé Badauê and performed frevo and reggae-ijexá during Carnaval. He also incorporated reggae into songs like 1986's "Pernambuco, Jamaica e Bahia," which included percussion by rising stars Carlinhos Brown and Tony Mola and guitar by Luiz Caldas. Moreira has written several Carnaval smash hits that celebrate Salvador and Bahian culture. His most famous composition to date is the ecstatic frevo "Festa do Interior" (Party in the Interior), written with Abel Silva, which became a huge success when interpreted by Gal Costa in 1981.

Axé Music

In the 1980s a new category of popular music emerged in Bahia that fully came of age in the next decade when it gained the name *axé music*, incorporating the Yoruba word *axé* (life force or positive energy). Olodum, Carlinhos Brown, and Daniela Mercury are among the most prominent exponents of axé music, an umbrella term for several different styles, with samba-reggae being the most significant. Primary ingredients in the mix are samba, ijexá, frevo, and reggae, and other elements can include merengue, salsa, *soca*, and *carimbó*. Several

factors helped local musicians develop the new sound: the influence of the blocos afro, the free-wheeling experimentation of trio-elétrico musicians, access to improved recording technology, and regional support for Bahian music.

By the 1980s Bahia's musical scene had become thoroughly Africanized. The influence of the Filhos de Gandhi, Olodum, Ilê Aiyê, and other blocos inspired a surge in Afro-Brazilian consciousness. Bahian popular music was suddenly full of Yoruba words, candomblé images, and references to Africa and Jamaica. And the trios elétricos started to present *afro-elétrico* music, to use Antonio Risério's phrase.[20]

Bahian musicians playing in the blocos and the trios began to invent a plethora of new sounds with a strong dance beat. It helped that a number of Brazilian and Caribbean forms mesh quite well together rhythmically. Reggae was an especially big outside influence in the 1980s and fit together well with various Brazilian grooves. Olodum used it to create samba-reggae, the most influential new Brazilian style of the 1980s. Meanwhile, the trio elétrico groups, the training ground for many young Bahian musicians, were throwing every musical reference they had into their frenetic, high-volume presentations.

The fast-paced creativity going on in Salvador was aided at this time by a regional market that eagerly absorbed locally produced music. Another factor helping musicians in Salvador was an improvement in technology. Cheaper and better synthesizers became available, and Bahian artists in general had increased access to modern recording studios. In many cases they didn't wait for deals with the big labels and instead put out their own independent records.

One such example was the singer-songwriter Luiz Caldas, who was born in Feira de Santana in 1963 and had moved to Salvador at age eighteen to play with the trio elétrico Tapajós. In 1985 Caldas released his debut album, *Magia* (Magic), on a small label, then talked PolyGram into picking up the distribution. The album included the song "Fricote," which used the *fricote* rhythm (also called *deboche*), in which Caldas concocted his own mixture of ijexá and reggae, juicing up the tempo and creating a new beat. The song was a forerunner of axé music and arguably its first major hit—before the category had a name. Caldas found himself with a platinum-selling album on his hands, with most of the sales coming from record stores in Bahia and the Northeast. He became a major star and scored another commercial success in 1986 with *Flor Cigana* (Gypsy Flower), which featured the fricote tune "Eu Vou Já" (I'll Go Soon).

Chiclete com Banana, Gerônimo, Banda Mel, and Banda Reflexu's were also helping to create the new Bahian sound at this time, which received a further boost from Olodum's introduction of samba-reggae. Sarajane, Abel Duerê, Cid Guerreiro, Lazzo Matumbi, Roberto Mendes, Missinho, Carlos Pita, Djalma Oliveira, Raízes do Pelô, Simone Moreno, Banda Eva, Netinho, Banda Cheiro de Amor and Márcia Freire (its former lead vocalist), and Bragadá (led by Tony Mola) were among the other key artists and groups recording the emerging styles. For the most part, rhythm has been the key ingredient in their songs, which typically feature simple melodies and harmonies. It is energetic, good-time party music, designed for dancing and Carnaval.

While serious themes have been explored in songs like "Faraó," most axé music tunes feature lyrics that focus on romance, sex, and Carnaval. The Bahian bands Gera Samba and Companhia do Pagode also epitomize this tendency. They recorded pop versions of styles like samba de roda, and their songs were extremely popular in Salvador's Carnaval in the mid-1990s and widely performed by other Bahian artists. Gera Samba's "É o Tchan" sold one million copies throughout Brazil, and a short time later part of the group spun off a second band, É o Tchan, which took the name of the hit song. Companhia do Pagode's "Na Boquinha da Garrafa" was another best seller. The two songs, with their infectious dance rhythms and sly erotic lyrics, generated the *dança do bumbum* (fanny dance) and the *dança da garrafa* (bottle dance), respectively, which were hit dances in Salvador's Carnaval. They joined other popular Bahian styles, like *dança da tartaruga* (turtle dance), to form what some call *axé dance*, the dance movements that accompany axé music. These are drawn from a wide variety of sources, including Brazilian folkloric dances and hip-hop, jazz dance, modern dance, and even aerobics.[21]

Daniela Mercury and Margareth Menezes

While axé music was dominating the airwaves in Salvador, it also began to appear on the albums of veteran MPB stars. In the late 1980s Beth Carvalho recorded the afoxé "O Encanto do Gantois" and the Ara Ketu tribute "Majestade Real." At the start of the 1990s Gal Costa released the samba-reggae "Salvador Não Inerte," "Revolta Olodum" with Raízes do Pelô, and Gerônimo's afoxé "É d'Oxum" with the Filhos de Gandhi. At that time many MPB singers also covered compositions by Carlinhos Brown. But it was not until the arrival of Daniela Mercury (Daniela Mercuri de Almeida Póvoas) that the new music from Bahia really took hold of all Brazil.

▼ Luiz Caldas. *(Photo by Paulo Ricardo. Courtesy of PolyGram.)*

▲ Daniela Mercury. *(Photo by Mario Cravo Neto. Courtesy of EMI Music Brazil.)*

Mercury was born in Salvador in 1965 and began her career singing in bars, favoring MPB standards by her idols Caetano Veloso, Gilberto Gil, Chico Buarque, and Elis Regina. Daniela's talent impressed Bahian singer-songwriter Gerônimo, and she sang backup vocals in his band for a year. In 1987 she performed as a singer for the trio elétrico associated with the bloco Eva, then recorded two albums with the group Companhia Clic. Daniela released her debut solo album, *Daniela Mercury,* in 1991. It features the hit song "Swing da Cor" (Swing of Color), written by Luciano Gomes, which Mercury sings dynamically atop the propulsive samba-reggae beat made famous by Olodum. The album (also referred to as *Swing da Cor*) was a best seller in Brazil that took samba-reggae's national popularity to a new level. Radio stations and bars that had previously ignored axé music now played Mercury's music nonstop. The next year, *O Canto da Cidade* (The Song of the City) added to her success, and its title song, co-written by Mercury, was another hit.

Some Brazilian critics suggested that much of Daniela's popularity was due to her being light-skinned and beautiful. Yet many black performers, including Gilberto Gil and Margareth

Menezes, have defended Mercury's success and talent.[22] Daniela is a kinetic performer with a sensual flair and effervescent charisma on stage. She is a fervent vocalist who expanded her musical range in the 1996 album *Feijão com Arroz* (Beans with Rice). On the album Mercury adeptly interprets well-produced axé music and adds new touches that include "À Primeira Vista" (At First Sight), a romantic ballad by northeastern bard Chico César, and "Vide Gal," a propulsive Carlinhos Brown samba with blazing horns and Rio-style percussion. Music writer Bruce Gilman says of Mercury that "her studio recordings never fail to create the sensational energy level of a live performance, one of the widely recognized merits of her work."[23]

Even before Mercury conquered Rio with her axé music, the genre was carried overseas by fellow Bahian singer Margareth Menezes (born in 1962). Menezes's deep, powerful voice was well

▼ Margareth Menezes. *(Photo by Livio Campos. Courtesy of Mango/Island.)*

suited to carrying a tune atop the propulsive drums in samba-reggae. After performing as a vocalist with trios elétricos, she made her solo debut in 1988 with the album *Margareth Menezes*. Her career received a jump start when she was invited by David Byrne (the former leader of the rock group Talking Heads) to accompany him on a world tour. This led to a deal with the Mango label and her first international release, *Elegibô*. Its title song, written by Rey Zulu, is an uplifting hymn to an ancient Yoruba city of the same name and might be described as *samba-reggae-exaltação* (exaltation samba-reggae).

In the years to follow, Margareth released well-regarded albums such as *Afropopbrasileiros* (2002), produced by Carlinhos Brown. Menezes introduced axé music to foreign audiences and helped pave the way for the success of other Bahian musicians, both nationally and internationally. Another female singer who helped spread the sounds of Bahia to the world was Virginia Rodrigues, whose album *Sol Negro* (Black Sun, 1998) showcased her otherworldly contralto voice, rooted in the music of the Catholic Church, as she interpreted sacred music, samba, and MPB with a sparse backing of harp, berimbau, and Bahia percussion.

Axé's Ups and Downs, and Ivete

Axé music peaked commercially in the 1990s. During that decade, artists like Daniela Mercury, Chiclete com Banana, Banda Eva, Banda Mel, Asa de Águia, Netinho, and others mentioned earlier sold millions of albums, were omnipresent on TV shows and on the airwaves, played for huge crowds in arenas, and performed in numerous *micaretas* (off-season carnival celebrations). The musical style created in Salvador, Bahia, had become a significant industry that generated millions of dollars annually. In the first years of the new century, things began to change nationally as the axé wave subsided. Overexposure and lack of renovation and creativity are two of the possible reasons. Daniela Mercury, Carlinhos Brown, and Olodum were among those who managed to re-

▲ Ivete Sangalo. *(Photo by Cacau Mangabeira. Courtesy of Universal Music Brazil.)*

tain their national popularity. A few others, like Ivete Sangalo and the band Babado Novo, led by singer Claudia Leitte, rose to an even higher degree of popularity, but most axé music artists have the bulk of their followers in the Northeast.

Ivete Sangalo, who has reached the top of national sales charts, was born in 1972 in Juazeiro, Bahia, also the birthplace of bossa nova's João Gilberto. She has a powerful voice and is an entertainer who puts on high-energy, big-production shows when performing live. She started as a solo artist (one of her first gigs was a micareta in the city of Morro do Chapéu), then joined Banda Eva as their leader singer in 1993 and recorded six popular albums with the group, including their best-selling album to that point, *Banda Eva ao Vivo*. Ivete resumed her solo career with a successful self-titled album in 1999. Her 2004 album *MTV ao Vivo: Ivete Sangalo* included Gilberto Gil and Margareth Menezes as guests and sold a million copies in Brazil, helping to secure her position as the most commercially successful axé music performer and the most popular female singer in Brazil. Three years later her DVD *Ao Vivo no Maracanã*, which captured her live performance at Rio's famed soccer stadium, was the best-selling music DVD of the year, according to Universal Music.[24]

Carlinhos Brown and Timbalada

Mercury, Caldas, Menezes, Marisa Monte, Maria Bethânia, Gal Costa, Caetano Veloso, and Cássia Eller are among those who have recorded songs by Carlinhos Brown (Antonio Carlos Santos de Freitas), an innovative songwriter, bandleader, and percussionist. Brown mixes axé music with funk, embolada, bossa nova, and other styles in idiosyncratic and rhythmically rich tunes that he describes as "Afro-Brazilian popular music without prejudice. In my sound there's space for everything from Noel Rosa to Pintado do Bongô to Villa-Lobos."[25]

Carlinhos was born in 1963 in Salvador and grew up in Candeal, an area in the Brotas neighborhood. His mother was an evangelical Protestant and his father practiced candomblé. Brown grew up listening to a wide range of music. He favored Luiz Gonzaga, the Beatles, merengue, Tropicália, Jorge Ben (later known as Benjor), and the Jackson 5, and he also absorbed *violeiros* in the streets, candomblé music coming from a terreiro near his parents' house, and Gregorian chants echoing out of a Catholic monastery atop a nearby hill.

As a youth, Brown studied with a percussion master named Pintado do Bongô (Osvaldo Alves da Silva), who played with the group Baticum. Carlinhos told us, "Pintado lived near me. At the time, I liked to dance and beat my cans and buckets but still hadn't discovered myself as a musician. But when I saw him play I was really impressed. I used to go to his place against my mother's will. As a Protestant, she always connected drum beating to candomblé." As an evangelical, she considered Afro-Brazilian religion pagan and evil.

▲ Carlinhos Brown. *(Photo by David Glat. Courtesy of Sony/ BMG Brazil.)*

"This was the time of Black Power," Brown continued. "I had Afro hair and loved Toni Tornado [a Brazilian funk singer and dancer] and James Brown." The latter also supplied Carlinhos with his stage name. "I was dancing at a party and started to attract everybody's attention. The guy who was throwing the party didn't like it at all. He turned off the stereo and asked, 'Who is that James Brown?' My friends started to make fun of me, calling me Brown, so I became Carlinhos Brown."

Carlinhos continued his lessons with Mestre Pintado, whom Brown described as a "master of *sambão*, a mixture of samba with mambo. The first Caribbean connection in Bahia was sambão, long before fricote. When I played with Luiz Caldas, he didn't know about sambão. He had a fantastic versatility but didn't know what was going on in the streets. When he got in touch with all that, he interpreted it quite well and created those mixtures, the most famous one being fricote. But it all started with sambão." The sambão beat went largely unrecorded, as far as Brown knows, but he did use it in his song "Guia Pro Congal" on the *Bahia Black* album.

Carlinhos performed in bars and at parties with Mestre Pintado, and—as he entered his teenage years—played with the female vocal group Clara da Lua (White of the Moon) and the rock band Mar Revolto (Stormy Sea). Then came a tour of duty with trios elétricos and work as a studio musician. In the 1980s he played percussion—claves, congas, agogô, pandeiro, timbales, afoxê, and more—on albums by Luiz Caldas, Moraes Moreira, Maria Bethânia, Caetano Veloso, and others. Brown achieved his first radio hit with the song "Visão do Ciclope" (Cyclops Vision) co-written with and recorded by Luiz Caldas, who included the song on his *Magia* album. By the middle of the decade, covers of Brown's tunes were garnering prodigious amounts of radio play on Bahian and northeastern radio stations. He was a part of Caetano Veloso's band in the late 1980s, playing on both *Caetano* and *Estrangeiro*. On the latter album, Veloso sang Brown's "Meia-Lua Inteira" (Entire Half Moon), which was used as the theme song for a TV novela and was a big hit in Brazil. Carlinhos also toured with Djavan, João Gilberto, and João Bosco.

But after getting his foot in the door of the Brazilian recording industry, Brown decided to head back home to Candeal. "Because I had received so much, I had to do something in return," he said. Brown started a percussion school for children, and the most musically talented of his students eventually became the band Vai Quem Vem, which would record on several albums with Carlinhos. One of their first appearances was on "Carro Velho" (Old Car), on the album *Os Grãos* by the Paralamas do Sucesso.

In 1992 Brown gained his first major exposure as a recording artist. He appeared on *Bahia Black: Ritual Beating System*, the intriguing group album produced by Bill Laswell that mixed axé music with funk and jazz. The recording focused largely on Carlinhos, featuring five of his songs and teaming him with Olodum and U.S. jazz artists Wayne Shorter and Herbie Hancock (who had created the landmark *Native Dancer* album two decades earlier with Milton Nascimento).

Sérgio Mendes's Grammy-winning *Brasileiro*, released later the same year, also showcased Brown's talent and reached an even wider global audience. Carlinhos and Vai Quem Vem provided the rhythmic underpinnings of *Brasileiro*, an innovative fusion of Rio samba, Bahian axé music, funk, and MPB. Brown wrote and contributed lead vocals to five of the album's songs, which ranged stylistically across the mixture of baião and samba-reggae in "Magalenha," the ijexá rhythm and pop-jazzy chorus of "Barbaré," and the intertwining of samba-reggae and merengue in "Magano." Another interesting sonic adventure was the Bahian-style rap song "What Is This?" composed and sung by Vai Quem Vem's Carmen Alice, with hip-hop rhythms played on berimbau and surdos.

At this time, the always hyperactive Carlinhos was also developing another musical entity—Timbalada, a group that began with about thirty musicians and grew to include a few hundred. In 1993 Timbalada released their debut album, *Timbalada*, co-produced by Carlinhos and Wesley Rangel. It included several Brown tunes, his arrangements, and waves of surging axé music rhythms propelled by *timbau* drums (similar to the pagode tan-tan), surdos, and percussion. Most songs featured vocalists Patrícia Gomes, Xexéu, or Augusto Conceição engaging in call-and-response vocals with a male chorus singing in unison. The beautiful northeastern-style ballad "Filha da Mãe" (Mother's Daughter) featured a special guest on pandeiro: Brown's former teacher, Mestre Pintado do Bongô.

The following year, the bloco performed its songs with rousing energy in Salvador's Carnaval. The upper bodies of its musicians (including singer Patrícia's bare breasts) were painted with white dashes, dots, and spirals that recalled the art of Keith Haring, the group's drums were decorated with bright colors, and Carlinhos roamed the percussion section, attracting attention with his unruly dreadlocks, nose rings, and omnipresent sunglasses. Timbalada's next album, *Cada Cabeça É Um Mundo* (Every Head Is a World), again featured a riot of thundering rhythms, but the overall sound was more polished and was augmented by a prominent horn section. Several songs had Caribbean or northeastern elements; one of the most unusual was "Convênio com Cristo" (Pact with Christ), which mixed berimbau and percussive effects with the singing of *repentista* Bule-Bule.

Around this time Brown also started to collaborate with Marisa Monte, whose outstanding albums in the mid-1990s featured several of his songs. Monte's *Cor de Rosa e Carvão* (Rose and Charcoal) in 1994 included "Maria de Verdade" and "Segue o Seco" by Brown and "Na Estrada" by Brown, Monte, and Nando Reis. *A Great Noise*, released two years later, included Brown's "Arrepio," "Magamalabares," and "Maraçá," as well as a live version of "Segue o Seco."

In 1996 Carlinhos released his first solo album, *Alfagamabetizado* (AlphaGammaBeta-ized), a singular effort that smoothly combines axé music drumming, northeastern rhythms, 1970s-type funk, bossa nova, and jazz fusion sonorities. Wally Badarou and Arto Lindsay produced *Alfa*, recorded in Salvador, Paris, and Rio. One can see the progression from Brown's earlier work with Timbalada and the *Bahia Black* collaboration, but overall *Alfa* is a distinctive effort that sounds quite unlike anything previously recorded in Bahia, or Brazil for that matter.

The dense rhythms in the Timbalada style shake the earth in tunes like "O Bode" and "Bog La Bag," but *Alfa* also contains soft ballads, acoustic guitar, cellos, violins, and strange ambient noises. In "Angel's Robot List," Alexandra Theodoropoulou ethereally recites the Greek alphabet while Kouider Berkane idly warms up on violin and dozens of surdos are dragged screeching across a floor. In "Pandeiro-deiro" Brown delivers embolada vocals (which sound like rap to North American ears) atop a driving beat and electric guitar. Brown is joined in "Quixabeira" by Gal Costa, Gilberto Gil, Maria Bethânia, and Caetano Veloso, who add beautiful vocal harmonizing atop a public domain samba from Bahia's Recôncavo region, performed by a legion of Candeal percussionists and flavored with Maeka Munan's fluid electric guitar. It is the only composition on the album not written by Brown.

On *Alfa*, Carlinhos handles lead vocals and arrangements and plays guitar and a wide variety of percussion instruments. He is backed by an abundance of talented guest artists, such as singer Marisa Monte, guitarist Roseval Evangelista, trombonist Sérgio Trombone, saxophonists Rowney Scott and Leo Gandelman, and noteworthy African artists like bassist N'Doumbe Djengue, accordion player Cadah Mustapha, and drummer Mokhtar Samba. *Alfa* is a remarkable work, with its excellent musicianship, dense yet subtle textures, and smooth melding of axé music and mellow ballads.

Since *Alfa*, Carlinhos has continued working with the nonprofit Pracatum Music School, which he founded in the Candeal neighborhood (Pracatum has won UNESCO recognition), released crossover albums that incorporated salsa and electronic textures (*Carlinhos Brown É Carlito Marrón* and *Candyall Beat*), and co-created the mellow, melodic, well-received *Tribalistas* album with Marisa Monte and Arnaldo Antunes in 2002.

Brown's view of life and art is eclectic, all-embracing. He credited the bloco afro Ilê Aiyê as "the one that opened the road for all the others, but I was never in favor of their racial approach. I cannot admit this separation of blacks and whites. We have to look for understanding. We're all human beings. People need to go back to the basics, to communicate. That's why we need the drums, our first language. If everybody stopped trying to communicate through different languages, they would find in the drums the rhythm of life, the universal language, the *pulse*."

Carlinhos Brown's philosophical vision is more cosmic than that of the typical musician, but his open-minded musical approach is characteristically baiano. Salvador receives the influences of all continents, infuses them with its own special swing, and sends them back out to the world.

NORTH BY NORTHEAST

7

Today, many miles away
In a sad solitude
I wait for the rain to fall again
For me to return to my sertão

Luiz Gonzaga and Humberto
Teixeira, "Asa Branca"

During the 1940s the most popular music in Brazil consisted largely of either samba-canção songs or imported genres—tangos, boleros, fox-trots, and waltzes. The accordionist Luiz Gonzaga changed all that when he achieved national commercial success late in the decade with two singles that pulsed with boisterous northeastern rhythms and were charged with a raw poignancy—"Baião" and "Asa Branca."

Gonzaga sang stories about Brazil's Northeast over accordion riffs that were long and melancholy on slow tunes or festive and tumbling over each other on dance numbers. His songs captured the imagination of the country. "Asa Branca" has a haunting melody and lyrics that describe a disastrous drought in the *sertão*, the vast arid interior of northeastern Brazil. The song's title refers to a type of pigeon that, according to local belief, is the last bird to abandon the sertão during droughts. "Asa Branca" became an unofficial anthem of the Northeast and has been covered by innumerable artists, including Elis Regina, Caetano Veloso, Lulu Santos, Sivuca, Hermeto Pascoal, and Baden Powell.

Gonzaga helped introduce Brazil to the sounds and culture of its Northeast—an area that is rich in folklore and possesses a remarkable musical tradition. It is a region that is quite different from the cosmopolitan urban centers of Rio and São Paulo to the south; in many ways the Northeast is like another country. The region

▲ Luiz Gonzaga in his trademark outfit. *(Courtesy of BMG.)*

has nearly forty million inhabitants, living in Salvador, Recife, Fortaleza, and other cities on the lush coast, and in towns and farms in the sertão.

THE SERTÃO

Brazil's Northeast is divided by Brazilian geographers into three principal geographical zones. Bordering the coast is the *zona da mata*, a lush area once covered by Atlantic rainforest (*mata atlântica*) that is well suited to sugarcane fields and cocoa tree groves. Just inland from that is the *agreste*, which receives less rainfall but is still good for farmland. And the sertão is the hot, dry interior—an area that covers some 1.5 million square kilometers.

The sertão has a mostly poor, often illiterate population who tend their own small plots of land or work for powerful landowners who rule their communities in a feudal manner. Much of this drought-stricken hinterland is covered by a thorny, dense brush called *caatinga*. Cowherds (vaqueiros)

must wear head-to-foot leather to protect themselves from the spines and barbs of the caatinga and often cover their horses' chests with cowhide as well. In the sertão, crops are picked by hand, day-to-day existence is hard, and life expectancy is short. Machismo is strong there, and blood feuds last for decades. *Sertanejos* (those who live in the sertão) are stoic, passionate, and given to mysticism. Many are strongly religious, attending Catholic church and praying to myriad saints. They are also a generous people. Whether they live in a big ranch house or a dirt-floored hovel, sertanejos are renowned for their warmth and hospitality. It is almost impossible to visit a home there and not be asked to dinner or offered a place to sleep if the hour is late.

Early in the twentieth century, some poor sertanejos took to banditry rather than accept the humble misery that was their lot; they would raid towns and farms, then escape on horseback to hiding places in dense tangles of caatinga in the rugged sertão. One such *cangaceiro* (outlaw) was the legendary Lampião (1898–1938), famed for his ruthlessness, sadistic excesses, and fighting skills, and for his courage, generosity, and musical ability. He sang and played the accordion well and often danced all night at parties. According to legend, he and his band of outlaws popularized the *xaxado*, a men's dance. He is revered today by many sertanejos as a bandit-hero and has been the subject of songs, movies, plays, books, and even a TV Globo novela.

Roughly every ten years, the usual January-to-May rains fail to refresh the parched sertão. When this happens, the caatinga shrivels in the tropical sun, rivers dry up, cattle drop dead, and hundreds of thousands of people go hungry. Many relocate to overcrowded refugee shantytowns in the northeastern capitals. Countless others emigrate to Rio and São Paulo in search of food and work. There they toil in factories and construction sites, as maids and as doormen, generally discriminated against because of their strong accents and lack of education. They stay in overcrowded favelas and wait for rain to return to the sertão so they can go home. Northeasterners

▲ Lampião (*third from left, front row*), the bandit hero who was admired by the poor and feared by the rich in the sertão, which he roamed and looted in the 1920s and 1930s, pictured with his gang and (*to his right*) his woman, Maria Bonita. (*Public domain image.*)

in the big southern cities often gather in weekly fairs to eat their own regional specialties, drink cachaça (sugarcane liquor), sell their wares, and dance to the galloping rhythms of earthy, accordion-driven forró (a generic term for dance-oriented northeastern styles).

LUIZ GONZAGA

Luiz Gonzaga (1912–1989) served as a spokesman for the rural Northeast, its history and its culture, singing tales of the sertão to urban audiences in the industrialized, rapidly growing cities of Rio and São Paulo. Born on the Caiçara ranch just outside the small town of Exu in the Pernambuco sertão, Luiz Gonzaga do Nascimento was the son of a farmworker who was well respected in the re-

gion for his accordion playing. Young Luiz was already tilling the fields at age seven, and soon after was traveling with his father to various local dances, parties, and festivals, where he mastered the accordion and other instruments. As a boy, Gonzaga admired the freedom and audacity of the cangaceiros; his idol was Lampião, then in the prime of his outlaw fame.

At age eighteen Luiz fell in love with the daughter of Raimundo Delgado, a wealthy and important man in Exu. But when Gonzaga went to ask for the girl's hand in marriage, her father reacted violently to the budding romance. Raimundo seethed, "A devil that doesn't work, that doesn't have farmland, that has nothing, that only plays the accordion, how is it that he wants to marry?"[1] He added a few racist remarks about Gonzaga's dark skin. Enraged, Luiz left and returned to defend his honor (with a knife, by some accounts). But Raimundo managed to talk him down and later told all to Santana, Gonzaga's mother. Furious, she whipped Luiz until he collapsed onto a stool. Humiliated, he decided to give up his romance and leave for Ceará, where he joined the army.

He remained an enlisted man for nine years, until 1939. Gonzaga played the cornet in the army band and studied accordion with Domingos Ambrósio, who taught him the popular music of the Southeast: polkas, waltzes, and tangos. After leaving the military, Gonzaga moved to Rio and survived by playing his accordion in clubs and bordellos. He got on the radio but did not make much of an impression, until one night a group of Cearense students asked him to play some music from the sertão. So, on Ary Barroso's show, Gonzaga played a *chamego* he had written, "Vira e Mexe" (a chamego, according to Luiz, was a choro with northeastern inflections in the rhythm and harmony).[2] It won first prize, and he was asked by an enthusiastic audience to do an encore. That year (1941) he recorded two 78-rpm singles for RCA and was on his way.

Over the next five years Luiz cut around seventy singles, most of them waltzes, polkas, mazurkas, and chamegos. Then came the chance to bring the musical heritage of his home state to the forefront, when Gonzaga achieved a breakthrough that transformed his career and had a significant impact on Brazilian popular music.

In 1946 Gonzaga recorded the revolutionary "Baião," whose title became the name of a new genre. Written by Gonzaga and Humberto Teixeira, a lawyer from Ceará, the tune exhorts listeners to try the new dance.

> I'm going to show all of you how you dance
>   a baião
> Whoever wants to learn please pay attention

Gonzaga and Teixeira's baião was derived from an older, folkloric baião or baiano, a northeastern circle dance of African origin. In the interior of Pernambuco, this dance would be performed as a prelude to a desafio, a sung poetic contest, between two sertanejo singer-guitarists. The instrumental musical introduction that accompanied the dance came to be called baião or *rojão*.

Gonzaga and Teixeira urbanized the baião, taking its syncopated 2/4 rhythm and expanding it into an entire song form of its own. They added a steady beat from beginning to end, making it easier to dance to. They changed the instrumentation, replacing the guitar with an accordion, and adding a triangle and *zabumba* bass drum. And they introduced a melody that used a natural scale with a raised fourth and flattened seventh, sometimes mixing this with a minor scale.

Some refer to the flat seventh as the *sétima nordestina* (northeastern seventh), and it is usually attributed to African influences, as are the flattened third and flattened fifths or sevenths in North American blues. Other tonal peculiarities of the baião are thought by scholars, such as the conductor Júlio Medaglia, to resemble medieval modes used in Gregorian chant.[3]

Gonzaga had created a vivid new dance music, whose accordion-bass-drum-triangle instrumentation gave it a rocking, earthy sound, akin to Louisiana zydeco. He followed "Baião" with a string of hits—performed by himself as well as others—and within a few years the baião style was heard as often as the samba on the radio throughout Brazil. One Gonzaga-Teixeira success from 1950 was the lively "Paraíba," the name for a person from Paraíba state. The song paid tribute to the courage and stoicism of a wife left behind in the sertão when her man traveled south to find work. It was recorded by many artists in that era and became a standard that was given a great interpretation four decades later by Chico César on his *Aos Vivos* album.

> When the mud turned to stone and the
>   mandacaru cactus dried up
> When the dove became thirsty, beat its
>   wings and left
> It was then that I went away, carrying my
>   pain
> Today I send a hug to you, little one
> Manly Paraíba woman, very macho, yes sir

Around this time, Gonzaga's songwriting partnership with Teixeira ended, when Humberto was

► Gonzaga, with Dominguinhos in the background. *(Photo by Conceição Almeida. Courtesy of BMG.)*

elected a federal congressman and became busy with governmental matters. Luiz had written "Vem Morena" with Zé Dantas, a doctor from Pernambuco, and they continued to collaborate in the 1950s, as Gonzaga's success continued. Besides the baião, Gonzaga popularized the xaxado (the dance favored by Lampião), and *xote* (another very danceable 2/4 rhythm).

Nowadays, much of Gonzaga's music is often referred to as forró, a word that originally meant a party or place to play dance music. Its etymology is the subject of much speculation, but it probably derives from *forrobodó*, a word for revelry or a party that may have been in use as early as 1833, according to folklorist Luis da Câmara Cascudo.[4] Forró came to be used as a generic tag for danceable northeastern styles such as *coco*, xote, and xaxado. According to some, forró refers specifically to a faster, livelier type of baião, introduced by Gonzaga in tunes such as "O Forró de Mané Vito" and "O Forró de Zé Antão."

By the 1960s Gonzaga's songs had fallen out of favor with the critics and the urban public, who were more interested in bossa nova and the new artists emerging from the music festivals. But Luiz's career was revived when he was championed by Gilberto Gil and Caetano Veloso, both of

whom recorded covers of his songs. Veloso startled his hip fans by proclaiming the out-of-style Gonzaga "a genius." Many MPB artists covered his tunes in the following years. "Vem Morena" reappeared in two superb new renditions—by Gil in 1984 and by Gonzaga himself, with Fagner, in 1988.

Late in his life Gonzaga became a musical legend in Brazil, and even more than that for the Northeast. One incident aptly illustrates his almost mythic stature in the region of his youth. In June 1978 a member of the Sampaio clan killed Zito Alencar, the mayor of Exu, reigniting a twenty-year-old war between the two families. Gonzaga, armed only with his accordion, decided to be a peacemaker. He returned to his native city for the first time in almost fifty years and succeeded in calming the tensions there between the Sampaios and the Alencars. It was something perhaps only Gonzaga could have done, for he had now become as famous in the sertão as the idol of his youth, the bandit Lampião.

When Luiz died in 1989, his body lay for two days in an open coffin in the legislative assembly hall of Recife. Thousands came to pay their respects, and all of Brazil mourned his passing. At the vigil, Dom Hélder Câmara, the archbishop of

Olinda and Recife, said, "I have certainty that with so good a soul, with such an understanding of the common people, that Gonzaga was received with a great party there in heaven."[5]

JACKSON DO PANDEIRO

While Luiz Gonzaga brought the rural sounds of the Northeast to the attention of all Brazil, his contemporary Jackson do Pandeiro (José Gomes Filho, 1919–1982) did much to popularize the Northeast's coastal and urban sounds, especially the coco. Jackson is mentioned repeatedly by contemporary Brazilian artists as an important influence. Born in Alagoa Grande in the state of Paraíba, the singer-percussionist played good-time music with an uncanny rhythmic sense. He was a master of the coco, a lively, merry Afro-Brazilian song style and circle dance known to have been present on the northeastern littoral as far back as the eighteenth century. It has a stanza-and-refrain structure and pulls the listener along with a fast tempo and irresistible syncopation. In the coco, singers and dancers form a ring, with solo dancers sometimes inside it, sometimes not. The coco can include the umbigada movement, the navel-touching invitation to the dance.

Singer-songwriter Manezinho Araújo believed that the coco originated in the Palmares quilombo in the backlands of Alagoas in the seventeenth century, from a work song sung by African-Brazilians breaking coconuts on rocks.[6] Its rhythm is typically in 2/4 time and can be maintained by the clapping of hands, the clacking of coconut shells, or with ganzá, pandeiro, and atabaque. Depending on the rhythmic variations and instrumentation, there are many variations: *coco de praia* (beach coco), *coco de roda* (circle-dance coco), *coco de sertão* (sertão coco), and others.

Many of Jackson's biggest hits were recorded in the 1950s and 1960s. They include "Sebastiana," "Forró em Limoeiro" (Forró in Limoeiro), "Cantiga do Sapo" (Song of the Toad), "Um a Um" (One to One), "Vou Gargalhar" (I'm Going to Laugh), and "O Canto da Ema" (Song of the Rhea). Some were interpretations of tunes by Gordurinha, João do Vale, and others. Jackson also co-wrote many of his own successes but registered them in the name of his wife, Almira Castilho. One such tune was the famed "Chiclete com Banana" (Bubblegum with Banana), co-written with Gordurinha and recorded by Jackson in 1959. It is a clever jab at American cultural attitudes, and rather prophetic. The song was covered by many artists in later years and provided the name for a popular Bahian axé music band in the 1980s.

▼ Jackson do Pandeiro. *(Photo by Hugo. Courtesy of Agência JB.)*

> *I'll only put bebop in my samba*
> *When Uncle Sam plays tamborim*
> *When he gets a pandeiro and zabumba*
> *When he learns that samba isn't rumba*
> *Then I'll mix Miami with Copacabana*
> *I'll mix bubblegum with banana*

Besides being a great musician, Jackson was a funny guy and could make audiences laugh at his crazy dance steps and his humorous facial expressions while he sang.[7]

EMBOLADA AND DESAFIO

Jackson was also a master of another important northeastern song form, the embolada, which is structurally quite similar to the coco (indeed, many scholars consider it to be essentially a more sophisticated form of the coco). The embolada is typically accompanied by pandeiros or ganzás. With a rapid tempo and small musical intervals, it rolls on at a breathless pace. Whereas the coco usually tells a simple, intelligible story, the embolada often employs improvised, tongue-twisting lyrics.

The embolada has set refrains that allow the singer to organize his next improvised stanza. Alliterative and hard-to-pronounce words are often used, and the lyrics may be comical, satirical, or descriptive. The tempo is gradually increased until the singer's words are pronounced so fast that they are almost unintelligible: they become *emboladas* (mixed together). Manezinho Araújo (1910–1993), born in Cabo, Pernambuco, was one of the greatest performers of the genre, known as the "king of the embolada" from the 1930s to the 1950s.

An embolada can be sung by a soloist or used by two vocalists for poetic song duels called desafios. Desafios share long improvisations, extended rhyming, and a spirit of bravado with American rap music, yet they are a more demanding poetic form. Such "song challenges" are also present in Venezuela (*porfias*), Argentina (*contrapunto*), Chile (*payas*), Spain, and Portugal, and have been around for centuries.

In public squares in the cities of the Northeast, crowds gather round embolada singers who are engaged in a desafio. Each keeps the rhythm with a pandeiro or a ganzá, as the improvised vocals fly back and forth. Sometimes they accompany themselves with violas, a ten-stringed folk guitar commonly used in regional music.

One singer poses a question, challenge, or insult; the other responds, trying to top his opponent, always in the same rigidly observed poetic form. The words are sung rather flatly, almost in a monotone. Sometimes riddles are posed; Luis da Câmara Cascudo quotes a famous stanza sung by João Izidro as a riddle to his desafio challenger (it rhymes in Portuguese).

To say you were never imprisoned
Is a well-known lie

You spent nine months
In an oppressive prison
A prison with only one entrance
Where was the exit?[8]

Gathered around the singers, the audience admires the verbal dexterity and laughs at the better jokes and insults hurled by the two. Afterward, a hat is passed to collect some coins.

Desafios can last hours or even entire nights. The participants are sometimes illiterate but demonstrate an astonishing capacity for wordplay and a remarkable grasp of regional culture. Their improvisations must follow certain rules, with the number of verses and syllables determined by the poetic form used. For example, the *martelo* has ten syllables per verse, and a *galope* is a martelo with six verses per stanza. Desafios may use the embolada song style as a structure or employ other musical forms.

The singers in the desafio are called repentistas, and they strive to come up with an improvised verse (a repente) that will break the concentration of their opponent and leave him unable to respond. The first repentista who is unable to invent and pronounce a fast response loses the desafio. An example of the repentista style wedded to a modern dance beat is found on Daúde's eponymous 1995 album, in the song "Quatro Meninas" (Four Girls), in which singer Daúde and repentista Miguel Bezerra try to outdo each other in reciting strings of girls' names.

JOÃO DO VALE

While repentistas express themselves through improvised performance, João do Vale worked for decades crafting popular songs that were brought to life in the recording studios by other artists. But for all the many famous tunes João has written, few people in the country know his name. For example, when Brazilians gather to play guitar at someone's house, they sometimes sing a beautiful, mysterious tune called "Na Asa do Vento" (On the Wing of the Wind), which was recorded by Caetano Veloso in 1975. But they probably won't

◄ João do Vale with Gonzaguinha (the son of Luiz Gonzaga).
(Photo by Frederico Mendes. Courtesy of Sony.)

know who wrote it, although they might guess that it was Caetano or maybe—if they're older—Dolores Duran, who sang the intriguing lyrics in 1956.

Love is a bandit
It can even cost you money
It's a flower that has no scent
That all the world wants to smell

João Batista do Vale (1933–1996), born in Pedreiras, Maranhão, co-wrote that song with Luis Vieira and composed hundreds of other recorded tunes, dozens of them standards. A few examples are "Carcará," "Pisa na Fulô" (Step on the Flower), "A Voz do Povo" (The Voice of the People), "Coroné Antonio Bento," and "O Canto da Ema" (The Rhea's Song). João's tunes were covered from the 1950s through the 1970s by artists such as Veloso, Duran, Bethânia, Nara Leão, Ivon Curi, Marlene, Alayde Costa, Tim Maia, Gilberto Gil, and Jackson do Pandeiro.

Although comparatively unknown, João was an important popularizer of northeastern song styles, along with Luiz Gonzaga and Jackson do Pandeiro, as well as a great lyricist. He told the story of his life and of the poor people of Maran-

hão in concise, poignant narratives filled with vivid images and the vernacular of the sertão (a dialect sometimes difficult for urban Brazilians to fathom). He could indulge in earthy good humor—as in the lascivious "Peba na Pimenta" (Armadillo in the Pepper), a playful tune full of lewd double entendres—or meditate lyrically about love and nature, as in "Na Asa do Vento."

In the 1960s João stepped into the limelight for a few years. Early in that decade Zé Keti took him to a hip musician's hangout—the restaurant Zicartola, run by the sambista Cartola and his wife, Zica. João began performing there and was invited to play a role in the 1964 musical theater piece *Opinião*, alongside Keti and Nara Leão. The play was a success, and one of its songs, João's stirring anthem "Carcará," launched Maria Bethânia (who replaced Leão) to fame the next year when she recorded it as a single. "Carcará" was about the *carcará* bird of prey that never goes hungry, even when millions of northeasterners are starving to death in the sertão during one of the region's frequent droughts.

Joao's song "Sina do Caboclo" (Fate of the Mestizo) concisely summarizes the fate of many northeastern men.

*I am a poor mestizo, I earn my living with a
    hoe
What I harvest is divided with he who plants
    nothing
If it continues thus, I will leave my sertão
Even with eyes full of tears and with pain in
    the heart
I will go to Rio to carry mortar for the
    bricklayer*

João did not have a great voice and achieved his success through his songwriting. By the late 1970s he had fallen out of the public eye, but his peers never forgot him. In 1981 several of his musical friends (Tom Jobim, Chico Buarque, Alceu Valença, Fagner, Clara Nunes, and Nara Leão among them) gathered with João to record *João do Vale*, a retrospective of his greatest hits. His hometown of Pedreiras named a street and a school after him. And in 1995 Buarque organized another tribute album, *João Batista do Vale*, in which Buarque, Valença, Edu Lobo, Maria Bethânia, and others interpreted João's classics.

Beside João, Luiz, and Jackson, other important northeastern musicians of their era who sang embolada, coco, baião, frevo, and other regional styles include Beija-flor and Oliveira, Catulo de Paula, Luis Bandeira, Patativa do Assaré, Otacílio and Lourival, Cego Aderaldo, Zé do Norte, Gordurinha, João Pernambuco, Jararaca and Ratinho, Venâncio and Corumba, and Lauro Maia.

NORTHEASTERN MUSICAL TRADITIONS

The history and folklore of the Northeast is kept alive in its music, in the *literatura de cordel* (handbound booklets of folk stories and moral tales in rhymed verse), and in its many processional and dramatic dances. Its culture derives from the usual Brazilian roots of Portugal, Africa, and the native Amerindians. But in the Northeast, this heritage mixed together for centuries in relative isolation, especially in the backlands, far from the cosmopolitan influences of Rio and São Paulo. The Northeast created its own traditions, some of which include archaic traits from Africa or Portugal that no longer exist in their places of origin.

Ancient Iberian musical elements often turn up in folk music from the region. Both Arabic scales (the Moors occupied Portugal for centuries) and medieval modes and harmonies have been noted in many northeastern songs by scholars such as Antonio José Madureira, co-founder of the 1970s group Quinteto Armorial. That band explored northeastern roots in a meticulously elaborated context in albums such as *Do Romance ao Galope Nordestino* (1974). The Northeast's rich musical heritage was also adeptly recapitulated by

▼ Four northeastern troubadours-Xangai, Geraldo Azevedo, Vital Farias, and Elomar-in concert. *(Courtesy of Kuarup.)*

Quinteto Violado in the 1970s and by troubadours Xangai, Elomar, Vital Farias, and Geraldo Azevedo in their 1980s albums *Cantoria* (Song Feast) and *Cantoria 2*.

The Power of Maracatu

One of the Northeast's most important genres is maracatu, an Afro-Brazilian processional dance from Pernambuco that is performed there and in other northeastern cities during Carnaval. In maracatu, participants sing and dance to a heavy, driving, almost trance-inducing rhythm, played usually on alfaias (large, double-headed bass drums), snare drums, chocalhos, and gonguês (bells). Colorfully clad participants parade in what resembles a royal procession of an African nation.[9] A standard-bearer is followed by a "king" and "queen" and other members of the court. Also present is the *dama de passo*, a woman who carries the *calunga* cloth doll, a figure of a black woman dressed in white.

In Recife and Olinda, the type of maracatu practiced is called *maracatu de baque virado*

▼ Maracatu dancers. *(Photo by Chris McGowan.)*

(turned-around beat maracatu), or *maracatu de nação*, and it is associated with Afro-Brazilian religious centers. One of the oldest such organizations is Maracatu Leão Coroado (Crowned-Lion Maracatu), founded in 1863. Other venerable maracatu groups include Nação Elefante, Nação Estrela Brilhante, and Nação Porto Rico. The rhythmic patterns played in maracatu are called toques or baques.

Maracatu groups in rural areas outside of Recife perform *maracatu de baque solto* (loose-beat maracatu), also called *maracatu rural* or *maracatu de orquestra*, a different tradition that incorporates wind instruments. Musicologist John P. Murphy describes maracatu rural: "the vocal music typically consists of composed and improvised verses by two master singers in friendly competition, accompanied by a small brass ensemble and a percussion group consisting of snare drums, metal bell and cuíca that plays a fast rhythm that might remind contemporary listeners of drum 'n' bass."[10]

Maracatu appears often in Brazilian popular music, especially in that of Alceu Valença, Naná Vasconcelos, Lenine, and Mestre Ambrósio. Nação Zumbi is among the groups that have married maracatu's powerful rhythm to rock and hip-hop. Adryana BB (Adryana Barbosa Bezerra) is a singer, songwriter, and guitarist from Recife who incorporates the style in her own music and in 2006 launched the Pernambatuque project—live presentations of maracatu and other traditional Pernambucano music and dance styles. She organized the first maracatu parade for Rio's Carnaval, and was associated with the formation of the award-winning Rio Maracatu group in 1997. "Pernambuco has a lot to be discovered! The rhythmic diversity is immense," she comments. "I believe I'm part of a generation that's going back to basics, and to rootsy instruments."[11]

Congadas, Caboclinhos, and Pífanos

Some scholars think that maracatu may derive from an early form of the Afro-Brazilian processional dances congo and congada. Congos are found in the North and Northeast, while congadas are typical of central and southern Brazil. They derive from a mixture of African, Portuguese, and Spanish practices. Congos feature characters dressed as African royalty and their courts and ministers. Participants enact various scenarios of war and peace, singing their lines to an accompaniment of drums, chocalhos, pandeiros, and guitars.

Caboclinho groups have been active in the Northeast since at least the late nineteenth century. Inspired by the legacy of the Brazilian Indians, caboclinhos parade during Carnaval in Pernambuco, Bahia, Ceará, and other northeastern states. Their performers dress as stylized Indians and dance in the street to the sound of flutes, fifes, and arrows banging on bows. They perform dramatic dances, with assorted characters and a varied choreography that illustrate stories taken from Brazil's colonization era.

Other important exponents of northeastern folkloric music are the fife-and-drum ensembles called *bandas de pífano* (fife bands), which typically perform forró for dance events as well as devotional music for novenas (prayer sessions devoted to saints) and religious processions. The Banda de Pífanos de Caruaru and the Banda de Pífanos Dois Irmãos (led by João do Pife), are two well-known such ensembles, and Carlos Malta has incorporated pífano playing into his jazz and instrumental music.

Music for the Magical Ox

Bumba-meu-boi is a colorful folk drama that revolves around a magical ox. In some cases the ox dies and is resurrected; other times, the ox falls ill and is healed. Full of elaborate costumes and choreography, it is a folk performance identified especially with northeastern states. The earliest known mention of bumba-meu-boi appears in an 1840 publication from Recife.[12] The story[13] often unfolds in the form of toadas and other rural styles, with singing underpinned by lively fifes, fiddles, pandeiros, and *bombo* bass drums, and the rhythmic clacking of *matracas*, pairs of wood blocks

carried by participants who are not in the bateria (drum-and-percussion section).[14]

Bumba-meu-boi is called *boi-de-mamão* in Santa Catarina and *boi-bumbá* in the Amazonian region, and acquires different characteristics in each area. The genre is a part of the repertoire of nationally famous performers such as singer Alcione; she hails from São Luis do Maranhão, which has a rich bumba-meu-boi tradition.

A boi-bumbá folkloric festival takes place every June in the city of Parintins in Amazonas state. It is a big, colorful event that revolves around a competition between two groups (called *bois*), Boi Caprichoso and Boi Garantido, founded in 1913–1914, by most accounts. In recent decades they have grown into large organizations of a few thousand members each. They stage three-hour boi-bumbá performances in the Bumbódromo stadium, which can hold thirty-five thousand spectators. Participants wear costumes that are as extravagant as those of Rio's samba schools and sing toadas that tell the story of the mythical ox. There are parade floats, giant puppets, and a few hundred drummers and percussionists who underpin the music.

The boi-bumbá sound was popularized internationally by the group Carrapicho, which released the song "Tic Tic Tac" in France in the summer of 1996, selling more than one million copies worldwide, according to *Veja* magazine.[15] The single was included in their album *Fiesta de Boi-Bumbá*. Most Brazilians outside the Amazon region heard about Carrapicho for the first time in reports filed by European correspondents.

Frevo: The Boiling Point

Frevo is a musical genre developed in the Northeast that has become an important part of Brazilian popular music and a Carnaval mainstay in states like Bahia, Ceará, and Pernambuco. Frevo derived its name from the verb *ferver*, which means to boil, and originated in the first decade of the twentieth century. Zuzinha (Captain José Lourenço da Silva, 1889–1952), the director of the Pernambuco Military Brigade band, is usually credited with transforming the polka-marcha into frevo by heightening the syncopation, increasing the tempo, and creating a vigorous new form that lent itself well to instrumental improvisation.[16] Some accounts place its invention in 1909, while others believe frevo may have been performed in Recife's Carnaval as early as 1907.[17] "Frevo is full of nuances," singer-songwriter Alceu Valença told us. "It was the most sophisticated invention of the Pernambucano people."[18]

Nelson Ferreira (1902–1976) helped popularize the genre on national radio with his frevo songwriting. His "Não Puxa Maroca" won a competition in 1928 and a year later was recorded by the Orquestra Victor Brasileira, arranged by the famed Pixinguinha, a master of the samba and choro genres; Ferreira composed various frevo hits over the next three decades and directed a radio orchestra in Recife for many years. Pixinguinha also popularized frevo by directing the recording of several instrumental frevos by the group Os Diabos do Céu.

Frevo-canção was a commercial song version of frevo that appeared in the 1930s.[19] Capiba (Lourenço da Fonseca Barbosa, 1904–1997) was a Recife composer who did well with the new style and had songs turned into national hits by singers Mário Reis, Francisco Alves, and other popular artists.

Frevo was the music of choice for Dodô and Osmar, who introduced the trio elétrico to the Bahian Carnaval in the 1950s (see Chapter Six). It has been further popularized nationally by Moraes Moreira, Alceu Valença, and Elba Ramalho. During Carnaval in Recife, the frevo dance is performed by brightly costumed dancers called passistas, who perform energetic, complicated steps (incorporating high leaps) and carry small shiny parasols. Frevo de rua is a breakneck instrumental form, performed by brass ensembles, percussion, and wind instruments, while frevo de bloco is a melodic style sung by female choruses and accompanied by an orquestra de pau e corda (string and wind orchestra).

Frevo is one of the specialties of Antônio Nóbrega, a Quinteto Armorial alumnus who is a unique guardian of northeastern culture. Born in Recife in 1952, Nóbrega is a singer, fiddler, actor, dancer, and acrobat whose energetic one-man theatrical shows move fluidly between different art forms, both erudite and popular. Nóbrega was a classical violinist before joining Quinteto Armorial, in which he played rabeca (fiddle) and violin. He emulated masters of traditional forms, such as Capitão Antonio Pereira, a famous performer of the bumba-meu-boi dance. Nóbrega began performing his syncretic presentations in 1976, bringing together his many talents—telling stories, frevo dancing, and creating mythical characters as he journeyed through northeastern traditions. His performance Lunário Perpétuo was released on DVD by Trama in 2003.

Frevo, maracatu, bumba-meu-boi, embolada, and the other traditions mentioned above provided the roots for contemporary musicians who would mix their northeastern culture with modern influences and instruments to add a fresh new sound to Brazilian popular music.

THE NORTHEASTERN WAVE

At the beginning of the 1970s, a new and more cosmopolitan generation of singers and musicians swept down to Rio from Fortaleza, Recife, and other points close to the equator. Inspired by bossa, rock, and Tropicália, this generation of northeastern artists added keyboards, electric guitars, pop arrangements, and other influences to baião, xote, maracatu, and embolada. Among these musicians were Alceu Valença, Geraldo Azevedo, Fagner, Elba Ramalho, Zé Ramalho, Belchior, Amelinha, and Ednardo. "After bossa nova and Tropicália, there was a strong northeastern movement. It didn't have a name, but I think it was as important," recalled singer-songwriter Geraldo Azevedo.[20]

Alceu Valença

Alceu Valença was one of the key figures in the northeastern musical invasion. Some music critics have called his kinetic style forrock, to describe

► Alceu Valença recording with his hero, Jackson do Pandeiro. *(Photo by Ronaldo Theobald. Courtesy of Agência JB.)*

Alceu's driving mixtures of forró and embolada with electric guitar and drums. On stage, Alceu often takes on a trickster's persona and dresses as a court jester. His visceral, imaginative music and theatrical presentations have made him a popular MPB performer in Brazil and overseas.

Alceu was born in 1946 to a middle-class family in São Bento do Una, a small village in Pernambuco located between the sertão and the agreste. His father was a farmer, lawyer, and politician. Alceu absorbed the unrecorded but vital music played by local groups and troubadours, and viewed the "street theater" of bumba-meu-boi and *chegança*. He also had a musical family. "My grandfather played guitar," Alceu told us. "He was more or less a repentista and influenced me with the sonority of the region. He passed this taste for popular music to me, and then on the coast I observed the black culture."[21]

At age nine, Alceu moved with his family to Recife, the capital of Pernambuco, and five years later he began to play guitar. "In the big city, Recife, a million folkloric things passed by on my street, Rua dos Palmares. But on the radio they didn't play that kind of music. What they played came from Rio, as well as international music." Valença was heavily influenced musically by Luiz Gonzaga and Jackson do Pandeiro; he absorbed

Jackson's clownish spirit and would later record cocos in his style. And two foreign singers made a deep impact on the young Valença: Ray Charles and Elvis Presley.

Alceu's career began in Recife, where he liked to play the northeastern music that was out of fashion with his well-off peers. "The middle class was ashamed of the baião," he recalled. "They wanted what was imported, canned." Valença attended college and obtained a law degree but was unenthusiastic about entering the legal profession. He made the obligatory pop musician's journey to Rio in 1970 and began to enter his songs in the music festivals. In 1972 he and Geraldo Azevedo recorded an album together, with Rogério Duprat (who had often worked with the Tropicalistas) handling the orchestration. Then Alceu made his solo debut with *Molhado de Suor* (Wet with Sweat) in 1974, chosen by critics as one of the year's top three albums. Alceu's spirited blend of blues, rock, and northeastern styles began to win great acclaim. His 1978 rock-embolada "Agalopado" displayed the vivid romanticism of his lyrics.

I sing the pain, the love, the disillusion
And the infinite sadness of lovers
Don Quixote free of Cervantes
I discover that the windmills are real

▲ Alceu Valença in concert.

Between beasts, owls, jackals
I turn to stone in the middle of the road
I turn into a rose, path of spines
I ignite these glacial times

In 1982 came perhaps his finest work to date, *Cavalo de Pau* (Stick Horse), and an appearance at the Montreux Jazz Festival in Switzerland.

Mixing Luiz Gonzaga and Elvis Presley, maracatu with synthesizers, coco with electric guitar, Alceu concocts exhilarating musical blends. Atop them, he sings vivid lyrics in which he seeks to create what he describes as "a hybrid language, urban and rural." In his concerts, he strives for an "almost operatic" climate in which he improvises a great deal and assumes many roles. "I have the clown side and the more cool side," he reflected. "I have various persons inside me, faces, masks, and my music is this—frevo to maracatu to something totally romantic."

Geraldo Azevedo

Another key figure in the "northeastern wave" was Alceu's partner on his first album, singer-song-writer Geraldo Azevedo. His light, clear songs center on his voice and guitar, with lyrics evoking the beaches, jangadas, and coconut trees of the northeastern coast. Azevedo bases his songs on styles such as toada, xote, and reggae, which he augments with bossa vocal influences and modern arrangements. The result is suave, carefully constructed music that is gentle, romantic, and reflective.

Born in 1945 in Petrolina, Pernambuco, on the banks of the São Francisco River, Geraldo grew up in a musical household where everyone played instruments or sang. "The folklore of the region—maracatu, coco, repentistas—it's in all of us without our perceiving it," he remarked. As a teenager, he listened to Luiz Gonzaga and Jackson do Pandeiro, as well as such diverse musicians as Johann Sebastian Bach, classical guitarist Andrés Segovia, bossa guitarist Baden Powell, and romantic crooner Nelson Gonçalves. But it was the bossa nova singer João Gilberto who inspired Geraldo to become a professional musician. "He made me more serious about looking into harmony. We didn't have those [bossa nova] harmonies in Petrolina."[22]

At eighteen Azevedo traveled to Recife to attend college, and while there he performed with the members of Grupo Construção, which included Naná Vasconcelos, Teca Calazans, and Paulo Guimarães. Five years later, in 1968, he moved to Rio and formed the group Quarteto Livre (Free Quartet) with Vasconcelos and others to back up singer-songwriter Geraldo Vandré, the aforementioned hero of the 1960s song festivals who sang protest lyrics against social problems and the dictatorship.

Then the infamous Institutional Act No. 5 clamped down hard on dissent and made it impossible for Vandré and Quarteto Livre to record. Vandré left the country and Azevedo went to prison. Azevedo was not politically militant, but his friendship with loudly dissenting musicians and artists caused him to be seized clandestinely and placed under arrest in 1969. When he came out of prison after forty-one days, he felt depressed and beaten down and almost gave up music for good. The next year was a bleak year for Azevedo, but near its end he re-encountered Alceu Valença, who gave Geraldo "a force, a strong push."²³

Azevedo made his debut in 1972 with the aforementioned *Alceu Valença e Geraldo Azevedo*, which included one of his most memorable songs, the haunting "Novena," a toada written with Marcus Vinícius. In this song Azevedo poetically evoked the fervent Catholicism of his childhood.

While the family prays
Someone follows the novena into the chasm

▼ Geraldo Azevedo. *(Photo by Livio Campos. Courtesy of BMG.)*

Of owed prayers
Of the whisper of an agony without end

Placing songs on numerous television novelas over the next few years brought him great attention, as it did Alceu. In 1976 he released his first solo album, *Geraldo Azevedo*, which included the beautiful and melancholy Azevedo-Valença tune "Caravan."

Life is a gypsy woman
It's a caravan
It's a stone of ice in the sun
Thaw your eyes
They are alone in a sea of clear water

Since then Azevedo has recorded many albums that show off his evocative songwriting, including *Bicho de Sete Cabeças* (Seven-Headed Animal), *De Outra Maneira* (Another Way), and *Eterno Presente* (Eternal Present).

Elba Ramalho

Born in 1951 in Conceição do Piancó, Paraíba, Elba Ramalho is one of the foremost vocalists to come from the Northeast. She is also an actress who has appeared in plays such as *Lampião no Inferno* (directed by Azevedo) and in the Ruy Guerra film *Ópera do Malandro*. Elba was a national-class handball player, a drummer in an all-girl rock band, and a sociology student before her stage acting earned her an invitation to perform with Quinteto Violado in Rio. There, she also was a backup singer for Alceu Valença and made further theatrical appearances before launching her first album on CBS in 1979, *Ave de Prata* (Silver Bird). With her ability to interpret a wide range of northeastern styles, her high-energy performing style, and her flamboyant, theatrical concerts, she soon became a national star. Her popularity soared in 1984 with the album *Do Jeito Que a Gente Gosta* (The Way We Like It), with its infectious forrós and maracatus, and the biting, politicized repentista-style track "Nordeste Independente" (An Independent

▲ Elba Ramalho. *(Photo by Livio Campos. Courtesy of PolyGram.)*

ings, northeastern flavors, and esoteric lyrical imagery in his own singular pop music hybrid.

The so-called Pessoal do Ceará (People of Ceará) included Fagner, Ednardo, Belchior, and Amelinha, all of whom began their musical careers in Fortaleza, the capital of Ceará state. Raimundo Fagner (born in 1950 in Orós, Ceará) has ventured far into commercial pop at times but also has been an excellent interpreter of local styles, especially on his albums in the 1970s and in later works such as the 1988 release *Gonzagão & Fagner*. Other noteworthy northeastern musicians of the late twentieth century included singers Castanha and Caju, accordion virtuosos Baú dos 8 Baixos and Pinto do Acordeon, producer and flutist Zé da Flauta, Trio Nordestino, singer-songwriter Nando Cordel, and vocalists Genival Lacerda, Anastácia, Jorge de Altinho, Clemilda, and Amelinha.

THE NORTHEAST: NEW GENERATIONS

Chico César and Zeca Baleiro are two contemporary artists who have added to the musical achievements of Valença, Azevedo, and their peers from the Northeast. Chico's songs have been recorded by many MPB artists; he established his recording career with *Aos Vivos* (1995) and *Cuscuz Clã* (1996). Chico (a.k.a. Francisco César Gonçalves) was born in 1964 in Catolé do Rocha, a town of twelve thousand inhabitants located in the sertão of Paraíba state. He drew attention with bright, heavily embroidered clothes and a shock of hair that springs straight up from an otherwise shaved head. But it was his music that won over the public. Chico has a high, expressive voice and writes powerful, well-crafted songs. His lyrics at times resemble kaleidoscopic collages; they explore personal and profound themes with clever wordplay and verbal invention. He fuses diverse musical elements in ways that seem utterly natural and harmonious: his work integrates MPB, reggae, bossa, soca, and jazz with reisado, carimbó, embolada, and repente. "Mulher Eu Sei" (I Know Woman), "À Primeira Vista" (At First Sight), and "Mama

Northeast). In subsequent years Elba expanded her repertoire, adding Caribbean and other new rhythms to her song list, and also enlarged the range of northeastern music with her instrumental and vocal arrangements.

More of the Northeastern Wave

Along with Elba and the late Gonzaga, Dominguinhos has been one of the top *forrozeiros* (forró makers) of Brazil in recent years. Born in 1941 in Garanhuns, Pernambuco, Dominguinhos has written standards such as "Só Quero um Xodó" and is one of Brazil's greatest accordionists. He has made numerous appearances on other artists' albums (including many of Luiz Gonzaga's) when the perfect accordion touch was required.

Also important in the 1970s northeastern wave were singer-songwriters Marcus Vinícius and Zé Ramalho. Vinícius has been described as "a popular composer of the vanguard." His sophisticated music is a meeting of northeastern roots with modern classical music and other influences. Zé Ramalho combines repentista poetry, Jovem Guarda and Beatles influences, Dylanesque styl-

África" (Mother Africa) are some of his most popular songs.

Chico's old songwriter partner Zeca Baleiro (José Ribamar Coelho Santos) was born in 1966 in Arari, Maranhão, not far from the hometown of João do Vale. As young musicians, Baleiro and César wrote songs and performed at clubs together in São Paulo. Baleiro has reached a wide audience with his deep, raspy vocals, lyrics laden with irony and subtle humor, and a compelling fusion of reggae and rock with embolada and northeastern sounds. Two successful early albums for Baleiro were *Por Onde Andará Stephen Fry* (1997) and *Vô Imbolá* (1999). His 2003 collaboration with Fagner, *Raimundo Fagner e Zeca Baleiro*, is especially noteworthy.

Updating Pernambuco: Mangue Beat and Mestre Ambrósio

Chico Science (Francisco de Assis França, 1966–1996) was an innovative artist from Recife whose life was cut short by an automobile accident. He and his band Nação Zumbi (Zumbi Nation) and the group Mundo Livre S/A started the mangue beat movement (originally "mangue bit," referring to the Portuguese word for mangrove and to the computer bit). They sought a fusion of local culture with high technology and foreign influences; their key image was a parabolic antenna rooted in the tideland mud, picking up signals from around the planet. Musically, they primarily mixed together maracatu and embolada from Recife with rock, especially heavy metal and hard rock, and hip-hop. The result was a harsh and aggressive sound, quite different from the melodious MPB songs incorporating rock that came from artists like Alceu Valença or Gilberto Gil.

Chico Science and Nação Zumbi's mangue beat music debuted on *Da Lama ao Caos* (From Mud to Chaos) in 1994. They followed that with 1996's *Afrociberdelia*, an album their fans consider their masterpiece. It takes its name from the words Africa, cybernetics, and psychedelia. The lyrics are written by Chico, who shares credit on the music-writing side with the rest of the band. *Afrociberdelia* takes Recife headlong into acid jazz, heavy metal, and cyber culture. In most of the songs, booming maracatu rhythms on alfaia drums bolster raging electric guitars and monotone embolada-style vocals growled out by Chico. There are strange looping effects, and tracks embellished by baião and ciranda, rap and funk, psychedelic guitar, and lounge music. Chico's life ended later that year, when his car struck a pole on a road near Olinda. Nação Zumbi carried on the mangue beat tradition after Chico's death, with albums such as *Fome de Tudo* in 2007.

Mestre Ambrósio has taken a different approach to upgrading Pernambucan sounds and has done it with attitude and embellishment, while sticking mostly to traditional instruments and genres. The group took its name from the master of ceremonies in the folk drama called *cavalo-marinho*, practiced in Pernambuco and nearby northeastern states. The rabeca (fiddle) is the lead melodic instrument for cavalo-marinho, which typically features baiano as its dance music, according to musicologist Larry Crook (as mentioned earlier, Luiz Gonzaga drew on the baiano to create the baião).[24] Mestre Ambrósio was founded in 1992 by Siba (Sergio Veloso), who plays rabeca and guitar. Hélder Vasconcelos handles the *sanfona* for the sextet, and five of the members pitch in with drums or percussion. The band explores the rich musical traditions of Pernambuco, including cavalo-marinho, maracatu, coco, and forró, and adds electric guitar (occasionally rather psychedelic in feel) and contemporary seasoning (Lenine co-produced their first album, and Suba their second). According to Crook, Mestre Ambrósio wields a "pan-northeastern percussion lineup (zambumba, triangle, pandeiro, reco-reco, agogô)" and "launched a type of forró that had never been popularized commercially: *forró de rabeca*."[25]

Mestre Ambrósio fuses Pernambuco's rural folk styles and plays them with the intensity of rock and roll. In reference to its urban flavor, the group's music has also been called *forró pé-de-calçada* (sidewalk forró), which alludes to the designation of *forró pé-de-serra* (foothill forró) for the

◄ Mestre Ambrósio.
(Photo by Mauro Ferreira.
Courtesy of Biscoito Fino.)

style played in rural areas. This was a nickname bestowed on the band by the legendary Tavares da Gaita, a composer-percussionist-harmonica player from Caruaru, Pernambuco.[26] One of Mestre Ambrósio's best albums to date is *Fuá na Casa do Cabral*, from 1999. Eight years later the group's founder, Siba, released *Toda Vez Que Eu Dou Um Passo/O Mundo Sai Do Lugar*, his second album with the group Fuloresta, a work that was yet another imaginative reworking of traditional idioms from Pernambuco.

Several other noteworthy contemporary artists are also updating traditional styles from Pernambuco and the Northeast. Silvério Pessoa, an ardent fan of Jackson do Pandeiro, founded Cascabulho in 1994; the band fuses electric rock instruments, northeastern percussion, and regional styles in what has been described as *mangue forró*.[27] Cabruêra, from Paraíba, brings together rock, funk, coco, ciranda, repente, and maracatu, while employing idiosyncratic embellishments such as leader Arthur Pessoa's "ballpoint guitar" (guitar picked with a ballpoint pen). Recife's Mundo Livre S/A, founded by Fred 04 (Fred Montenegro) presents mangue beat sounds with politically engaged lyrics.[28] Singer-songwriter Otto is also

from Pernambuco and is a former percussionist of Nação Zumbi and Mundo Livre S/A; he has released several well-regarded solo albums, in which he blends maracatu, repente, and samba with drum 'n' bass and rap.

THE NORTH: RHYTHMS OF AMAZONIA

The western edge of Maranhão state borders Brazil's northern region, a vast area that is hot and humid and includes much of the Amazon rainforest. Pará and Amazonas are the two biggest states in the North, and each would make a good-sized nation. Roraima and Amapá lie above the equator, and Acre and Rondônia border Peru and Bolivia, respectively. The North is a long way from Brazil's media and financial centers like Rio de Janeiro and São Paulo, and is the most culturally distinctive part of the country. The indigenous peoples of the Amazon Basin have their own music, which has never been widely available as commercial recorded music, in or outside of Brazil.

The popular and folk music of the North is quite varied, and includes the styles carimbó, *siriá*, *marabaixo*, *lundu marajoara*, guitarrada (and lambada), boi-bumbá (see the previous bumba-meu-boi section), *calípso* (not be confused with Trinidad's calypso), and technobrega. Paraense music has maintained itself outside Brazil's mainstream recording industry and achieved a home-grown commercial boom during the digital age, as we shall see.

Some of the North's most intense musical activity has taken place recently in Belém, the capital of Pará. It is a bustling port city located just downstream from where the huge Tocantins River converges with the even mightier Amazon, as both rivers flow into the Atlantic Ocean. Marajó Island, around which the estuaries of the Tocantins and Amazon flow as they reach their ocean destination, is the size of Switzerland. Marajó and the environs of Belém are the home of carimbó, a lively Afro-Brazilian song-and-dance form of uncertain origin that dates back at least to the beginning of the twentieth century, perhaps much earlier.[29] It has also made its way to São Luis, in nearby Maranhão state.

Carimbó's fast-tempo 2/4 meter is typically anchored by two carimbó drums, hollowed-out tree-trunk sections covered with deer skin,[30] and accompanied by percussion, wind, and string instruments. The carimbó dance features barefoot dancers (the women wear long, colorful skirts) who form a circle and take solo turns in the center of the group. At one point, a woman drops her handkerchief to the floor and her partner must pick it up with just his mouth.

In recent decades the singer-songwriter Mestre Verequete (Augusto Gomes Rodrigues), born in 1916 in Bragança, has been the leading exponent of traditional carimbó. His group Uirapuru performs the style with a lineup of guitar, flute, clarinet, banjo, and percussion. Other important carimbó musicians include singer-songwriter Pinduca and composer and multi-instrumentalist Mestre Curica (who favors the banjo and was an arranger for Uirapuru). Singers Fafá de Belém and Nazaré Pereira helped popularize the genre nationally and internationally. Carimbó is a component of guitarrada, which gained world fame initially under the moniker of lambada.

The Birth of Lambada

Pará state receives musical influences from nearby countries in the north of South America and in the Caribbean; for example, *cumbia* and *merengue* are two styles that have long been locally popular. Guitarist Mestre Vieira (Joaquim de Lima Vieira, born in 1934) is a Paraense musician who blended the two foreign rhythms with carimbó in the 1970s. He grew up in the riverbank town of Barcarena, outside Belém, and played regional music and choro (the latter on mandolin) before creating his own new sound. Vieira brought together elements of merengue, cumbia, and carimbó, added influences from choro and the simple '60s rock of Jovem Guarda (the movement led by Roberto Carlos and Erasmo Carlos), and incorporated a rock-and-roll format of electric guitar, bass, drums, and voice.[31] The result was a new style that is now called guitarrada, which emphasized his upbeat electric guitar solos with a Caribbean lilt and Brazilian swing. Vieira created the sound in the mid-1970s and first recorded it on the album *Lambada das Quebradas*, released in 1978. As one can deduce, the style was initially called lambada, a name that has now fallen out of favor.

According to bassist Bruno Rabelo of the group Cravo Carbono, Vieira's guitar phrasing was influenced by both choro and the percussion and wind instruments of carimbó. Cravo Carbono is a contemporary group from Belém that incorporates guitarrada into its sound. Its vocalist-lyricist Lázaro Magalhães told us that guitarrada adapted foreign rhythms for local tastes, "in the best cannibalistic sense." He feels that Vieira's guitar work is so influential that "in Brazil today there exist two schools of original electric-guitar technique" with distinctive accents. One is the guitarrada of Pará and the other the *guitarra baiana* (Bahian electric guitar) of Dodô and Osmar, popularized by the trio elétrico groups.[32]

Vieira's compositions were called lambadas, which was a fluid label from the start. Around the same time that Vieira was creating his style, disc jockey Haroldo Caraciolo of Belém's Clube AM station was programming music with Caribbean rhythms and calling all of it "lambada," which in Portuguese means "slap" or "shot of cachaça."[33]

In any event, the instrumental lambada played by Vieira began to catch on and be transformed by other local musicians. Aldo Sena played the style on his *Populares de Igarapé-Miri* in 1981, and popular carimbó composer Pinduca (Aurino Quirino Gonçalves) also performed lambadas and later claimed to have invented the new style. Lambada's popularity grew quickly and spread in Belém through *festas de aparelhagem*—"sound parties" in which DJs would set up enormous sound systems for one-night dances—and by radio.

A lambada dance appeared: it was also a new hybrid, mixing elements of the merengue, maxixe, samba, and forró dances. In it, couples press tightly together, the right thigh of each between the other's legs, and dip and swirl sensually. The new rhythm and dance spread to Manaus, the capital of Amazonas state, and Salvador, and eventually to Fortaleza, where it is said that the dance grew more erotic. In the late 1980s it hit São Paulo, where numerous dance clubs called *lambaterias* opened.

Lambada picked up more influences, including salsa and *zouk*; it was now a vehicle of songs as well as instrumental music; and its soloing spread from guitar to sax and keyboards. Teixeira de Manaus was a popular saxophonist from the state of Amazonas who was recording lambadas in the early 1980s. In that decade saxophonist Manezinho do Sax and vocalists Beto Barbosa, Betto Douglas, Carlos Santos, Alípio Martins, Márcia Rodrigues, and Márcia Ferreira were successful lambada performers from Pará. Ferreira had a hit with "Chorando Se Foi," which would later gain global fame as "Lambada," performed by Kaoma.

Lambada was about to expand its audience beyond the North and Northeast of Brazil. It would conquer the world, if only for a short time.

The Lambada Boom and Scandal

In 1989 the daring, sexy lambada dance emerged in the nightclubs of Europe. On the continent that year, especially in France and Germany, lambada seemed the essence of tropical passion. The international lambada fad was ignited through marketing by two French music entrepreneurs named Jean Karakos and Olivier Lorsac (Olivier

Fafá de Belém

Early on, lambada had a booster in Fafá de Belém (Maria de Fátima Palha de Figueiredo), who has long been a sort of cultural ambassador from Brazil's North to the rest of the country. Born in 1957, she has a strong, appealing voice with which she interprets a wide variety of popular songs, with a focus on romantic ballads. But her regionality has set her apart; she was probably the first major MPB star to record carimbó (an example can be found on *Tamba-Tajá* in 1976) and lambada (*Atrevida*, from 1986, has a lambada medley)

▶ Fafá de Belém. *(Photo by Márcio Rodrigues. Courtesy of Som Livre.)*

Lamotte d'Incamps). While visiting Brazil in 1988, the two visited the Bahian resort town of Porto Seguro and first heard and saw the exotic new style. At the time, lambada was a regional success—like the fricote of Luiz Caldas—popular in the North and Northeast.

Karakos and Lorsac knew they were on to something, and back in France they organized a multinational group called Kaoma to sing lambada songs in Europe (Kaoma's lead singer was a Brazilian named Loalwa Braz). Kaoma recorded a cover of Márcia Ferreira's hit "Chorando Se Foi," her Portuguese-language adaptation of "Llorando Se Fue," a Bolivian *saya* tune written by the brothers Gonzalo and Ulises Hermosa. They had recorded it originally in 1982 with their group Los Kjarkas, on the album *Canto a la Mujer de mi Pueblo*.[34] Karakos and Lorsac renamed the Ferreira version, and Lorsac registered it with SACEM (the French performing rights society) under the pseudonym Chico de Oliveira.[35] They filmed a music video for the tune that served as a commercial for the soft drink Orangina, which got them lots of television exposure, and arranged a record deal with CBS.

"Lambada" was the sensation of the summer and fall on the continent. It hit number 1 on the charts in fifteen countries, was number 1 on the *Music & Media* pan-European pop chart for months, and sold five million units (the album sold two million copies). Kaoma's single was a hybrid, mixing a Bolivian folk theme with lambada, and having a pronounced flavor of northeastern Brazil as well. The issue of what was and was not "lambada" became even more confused when record labels started sticking the "lambada" label on anything that was Brazilian—even bossa nova.

By 1990 nightclubs in New York and Los Angeles offered "lambada" nights, and Kaoma's album (called *World Beat* in the United States) went gold and hit number 1 on the *Billboard* Latin music chart. Publicists outdid themselves in the hype department, spreading ridiculous stories about how lambada had been banned as "immoral" in Brazil in the 1930s. Two lamentable low-budget exploitation movies (*The Forbidden Dance* and

▲ Two dancers from the Brazilian-European band Kaoma performing lambada. (*Courtesy of Epic.*)

Lambada: Set the Night on Fire) attempted to cash in on the craze.

The international attention helped increase lambada's popularity in Brazil. Many leading Brazilian pop artists, especially those from Bahia, added at least one lambada to their albums in 1989 and 1990. In Salvador the style was augmented with synthesizers and local rhythms, while the lambada from Pará generally retained a lighter, simpler sound.

Meanwhile, the publishing scheme hatched by Lorsac and Karakos finally backfired on them, and they were sued by EMI Music, which represented the interests of the Hermosa brothers. The two Frenchmen came to an agreement with EMI and relinquished the authors' earnings from "Lambada." Lorsac received a reprimand from SACEM, the French performing rights society.[36] Ulises Hermosa never benefited financially from his global hit; he died in 1992. Lambada soon disappeared from the international spotlight, a victim of hype and exploitation.

Lambada to Guitarrada

Lambada also faded away in Brazil, at least as a musical label. But it would live on in its other identity—guitarrada, a new name for the original style invented by Vieira. "Lambada was born instrumental in the hands of Mestre Vieira," comments Cravo Carbono guitarist Pio Lobato.[37] Instrumental lambada acquired the name guitarrada (from guitarra [electric guitar] plus lambada) only in 1985, when featured on a successful series of *Guitarradas* records released by Carlos Marajó. With the resurgence of the genre in Pará in the second half of the 1990s, as the style was reinterpreted by a new generation of musicians, the term *guitarrada* came into wider use, according to Magalhães, who agrees that lambada is now disappearing as a label.[38]

Another of guitarrada's showcases is a Lobato-produced album, *Mestres da Guitarrada*, which was released in 2004 and brings together Mestre Vieira, Aldo Sena, and Mestre Curica. The style also gained impetus in the hands of guitarist Chimbinha (Cledivan Almeida Farias, born in 1974), now famous as part of Banda Calypso. Prior to founding the group, he was a prolific session guitarist in high demand, who could be heard playing on hundreds of local albums in the late '90s. His playing stood out, with "rococo fingering, full of flourishes but clear and secure," according to journalist Hermano Vianna. He released a noteworthy solo album in 1998 called *Guitarras Que Cantam* (Guitars That Sing). Vianna comments, "It was an album of guitarrada, clearly an heir to the inventions of the masters Vieira and Aldo Sena, who were very popular in all the Amazon at the beginning of the '80s, before the lambada fever."[39]

The next year, Chimbinha formed a group that incorporated guitarrada into its sound and took Paraense pop to a national audience.

Guitarrada to Technobrega

In 1999 Chimbinha joined with singer-dancer Joelma Mendes (born in 1974 in Pará) to create Banda Calypso, which has been highly successful as an independent recording act, selling millions of CDs and DVDs outside the mainstream music industry. By 2005 they had become one of Brazil's most popular groups, ranking alongside big names such as Ivete Sangalo and Zeca Pagodinho. Banda Calypso's bouncy, up-tempo music fuses guitarrada with *brega paraense* (the *brega* from Pará) and other ingredients. Whereas brega in Brazil has long been a pejorative label for unsophisticated romantic songs, in Pará it now refers to a more specific musical style and rhythm.

"Originally, the rhythm was tied to Brazil's Jovem Guarda, which was influenced by English and North American rock in the '60s. In the '70s, a big roster of romantic and popular composers availed themselves of this format of guitar, bass, drums, and voice, and created a particular song style in all Brazil, very popular and tied to the poorer levels of the population and cities that were far from the big urban centers. In general, this genre was always branded by the big national music industry and big media as something of lesser value" comments Magalhães.[40]

"Curiously, in Pará, the genre inaugurated by Jovem Guarda had a special development in terms of musical structure," he adds. The 4/4 beat and instrumental format were adapted for local needs, the tempo was progressively accelerated over the decades, original guitar work was created for the genre (especially by Chimbinha), and further mutations occurred, "beginning with fusions with other rhythmic cells, like carimbó and, more recently, electronic music."[41]

In Pará, the transformed brega achieved popularity with albums like singer-songwriter Roberto Villar's mid-1990s releases *A Nuvem* (The Cloud) and *Ator Principal* (Main Actor), both of which featured Chimbinha on electric guitar. "From then until now, the albums were produced with great care, the guitars were doubled, and the rhythm accelerated," observes Vianna.[42] Rabelo gives credit to Chimbinha, saying that he "redefined brega paraense in the middle of the '90s. He blended guitarrada, one of his big influences, with the brega of the '80s, creating a more danceable, swinging style."[43]

This "novo brega" or "brega pop," distinctive to Pará, also grew in popularity because of the introduction of an accompanying brega dance that resembles a curious fusion of '50s rock-and-roll dancing (with a lot of partner twirling) and a less erotic form of lambada. Wanderley Andrade and Chimbinha were two musicians who popularized the new brega, which gained another name: calipso (or calypso), which was given to it in the Northeast, "where the movement is as intense as in Pará," says Magalhães.[44] The new label of calipso or calypso, which is different from Trinidad's genre of the same name, was applied to Chimbinha's new group, Banda Calypso, which is probably the most successful independent act of all time in Brazil.

Playing some three hundred shows per year, Banda Calypso distributed its CDs outside traditional distribution networks and the mainstream music industry. After expanding its success to the rest of Brazil, it began appearing on national television and soon became a mainstay on popular TV Globo variety shows. Along with the group's high-energy sound, the tireless Joelma is backed by an array of dancers (she choreographs the stage show). The sound and presentation are now much imitated in Brazil.

The new brega gave birth to Pará's technobrega movement, which is "electronic music (electronic drums and synthesized sounds with diverse effects) made with elements of brega paraense and fragments of American music," according to Rabelo.[45] The mix can include samples downloaded from the Internet or pirated from video games. Some technobrega songs have highly accelerated tempos, reaching 170 beats per minute, according to journalist Vladimir Cunha. As a result, the subgenre of slower, more romantic technobrega is now called *melody*.[46] Interestingly, the name brings to mind Rio's milder variety of funk, called *funk melody*.

Technobrega musicians have achieved fame as independents, but in a more radical fashion than that of Banda Calypso, and have created a new paradigm for music success. Technobrega artists take advantage of cheap available technology, often using personal computers as home "studios," and take their music tracks to DJs who put on the festas de aparelhagem, in which they take sound systems from location to location and stage shows that can include smoke machines, laser displays, and giant video screens. According to Cunha, there are about three hundred festas de aparelhagem in greater Belém, and their DJs can turn unknown songs into instant hits.

The composers freely allow the DJs or producers to copy the music and sell it on CDs that cost as little as $1 apiece. The "pirates" become distributors, and the artists gain exposure (but zero royalties) through the distribution of their work to the public. Hitherto anonymous artists can then put together bands that may consist of just a keyboardist and vocalist, and go to play at the festas de aparalhagem and in clubs. "A market is thus formed, and strengthened, that doesn't need radio, music companies or TV for promotion," adds Rabelo.[47] The new model is so successful in Pará that Ronaldo Lemos, a law professor at the Getúlio Vargas Foundation, estimated that technobrega artists would release four hundred albums in 2007.[48] That's remarkable considering that Belém, the state's biggest city, has only about two million inhabitants in its metropolitan area.

More Paraense Fusions

The music in Pará is being blended in different ways by the group Cravo Carbono, formed in Belém in 1997 and consisting of the previously quoted Lázaro Magalhães, Pio Lobato, and Bruno Rabelo, plus drummer Vovô. Their music on albums like *Córtex* (2006) is wildly eclectic, yet based in rock and guitarrada. For example, "Café BR" has a *technoguitarrada* sound (which Lobato defines as technobrega plus guitarrada); "Canção à Prova D'Água" (Waterproof Song) starts as a bossa nova and ends as a rock ballad, with a hint of Robert Fripp; Lobato describes "Marx Marex" as a "carimbó with riffs" (it is reminiscent of the group Karnak); "Arraial" is a mix of rock ballad with zouk; "Vale Quanto Pesa" has elements of King Crimson and the Filhos de Ghandi afoxé; and Rabelo identifies "Alto do Bode" as a meeting of carimbó, *maculelê*, and reggae.[49]

The singer-songwriter-banjo player Marco André, also originally from Belém, released *Amazônia Groove* in 2005. The award-winning album took listeners on a musical tour of the North, exploring carimbó, marabaixo (from Amapá state), *samba de cacete* (from the city of Cametá in Pará), and boi-bumbá, as well as locally popular foreign rhythms of merengue and zouk. Iva Rothe-Neves is a local singer, composer, and keyboardist who mixes regional sounds with MPB in works such as *Aluguel de Flores* (2001). Marlui Miranda (known for her work with indigenous music); Arraial do Pavulagem and Ronaldo Silva (interpreting northeastern styles); composer Walter Freitas; guitarrada group La Pupunã; and technobrega band Tecnoshow are other notable northern artists.

Regarding technobrega, Cravo Carbono's Rabelo asks, "Will it change Brazilian music? I don't know. But certainly the style will survive independently of what happens in the declining Brazilian phonographic market."[50] Brazilian music is less dominated now by the tastes and trends of Rio de Janeiro and São Paulo, where the national music industry has traditionally been centered. The music of the North, especially in the state of Pará, has carved out its own business model and cultural identity, both of which look to keep evolving.

BRAZILIAN INSTRUMENTAL
MUSIC AND JAZZ

Instrumental music has always been a richly varied and important part of the Brazilian sound, from Pixinguinha's elegant and lively compositions to Uakti's primordial chamber music, played on specially designed instruments. And part of the instrumental spectrum in Brazil is jazz, which its musicians have absorbed and expressed in their own way. Conversely, many of the world's leading jazz and instrumental artists have been heavily influenced by Brazilian music. Before we delve into such subjects, it is necessary to take a side trip back to the late nineteenth century, to explore the origins of the Brazilian genre that provides the backbone of much of its instrumental music. It is called choro.

CHORO

In the late nineteenth century in Rio, a new musical style emerged that would become one of the most creative musical manifestations in Brazil. Choro is primarily an instrumental form, and to a North American ear might sound a little like a small Dixieland jazz combo playing with strange rhythms, extreme melodic leaps, unexpected modulations, and occasional breakneck tempos. Choro and jazz are both characterized by their use of improvisation and mixture of African and European musical elements. Interestingly, choro's early development arguably predates that of both ragtime, which first appeared in the 1890s, and jazz, which emerged at the start of the twentieth century.

The first *chorões* (musicians who played choro) began to play in Rio around 1870. In its early days choro was less a genre than a style, with Afro-Brazilian syncopation and a Brazilian flair added to fashionable European dance music of the time, including waltzes, polkas, schottishes, quadrilles, and mazurcas. The pioneering figure Joaquim Antônio da Silva Calado (1848–1880) founded the group Choro Carioca in 1870, the same year that he was appointed a teacher at Rio's Imperial Conservatory of Music. Choro Carioca, the most popular choro band of that decade, was an ensemble that initially consisted of flute, two guitars, and a cavaquinho.

Calado was a virtuoso flutist whose solos featured spectacular octave leaps and mercurial key changes. He could create the "illusion of two flutes playing simultaneously an octave apart," according to musicologist David Appleby. Another aspect of his performance style was the *ganha-tempo*, a "stalling for time" in which a melodic or rhythmic passage would be played languidly, with a "deliberate indolence and indeterminancy."[1] Few of Calado's many compositions were published, but those that were exerted a great influence on his peers. Other key figures from the first generation of chorões included the flutist-composers Viriato da Silva, Virgílio Pinto da Silveira, and Luizinho.

The first choro musicians were usually not professionals. They didn't mind playing all night long at parties, provided there was a lot of food and drink. Between 1870 and 1919 hundreds of chorões in Rio spent nights moving from house to house, party to party. When these musicians played a song with vocals, it was usually termed a seresta (serenade), whereas an instrumental piece was called a choro. José Ramos Tinhorão wrote that the new style may have gained its name from the common use of low guitar notes and "plaintive tones."[2] Choro also means "the act of weeping, crying, or sobbing" in Portuguese. Others think the name derives from *xolo*, a word used long ago by some Afro-Brazilians for their parties and dances.

The early choro bands usually followed Choro Carioca's format of flute, guitar, and cavaquinho.

The flute acted as the soloist, the guitar supplied the lowest tones with its bass strings, and the cavaquinho handled the rhythm. Other instruments would be added later. Choro musicians improvised upon European rhythms and melodies and developed a dialogue between the soloist and other instruments in which the objective was the *derrubada* (drop)—the moment at which the accompanying musicians could no longer follow the soloist's creative and unpredictable riffs.

The popular "Caiu, Não Disse?" (Didn't I Say You'd Fall?) was a choro-type song composed in 1880 by Viriato da Silva (1851–1883). It was a polka with prominent derrubada sections that emphasized the virtuosity of the flute soloist. This competitive characteristic of choro would be reflected in later choro titles such as Ernesto Nazaré's "Apanhei-Te Cavaquinho" (I Got You, Cavaquinho) and Pixinguinha and Lacerda's "Cuidado, Colega" (Careful, Pal).

Another early composition in the choro style was Chiquinha Gonzaga's 1877 polka "Atraente" (Attractive), which some critics later termed a *choro-polca*. Appleby notes that "Atraente" was Gonzaga's "first successful attempt to write in the improvisational style of the *chorões*." It included some chromaticism and a few wide leaps and repeated notes in the melodic line characteristic of Calado's compositions. In addition, "the use of alternation of melodic elements among flute, clarinet, and cavaquinho also is suggestive of the style of the choros."[3]

Gonzaga was the daughter of Marshall José Basileu Neves Gonzaga, a high-ranking military official. A prolific and brilliant composer in nearly every idiom, she was a tremendously influential figure in Brazilian popular music, which at that time was almost exclusively a male domain. In 1889 Chiquinha published a composition called "Só no Choro" (Only in Choro) that seemed to give the new genre "proof of existence," according to Tinhorão.[4] She went on to write many choros, including the classic "Forrobodó" in 1912. Chiquinha, known for her independent spirit and disregard for convention, was the first woman in Brazil to conduct a military band and a theater orchestra and was the author of the landmark marcha "Ô Abre Alas," the first song composed especially for Carnaval. She was also politically active and, when young, worked for both the abolitionist and the republican causes in Brazil.

By the turn of century choro had developed into an independent genre with its own basic characteristics, although choros were still labeled according to the polkas and other dances that provided the underlying rhythm. Each choro was typically divided into three parts, in three different tonalities, repeated in the sequence ABACA, with a medium to fast tempo. Only one instrumentalist in choro performed the solos, a marked contrast with jazz. The flute took the solos in choro's early years, and later the clarinet or guitar could assume this role. The new genre displayed the derrubada and other characteristics mentioned earlier.[5]

Ernesto Nazaré (1863–1934) took the style pioneered by Calado, Gonzaga, and others and developed it further, penning sophisticated compositions with strong melodies. Ernesto, like Gonzaga, was classically trained and wrote in various popular styles for the piano. He composed many classic choros and maxixes that were usually designated "Brazilian tangos." Nazaré (the old spelling of his name is "Nazareth") will always be remembered for "Odeon" (1909) and "Apanhei-te Cavaquinho" (1913), which became standards in the choro repertoire. Zequinha de Abreu (1880–1935) was another composer from this era and in 1917 wrote the scintillating "Tico-Tico no Fubá" (Tico-Tico Bird in the Cornmeal), one of Brazil's all-time most popular songs. It hit Hollywood in 1947, when it was sung by Carmen Miranda in the film *Copacabana*.

Pixinguinha and Os Oito Batutas

The legendary Pixinguinha (Alfredo da Rocha Vianna Jr., 1898–1973) was both a founding father of samba and a superb choro flutist-composer. Many consider him the greatest choro musician of all time. Pixinguinha wrote many of the most fa-

▲ An album of Pixinguinha standards released by Brazilian independent label Kuarup. *(Courtesy of Kuarup.)*

mous standards in the genre, including "Carinhoso" (Affectionate), "Rosa," and "Sofre Porque Queres" (You Suffer Because You Want To). He was a pioneer in taking Brazilian music overseas, touring Europe and South America.

Pixinguinha was the son of a civil servant who worked in the department of telegraphs and liked to play flute at home with friends. The Vianna household was always packed with friends and often was the site of all-night choro sessions. Pixinguinha showed musical talent as a boy, and his father bought him a beautiful flute imported from Italy. He began studying with the music teacher Irineu de Almeida, who stayed for a while with the Vianna family. By the age of twelve, the young prodigy had already composed his first choro, "Lata de Leite" (Milk Can), and played with the Carnaval group Filhas da Jardineira. His development continued, and as a teenager in 1915 he made his first recording—interpreting Irineu's *tango brasileiro* "São João debaixo d'água" (St. John Under the Water) with the group Choro Carioca.

By 1917 the nineteen-year-old Pixinguinha had his own band, Choro Pixinguinha. The industrious young musician also played with the Carnaval bloco Grupo do Caxangá, which included friends who often jammed with Pixinguinha at Tia Ciata's legendary house. Several members of the bloco would subsequently join Pixinguinha's next group, which he formed when the manager of the movie theater Palais asked him to organize a small orchestra to play in the foyer. At first the flutist was a little incredulous, since it was unheard of to have a black band play in such an elegant setting. But he went ahead and recruited several of his most talented colleagues from Grupo do Caxangá. In 1919 his instrumental ensemble Os Oito Batutas (The Eight Masters) made its debut at the Palais, playing various popular styles, including choros, maxixes, lundus, and modinhas. The Batutas were extremely well received, and even Ernesto Nazaré came to hear them play after he was done with his own gig at the Odeon Theater.

The Oito Batutas was the first ensemble of its type to incorporate the percussion instruments ganzá, pandeiro, and reco-reco. The early formation of the band included Nelson Alves (cavaquinho), José Alves (mandolin), Raul Palmieri (guitar), Luís Silva (mandolin and reco-reco, China (Pixinguinha's brother Otávio Viana, on piano, guitar, and vocals), Jacó Palmieri (pandeiro), and Donga (Ernesto dos Santos, on guitar), co-author of the first registered samba, "Pelo Telefone."

With a slightly different lineup, Pixinguinha and the Batutas took a boat to Paris for a highly successful six-month stay, playing choros, sambas, and maxixes. They accompanied Duque (the Bahian ex-dentist Antônio Lopes de Amorim Diniz) and Gaby (a French ballerina), a pair of dancers who had already become famous performing maxixe in Europe in the previous decade. Once in Paris, the Oito Batutas were influenced by the fox-trot orchestras they heard there; they returned home and added saxophone, clarinet, trombone, and trumpet to their instrumentation, and fox-trots and ragtime to their repertoire. With new members in the group, the Batutas continued playing until around 1928 and left a musical legacy that had a tremendous impact on the development of choro and Brazilian popular music. A few years later, Pixinguinha founded another influential group, Grupo da Guarda Velha, which included Donga, Luís Americano, and João da Baiana in its all-star lineup.

Choro: The Genre Broadens

The guitarist Garoto (Annibal Augusto Sardinha, 1915–1955), advanced the choro genre in the 1930s and 1940s with his songwriting and innovative playing. Born in São Paulo, Garoto was adept with guitar, banjo, mandolin, and cavaquinho. He played with chorões as a young man and became known for the challenging harmonies that he added to the music. In 1939 Garoto journeyed to the United States to join Carmen Miranda's Bando da Lua. He performed with them on stage and in the film *Down Argentine Way*. Twenty-four of his compositions can be heard on Paulo Bellinati's 1991 album *The Guitar Works of Garoto*.

Choro's popularity had waned somewhat by the start of the 1940s, but a new generation of choro musicians appeared in that decade to ensure the continuation of the genre. Flutists Benedito Lacerda and Altamiro Carrilho, mandolin virtuoso Jacó do Bandolim, clarinetist and alto saxophonist Abel Ferreira, bandleader Severino Araújo, and cavaquinho master Valdir Azevedo were responsible for a choro revival.

Another chapter in the genre's story that decade occurred when Pixinguinha, apparently out of financial necessity, joined Lacerda's group, concentrating on sax while Lacerda handled the flute. This was a subordinate role for Pixinguinha, but the collaboration popularized several of his compositions, including "Um a Zero" (One to Zero), "Ingênuo" (Naive), and "Segura-ele" (Grab Him). Unfortunately, he had to share their authorship with Lacerda. They were among the many choro standards composed in the 1940s; another example is the beloved "Brasileirinho" (Little Brazilian, 1947) by Azevedo.

Choro's fortunes again declined, but another revival would begin in the mid-1970s, stimulated by musicians like Paulo Moura, Turíbio Santos, Arthur Moreira Lima, Raphael Rabello (1962–

1995), Marcos Ariel, Paulinho da Viola, Hermeto Pascoal, and the Novos Baianos, all of whom included choros on their records. Nó em Pingo D'Água (Knot in a Drop of Water) was an instrumental group founded in 1978 that modernized choro in several eclectic albums. In addition, choro was part of the vocabulary of the instrumental group A Cor de Som and their mandolin player, Armandinho, who mixed it with frevo, rock energy, and a trio elétrico sensibility (see "Bahia"). Armandinho and guitarist Rabello, both brilliant at improvisation, would team up for some memorable progressive choro concerts later in their careers.

The 1988 album *Noites Cariocas* is an excellent introduction to the genre. On it, Altamiro Carrilho (flute), Chiquinho (accordion), Joel Nascimento (mandolin), Paulinho da Viola (cavaquinho), Paulo Moura (clarinet), and Paulo Sérgio Santos (clarinet and sax) perform seventeen choro standards. Outside of Brazil in the 1980s and '90s, Laurindo Almeida, Carlos Barbosa-Lima, Charlie Byrd, and Richard Stoltzman are among those who recorded classic choros for North American audiences. David Grisman released two volumes of Jacó do Bandolim choros on his own label. And mandolinist Mike Marshall and cellist Yo-Yo Ma have both explored the genre in recent years.

Twenty-First Century Choro

The first decade of the twenty-first century witnessed the rise of a plethora of innovative new musicians who took choro in new directions. One of them is the trumpet player Joatan Nascimento, who played with the Symphonic Orchestra of Bahia before releasing the album *Eu Choro Assim*.

Cavaquinho player Henrique Cazes, born in 1959, cannot be considered a newcomer—he

started his career in 1976 with the Coisas Nossas band—but he released his most innovative works in the 2000s. A good example is the 2002 album *Eletro Pixinguinha XXI*, which features eleven Pixinguinha themes played with samples, loops, and a cavaquinho connected to a MIDI synthesizer.

Guitarist Caio Márcio and his band Tira Poeira, based in Rio's lively Lapa nightclub scene, stir up the genre with samba, Cuban, flamenco, and jazz influences. Caio has also experimented with fusions of choro and jazz-rock on his eponymous debut solo album. Two other notable young guitarists are Zé Paulo Becker, who interprets choro and other genres on the well-regarded *Lendas Brasileiras*, and Rogério Caetano, who won accolades for his 2006 debut album, *Pintando o Sete*. The group Pagode Jazz Sardinha's Club, with saxophonist-flutist Eduardo Neves, cooks up an original stew that mixes choro, funk, samba, and maxixe, with apparent inspiration from Paulo Moura's seminal *Confusão Urbana, Suburbana e Rural*.

The new generation is giving choro a facelift, adding new life to a style that many considered old-fashioned. Although its mass appeal has risen and fallen in cycles, choro remains a fundamental part of the musical vocabulary of most Brazilian instrumentalists.

Hamilton de Holanda and Yamandú Costa

Hamilton de Holanda, born in 1976 in Rio de Janeiro but raised in Brasília, is heir to the Brazilian mandolin legacy of masters like Jacó do Bandolim, Joel Nascimento, and Armandinho. No less than Hermeto Pascoal has called him the best mandolin player in the world. Known for his stage charisma and rock-and-roll energy, Hamilton was a choro prodigy when he made his first appearances at revivalist festivals in the mid-1990s. "Hamilton's distinctive manner of performance drew as many remarks as his technical prowess; dressed in neon colors, he strutted around the stage while playing in a manner not unlike the electric bandolinist Armandinho of A Cor do Som, who had shocked audiences and judges twenty years earlier," note the authors of *Choro: A Social History of a Brazilian Popular Music.*[6]

Hamilton plays a ten-string custom mandolin,

◄ Guitarist Marco Pereira and mandolinist Hamilton Holanda. *(Courtesy of Kuarup Records.)*

▼ Yamandú Costa. *(Courtesy of Biscoito Fino.)*

extracting from it rich harmonic, textural, and percussive effects. He is highly regarded as a composer of modern Brazilian instrumental music and, along with his short pieces, has written a concerto for orchestra and mandolin. He cites Guinga, Baden Powell, and Luiz Gonzaga as major influences. By 2006, at the age of thirty, Hamilton had already released eight acclaimed albums, including *01 Byte 10 Cordas* and *Samba do Avião*, ranging through choro, samba, and MPB. He has also performed with some of Brazil's greatest instrumental musicians, including guitarists Marco Pereira and a fellow prodigy with the unusual name of Yamandú.

Yamandú Costa is a guitar virtuoso who has mastered the choro idiom and also ranges into bossa nova and styles popular in his native Rio Grande do Sul like tango, *milonga*, *zamba* and *chamamé*. Born in 1980 into a family of musicians, he moved to Rio "to be close to the wonderful artists who were creating new harmonies for old songs."[7] When Yamandú plays live, he often seems caught in a trance during one of his fast, surprising, often dissonant solos. He can sound like Baden Powell meets Jimi Hendrix meets John

McLaughlin. With prodigious technique he discovers new tones, slows down the tempo, speeds it up, and turns the guitar into a percussion instrument.

Both Yamandú and Hamilton are helping to reinvigorate choro, yet they cannot be labeled only choro artists, as they roam widely across many instrumental genres. In that respect, they are like their formidable musical predecessor, Paulo Moura.

PAULO MOURA

Moura is a good example of how Brazilian musicians have dexterously woven choro together with a variety of other styles. Moura plays both saxophone and clarinet, and can coax refined, raucous, or soulful sounds from both instruments, depending on the occasion. He is a master of many idioms besides choro, including jazz, bossa, classical music, and *samba de gafieira*, an orchestrated style performed in dance halls.

Born in 1933, Moura began as a classical clarinetist with the Municipal Theater Orchestra of Rio and later ventured into jazz-bossa with Sérgio Mendes's Sexteto Bossa Rio. Since the 1960s Paulo has been a highly influential force in Bra-

zilian popular music. He has taught music theory to the likes of Wagner Tiso and Mauro Senise, arranged albums by Elis Regina, Fagner, and Milton Nascimento, and appeared as a sideman on many important recordings, including Marisa Monte's debut album. And he has recorded several exceptional solo albums, such as *Confusão Urbana, Suburbana e Rural* (Urban, Suburban, and Rural Confusion) in 1976.

Confusão is an intriguing tour through landscapes of modern and traditional Brazilian music. In the Severino Araújo choro "Espinha de Bacalhau" (Cod Spine), Moura's capricious soprano sax leaps and winds spectacularly across the strumming of cavaquinho and guitar. The samba "Notícia" (News) swells with a big band sound, as Paulo's sax follows the slow and sentimental arrangements, while an insistent cuíca yelps, calls, and whoops amid the orchestration. "Bicho Papão" (Bogeyman) features a wild, fast beating of bass and hand drums, a rather unsettling jazzy sax solo, and an urban traffic jam of a horn section. "Tema do Zeca da Cuíca" (Cuíca Zeca's Theme) is a variegated montage of elec-

▼ Clara Sverner and Paulo Moura performing choros at Rio's Mistura Up club in 1989. *(Photo by Chris McGowan.)*

tric guitar riffs, cuíca gasps, wistful flute playing, and intermittent Gil Evans–like strings, all coalescing into a rolling, breathless batucada. "Carimbó do Moura" balances Paulo's joyful clarinet playing with the rollicking carimbó rhythm from Pará. And "Se Algum Dia" (If One Day) is an earthy, tender reading of a sentimental samba by Martinho da Vila. With such variety and virtuosity, *Confusão* was one of the most creative and accomplished Brazilian albums of the 1970s.

One of Moura's more traditional works came in 1988, when he and a pianist friend paid homage to choro's greatest exponent with the album *Clara Sverner & Paulo Moura Interpretam Pixinguinha*. Other noteworthy releases have included the tribute albums *Paulo Moura e Ociladocê Interpretam Dorival Cayimmi* (1991) and *Paulo Moura Visita Gershwin e Jobim* (2000). In 2003 he collaborated with guitarist Yamandú Costa on *El Negro del Blanco*. Moura describes that album as "an attempt to join the influence of Africa in Latin American music and the Iberian stream brought by Portuguese and Spanish settlers."[8]

LAURINDO ALMEIDA

Laurindo Almeida was from an older generation than Moura but also displayed a great facility for meshing old and new instrumental styles. Laurindo José de Araújo Almeida Nobrega Neto (1917–1995) was born in the village of Prainha, near São Paulo. He was a guitarist known for his harmonic mastery, subtle dynamics, rich embellishments, and adept improvisational skills in a variety of idioms. Although he never was a household name in Brazil or abroad, his playing was ultimately heard by millions around the world, thanks to decades of studio work in Hollywood for film and television.

Almeida's career spanned several decades. In the 1930s the self-taught young musician formed a guitar duo with Garoto, playing choros and sambas while adding chords that were harmonically advanced for the time. In 1947 Almeida left for the United States and began his career there. He

▲ Laurindo Almeida in 1951 on the cover of *BMG* magazine. *(Courtesy of Laurindo Almeida.)*

was invited to play with Stan Kenton's orchestra and was its featured guitarist for three years.

Laurindo settled in Los Angeles and began a recording career. In 1952 he led a trio that added jazz edges to choro, baião, and samba. He teamed with saxophonist Bud Shank to cut *Laurindo Almeida Quartet Featuring Bud Shank*, in sessions that took place in April 1953. A pair of ten-inch records on the Pacific Jazz label were released in 1954 and then combined in 1961 into a twelve-inch World Pacific disc called *Brazilliance*. On that innovative work he mixed cool jazz with Brazilian idioms.

Almeida and Shank's "jazz-samba" was not bossa nova, as some have claimed; it lacked the characteristic João Gilberto beat, the harmonic stamp of Jobim and others, and the economy of expression achieved by bossa. Quite simply, it had a different mood and sound. But Almeida and Shank's work was certainly valuable in its own right. They continued their jazz-samba collaborations with *Holiday in Brazil* and *Latin Contrasts*.

On other albums Almeida linked a variety of Brazilian genres to jazz and classical forms. For example, he explored modinha, choro, maracatu, and boi-bumbá in *Duets with the Spanish Guitar* in 1957. He also covered Villa-Lobos and Radamés Gnattali in *Impressões do Brasil* and played guitar transcriptions of Debussy, Ravel, and Bach in the Grammy-winning *Spanish Guitars of Laurindo Almeida*.

Though Almeida was several thousand miles away from the burgeoning bossa nova movement in Rio in the late 1950s, he adapted it to his own style when it was carried to American shores by Getz, Gilberto, Byrd, Jobim, and others. His 1962 album *Viva Bossa Nova!* was one of his commercial successes in the genre, and *Guitar from Ipanema* (1964) won a Grammy award for Best Instrumental Jazz Performance (Large Group). Almeida won a total of five Grammys, most of them coming in the late 1950s and early 1960s, and received an additional eleven Grammy nominations throughout his career.

In 1974 he and Shank formed the L.A. Four with bassist Ray Brown and drummer Chuck Flores, and the group recorded numerous albums together (Flores's place would be taken by Shelly Manne, then by Jeff Hamilton). Their varied repertoire included jazz, classical, and Brazilian-oriented material. Almeida also recorded with pianist George Shearing, singer Sammy Davis Jr., the Modern Jazz Quartet, and guitarists Sharon Isbin, Charlie Byrd, and Larry Coryell. And he wrote, arranged, and played on hundreds of scores for films and television shows. His electric guitar, mandolin, and lute playing could be heard in Elvis Presley films, *The Godfather*, *A Star Is Born*, *Camelot*, *Funny Girl*, and *The Agony and the Ecstasy*, and in the television shows *Bonanza*, *Rawhide*, and *The Fugitive*.

EGBERTO GISMONTI

Of Brazil's best instrumental musicians, few have followed as singular a path as Egberto Gismonti, who received formal training in the conservatory and also absorbed musical lessons in the Amazon

▲ Egberto Gismonti at the keyboard in 1986. *(Photo by Mabel Arthou. Courtesy of Agência JB.)*

jungle. Gismonti (born in 1945 in Carmo, a small city in Rio de Janeiro state) has been engaged in a life-long search for new musical languages. He started by taking fifteen years of classical piano lessons in Rio and then studying orchestration and composition in Paris with Nadia Boulanger and Jean Barraqué. But Egberto's interest in all kinds of popular music—jazz, samba, choro, baião, bossa—took him out of the conservatory and into a new musical world of his own making.

Gismonti can be intensely lyrical, sounding something like a highly rhythmic Ralph Towner on guitar or Keith Jarrett on piano, improvising atop baião and frevo patterns. He has written beautiful melodies that have been covered by many musicians; "Sonho" (Dream), for example, has been recorded by Henry Mancini, Paul Mauriat, and more than a dozen others. Then again, his music can be jarring, strange, and difficult. Nevertheless, Egberto is one of Brazil's most popular musicians internationally. *Dança das Cabeças* (Dance of the Heads), recorded with percussionist Naná Vasconcelos, has been released in eighteen countries and has sold more than two hundred thousand copies, an impressive sum for nonvocal experimental music.

Egberto plays acoustic and electric keyboards, eight- and ten-string guitar, sitar, accordion, violoncello, all kinds of flutes, and numerous other instruments he has come across in his world travels. Sometimes he records solo, other times in ensembles. He collaborated with bassist Charlie Haden and saxophonist Jan Garbarek on *Mágico* and *Folk Songs*, and with flutist Paul Horn on *Altitude of the Sun*. And Gismonti released *Academia de Danças* (Academy of Dances) and *Corações Futuristas* (Future Hearts) with Robertinho Silva (drums), Nivaldo Ornellas (sax and flute), and Luis Alves (bass).

Egberto has also recorded without accompaniment. *Solo* (1979) is a beautiful, lyrical effort that features him on acoustic piano and guitar. And in 1982's *Fantasia* he used sound samplers to simulate an entire orchestra. The opening two cuts on that album—"Overture" and "Infância"—demonstrate the range Egberto may explore in just a few minutes. The overture begins with a foundation of sustained chords over which dissonant harmonic clusters are juxtaposed with nervous rhythmic patterns. This anxious mood then mellows as "Infância" begins; the main theme is introduced and worked through many variations, and the composition ends up with a rambunctious baião-like feeling that evokes images of children dancing and playing.

"For me personally, Egberto has been a kind of model, in that he is willing to use a child singing one minute and then have a chamber orchestra the next, then a whole bank of synthesizers," keyboardist Lyle Mays told us. "He has a raw edge that sometimes puts people off, but to me the vision behind his music is just astounding."[9]

▼ Egberto Gismonti on guitar. *(Courtesy of ECM.)*

Another adventurous Gismonti album, *Sol do Meio Dia* (Noonday Sun), released in 1978, was influenced by his friendship with Sapain, a shaman from the Yawalapiti tribe in the Amazon jungle near the Xingu River. Egberto stayed with the Yawalapiti for several weeks in 1977 and learned much about their music from Sapain. Because of the experience, he sought to make his own music more spontaneous and to find a perfect integration between musician, music, and instrument.

Watching Egberto play live is an unforgettable experience. His improvisations on guitar and on piano (on which he is equally proficient) are consistently surprising and imaginative. On guitar, he can play with a blinding speed and can also elicit a wide range of timbral effects. Sometimes he plays the guitar like a piano or percussion instrument, using his left hand to pluck and "hammer" the strings. He also sings in a gentle voice, often with lyrics composed by the poet Geraldo Carneiro. But words in Gismonti's music are primarily part of the sound, functioning like another instrument.

Egberto has written music for solo performances, ensembles, films, theater, and ballets. His 1997 album *Meeting Point* is "an orchestral work that juxtaposes dramatically dense textures with quiet passages of austere beauty and clarity," writes musicologist-critic Bruce Gilman. "The string writing is intense and lyrical, percussion and woodwind parts pointed and impetuous, [and] the brass is aggressive, bringing to mind the work of both Stravinsky and Edgard Varèse."[10]

ECM has a large catalog of much of Gismonti's best work, and several of his most experimental albums have been released on his own label, Carmo. The prolific Gismonti has written scores for several dozen movies and ballets, and released sixty albums, distributed in forty-two countries. There is obviously a wide demand for his work, despite its having been labeled as too difficult or experimental by some critics. About this, Gismonti has commented, "Music can only be divided into two categories: music that is good for the soul and music that is not."[11]

HERMETO PASCOAL

One of Brazil's most colorful musical figures is Hermeto Pascoal, born in 1936 in Lagoa da Canoa, a neighborhood in the town of Arapiraca in Alagoas. When he performs, Hermeto cuts a striking figure. He is an albino with a flowing white beard and long, luminous white hair, and he tends to dart from instrument to instrument on stage, full of energy and inspiration as he follows each musical impulse wherever it leads him. His music is not for those with a lazy ear: he may shift from a merry frevo played by horns and guitars to a droning, dolorous toada on the accordion, then swing between xaxado and maxixe, plunge into a free-jazz piano interlude, and finish with a cuíca and saxophone giddily chasing each other all over the scales.

Like Gismonti, Pascoal has an uncanny ability to create new sounds. But while Egberto will often accomplish this by playing conventional instruments in unusual ways, Hermeto will do it by making ordinary household objects into instru-

▼ Hermeto Pascoal in 1988. *(Courtesy of Som da Gente Records.)*

ments. He can elicit interesting and uncanny tones from pots, pans, jars, whatever is available.

On the 1984 composition "Tiruliruli" he took a phrase from a Brazilian soccer announcer's on-air play-by-play report and repeated it over and over, gradually adding more and more harmonium embellishments until he had created a quirky but strangely affecting short piece. In Hermeto's world, everything has musical possibilities. Percussionist Airto Moreira calls him "the most complete musician I ever met in my life" and "a genius."[12]

"His harmonic concepts are a new way to look at music," explains Jovino Santos Neto, an alumnus of Hermeto's band O Grupo. "The idea of one tonal center or key signature that we have been using in music for centuries has been replaced with a much deeper and multilayered approach. His music can be folkloric, regional, popular, jazzy, atonal, but the concept remains as a guiding force. It's hard to explain without an instrument, but its basis is the juxtaposition of simple triads and the avoidance of linear forms such as scales or modes. You can employ it to play all existing music, but it can lead to creation at a much higher level."[13]

Pascoal was a child musical prodigy. He started with a flute and then, at the age of seven, learned to play the accordion. By eleven he was already playing at the dances and forrós in the region around Arapiraca. When he was fourteen his family moved to Recife, and Hermeto began to earn money performing on radio programs there. At sixteen he moved to Caruaru, a city famous for its regional music. There Hermeto played his accordion on the local radio and at dances, returning to Recife a few years later. Although he was self-taught, Hermeto's musical development continued at a rapid pace: the piano came next, followed by various wind and percussion instruments. Pascoal moved south and struggled to make a living by playing any and all types of music in Rio and São Paulo in the late 1950s and early 1960s.

In 1964 he formed the Sambrasa Trio with bassist Humberto Claiber and percussionist Airto Moreira, who recalled, "We would often stay up all night talking about music." Later, Airto was in a band called Trio Novo with guitarists Heraldo do Monte and Théo de Barros. Hermeto joined them and the group changed its name to Quarteto Novo (New Quartet) and dedicated itself to a progressive reinvention of northeastern song styles. "We played baião, xaxado, other northeastern Brazilian rhythms, but the arrangements were very jazzy, in 4/4 time with modern harmonies," recalled Airto.[14] The band released just one album, *Quarteto Novo*, in 1967.

After the group split up, Hermeto journeyed to the United States. He was invited to record by jazz legend Miles Davis. Hermeto played piano on Miles's *Live-Evil* album (1970). That same year he cut the acclaimed solo album *Hermeto* with Buddha Records. While in North America, the multi-instrumentalist drew raves for his extraordinary improvisational abilities in concert and his idiosyncratic and original compositions. Gil Evans and the Berlin Symphony recorded his material at this time. Pascoal's songs explored choro, frevo, maxixe, baião, jazz, and many other forms, mixing them freely and in unusual combinations. He included surprising modulations, eccentric instrumentation, shifts of meter, and multiple rhythms within individual songs. Hermento's singularity was especially evident in his 1976 album *Slaves Mass*, in which he included the grunts of little piglets in his music and employed the human talents of Airto, Flora Purim, Laudir de Oliveira, Raul de Souza, David Amaro, Ron Carter, and Alphonso Johnson.

In the years since, Pascoal's own recordings have continued to be freewheeling and uninhibited, incorporating an ever-expanding array of found instruments, animate or inanimate: parrots, chickens, teapots, and bowls of water. In concert, Hermeto has always been unpredictable. He may stalk off the stage in a rage if the sound is inadequate or the audience is clinking their cocktail glasses and talking too loudly. But more than likely he will give a unique performance—unique because his group has a large repertoire of tunes and on any given night may perform any number of them in any order, always enlivened with im-

provisation, humorous comments between songs, and the unpredictable results of Hermeto's ability to make music with almost any animate or inanimate object on this earth.

Other Pascoal albums include *A Música Livre de Hermeto Pascoal* (1973), *Cérebro Magnético* (1980), *Lagoa da Canoa, Município de Arapiraca* (1984), *Só Não Toca Quem Não Quer* (1987), and *Festa dos Deuses* (1992). On the solo work *Eu e Eles* (1999), Hermeto played everything himself, including piano, cavaquinho, soprano sax, accordion, flugelhorn, mandolin, and flutes, not to mention surdo, triangle, pandeiro, and whistles. And, lest we forget, bottles and water-tuned pots.

Because of his eclecticism and radical experimentation, Hermeto has been a cult figure among musicians. Lyle Mays finds him "worth listening to just for his wild creativity. His music tends to show me that there are possibilities that I should try to open myself up to explore. He has a real devotion to the making of music and it comes across—let's go for it, let's do everything we can!"[15]

O Grupo and Jovino Santos Neto

Hermeto has mentored many contemporary Brazilian musicians, members of O Grupo above all. Jovino Santos Neto was a vital part of Hermeto's ensemble from 1977 to 1992, functioning as a pianist, flutist, composer, producer, and arranger for O Grupo. Looking back fifteen years later, Jovino recalled how Hermeto expanded his sonic universe. "Hermeto was my school for fifteen years, and I continue to learn from him by studying, practicing, and analyzing his music. His importance as a mentor to several generations of Brazilian musicians is undeniable. As a teacher, he never 'taught,' but instead he knew exactly what kind of challenge to place in front of a musician. He knew what kind of language to employ with each one, and how to make musicians with widely different levels of expertise play together harmoniously."[16]

About rehearsals, Jovino remembers, "Every day was different. We often would spend entire

▲ Jovino Santos Neto. *(Photo by Lara Hoefs. Courtesy of Jovino Santos Neto and Liquid City Records.)*

days working on one challenging passage, learning it individually and collectively. He often composed the music in front of us, so we also got to know how to compose, arrange, score, and lead a group. At other times he would dismantle the rehearsal by starting some wacky improvised piece of music, and this could lead to new written music. There was never a dull day in the Grupo." Performances were also unpredictable. "Our sets were never predetermined. We would often change a piece in the middle into another one. Often there would be guest musicians sitting in with us, or new compositions would be premiered right there in front of the audience. We have played concerts as long as five hours, so this was certainly a stamina-building exercise."

Neto eventually embarked on a solo career, relocating to Seattle, Washington. He has fused jazz, Brazilian, and classical music in his albums *Canto do Rio* (2003) and *Roda Carioca* (2006), each of which garnered a Latin Grammy nomination in the Best Latin Jazz Album category. Jovino's analysis of several songs on *Canto do Rio* shed

light on his "universal music" approach, heavily influenced by his work with O Grupo.

"If you listen to the opening track, 'Guanabara,'" says Jovino, "it starts with a choro groove with pandeiro and clarinet, but the main theme has the hits and the melody of a maracatu for a bit, then it becomes a samba and the improvisation section in 7/4 meter is something else. I personally don't keep track of these transitions; the process is more organic and fluid during the composition and arranging stages of the creation. 'Pedra Branca' is another maracatu with two simple parts that get different harmonies and textures as the tune develops. 'Primavera em Flor' is a baião for most of [it], but at one point there is an abrupt change into a xote, where the solos happen. 'Sempre Sim' is a simple theme in 7/4 built over a pedal vamp, and the band just played it in a loose way, where everyone improvises at once."

Neto now mentors others at the Cornish College of the Arts, where he teaches piano, composition, and jazz ensemble. He continues to collaborate with Hermeto Pascoal, coordinating international performances of Pascoal's big-band music. He is a caretaker of Pascoal's vast body of work, most of which is still unrecorded. Jovino has collected all of Pascoal's original manuscripts, annotating or transcribing more than a thousand compositions. He edited *Tudo É Som* (All Is Sound), a collection of Pascoal compositions published by Universal Edition. "This work of preparing and notating Hermeto's music," says Jovino, "will probably take many more years, since there is so much material, but I do it one day at a time."

CARLOS MALTA

Jovino's fellow Grupo alumnus Carlos Malta is a multi-instrumentalist who is adept with the entire saxophone and flute families and several regional instruments, such as the Brazilian northeastern pife ("fife," a small open-holed flute with a high-pitched sound). Born in Rio in 1960, Carlos is one of the most accomplished Brazilian reed musicians, and has made albums that cross over from Brazilian folk to jazz, applying his creativity and originality to make music that's true to both languages. Malta spent twelve years with O Grupo, which helped his skills as an instrumentalist, arranger, and composer mature, and prepared him for his first solo album, *Rainbow* (1995). One of his most successful creations was Pife Muderno, a band that takes the listener on a trip through Brazilian northeastern folk music, dressing it in contemporary clothing. Malta and his companion flutist Andrea Ernst Dias play their fifes with happy energy as their ideas flow forth continuously at breathtaking tempo on *Carlos Malta and Pife Muderno* (1999) and *Paru* (2006). Carlos has also ventured into more classical jazz territory: *Pimenta* (2000) is a tribute to the late vocalist Elis Regina, taking songs made famous by her and adding inspired and bold improvisations, fusing the rhythms and harmonies of Brazilian music with the language of jazz. Music critic Bruce Gilman calls him "one of the world's fastest and most imaginatively advanced improvisers" and "an exciting tone colorist."[17]

AIRTO MOREIRA

While Sérgio Mendes was the most well known Brazilian musician in the United States in the late 1960s, husband-and-wife team Airto Moreira and Flora Purim took the spotlight in the next decade, adding their Brazilian spirit to the burgeoning jazz fusion scene of those years. Airto spearheaded the Brazilian "percussion invasion" of the late 1960s and '70s that infused American jazz with new rhythms, percussive textures, and tone colors. Although drummers Milton Banana and Hélcio Milito had recorded with Americans during the bossa era, and Dom Um Romão and João Palma had played with Mendes in the mid-1960s, Airto would have the biggest impact outside his country of any Brazilian drummer or percussionist.

Airto was born in 1941 in Itaiópolis, Santa Catarina, and grew up in the city of Curitiba, Paraná. After playing with the bossa group Sambalanço Trio in the early 1960s, he was part of the aforementioned Sambrasa Trio and Quarteto Novo with Hermeto Pascoal. Airto was interested in both jazz and progressive interpretations of traditional Brazilian styles, and he was a multitalented instrumentalist who didn't fit into any one niche. "At that time, percussionists in Brazil were usually specialists," he told us. "One guy would play pandeiro really well, another guy would be a cuíca player, another would play surdo. But I mixed instruments and played everything."[18]

In Rio, Airto had met and fallen in love with a young singer by the name of Flora Purim. In 1968

▶ Airto Moreira (*center*), flexing his muscles backstage, with Cannonball Adderley and Flora. (*Photo by Phil Bray. Courtesy of Fantasy.*)

she decided to travel to the United States to pursue a jazz career, and Airto chose to follow her there, convinced that he could eventually persuade her to return to Brazil with him. That was not to be, but he and Flora did stay together, marrying in 1972 and settling permanently in California.

When he first came to the United States, Airto was prepared to work. "I brought all the hand percussion instruments I had," he recalled, "and the fact is that I came at the right time." Jazz was especially ready for him in the late 1960s: Miles Davis, Larry Coryell, Herbie Hancock, Tony Williams, Chick Corea, Weather Report, and other artists were creating new musical hybrids by mixing free jazz and bebop with funk, rock, and Latin styles. Brazil offered an alternative to Cuban music, which had heavily influenced many jazz musicians in the 1940s and '50s with rumba, charanga, and mambo rhythms, and congas, maracas, timbales, and bongos (following the Fidel Castro revolution in 1959, the American-Cuban interchange had slowed somewhat).

Airto spent his first several months in the United States studying with composer-arranger Moacir Santos, then began integrating himself into the American jazz scene, playing first with Paul Winter, one of the few Americans familiar with Brazilian hand percussion instruments. Later, he did session work with Wayne Shorter, Cannonball Adderley, and others.

Airto astonished the American musicians and producers with his vast array of percussion pieces—cuíca, berimbau, agogô, afoxê, ganzá, pandeiro (his strongest solo instrument), *pau de chuva* (rain stick), and various other rattlers, shakers, and drums, as well as musical devices that he had invented. Each instrument had different tones and textural possibilities, and their sum total—especially in Airto's dexterous hands—was all rather staggering for Americans who were seeing him perform for the first time.

When he would show up at a recording studio with all his gear in tow, "the producers would go crazy," Airto remembered. "They would go up to the pile of percussion instruments and say, 'I like this one. Play this.'"

Moreira played the berimbau on albums by Paul Desmond and others. He added cuíca to Paul Simon's "Me and Julio Down by the Schoolyard," a salsa-flavored hit single of 1972. About Simon, Airto recalled, "He said he wanted something different, like a human voice. I had the cuíca and he said, 'That's it!'"

Airto caught the attention of Miles Davis, who used him on the albums *At Fillmore* and *Live-Evil*, both recorded in 1970. He also played with Weather Report on their groundbreaking eponymous first album in 1971. He was invited to join the group permanently but was unable to because of his commitment with Miles; Dom Um Romão would replace him on Weather Report's next album, *Mysterious Traveller*.

Airto commented that Miles "really didn't want me to play rhythm all the time. He wanted me to play colors and sounds more than rhythm. I would play the cuíca to kind of tease him and he would feed off that and play more." By focusing on "atmosphere" with Miles, Airto greatly expanded the role of percussion. This would ultimately change his own musical direction and influence many jazz drummers and percussionists to follow.

"He was playing stuff that couldn't be played by anybody else," said jazz keyboardist George Duke. "I'd never heard a percussionist play like that, that free, and understanding how to play the right thing at the right moment."[19] Airto's success would trigger a northerly migration: "After I played for Miles, a lot of Brazilian percussionists started coming to the States and bringing all kinds of stuff and making their own instruments."[20]

Meanwhile, in between gigs with Davis, Airto found time for his first solo albums, *Natural Feelings* (1970) and *Seeds on the Ground* (1971). The next year, he and Flora joined bassist Stanley Clarke, saxophonist-flutist Joe Farrell, and keyboardist Chick Corea for Corea's seminal fusion album *Return to Forever* (the album's name would become the group's moniker). "When Chick heard the rhythms I was playing, it was a whole new thing for him. Brazilian music has a very different beat, and he really liked the way Flora was singing and phrasing. It was different from both jazz and Latin

◄ International musical travelers (*left to right*): Airto, Ndugu Chancler, Raul de Souza, Miroslav Vitous, Flora Purim, George Duke, and Cannonball Adderley. *(Photo by Phil Bray. Courtesy of Fantasy.)*

music."[21] Airto had an uncharacteristic role in the band, playing only drums, while Flora handled the percussion. The pair also played on Return to Forever's 1973 album *Light as a Feather*, and they gave both albums a strong Brazilian edge.

Airto then left the group because "Chick wanted to go more into electronics and I didn't want to do that, to play loud." Instead, with producer Creed Taylor's backing, Airto formed his own band, Fingers, which included David Amaro on guitar and lasted for two years. In 1975 came Airto's tour-de-force solo effort, *Identity*, considered one of the finest fusion albums ever. It inspired musicologist John Storm Roberts to effuse, "The texture of *Identity* was extraordinarily dense. Driving Afro-Brazilian percussion, berimbau musical bow, bossa nova vocals, almost purely Congo-Angola melodies, Amerindian wooden flutes, rich strings, rock drumming and guitar, shimmering free-rhythm bells and strikers, a kind of manic avant-garde scatting, were interwoven through multiple tracking in a series of compositions so rich in their references that they took on deeper meaning on every listening."[22]

After Moreira's performances with Miles Davis, Weather Report, and Chick Corea, many bands added a percussionist, and percussive color-

ation became standard in jazz and fusion. In fact, because of Airto, *Down Beat* magazine added a percussion category to its annual critics and readers poll awards. Moreira took top honors in many years from the mid 1970s on.

In 1979 Airto went to Brazil with George Duke, Ndugu Chancler, Stanley Clarke, Raul de Souza, Roland Batista, and other fusion stars to give a concert in Rio. Recalled George, "It was the first time Airto had been back to Brazil in a long time. He was nervous, because everybody was waiting to hear him. And he played a solo that night by himself that was the most incredible, magnificent percussion solo I've ever heard, bar none. It was an experience."[23]

Airto's concerts are always vivid experiences. Audiences are fascinated by his vast array of musical objects, the strange new sounds he can generate, the virtuoso solos he offers on pandeiro, his bird calls and otherwordly chanting, and the near-trance intensity with which he creates his exotic, incredibly rhythmic musical atmospheres. Airto and Flora have teamed on many joint albums, and Moreira has recorded and toured with the Crusaders, Freddie Hubbard, Carlos Santana, Herbie Hancock, Gil Evans, Mickey Hart, and Babatunde Olantunji.

NANÁ VASCONCELOS

Naná Vasconcelos is another Brazilian percussionist who has left his mark on global music. Naná, whom Airto calls "the best berimbau player in the world,"[24] has gained international critical acclaim for his work with Egberto Gismonti, Codona, and the Pat Metheny Group.

Naná (born in Recife in 1945) was part of Quarteto Livre with Geraldo Azevedo in the late 1960s, then lived in Europe throughout much of the 1970s. There he toured with saxophonist Gato Barbieri and also spent a few years in Paris working with disturbed children in a psychiatric hospital, using music as a form of creative therapy. Back in Brazil, he was part of the notable Som Imaginário band, then toured and recorded with Egberto Gismonti. In 1979 he formed Codona with trumpeter Don Cherry and percussionist Collin Walcott. The trio released three highly regarded albums that mixed free jazz and cross-cultural improvisation.

▼ Naná Vasconcelos with a berimbau slung over his shoulder. *(Photo by Nick White. Courtesy of Antilles/Island.)*

Naná next played percussion and sang with the Pat Metheny Group, adding a significant amount of rhythmic density and atmosphere to the albums, especially 1981's *As Falls Wichita, So Falls Wichita Falls*, on which Naná was part of a trio with guitarist Metheny and keyboardist Lyle Mays. "He was a total joy to work with," said Mays. "One of the things that I most enjoyed about playing with Naná was that he was interested in working with me as a synthesizer player to come up with combination textures that neither of us could do alone. He took things a step further, using his voice together with his instrument and with my instruments. Naná broadened our soundscape, and he added charisma, another focal point of attention on stage."[25]

Vasconselos can create a dense musical atmosphere of rustles, rattles, whispers, and rumbles, moving with irresistible rhythm or clashing in unearthly cacophony. And, as Airto notes, Naná can wield the berimbau like no other, turning it into a unique solo voice. His best works, among them his 1989 solo album *Rain Dance*, are like sound encyclopedias, beautiful elaborations of rhythmic and textural possibilities. On *Chegada* (2005) he continued to explore familiar rhythms—maracatu, samba, baião—while searching for new rhythms within them; the ambitious album also included an interpretation of "O Canto do Cisne Negro" (The Song of the Black Swan) by Brazilian composer Heitor Villa-Lobos. About his work, Naná commented, "it's all very simple, but it's hard to be simple."[26]

FLORA PURIM

Airto's wife, Flora Purim, was the most successful jazz-fusion singer of the 1970s, both artistically and commercially. Many were the jazz fans in that decade who tuned in one of Flora's songs on the radio and were astonished and delighted by what they heard. She sang with great passion in Portuguese and accented English, with a sensuous voice that was alternately smooth and husky. Flora used an amazing array of vocal effects: squeaks, moans, cries, electronic distortions, freeform scatting, and precipitous glissandi. A new type of jazz singer, she could serve as a lead vocalist or as another instrument interacting with the flute, guitar, and percussion. Flora was ideally suited to collaborate with the creative talents of Airto, George Duke, Chick Corea, Hermeto Pascoal, and Stanley Clarke.

Born in 1942, Flora grew up listening to jazz and blues, as well as samba and classical music. She sang in various clubs in and around Rio in the 1960s, during which time she met Hermeto Pascoal, who suggested she try wordless vocal improvisations. After moving to New York in 1968, she sat in on jam sessions with the likes of Herbie Hancock and Thelonious Monk. Her first gigs involved singing jazz-bossa in Europe with Stan Getz and recording with Duke Pearson and Gil Evans.

Then Corea invited Purim and Moreira to play on the *Return to Forever* album, and she stayed with that band for two years, singing and writing lyrics for songs such as "Light as a Feather." George Duke observed that "she was so free melodically that she sounded like a horn player. It was absolutely new music. I don't think there's anybody that sings quite like her. Free as a bird."[27]

In 1973 Purim recorded her solo debut, *Butterfly Dreams*. The album's opening notes—Airto's cuíca and Stanley Clarke's funky bass playing off each other—foreshadowed the jazz-fusion feast to follow. The album's personnel also included keyboardist Duke, guitarist Amaro, flutist Joe Henderson, and zither player Ernie Hood. Collectively they mixed funk-Brazilian grooves with uninhibited free-form soloing to create one of the era's most noted works. Highlights included Purim's lovely rendition of Jobim's beautiful "Dindi" and the ballad "Love Reborn," with its bossa-like guitar, Flora's romantic vocals, and Henderson's languid sax.

Flora cut a live album in Montreux, finished another studio work, *Stories to Tell*, and then was awarded *Down Beat* magazine's 1974 award for best female jazz vocalist. In 1976 she recorded *Open Your Eyes, You Can Fly*, whose title song became one of her most popular standards. That album included Duke, Airto, Pascoal, Gismonti, bassist Alphonso Johnson, and drummers Ndugu and Robertinho Silva.

In later decades Flora released several more albums and was a frequent performer at events such as the Montreux Jazz Festival. She has worked frequently with Airto, including in their group Fourth World with saxophonist-flutist Gary Meek and acoustic guitarist José Neto. She also teamed with Mickey Hart and Airto on the intriguing *Dafos* (1989) and added vocals to Hart's world music drumming-and-percussion fest *Planet Drum* (1991). In the first decade of the new century, she continued to blur the lines between jazz and world music with *Speak No Evil* (2003) and *Flora's Song* (2005).

ITHAMARA AND LUCIANA

In 2000, with the release of the album *Serenade in Blue*, North Americans listeners were introduced to jazz singer Ithamara Koorax, and they liked what they heard. *Down Beat* magazine's readers voted her one of the top ten female jazz singers of the year, an honor that had previously gone to

▼ Ithamara Koorax. *(Courtesy of Milestone Records.)*

only one other Brazilian singer: Flora Purim. *Down Beat* readers honored her again in 2002.

Born in 1965 in Niterói (Sérgio Mendes's birthplace), Ithamara had been amassing cult followers for some time—first in Brazil, where she had worked with Paulo César Pinheiro and Guinga, and then in Europe and Japan. She released her first solo album, *Luiza/Live in Rio,* in Japan in 1994. Two years later she collaborated with Bonfá, Ron Carter, Larry Coryell, Sadao Watanabe, and Eumir Deodato on *Almost in Love/Ithamara Koorax Sings the Luiz Bonfá Songbook,* setting the stage for her mainstream acceptance in the new millennium. Brazilian pianist and composer Mario Castro-Neves praised her "amazing vocal range" and "the uniqueness of her interpretation and the crystalline beauty of her voice."[28]

Luciana Souza is another Brazilian vocalist who followed in the footsteps of Flora Purim and has been embraced by the jazz world. Born in 1966 to a family of musicians in São Paulo, Luciana began recording as a child and by the age of sixteen had already recorded two hundred commercial jingles. When she decided to take music more seriously, she moved to the United States, where she studied jazz at the Berklee College of Music and the New England Conservatory. Luci-

▼ Luciana Souza. *(Courtesy of Sunny Side Records.)*

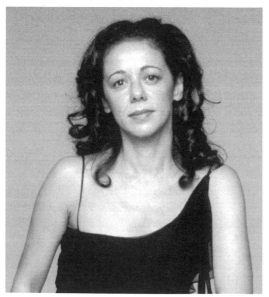

ana employed her musical knowledge and her expressive, pitch-perfect alto voice on albums that brought together jazz, Brazilian classics, thoughtful lyrics, and poetry. Some of her work is beautifully spare: *Brazilian Duos* (2002) has just voice and guitar, with Luciana accompanied by the playing of Marco Pereira, Romero Lubambo, and her father Walter Santos. She won Grammy nominations for that album and the three that followed it: *North and South, Neruda,* and *Duos II.* Luciana was picked as Female Jazz Singer of the Year in 2005 by the Jazz Journalists Association, and has also crossed over into classical music, performing with several symphony orchestras.

THE BRAZILIAN WAVE

Of the prolonged interchange between Brazilian and American music, Sérgio Mendes told us some twenty years ago, "It's interesting for me today to see Herbie Hancock doing things with Milton Nascimento. It's a kind of mutual curiosity between two different worlds. I still listen to Horace Silver and Bud Powell. And Stevie Wonder, Henry Mancini, Burt Bacharach, Pat Metheny—who has not been influenced by Brazilian music?"[29]

Latin American and Caribbean music strongly influenced American jazz and popular music throughout the twentieth century, as was painstakingly documented by musicologist John Storm Roberts in *The Latin Tinge.* Jelly Roll Morton used the habanera rhythm in many songs, Cole Porter incorporated the rumba, and Professor Longhair and Fats Domino both had Latin-influenced piano styles. Rocker Bo Diddley's trademark beat was a pounding rumba rhythm, with Jerome Green on maracas. And jazz musicians Dizzy Gillespie, Duke Ellington, Stan Kenton, George Shearing, and Bud Shank experimented with Latin (especially Cuban) rhythms, percussion, and song styles in the 1940s and '50s.

The Brazilian Percussion Invasion

Brazilian music—its rhythms, instruments, harmonies, melodies, and textures—had an enormous influence on American music from 1962 on. Percussionists were a large part of that impact. Brazilian music helped create a new rhythmic emphasis in jazz and became an important element in the emerging style called "jazz fusion." As noted above, Airto Moreira led the way in this rhythmic revolution, and Naná Vasconcelos had a strong impact a few years later. Other influential Brazilian drummers and percussionists in the 1960s and '70s were Dom Um Romão (1925–2005), Édison Machado (1934–1990), Milton Banana (1935–1999), Laudir de Oliveira, and Guilherme Franco, all of whom recorded and toured with numerous jazz, rock, and pop artists in the United States. Paulinho da Costa (born in 1948) settled in Southern California in 1973, played with Sérgio Mendes for four years, and then was one of L.A.'s most active session players in the late 1970s and '80s. He added drums and percussion to hundreds of pop albums, working with Quincy Jones, Michael Jackson (Paulinho was the percussionist on *Thriller* in 1982), Sting, and Madonna, and also recording with notable jazz artists.

"In all fusion bands, the drummers slip into a jazz-Brazilian groove almost automatically," observed jazz flutist Herbie Mann. And in the 1970s, "it became almost matter of fact for every band to have a percussionist. But all the colors were Brazilian-influenced. Before that, the Latin drummers just played congas, timbales, and bongos."[30]

Speaking of samba and its cousins in 1989, George Duke commented, "I think you can find these Brazilian rhythms everywhere; they've gone into TV and film scoring. And percussion has become so strong in dance music; all that stuff on top is Brazilian stuff that sounds like a batucada— shakers, agogôs, and those kind of rhythms. In a strange sort of way, it infiltrated the modern pop world without them even knowing it."[31]

The Pat Metheny Group is an example of a band that consciously incorporated many Brazilian elements into its sound. "During the first half of the group's history, one hundred percent of the music we did had that straight-eighth rhythm, which comes from Brazilian music," observed Lyle Mays, noting that most jazz has the charac-

teristic "swing eighth note." Mays was the keyboardist for the group and co-wrote its material with Metheny. "You can hear it in 'San Lorenzo,' 'Phase Dance,' and then it is even more evident in the album *Watercolors*. We played on electric guitar and keyboards, but under the surface the actual rhythms had a whole lot to do with Brazilian music. I don't mean that to sound like we were pioneers. It was a thing happening in jazz in general, such as with Gary Burton, which is where Pat got it from. There was some Latin influence going around too, all the way back to Dizzy Gillespie. But the Brazilian rhythms are a little more subtle and translated into a music that sounded like a hybrid. It wasn't so obvious it was Brazilian-based."[32]

While such influences were "covert," as Lyle saw it, a more "overt" impact began when Brazilian musicians began to join American bands. A good example is the effect Vasconcelos had on the Pat Metheny Group. In 1981 Metheny and Mays started to work with Naná, who stayed with them through *Travels* (1983). He made a vivid atmospheric contribution to their sound; and, rhythmically, some of their tunes, such as "Are You Going with Me?" and "Straight on Red," became more obviously samba-based.

Vasconcelos left the group after a few years but would later play on Lyle Mays's 1986 eponymous solo album and Pat Metheny's 1992 solo effort *Secret Story*. The latter album also featured Brazilian percussionist Armando Marçal, who took Naná's place in the Pat Metheny Group in the mid-1980s and appeared on albums such as *Still Life (Talking)* and *Letter from Home*.

"I think that Naná was more interested in sounds and textures, while Armando is more interested in rhythms. Armando is almost like an entire samba school," said Mays. "He has maybe the strongest rhythmic clock of anybody I've ever heard, just relentless, incredible. He does everything from rock tambourine parts to more tradianal samba."[33]

Keyboardist-composer Don Grusin and his brother Dave Grusin have both been inspired by the Brazilian sound. "It started in the 1960s, when I first heard Astrud Gilberto and Stan Getz and

Brazilian Rhythm Masters and International Music

Brazil turns out great drummers and percussionists the way it turns out great soccer players. Some of the best, past and present, with careers primarily within Brazil include Marcos Suzano, Robertinho Silva, Pascoal Meirelles, Milton Banana (Antonio de Souza), Jorginho do Pandeiro, Wilson das Neves, Hélcio Milito, Paulinho Braga, Chico Batera, Dom Chacal, Gordinho, Sidinho, Jurim Moreira, Marcelo Costa, Toninho Pinheiro, Ovídio Brito, Simone Soul, and Firminho. Other Brazilian rhythm masters have performed a great deal overseas, and the following is a sampling of the recording and touring activity of a select few in recent decades. The name of the Brazilian artist (or ensemble) is followed by some of the international artists with whom they toured or recorded.

Waltinho Anastácio: JoAnne Brackeen, Gerry Mulligan, Keiko Lee, Lee Konitz.

Mingo Araújo: Paul Simon, Edie Brickell, Willie Nelson.

Cyro Baptista: Paul Simon, David Byrne, Ambitious Lovers, Herbie Mann, Paula Robison, Ryuichi Sakamoto, Kathleen Battle, Gato Barbieri, Dr. John, Brian Eno, Robert Palmer, Melissa Etheridge, Laurie Anderson, John Zorn, James Taylor, Carly Simon, Michael Tilson Thomas, Daniel Barenboim, Bobby McFerrin, Wynton Marsalis, Yo-Yo Ma, Spyro Gyra, Trey Anastasio of Phish, Jay-Z, Santana, Sting, the Chieftains, Cassandra Wilson, Richard Stoltzman, Herbie Hancock.

Carlinhos Brown: Bill Laswell, Wayne Shorter, Herbie Hancock.

Café (Edson Aparecido da Silva): Elements, Sadão Watanabe, Roberta Flack, David Byrne, Herbie Mann, Larry Coryell, Michael Brecker, Randy Brecker, Richard Stoltzman, Paul Winter, Stevie Winwood, Gato Barbieri, Michael Franks, Harry Belafonte, Chuck Mangione, Ernie Watts, Paquito d'Rivera, James Taylor, Stevie Wonder.

Djalma Correa: Peter Gabriel, the Manhattan Transfer.

Mayuto Correa: Charles Lloyd, Gabor Szabo, Hugh Masakela, Freddie Hubbard, Donald Byrd.

João Gilberto," recalled Don, who produced and arranged albums for Gilberto Gil, Simone, Rique Pantoja, and other Brazilian artists. He sees Brazilian music as having strongly influenced the jazz of his era. "I hear a kind of hybrid sound in my music and that of Dave, Lee Ritenour, Ronnie Foster, Harvey Mason."[34]

The Melodic-Harmonic Impact

"I think Brazilian music has affected jazz musicians and songwriters a lot, including how they melodically approach their music," George Duke commented. "I know that when I was in Brazil in the 1970s, I bought every Milton, Ivan Lins, Edu Lobo, and Simone record I could find. I brought them back and played them for my friends. And then I sat down and tried to emulate those songs, to compose in that area, and you can hear that on some of my early records. The same way I learned to play jazz, I learned to play Brazilian music; you have to learn the fundamentals first. And I know that Cannonball Adderley was totally immersed in that music before he died. He felt the same way."[35]

Duke collaborated on many recordings with Brazilian musicians. His album *A Brazilian Love Affair* (1977) featured Milton, Airto, and Flora Pu-

Paulinho da Costa: Dizzy Gillespie, Milt Jackson, Ella Fitzgerald, Joe Pass, Quincy Jones, Michael Jackson, Madonna, Sting, Barbra Streisand, Lionel Richie, and hundreds of others.

Alyrio Lima Cova: Webster Lewis, Weather Report, Pat Martino.

Duduka da Fonseca: JoAnne Brackeen, Herbie Mann.

Guilherme Franco: Gato Barbieri, Keith Jarrett, McCoy Tyner, Elvin Jones, Don Pullen, Paul Winter.

Téo Lima: Yutaka, Hendrik Meurkens, Toots Thielemans.

Édison Machado: Herbie Mann, Stan Getz.

Armando Marçal (Marçalzinho): The Pat Metheny Group, Paul Simon.

Airto Moreira: Miles Davis, Weather Report, Return to Forever, Stan Getz, Paul Simon, George Duke, Paul Desmond, Mickey Hart, Bob James, Bobby Hutcherson, Cal Tjader, Cannonball Adderley, Santana, Chaka Khan, Chick Corea, Charles Rouse, Dee Dee Bridgewater, Diane Reeves, Dizzy Gillespie, Donald Byrd, Freddie Hubbard, George Benson, Hubert Laws, John McLaughlin, Joni Mitchell, Joe Farrell, Wayne Shorter, Tina Turner, Stanley Turrentine.

Laudir de Oliveira: Chicago, Nina Simone.

Olodum: Paul Simon, Bill Laswell, Herbie Hancock, Wayne Shorter.

João Parahyba: Michel LeGrand, Dizzy Gillespie.

Dom Um Romão: Cannonball Adderley, Tony Bennett, Paul Horn, Weather Report.

Jorge da Silva: John Zorn, Arto Lindsay, David Byrne.

Naná Vasconcelos: Don Cherry, Miles Davis, Art Blakey, Tony Williams, Ralph Towner, Gato Barbieri, the Pat Metheny Group, Paul Simon, B. B. King, the Talking Heads, Leon Thomas, Jean-Luc Ponty, Jon Hassell, Harry Belafonte, Claus Ogerman, Ginger Baker, Jack DeJohnette, Jan Garbarek, Lyle Mays, Carly Simon, the Yellowjackets.

rim. Duke, like many jazz artists, turned to Brazil in the 1970s and 1980s for great melodies to cover, because so much of the music sounded fresh and original. It is arguable that in recent decades American composers have not been writing popular songs that have the melodic-harmonic quality of the standards produced by the likes of George Gershwin, Duke Ellington, Cole Porter, and Billy Strayhorn earlier in the twentieth century. "The U.S. is becoming more of a rhythm nation than a melodic nation," noted Duke, speaking twenty years ago. "Brazil is both."[36]

In recent years the songs of Tom Jobim, Milton Nascimento, Ivan Lins, Gilberto Gil, Djavan, and other composers from Brazil have been covered extensively overseas. Numerous jazz musicians have also been mining the musical treasures of the choro and samba-canção eras, recording the standards of Pixinguinha, Jacó do Bandolim, and Ary Barroso.

Over the past few decades, noteworthy international artists not mentioned at length elsewhere in the book who have covered Brazilian songs include the Crusaders, Joe Pass, Carmen McRae, Diane Schuur, Sadao Watanabe, Al Jarreau, Al Di Meola, Willie Bobo, Larry Coryell, Quincy Jones, Ella Fitzgerald, Toots Thielemans, Mark Murphy, Lee Ritenour, Ernie Watts, Patti

Austin, Hendrik Meurkens, Terence Blanchard, Joe Henderson, and Kenny Baron.

KEYBOARDS AND ACCORDION

One of the most influential Brazilian musicians in North America in the 1970s was Eumir Deodato, a pianist-arranger born in Rio in 1943. Eumir scored a smash hit with his funky-jazzy rendition of Richard Strauss's "Also Sprach Zarathustra" in 1973 (which at the time was on the public mind because of Stanley Kubrick's film *2001: A Space Odyssey*). Deodato's hip version went to number 2 on *Billboard*'s pop singles chart, and the album it was from, *Prelude* (1972), hit number 3.

Deodato also played an important part in launching Milton Nascimento's career in Brazil by arranging Milton's songs for his debut at the International Song Festival in Rio. In the United States, Eumir helped shape the pop sound of the 1970s and '80s through his work as a producer or arranger for acts such as Kool and the Gang, Earth, Wind and Fire, Roberta Flack, Bette Midler, Stanley Turrentine, Björk, and Aretha Franklin.

Singer-songwriter-pianist Tania Maria (born in 1948) was a familiar figure on jazz radio in the 1980s, achieving great success with a spicy combination of Brazilian and Cuban rhythms, funk and rock influences, a percussive piano attack, and vigorous vocals. Tania started her career in France by launching several albums there, then moved to the United States. She released her first album, *Piquant*, there in 1981, produced by Latin-jazz legend Cal Tjader. Later came a string of hit albums, notably *Come with Me* and *Love Explosion*, that established her as a compelling new jazz voice.

Pianist-composer Eliane Elias established her career in the 1980s with a style steeped in traditional jazz. She has been lauded for her impressive piano technique, harmonic inventiveness, and compositional skill. Born in 1960 in São Paulo, Eliane was a child prodigy who at the age of twelve could play challenging jazz standards on the piano. At seventeen she started playing be-

▲ Eliane Elias. *(Photo by Paul D'Inmocenzo. Courtesy of Blue Note.)*

hind Vinícius de Moraes and Toquinho and stayed with their group for three years. In 1981 in Paris she met bassist Eddie Gomez, then a member of the fusion group Steps Ahead. She subsequently moved to New York and began a one-year stint with the band. She married American trumpet player Randy Brecker, with whom she recorded *Amanda* (named for their daughter) in 1985. On her first solo album, *Illusions* (1987), Elias delved into bebop, ballads, and choro, backed by Gomez, Al Foster, Stanley Clarke, Lenny White, and Toots Thielemans. *Cross Currents* (1988) was heavily jazz-oriented, while *So Far, So Close* (1989) included more samba, choro, and bossa. *Eliane Elias Sings Jobim* (1998) is an album dedicated exclusively to Tom Jobim's songs. Herbie Hancock has said of Elias, "She plays so beautifully that it makes me cry. I love the harmonies she uses."[37]

Antonio Adolfo started his career in the mid-1960s with the trio 3-D and went on to become a leading keyboardist, songwriter, and music teacher. His song "Sá Marina" was given English lyrics by Marilyn and Alan Bergman, and (as "Pretty World") was recorded by Stevie Wonder, Sérgio Mendes, Herb Alpert, and Earl Klugh, among others. In 1977, frustrated by the indifference of major record companies in Brazil to instrumental music, Adolfo financed and released his own album, *Feito em Casa* (Homemade), and its success proved there was a small but eager market for such works. Many other artists subsequently launched their own albums, triggering a boom in independent recording. Adolfo later released the accomplished albums *Cristalino* (1989), *Jinga* (1990), and *Chiquinha com Jazz* (1997), the last reviving the works of the important turn-of-the-century composer Chiquinha Gonzaga.

Sivuca (Severino D'Oliveira, 1930–2006) was an accordion virtuoso who also sang and played piano and guitar. Born in Itabaiana, Paraíba, he recorded numerous albums featuring forró, choro, waltzes, and other genres interpreted with a folksy, jazzy style and embellished with rich improvisation. He was a fixture on the international jazz scene from the 1960s on and toured and recorded with Miriam Makeba, Harry Belafonte, Oscar Brown Jr., Airto Moreira, and Toots Thielemans.

Other notable contemporary Brazilian piano and synthesizer players include João Carlos Assis Brasil, Wagner Tiso, Amilson Godoy, Amilton Godoy, Manfredo Fest, Dom Salvador, Cido Bianchi, César Camargo Mariano, Nelson Ayres, Gilson

▼ The cover of Sivuca's *Som Brasil* album. *(Courtesy of Sonet Records.)*

Peranzzetta, João Carlos Assis Brasil, Marcos Ariel, Tulio Mourão, Lincoln Olivetti, Luiz Avellar, Ricardo Leão, Marcos Silva, Marcos Souza, Rique Pantoja, Guilherme Vergueiro, Paulo Calasans, Paulo Braga, Jota Morais, Marcio Miranda, William Magalhães, and Marinho Boffa. A few of Brazil's many outstanding accordion players are Dominguinhos, Renato Borghetti, Chiquinho do Acordeon, Baú dos Oito Baixos, Orlando Silveira, and Severo.

GUITAR AND STRINGS

If there is one musical instrument that most typifies Brazil, it is the guitar. Brazil has produced many greats on that instrument, from Garoto, to Baden Powell, to Yamandú Costa. Two guitarists who are largely forgotten in Brazil today but once were popular around the world were Los Indios Tabajaras, a duo consisting of the brothers Natalício Moreira Lima (Erundi) and Antenor Moreira Lima (Mucaperê), members of the Tabajara tribe in Ceará state. Self-taught musicians, they developed a successful nightclub act in which they played Brazilian folk songs and dressed up in ceremonial Indian costumes. They toured Latin America and released albums through RCA's Latin American division. In the early 1950s they took a break to study erudite music, each with a different teacher, and added Villa-Lobos, Bach, and Albeniz to their repertoire. They began to release albums in North America and found a receptive audience for their easy-listening renditions of pop and light classical standards on classical guitar. Their version of "Maria Elena" (a tune first popularized by Jimmy Dorsey) was a Top 10 U.S. hit in 1958 and a success in Europe and Latin America (interestingly, Terry Gilliam initially wanted to use a Ry Cooder recording of "Maria Elena," a.k.a. "Maria Helena," for his movie *Brazil* before settling on Ary Barroso's "Aquarela do Brasil").[38] The brothers toured internationally and recorded albums together into the 1980s, with compilations of their greatest RCA hits still being released in subsequent years.

Bola Sete (Djalma Andrade, 1923–1987) was a guitarist who was adept at mixing jazz and samba and playing choro and bossa nova. Born in Rio, he studied classical music at the National School of Music and was influenced early in his career by Andres Segovia, Django Reinhardt, and Charlie Christian. He developed a versatile repertoire, playing in samba groups and composing choros ("Cosminho no Choro," for example). In 1959 he moved to the United States and lived there for the rest of his life, developing his own jazz-samba fusion. Bola toured with Dizzy Gillespie and recorded several albums for Fantasy Records (one of the best was *Autêntico!*).

Heraldo do Monte (born in Recife in 1935) was a member of Quarteto Novo with Airto Moreira

and Hermeto Pascoal. Heraldo is a master of the guitar and has a command of many other string instruments as well, including the mandolin and cavaquinho. In the 1980s he recorded the excellent solo albums *Cordas Vivas* (Live Strings) and *Cordas Mágicas* (Magic Strings), which show off his dazzling electric and acoustic guitar work and mix baião, xaxado, and other regional styles with choro and Tal Farlow influences.

The brothers Sérgio Assad (born 1952) and Odair Assad (born 1956) perform on classical guitar and have arguably been the world's most famous guitar duo since the 1990s, when they drew international attention with a series of outstanding releases on Nonesuch Records. Their wide range encompasses classical music (Rameau, Scarlatti, Bach), choro, Hungarian folk tunes, flamenco, and Brazilian composers from Heitor Villa-Lobos to Egberto Gismonti. Their Latin Grammy award–winning *Sérgio and Odair Assad Play Piazzolla* interprets Astor Piazzolla, and a collaboration with violinist Nadja Salerno-Sonnenberg features pieces written by Sérgio that were inspired by gypsy folk tunes from Europe. They have also appeared on notable albums by others, such as cellist Yo-Yo Ma's *Obrigado Brazil*.

Sérgio and Odair's younger sister, Badi Assad (born in 1966), has the same solid background in classical guitar as her siblings but has branched

▲ Bola Sete (guitar), Paulinho (drums), and Sebastião Neto (bass) on the cover of an album recorded for Fantasy in the 1960s. *(Courtesy of Fantasy.)*

◄ Sergio and Odair Assad. *(Courtesy of GHA Records.)*

▶ The guitar trio D'Alma in 1988 (*left to right*): Andre Geraissati, Ulisses Rocha, and Marco Pereira. *(Photo by Paulo Vasconcellos. Courtesy of Som da Gente Records.)*

further into the realms of MPB, jazz, and international pop. She established herself overseas with the mid-1990s albums *Solo* and *Rhythms*, interpreting Brazilian works. Moving to the United States in 1997, where she would live for the next seven years, she expanded her work as a composer with the album *Chameleon*, then collaborated with jazz guitarists Larry Coryell and John Abercrombie on *Three Guitars*. She subsequently signed with Edge Music, an imprint of the prestigious Deutsche Grammophon classical label, and released *Verde* (2005), with songs by Björk and U2. Her *Wonderland* (2006) was a crossover work emphasizing Badi's vocals along with her guitar work on international and Brazilian songs, ranging from Tori Amos to Lenine. The album was produced by Jacques Morelenbaum and featured Carlos Malta (saxophone and flute) and Marcos Suzano (percussion).

Paulo Bellinati is an accomplished Brazilian contemporary guitarist, as well as an important composer and arranger. Born in 1950, he studied with Isaias Sávio (1900–1977), a renowned guitar teacher from Uruguay who settled in São Paulo and also taught Luiz Bonfá. As a composer, Bellinati has enhanced lundus, sambas, modinhas, jongos, maracatus, frevos, xaxados, and other traditional Brazilian forms with modern compositional techniques and harmonies. His works have

been recorded and performed by John Williams, the Los Angeles Guitar Quartet, and fellow brasileiros Badi Assad, the Assad Brothers, Cristina Azuma, and Carlos Barbosa-Lima.

Paulo has arranged many prize-winning albums and has made important contributions to the field of musical scholarship. He spent eight years researching, transcribing, and recording the music of the great Brazilian guitarist-composer Annibal Augusto Sardinha (Garoto), and won praise for his recording of *The Guitar Works of Garoto* and publication of printed music of Garoto's compositions.

Carlos Barbosa-Lima (born in 1944) is another Brazilian master of the classical guitar. He made his recording debut at age twelve. He studied with the aforementioned Sávio and later with the legendary Andrés Segovia. In the early 1990s he recorded solo albums and collaborations with Charlie Byrd, Laurindo Almeida, and Sharon Isbin. Paris-based Cristina Azuma, born in 1964 in São Paulo, is another notable classical guitarist from Brazil.

Marco Pereira (born in 1956) has applied his impeccable guitar technique to albums such as *Círculo das Cordas* (Circle of Strings, 1988), a compelling meeting of classical guitar and jazz improvisation. Pereira, a respected composer, arranger, and teacher, has recorded solo works and collaborations with pianist Cristovão Bastos and mandolinist Hamilton de Holanda, and has teamed up with fellow guitar masters André Geraissati and Ulisses Rocha in the acoustic guitar trio D'Alma.

Despite a premature death at age 32 in 1995, guitarist Raphael Rabello left behind a formidable body of work and enlivened choro and other Brazilian idioms with his exuberant talent and superlative technique.

Other Brazilian guitarists of note, past and present, include Dilermando Reis, Dino 7 Cordas, *viola caipira* specialists Helena Meirelles and Roberto Corrêa (see Chapter Ten), Nonato Luis, Cristóvão Bastos, Olmir "Alemão" Stocker, Hélio Delmiro, Durval Ferreira, Victor Biglione, Almir Sater, Fredera, Turíbio Santos, Paulinho Soledade, Natan Marques, Romero Lubambo, João Lyra, Nelson Faria, Luiz Brazil, Eduardo Gudin, Canhoto da Paraíba, Francisco Soares de Araújo, Tavinho Bonfá, Jaime Alem, Luiz Brasil, Ricardo Silveira, Heitor T. P. (guitarist-composer Heitor Teixeira Pereira), and Torcuato Mariano (who was born in Argentina but moved to Brazil at age fourteen). On the bass guitar, some of the best are Luis Alves, Nico Assumpção, Jorge Degas, Zeca Assumpção, Pedro Ivo, Arismar do Espírito Santo, Artur Maia, Luizão Maia, Nilson Matta, Rubão Sabino, Yuri Popoff, and Jamil Joanes.

WIND INSTRUMENTS AND COMBOS

Pixinguinha was not the last notable wind musician to come from Brazil. Cláudio Roditi, a trumpeter who has been part of the international jazz scene since the early 1970s, has appeared on albums by Charlie Rouse, Slide Hampton, Herbie Mann, and Paquito D'Rivera. His solo albums *Gemini Man* and *Slow Fire* display his unique bebop-Brazilian blends. Raul de Souza is a trombonist who was a strong presence in the jazz world in the 1960s and '70s, recording with the Crusaders and Sonny Rollins, among others.

Moacir Santos (1926–2006), who taught music theory to both Airto Moreira and Flora Purim, became an influential music professor and men-

▲ Moacir Santos, as pictured on the cover of one of his albums.

▲ Progressive-jazz band Azymuth (*left to right*): Ivan Conti, José Roberto Bertrami, and Alex Malheiros. (*Courtesy of Milestone Records.*)

tor for many young Brazilian musicians when he moved to the United States in 1969. He scored a big hit in Brazil with "Naná" in 1964, and in the United States recorded three albums for Blue Note in the early 1970s (including *Maestro*, for which he received a Grammy nomination). Moacir lived in Pasadena, California, for forty years, rarely returning to Brazil. He was known for

▲ Jazz ensemble Cama de Gato performing at the Jazzmania club in Rio (*left to right*): Rique Pantoja, Arthur Maia, Mauro Senise, and Pascoal Meirelles. *(Photo by Chris McGowan.)*

his esoteric mixes of jazz, Brazilian idioms, and complicated rhythms, often in large-ensemble arrangements. *Coisas*, Moacir's 1965 album, was included in *New York Times* jazz critic Ben Ratliff's list of the top one hundred jazz albums of all time.[39] *Ouro Negro* (2001) is a noteworthy tribute to his music produced by Mario Adnet and Zé Nogueira.

Saxophonist Leo Gandelman's smooth, swinging playing style and mixing of jazz, technopop, and Brazilian genres made him the most popular Brazilian instrumental artist of the late 1980s and early 1990s—voted into that position four years in a row by the Brazilian press. Gandelman's solo albums *Solar*, *Visions*, and *Made in Rio*—featuring both standards and songs written by himself and keyboardist William Magalhães—reached a wide national audience. Trumpeter Márcio Montarroyos (1948–2007) was a valued session man in Brazil and on North American jazz recordings,

and his solo albums, among them *Samba Solstice*, found an international audience.

Other prominent Brazilian wind musicians include harmonica players Mauricio Einhorn, Flavio Guimarães, and Rildo Hora; saxophonist-flutists Teco Cardoso, Nivaldo Ornellas, Roberto Sion, Mauro Senise, Dirceu Leitte, Marcelo Martins, and Raul Mascarenhas; trombonists Raul de Barros and Bocato; saxophonist-pianist Zé Nogueira; clarinetist Paulo Sérgio dos Santos; flutists Danilo Caymmi and Andrea Dias; trumpeters Guilherme Dias Gomes and Bidinho; and flutist-guitarist Edson Alves.

In terms of combos, the trio Azymuth was a popular international act in the 1980s that blended jazz, samba, and funk. The band featured José Roberto Bertrami on keyboards, Ivan Conti on drums, and Alex Malheiros on bass (all three were born in 1946). In 1979 they released *Light as a Feather*, and its single "Jazz Carnival" went gold in England. *Telecommunication* (1982) was a Top 10 jazz album. Azymuth went on to record many more albums, and the threesome also released numerous solo works on their own.

Cama de Gato (Cat's Cradle) released compel-

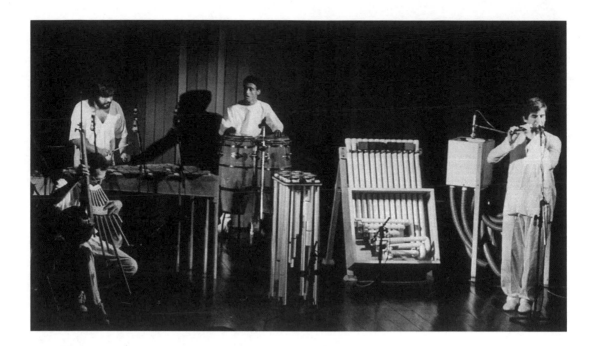

▲ Uakti in concert. *(Photo by Cristiano Quintino. Courtesy of Verve.)*

ling Brazilian "fusion" albums in the 1980s and was composed of four talented instrumental artists—bassist Arthur Maia, saxophonist-flutist Mauro Senise, drummer Pascoal Meirelles, and keyboardist Rique Pantoja. Nó Em Pingo D'Agua (Knot in a Drop of Water) is an instrumental combo that augments choro with samba, jazz, tango, and salsa. Its founder, flutist-saxophonist Mario Seve, is also a member of Aquarela Carioca (Rio Watercolor), which moves fluidly through the above styles and maracatu, pop, and reggae. Other accomplished instrumental groups from recent years include Funk Como Le Gusta, Orquestra de Cordas Dedilhadas de Pernambuco (Plucked String Orchestra of Pernambuco), Pau Brasil (Brazilwood) with bassist Rodolfo Stroeter and guitarist Paulo Bellinati, Orquestra de Música Brasileira, and Homem de Bem (Man of Good).

UAKTI

One of Brazil's most innovative Brazilian instrumental groups is Uakti, which takes its name from a mythological figure of the Toucan tribe in the Amazon rainforest. His story was recounted in the liner notes of the band's eponymous U.S. debut album. Uakti's body was perforated with holes, and when the wind blew through them an irresistible sound was produced that attracted all the Toucan women. Jealous, the men killed Uakti, burying his body in the ground in a place where tall palms later grew. From the wood of the palms the Indians fashioned instruments that could produce melodious and seductive tones like those once made by the wind passing through Uakti's body. Naturally, it was absolutely forbidden to play these flutes outside of secret male ceremonies.

The group Uakti, which also makes its own instruments, was formed in the mid-1970s by Marco Antonio Guimarães, who had studied at the University of Bahia with the legendary composer Walter Smetak, a sort of Swiss-Brazilian Harry Partch who created new musical systems and instruments. One of Smetak's creations was A *Grande Virgem* (The Big Virgin), a giant flute played by twenty-two persons.

When Guimarães returned home to Belo Horizonte, Minas Gerais, he gathered together a group of like-minded adventurous musicians, each of whom had classical training: Paulo Sérgio dos Santos, Artur Andres Ribeiro, and Décio de Souza Ramos. The foursome designed an orchestra of wholly original string, wind, and percussion instruments. Among them are the *planetário* (planetarium), a wooden box strung with latex bands; the *marimba de vidro*, a two-octave glass marimba; and the *trilobita* (trilobite), a cluster of tuned PVC tubes topped with drum skins. The sounds that come from them are as mesmerizing as what might have come from their mythological namesake. They mix together maracatu, samba, jazz, minimalism, and elements of medieval, Hindu, and Andean music; all this is then played upon their strange-looking and beautiful-sounding instruments, producing what sounds like chamber music from some lost civilization.

Uakti's early releases include the outstanding works *Tudo e Todas As Coisas* (All and Everything), *Mapa* (Map), and *I Ching*. The group also made appearances on albums by Milton Nascimento—most notably on *Anima*—in the 1980s and can be heard on the Manhattan Transfer's *Brasil* and Paul Simon's *The Rhythm of the Saints*. In 1993 the group was asked to perform "Águas da Amazônia" (Waters of the Amazon), an original work by American composer Philip Glass commissioned by Grupo Corpo, a Belo Horizonte dance company that had previously worked with Guimarães. The *Águas da Amazônia* album was released in 1999. Uakti also teamed with Glass on *Orion*, a multicultural collaboration featuring Glass and other composers, commissioned for the 2004 Athens Olympiad. In 2005 Uakti released *Oiapok Xui*, a rich, innovative, and at the same time accessible musical mix that includes standards such as Ary Barroso's "Aquarela do Brasil," Tom Jobim's "Águas de Março," and Milton Nascimento's "Cravo e Canela."

THE INTERNATIONAL IMPACT

Looking at the profound influence of Brazilian rhythms, songwriting, and percussion on global music, it is fitting to reiterate Sérgio Mendes's rhetorical question: "Who has not been influenced by Brazilian music?" A significant interchange has been going on for more than a century and has accelerated over the past few decades. Herbie Mann added, "It gets to the point where you have Djavan recording in Los Angeles, and Manhattan Transfer in Brazil, and they are all using people who have been listening to Herbie Hancock and Ivan Lins. That is, it all gets so crossed that each in turn re-influences the other."[40]

Oh, my God, what happened to MPB?
Everybody is serious
Everyone takes it seriously
But this seriousness sounds like a game to me

Rita Lee and Paulo Coelho,
"Arrombou a Festa" (Crashed
the Party)

Over the past several decades, rock has undergone as complex an evolution in Brazil as it has in the United States, its country of origin. Brazilian musicians have produced their own versions of bubble-gum rock, Beatles-style pop rock, hard rock, punk rock, folk rock, and heavy metal. They have also fused rock with Brazilian genres such as frevo, baião, samba, and maracatu, inventing new musical hybrids. Rock and roll has also met with sharp criticism from Brazilians who have resented the encroachment of American pop music into MPB territory. The band Os Mutantes, of which Rita Lee was a member, was an early target of nationalistic wrath.

As a whole, Brazilian rock came of age in the 1980s. One reason for this, perhaps, was that the new generation of *roqueiros* (rockers) had grown up listening to rock—American, English, and Brazilian—their entire lives. "It was like our generation was eating the whole rock history," commented singer Paulo Ricardo, ex-leader of RPM, the first rock act to sell more than two million units of a single album. "We had all that information in our minds and we couldn't wait to put it all together. We felt we were equal in some sense with rock in the rest of the world."[1]

Starting in that decade, Brazilian roqueiros had access to high-quality electric guitars and keyboards and high-tech recording equipment, and they demonstrated a great degree of professionalism in staging shows. They also began to benefit from increased support from music companies. These changes helped the leading Brazilian rock acts to realize their potential, producing innovative music of high technical quality. And the best Brazilian rock wordsmiths carried on the MPB tradition of great lyric writing, albeit with an angrier, more outspoken edge. Cazuza, Titãs, the Engenheiros, the Paralamas, Legião Urbana, and other bands from the new generation became enormously successful in Brazil.

Two other factors may have contributed to producing so many notable rock artists in that decade: the lifting of censorship imposed by the government, and the arrival of the socioeconomic crisis that slammed Brazil in the 1980s. During the military dictatorship's heaviest repression, roughly between 1968 and 1978, lyrics had to be free of political content or heavily coded, and MPB artists crafted elegant and metaphoric verses to voice their discontent. But in the next decade songwriters were by and large free to question the government and critique Brazil. Many rock groups used raw, direct, openly aggressive language to express their generation's dismay with Brazil's horrific problems.

Those problems were serious indeed, as Brazil plunged into the worst economic crisis of its history. Hyperinflation struck (topping 1,700 percent in 1989), widespread corruption continued at all levels of government and society, and the quality of life took a tremendous drop for both the poor and the middle class. Crime skyrocketed, as did the numbers of abandoned children, homeless people, and starving poor.

Brazilians in the 1980s were cynical and bitter. People had the feeling that the government had been making fools of everyone for quite a long time and no one had noticed. They were impatient for a return to democracy; they were sick and tired of governmental corruption and repression. This feeling was strongest among the youth, and the form of art that best expressed it, for the middle class, was rock. One such angry song was "Estado Violência" (State of Violence), by Titãs.

Violent state, hypocritical state
The law that isn't mine, the law I didn't
*   want . . .*
Man in silence, man in prison
Man in darkness, future of the nation

Yet diversity was also a hallmark of Brazilian rock at that time. Not all rock was full of outrage. After all, Brazilians have a remarkable capacity to make do with new circumstances, as well as to seize the moment and leave their sorrows behind, at least for a night of partying or an afternoon of soccer. And because Brazil has absorbed so many influences, national and international, there is not one Brazilian rock style, but many.

FROM COPACABANA TO THE UNDERGROUND

Brazilian rock dates to 1957, when Cauby Peixoto recorded the first domestically composed rock tune, "Rock 'n' roll em Copacabana." The next year, Celly Campello recorded Fred Jorge's giddy "Banho de Lua" (Moonlight Bath), which in its innocence seems light years away in attitude from the angry lyrics of rock artists such as Titãs and Cazuza in the 1980s.

I take moonlight showers
And turn snow-white
Moonlight is my friend
No one dares to reproach me
It's so good to dream about you
Oh, what a pure moonlight

During the next few years, Campello, Demetrius, Sérgio Murilo, Ronnie Cord, and others recorded a string of Portuguese-language covers of American and European rock tunes. In 1965 the Jovem Guarda (Young Guard) movement arrived, led by Roberto Carlos and Erasmo Carlos. Roberto, a singer and composer, had established a rock career two years earlier with "Calhambeque" (Old Heap) and a cover of "Splish Splash." By that time bossa nova musicians had largely turned to social and political themes, singing about the poverty

▲ Jovem Guarda-Erasmo Carlos, Wanderléia, and Roberto Carlos-at the microphone in 1968. *(Photo by Wilson Santos. Courtesy of Agência JB.)*

by millions of curious and enraptured fans. On videotape the nation saw girls crying hysterically, boys dancing madly, and on stage—under Roberto and Erasmo's command—young singers like Wanderléia, Eduardo Araújo, Rosemary, Ronnie Von, and Jerry Adriani.

Roberto and Erasmo scored hits with "Parei na Contramão" (I Parked the Wrong Way), "É Proibido Fumar" (No Smoking), "Garota do Baile" (Dance Girl), and Jovem Guarda's anthem, "Quero que Vá Tudo Pro Inferno" (I Want Everything to Go to Hell). It was a reply to the more nationalistic critics and other musicians who did not accept any mixture that defiled the "purity" of Brazilian music.

By 1969 the music business phenomenon of the *Jovem Guarda* television show was over, and each artist went off on his or her own path. In the 1970s Roberto made a transition from roqueiro to romantic singer and has since typically recorded mostly boleros and ballads on his albums. He achieved success with sentimental songs like "Detalhes" (Details), "Proposta" (Proposal), "Eu Disse Adeus" (I Said Goodbye), all written with his old partner and friend Erasmo (who continued as a rocker in his own career).

Roberto became the best-selling recording artist

▼ Roberto Carlos in concert in the 1980s. *(Photo by Mircea Dordea. Courtesy of Sony.)*

and suffering of poor Brazilians. But a large portion of urban youth did not care about droughts in the Northeast or peasants without land. They worried about more immediate things in their own lives: cars, romance, clothes, and school. Jovem Guarda's rock and roll reflected these concerns.

Roberto Carlos (born in 1943) started out singing bossa nova but then met Erasmo Carlos (Erasmo Esteves, born in 1941), a true carioca rocker, and a long and fertile songwriting partnership was born. Roberto's romanticism blended perfectly with Erasmo's naive aggressiveness, shaping the format of Jovem Guarda music: upbeat, simple rock and roll. They recorded separately and together, but most of their many successes came through Roberto's singing their co-written tunes.

Fame resulted from the *Jovem Guarda* show on the TV Record network, a massive success that lasted from 1965 to 1968. Recorded live in São Paulo, the show was watched all over the country

in Brazil of all time, according to most accounts, with many albums selling more than one million copies in Brazil from the late 1970s on. He is also highly popular in Latin America and Europe, and claims to have sold more than a hundred million records (albums and singles) worldwide. In the early years of the new millennium, Roberto was still a major star, singing the same kind of repertoire he had embraced since the late '70s: romantic ballads and boleros. He had Brazil's best-selling album of 2001 (*Roberto Carlos Acústico*), and his other releases in that decade were usually among the top five best sellers for the year, according to the Brazilian Association of Record Manufacturers, which tracks reported sales of the biggest Brazilian music companies.[2]

Roberto and his colleagues translated and adapted rock to Brazil, to its language and culture. Jovem Guarda had taken American rock and reformulated it with Brazilian singers, composers, arrangers, and instrumentalists. They had a lasting impact on the popular music of Brazil in succeeding years.[3]

Os Mutantes

The next big step for Brazilian rock came with Tropicália, which mixed rock freely with domestic genres. The rock side of the movement was represented by the group Os Mutantes (The Mutants). Sérgio Dias Baptista (guitar and vocals), his brother Arnaldo Dias Baptista (bass, keyboards, and vocals), and Rita Lee (flute and vocals) formed the basic lineup of the first artistically important rock band in Brazil and arguably the first in the world to achieve a truly international sound, fusing psychedelic rock, Latin and Brazilian rhythms, found sounds, and avant-garde embellishments.

Founded in 1966, Os Mutantes made occasional appearances on the *Jovem Guarda* TV show before teaming up with Gilberto Gil, who would show them how they could mix rock and roll with

Brazilian culture. His song "Domingo no Parque," with its dazzling conjunction of influences, especially inspired the young band. Os Mutantes backed Gil in 1967 when he performed the song in the TV Record Song Festival, and their appearance—three long-haired kids playing electric instruments—provoked controversy. They outraged even more people when they wore plastic clothes and accompanied Caetano Veloso in 1968, as he sang "É Proibido Proibir" at the International Song Festival in São Paulo. Many irate nationalists wrote petitions to the event organizers asking them to ban Os Mutantes, who enjoyed the role of provocateurs.

In 1968 the group participated in the seminal recording *Tropicália ou Panis et Circensis* with Gil, Veloso, Tom Zé, and Rogério Duprat, and released their debut album, *Os Mutantes*, on which they fused rock and roll with baião, mambo, música sertaneja, and irreverent, sometimes surrealistic lyrics. A mixture of Bosch and Salvador Dali is how Arnaldo reportedly described it.

Many critics remained hostile toward the group. "In the beginning they called our music imperialistic, North American. We spent a lot of time proving it was Brazilian, putting Brazilian rhythms into rock and roll," recalled Lee.[4]

Good humor was always part of the group's personality: their philosophy was yes to nonconformity, no to anger. This spirit was maintained on their next several albums, as evidenced by the titles: *A Divina Comédia ou Ando Meio Desligado* (The Divine Comedy, or I'm Kind of Spaced-Out) in 1970, *Jardim Elétrico* (Electric Garden) in 1971, and *Mutantes e Seus Cometas no País dos Bauretz* (The Mutants and Their Comets in the Country of Joints) in 1972.

The band's song "Caminhando Noturno" (Night Walker) illustrates its Tropicalista tendency to create musical salads: it opens with a fanfare that leads into a waltz. Then a strong bass enters, introducing a rock pulse. The melody takes surprising twists and turns, the vocals sometimes natural and at other times quite artificially pinched, and the waltz rhythm comes and goes. A Mexican-flavored interlude is introduced by a

Herb Alpert and the Tijuana Brass–like arrangement. The song keeps throwing out surprises until it ends in a burst of sonorous paraphernalia that includes a soccer stadium crowd chant and the voice of the robot in the *Lost in Space* TV series repeating (in Portuguese): "Danger, danger . . ."

Rita Lee had already recorded two solo albums before she left the band in 1973 to follow her own path, and Arnaldo departed the next year. But Sérgio Dias, one of the best Brazilian guitarists of his time, stayed, added new players, and kept the band going. This new incarnation of Os Mutantes, with a bassist named Liminha, had nothing to do with the old band. They made two more albums, then broke up in 1978. Os Mutantes had a short career, but they had a tremendous impact on the next generation of roqueiros.

The world outside Brazil discovered Os Mutantes in the 1990s, and they acquired the status of a cult underground band a quarter century after their breakup. Kurt Cobain was a fan and sent a letter to Arnaldo Baptista, asking the Mutantes to reunite and play with Nirvana when it was in Brazil (they said no). Beck paid tribute to them with his 1998 album title *Mutations* and the song "Tropicália." Stereolab, the Posies, and Belle & Sebastian were also admitted Mutantes fans. Their newfound popularity expanded through U.S. college radio exposure, the 1999 release of the compilation album *Everything Is Possible*, and the international launch, in 2000, of the previously unreleased *Technicolor* album, originally recorded in late 1970 with most of its tracks in English (Sean Ono Lennon illustrated the cover).

In 2005 London *Times* journalist Rob Chapman wrote, "The band's music between 1968 and 1972 stands with the best to come out of Britain and America."[5] Brazilian music critic and film director José Emilio Rondeau commented, "Had the Mutantes happened in an English-speaking country, they would have been cherished worldwide from day one. When the rest of the world caught up with them, thirty-something years after their peak, everybody was much more open to non-English singing bands, and it was an epiphany. Their music was way ahead of their time but also a perfect representation of their time."[6]

In the years following the '78 breakup of Os Mutantes, Sérgio Dias embarked on an international career as a studio musician. He toured and recorded with violinist L. Shankar and was a member of the jazz-rock band Unit. In 1990 he teamed with Roxy Music veteran Phil Manzanera on *Mato Grosso*, in which the duo combined their guitar, keyboard, and production skills to create a rock-driven, New Age, Brazilian-flavored album of exotic soundscapes. Other former Mutantes members moved in different directions. Liminha became one of Brazil's top producers, working with domestic acts, including Os Paralamas do Sucesso, Gilberto Gil, Jorge Benjor, and Titãs, and foreign artists like Sigue Sigue Sputnik. Arnaldo Baptista, partially recovered from his drug-induced psychiatric problems, released a solo album in 2004 called *Let It Bed*.

In 2006 the band had a partial reunion tour. With singer Zelia Duncan substituting for Rita Lee (who frowned upon the project), the brothers Sérgio and Arnaldo Baptista played gigs in England, the United States, and Brazil.

Rita Lee

The press has labeled Rita Lee (Rita Lee Jones, born in São Paulo in 1947) Brazilian rock's First Lady since the beginning of her solo career in the 1970s. As she had with the Mutantes, Rita continued packing her lyrics with irony and irreverence. Little by little she moved in the direction of an upbeat, light pop-rock sound flavored with various Brazilian rhythms and touches. She had her first solo hits in 1976 with "Ovelha Negra" (Black Sheep) and "Arrombou a Festa" (Crashed the Party).

Babilônia (1978) was a major seller, and her following albums went consistently gold and platinum. Her many hits included "Chega Mais" (Get Closer), "Lança Perfume" (named for an ether-laden perfume frequently sniffed during Carnaval), "Saúde" (Health), "Baila Comigo" (Dance with Me), and the typically playful "Mania De Você" (Mania for You).

▲ Sérgio Dias and Phil Manzanera in 1990, while collaborating on the album Mato Grosso. *(Courtesy of Black Sun.)*

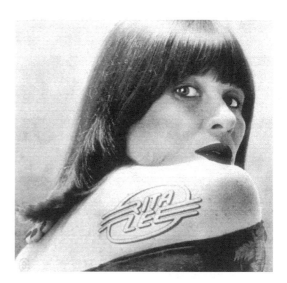

▲ A 1979 Rita Lee album. *(Courtesy of Som Livre.)*

Baby, you make my mouth water
Making up fantasies, taking your clothes off
We make love through telepathy
On the ground, in the sea, in the street, in
*   the melody*

By this time Rita had begun to write songs with her new husband, guitarist Roberto de Carvalho. Rita and Roberto combined the sensuous and the sarcastic, mixing catchy melodies with Brazilian rhythms, boleros, and rock beats. But there was

▲ Rita Lee in the 1980s. *(Photo by Bob Wolfenson. Courtesy of EMI.)*

The Underground

In the 1960s, rock artists were not considered real Brazilian musicians, and they didn't care. But then Tropicália came and absorbed the rock attitude (iconoclastic and free) and some of its musical characteristics into "authentic" Brazilian music. All of a sudden rock had lost its niche in the music scene.

At the time, rock musicians were very radical about their musical convictions. Like samba musicians, they wanted to keep their musical "purity," and so they hid. Their hideout was the underground, where it was good to be anyway during the 1970s because of government repression and brutal censorship. Recording companies and radio stations did not like to take risks with a musical genre that didn't fit the taste of the rulers.

With all doors closed, rock became music for aficionados. Groups played for small audiences at small theaters. Many never had access to recording. Most of these groups—O Terço (led by Flávio Venturini), O Som Nosso de Cada Dia, Vímana, and A Barca do Sol, for example—fell into the broad genre of "progressive rock."

often a serious undertone to their playfulness, as shown in the 1987 tune "Brazix Muamba" (*brasix* is a made-up word; *muamba* means contraband). In the song they bemoan Brazil's many problems and criticize Angra I and II, the nuclear power plant reactors built outside Rio.

> *Long live Brazix*
> *Dying of pain*
> *AIDS for those who make love*
> *Angra I, Angra II, III, and afterward*
> *The exterminating angel*

Rita Lee pioneered the "unplugged" style in Brazil with her *Bossa 'n' Roll* (1991), an acoustic album that featured many of her hits recorded the bossa nova way. Her 2000 project, *3001*, won a Latin Grammy for Best Rock Album.

▼ Ney Matogrosso. *(Photo by Mircea Dordea. Courtesy of Sony.)*

In terms of public recognition, only two rock acts were really successful in the '70s. One was the short-lived but very popular Secos e Molhados (Dry Ones and Wet Ones), which existed from 1972 to 1974; the band members decorated their faces with black-and-white makeup. Their androgynous lead singer, Ney Matogrosso, commanded attention with his unusual high-pitched voice and provocative dancing style. He sang lyrics and poems by the likes of Vínicius de Moraes, Manuel Bandeira, and Oswald de Andrade, surrounded by progressive rock that often used unusual fusions—for example, the tune "O Vira" mixed rockabilly with *vira*, a syncopated, high-spirited Portuguese folk style played on the accordion. After the group split up, Matogrosso became one of MPB's most popular vocalists.

Raul Seixas

Raul Seixas (1945–1989), born in Salvador, was a tragic figure who broke many musical boundaries. As a teenager he was fascinated with metaphysics, philosophy, and religion. He was not interested in music until he heard the Beatles on the radio, then decided he wanted to write songs instead of books. He formed a rock-and-roll band called Raulzito e os Panteras (Little Raul and the Panthers), which cut its first record in 1968. Dressing in a black leather jacket, he performed with total abandon, dancing, quivering, throwing himself on the stage, sometimes imitating the flamboyant Little Richard.

In the 1970s, living in Rio, Raul was invited to sign a contract with Philips/Phonogram by bossa nova figure Roberto Menescal, then working in A&R at the label, and Seixas released the solo albums *Krig-Ha Bandolo!* (1973) and *Gita* (1974). Raul was still a rocker but, like many Brazilian musicians of his generation, one with no use for boundaries or limitations. He was the first, along with Alceu Valença and Gilberto Gil, to mix 1950s American-style rock and Beatles-type pop with the northeastern styles baião, xote, and repente. His tunes often started in one rhythm and finished in another. Raul's first hit, "Ouro de Tolo" (Fool's Gold), was recorded in 1973.

▲ Raul Seixas. *(Photo by André Barcinski. Courtesy of Agência JB.)*

Far from the fences adorned with flags
That separate backyards
A flying saucer's sonorous shadow lands
On the calm summit of my seeing eye

Raul's lyrics were full of imagery of the occult, religion, and bizarre situations. Always he strove to provoke and challenge, as in the lyrics for "Metamorfose Ambulante" (Walking Metamorphosis), also from 1973.

I want to say now
The opposite of what I said before
I'd rather be a walking metamorphosis
Than to have that old fixed opinion about
*   everything*

The lyricist for many Seixas tunes was Paulo Coelho, now one of the world's best-selling novelists. The *Gita* album's title track, which referred to the dialogue between Krishna and Arjuna in the *Bhagavad Gita*, and "Sociedade Alternativa" (Alternative Society), inspired by the "do what thou will" philosophy of occultist Aleister Crowley, were among their collaborations. Coelho went on to write the mystical novel *The Alchemist* in 1987, a book that has been translated into sixty-four languages, according to the *New Yorker*'s Dana Goodyear, who reports that all of Coelho's books have sold nearly a hundred million copies worldwide.[7]

Seixas recorded more than two dozen of their co-written songs on his first four Phonogram albums. Goodyear says that Coelho introduced Seixas to drugs and that the two cultivated renegade personas. She cites Roberto Menescal as recalling that they invariably "dressed in combat boots and military garb, kept their hair long, and always wore dark glasses."[8]

Seixas was capable of extremely provocative performances. Marcelo Nova, in the liner notes of PolyGram's boxed-set collection *Raul*, recalled how in 1976, when Raul was performing in the Teatro Castro Alves in Salvador, he took off all his clothes on stage during a show. Proclaiming, "This is my homeland, and here I will be as I want," Raul ordered the audience to throw away their identity cards (as important in Brazil as a driver's license in the United States) and stated, "There are no frontiers on earth that transform human beings into numbers." This, recalled Nova, "provoked a true shower" of identity cards and "a terrible headache for those who needed them the next day."[9]

Seixas was committed to freedom and nonconformity. He ran for Congress in 1978 and dreamed of building a utopian city in Minas Gerais (based on the "Sociedade Alternativa" concept), but neither goal was achieved. He recorded seventeen albums in a career cut short by an early death from alcoholism. But his work would inspire many Brazilian rock artists who followed him.

THE EIGHTIES: THE THIRD WAVE

During Brazilian rock's underground period (1972–1981), its place in the hearts and minds of young people was usurped by MPB musicians like Alceu Valença, Belchior, Fagner, Zé Ramalho, and others who incorporated rock attitudes and instrumentation into their northeastern-rooted music. Most of these artists even had former rock musicians in their bands.

If Jovem Guarda and Os Mutantes were the first generation of Brazilian rock, and the underground groups the second, the 1980s saw the birth of the third wave: the strongest and most creative generation of rock musicians Brazil has ever seen. It was a generation that grew up listening not only to Anglo-American rock but also to modern MPB, which had already begun incorporating elements of rock and jazz.

There were also a few veterans from the 1970s who found success in the next decade. Two of them—Lobão and Lulu Santos—played together in a 1970s progressive-rock group called Vímana, along with Swiss musician Patrick Moraz (who had previously played keyboards for Yes) and singer-songwriter Ritchie. After Vímana broke up, English expatriate Ritchie briefly hit the top of the Brazilian charts with his pop rock. Lulu Santos went on to a solo career, recording his own style of "Brazilianized, tropicalized, Latinized rock" (as he called it), which incorporated boleros, ballads, bossa nova, reggae, and samba.[10] His appealing tunes had fluid melodies and high energy; a few examples are "De Repente Califórnia" (Suddenly California), "Tesouro da Juventude" (Treasure of Youth), and "De Leve" (Lightly). Lobão was another Vímana alumnus who went on to establish a solo career, but first he had a stint in an unusual group called Blitz.

Underground-theater actor Evandro Mesquita and guitarist Ricardo Barreto got together in the early 1980s to create the satirical pop-rock group Blitz, and the band's massive success opened the Brazilian market for many new native rock groups. Suddenly rock was mainstream. Soon came gold and platinum albums by Ritchie, Lulu Santos, Barão Vermelho, Marina, and Kid Abelha. Talented new groups like Os Paralamas do Sucesso (The Mudguards of Success) and Ultraje a Rigor (Formal Outrage) were also appearing on the scene. Rock wasn't underground any longer.

Rock in Rio

But its biggest boost was yet to come—a ten-day music festival called Rock in Rio drew 1.38 million fans in 1985, according to entrepreneur Roberto Medina, whose advertising agency, Artplan, staged the event. Rock in Rio took place in Janu-

BABY CONSUELO
SEM PECADO e
SEM JUÍZO

▲ Baby Consuelo, a Novo Baiano alumnus, who mixed rock with other styles in the '80s and also found time to nurse several babies. *(Courtesy of Sony.)*

ary in the Barra da Tijuca neighborhood on the outskirts of Rio. It was the biggest multiday rock event to date (a fact that went largely unreported in the North American press that year) and featured international acts such as James Taylor, Rod Stewart, AC/DC, and Queen. Playing with them were Blitz and fellow Brazilian artists Erasmo Carlos, Ney Matogrosso, Ivan Lins, Gilberto Gil, Elba Ramalho, Blitz, Baby Consuelo and Pepeu Gomes, Rita Lee, Lulu Santos, Moraes Moreira, Eduardo Dusek, Kid Abelha, Alceu Valença, Barão Vermelho, and the Paralamas do Sucesso.

At Rock in Rio, Brazilian rock lost its inferiority complex for good. Brazilian and foreign bands playing together on the same bill made comparisons possible, and some Brazilian bands gave better performances than the foreign acts. And the festival popularized native rockers in their own country via network television and heavy press coverage. André Midani, then managing director of WEA Brazil, observed, "Rock in Rio helped break acts in a big way, and life has never been the same since for the music business. I think that this new generation of Brazilian youth needed a new language, something to identify with."[11] WEA, along with EMI Brazil, signed many of these acts

in the 1980s. The middle-class and upper-class youth of Brazil began to tune in to their own country's rock, listening more to it than to the North American or U.K. variety. Rock in Rio took place two more times in Rio (in 1991 and 2001) and exported its format to Europe with festivals in Lisbon and Madrid.

Cazuza

Also from Rio, Cazuza (Agenor de Miranda Araújo Neto, 1958–1990) was one of the most incendiary songwriters of his time in Brazil. He started out as the vocalist and leader of Barão Vermelho (Red Baron), the only Brazilian rhythm-and-blues band to achieve widespread popularity to date. Two of the band's biggest hits, "Maior Abandanado" and "Bete Balanço," came in 1984. The latter was the theme song to a popular movie of the same name, in which the group also performed. Cazuza stayed with the band until 1985, then left to pursue a solo career.

On subsequent albums it was Cazuza's words that stood out, placed against a background of boleros and bossa mixed with blues and rock. In romantic songs he displays a bitter and desperate lyricism, as in "O Nosso Amor a Gente Inventa" (We Invent Our Love).

> *Your love is a lie*
> *That my vanity wants*
> *My love is a blind man's poem*
> *That you can't see*

Other songs are vivid attacks against deception and hypocrisy. In the electrifying "Brasil," Cazuza sums up the injustice of his country.

> *They didn't invite me to this lousy party*
> *That the men put on to convince me*
> *To pay, before seeing, for this entire droga*
> *That already was cut before I was born*

"Droga" has the double meaning here of "bummer" and "drug," while "cut" means to weaken a drug by adulteration. "Brasil" is one of Cazuza's

◄ Barão Vermelho at the start of their career, with Cazuza at far left. *(Photo by Frederico Mendes. Courtesy of Sony.)*

most corrosive songs, and its lyrics evoke the situation of most everyone in Brazil except the privileged upper class. The narrator of the song (the average Brazilian) has to stay outside the walls of the party (the good life from which he is excluded), which he is taught to crave, to yearn for, to support, but will never have. Cazuza asks who was paid off, who put Brazil in its terrible present state. The lyrics continue: "Will it be that my fate is to watch color TV in the village of an Indian, programmed only to say yes?"

In 1987 Cazuza discovered that he had AIDS. Between treatments over the next two years, he continued recording in the studio and performing in concert, even as his health deteriorated. He won prestigious Sharp Awards for his album *Ideologia* (Ideology) and song "Brasil." And he continued to compose songs, his natural irony and sarcasm becoming even more biting. In 1989 Cazuza achieved the greatest public acceptance of his career. His last two works, the double album *Burguesia* (Bourgeoisie) and the live album *O Tempo Não Pára* (Time Doesn't Stop), were released just before his death in 1990, and both achieved critical adulation and multiplatinum sales.

In 2004 the biographical movie *O Tempo Não*

Pára was launched. Directed by Walter Carvalho and Sandra Werneck, the film was an acute portrait of the life of restless singer, poet, and enfant terrible Cazuza.

Os Paralamas do Sucesso

Perhaps the most musically innovative Brazilian rock group of the 1980s was Os Paralamas do Sucesso (The Mudguards of Success), which managed to build solid musical bridges connecting Brazil, North America, Africa, and the Caribbean. Their music is upbeat party music with an edge, a seamless weaving together of rock energy, reggae, ska, and world-beat fusion. It is wrapped up in a tight pop format and delivered with infectious energy, a driving rhythmic sense, and a pinch of irony. Their sound, said leader Herbert Vianna, is "a collage that has created a style. Caribbean music, ska, reggae, samba. Lots of swing, very Latin, very Brazilian."[12]

The Paralamas, based on a simple trio format, were formed in Rio de Janeiro in 1982. João Barone (drums) and Bi Ribeiro (bass) are cariocas; Herbert Vianna (guitar and lead vocals) is from Paraíba. Early influences included the Specials, Madness, the English Beat, and the Clash. Their first two albums, *Cinema Mudo* (Silent Cinema) in 1983 and *Passo do Lui* (Lui's Step) in 1984, feature Herbert's raw, bittersweet vocals riding atop fast, compelling rock and ska riffs and rhythms. The latter album, coupled with exposure from the Rock in Rio festival, helped the Paralamas achieve commercial success. Herbert recalled, "With Rock in Rio we went to the top of the charts. We were known [before] in Rio, but not in the rest of Brazil."

Selvagem? (Wild?), released in 1986, was a creative leap forward for the trio, as they succeeded in infusing their rock and ska with a distinctively Brazilian accent, be it through suave arrangements or percussive touches. Veteran roqueiro Liminha produced and played keyboards on several songs. A notable tune was "Alagados," a Caribbean-Brazilian fusion that mixes elements of reggae, samba, and northeastern xaxado. It was a hint of things to come, both in its deft and natural mixing of genres and in Vianna's hard-hitting lyrics about the Alagados and Maré slums (in Salvador and Rio, respectively).

Alagados, Trench Town, Favela da Maré
Hope comes neither from the sea nor from
the TV antennas

▼ The Paralamas in 1989 (*left to right*): Bi Ribeiro, João Barone, and Herbert Vianna. (*Photo by Mauricio Valladares. Courtesy of Intuition/Capitol.*)

Art is to live out of faith
One just doesn't know what to have faith in

The album sold seven hundred thousand units in Brazil, according to EMI-Odeon, and they followed it up the next year with a live album recorded at the Montreux Jazz Festival. Their 1988 album *Bora Bora* was even more accomplished, a bold expansion of their world-beat experiments. "We used a horn section for the first time, and with that we could make our intentions clear and play the kind of music we wanted to play. It allowed us to use other rhythms, many from Brazil, such as lambada, afoxé, coco, congada," said Vianna.[13] With the added instrumentation, the Paralamas' new Caribbean-Brazilian blends grew heady indeed.

"Um a Um" (One to One) is an infectious cover of a classic Jackson do Pandeiro tune, in which Vianna carries the coco rhythm in his voice while he plays reggae chords on his guitar. "Sanfona" (Accordion), in Herbert's words, is "a fusion of lambada with baião." Other highlights included the reggae-dub "Don't Give Me That," in which Jamaican DJ Peter Metro adds vocals in English, and the delirious Caribbean-Brazilian instrumental "Bundalelê," which incorporates the Haitian *compas* rhythm.

More outstanding albums followed, including 1989's *Big Bang*, 1991's *Os Grãos*, and 1994's *Severino*, which included Tom Zé, Egberto Gismonti, and Phil Manzanera among the guest artists. The Paralamas made a memorable political comment in 1995 with the tune "Luiz Inácio (300 Picaretas)." The song was inspired by then presidential candidate Luiz Inácio Lula da Silva's accusation two years earlier that there were three hundred *picaretas* (charlatans) in the Brazilian Congress. Vianna's tune takes this as its theme and attacks corruption in Brasília. Federal judge Ionilda Maria Carneiro Pires censored the song, banning it from radio airplay and public shows. Ironically, the administration and political party of Lula (as he is called in Brazil), who was elected president in 2002, would later be accused of corruption, including allegations of bribing congressmen.

◄ Legião Urbana in 1987 with bandleader Renato Russo (*second from right*). *(Photo by Isabel Garcia. Courtesy of EMI.)*

In 2001 bandleader Herbert Vianna crashed his ultralight glider. His wife died in the accident and Vianna fell into a coma. He suffered brain damage, yet his musical skills returned. Despite being confined to a wheelchair, he continued to perform concerts with the Paralamas, which subsequently released two albums with new material, *Longo Caminho* (2002) and *Hoje* (2005).

Legião Urbana

Brasília, the capital of Brazil, is only three years younger than Brazilian rock, but it is already a metropolis. Inaugurated in 1960, Brasília was an instant city, designed by architect Oscar Niemeyer and built out in the middle of a high deserted plateau in Goiás state. Today it is the cosmopolitan home of around one million inhabitants and is culturally isolated from the rest of the country. Teenagers there, more than in other parts of the country, have tended to move toward the international youth language of the late twentieth century: rock. So, in 1978, while the rest of Brazil was dancing to disco music or listening to MPB, Brasília already had its punks.

The best-known punk bands in the capital were Aborto Elétrico (Electric Abortion) and Dado e o Reino Animal (Dado and the Animal Kingdom). Members from these two bands—Renato Russo (guitar and vocals), Dado Villa-Lobos (guitar), Renato Rocha (bass), and Marcelo Bonfá (drums)—formed Legião Urbana (Urban Legion). They came to Rio in 1983 and conquered the public with their poetic lyrics, driven by enraged energy.

Legião Urbana's songs had a hard, strong beat, guitar chords reminiscent of U2, and vocals influenced by the Cure. In concert they wore jeans and T-shirts, and disheveled, unshaven lead singer Renato Russo would whirl around on stage in a strange tribal dance, as if being stung by a thousand bees. Inspired by Legião Urbana's antifashion style and Dylanesque protest anthems, crowds went into frenzies.

Singing about unemployment, the army, urban violence, and social disillusion, Legião summed up the life of Brazilian youth with honesty and passion in songs such as "Geração Coca Cola" (Coca-Cola Generation).

Ever since we were kids
We've been eating commercial and industrial trash
Now it's our time, we'll spit it all back on you

By 1989 they had released three albums. The second, called simply *Dois* (Two), was a commercial success and sold more than seven hundred thousand copies, according to EMI. Legião's third album was an anthology of the group's first ten years, and one of its tracks became its biggest radio hit—the nine-minute "Faroeste Caboclo" (Mestizo Cowboy Movie)—an epic of a northeastern immigrant in Brasília who is oppressed by society. The band's career was cut short when leader Russo (Renato Manfredini Junior) died of AIDS in 1996 at the age of thirty-six. At the time he was Brazil's most popular rock star. Veteran music journalist José Emilio Rondeau called Russo one of the two biggest talents in the history of Brazilian rock, along with Arnaldo Baptista of the Mutantes.[14]

Titãs

São Paulo has long been a center of Brazilian rock and roll. It is a huge metropolis (more than fifteen million people live in Greater São Paulo) with immigrants from all over Brazil and the world: Bolivians, Italians, Lebanese, Portuguese, and Japanese. Accordingly, in terms of *paulistano* rock, there is no dominant style. Punk, experimental, progressive, rockabilly, technopop, and even Japanese-influenced bands are found there.

One paulistano band that made it big in Brazil for a while was RPM, a technopop band led by vocalist-composer-bassist Paulo Ricardo and keyboardist-arranger Luis Schiavon. In 1986 RPM produced the biggest-selling Brazilian album to that date, *Radio Pirata Live* (Live Pirate Radio), which sold more than two million copies. But the band's career was short-lived. In 1988 it cut the musically more ambitious album *Os Quatro Coiotes* (The Four Coyotes), which included Milton Nascimento and sambista Bezerra da Silva, but broke up the next year. In 2002 RPM made a comeback with the release of a live album, but the group soon disbanded again.

As RPM was fading away, another paulistano band was emerging that would become one of the

▼ Titãs inside São Paulo's Transamérica Studios.
(Courtesy of WEA.)

Sepultura: Heavy Metal from Minas Gerais

Heavy-metal band Sepultura (Grave) was Brazil's most popular recording act internationally in the closing years of the twentieth century. The quartet—Max Cavalera (vocals and rhythm guitar), his brother Igor Cavalera (drums), Andreas Kisser (lead guitar), and Paulo Jr. (bass)—came from Belo Horizonte and released their first full-length album, *Mortal Visions,* in 1986. Their apocalyptic intensity generated a cult following abroad, and their international audience was expanded by their 1989 album *Beneath the Remains* (released by an American label) and an appearance at Rock in Rio II (the 1991 follow-up to the first event). *Arise,* launched that year, sold more than one million copies worldwide. Two years later their album *Chãos A.D.* addressed social problems in Brazil and elsewhere. The song "Kaiowas" was about a tribe of Amazonian Indians who had committed suicide rather than be moved out of their rainforest home by the Brazilian government. "Manifest" was inspired by a revolt of inmates in the Carandiru prison in São Paulo, in which more than one hundred prisoners were massacred by police. "Biotech Is Godzilla" included lyrics by Jello Biafra, founder of the punk

▲ Sepultura. *(Photo by Gary Monroe. Courtesy of Epic.)*

band the Dead Kennedys. The band expanded its sonic experiments with *Roots* in 1996. In 1998 Derrick Green replaced Max Cavalera (who went on to form the group Soulfly), and Jean Dolabella took the place of Igor Cavalera in 2006.

most accomplished rock groups of its generation: Titãs (Titans). A group with multiple personalities, Titãs was composed of eight individuals who all wrote songs, five of whom were lead singers. Their pluralistic music went from romantic ballads, to two-chord punk, to reggae, to funk, to rap. Lyrics were evocative and often aggressively critical. During their dynamic shows, they took turns being up front on the stage. The band had no leader. "We are not a band with only one aesthetical choice. We are not reggae, nor funk, nor heavy. We are nothing. We kind of confiscate everything in a free and sincere way," said Nando Reis (vocals and bass). According to drummer Charles Gavin, the band recorded "everything from angry, aggressive songs to romantic, tacky ballads. We in-

spire feelings that range from pure romanticism to repugnance."[15] Their song "Sonífera Ilha" (Sonorous Island) is a romantic existential lament.

> I can't stay at your side anymore
> So I stick my ear to the radio
> To get in tune with you
> Alone on an island

"Bichos Escrotos" (Disgusting Pests) is one of their "repugnant" numbers, a rough-edged rock-funk piece that says that only the pests will inherit the earth.

> Animals, come out of the filth
> Cockroaches, let me see your paws

Rats, get in the shoes of civilized citizens
Fleas, come live in my wrinkles

On their third album, the acclaimed *Cabeça Dinossauro* (Dinosaur Head), Titãs consolidated their musical and thematic language. The album assaults modern social institutions with acid fury. In "Porrada" (Punch), they ridicule all those who uphold hypocritical society.

A mark of ten for the girls of the opposing
team
Congratulations to the academics of the
association
Salutations to those graduating in law
All due respect to the ladies
A punch in the face of those who do nothing

In 1989 the philosopher and law professor Willis Guerra Filho commented on the band's lyrics: "The words of the songs are like a critical register of the Brazilian way of life, of our society nowadays, with its great insecurity where the people are attacked from all sides, from bandits and the police, from insects and DDT, from the state and social agencies."[16]

Besides Gavin and Reis, the other members of the hydra-headed band were Arnaldo Antunes (vocals), Toni Bellotto (guitar), Paulo Miklos (bass, vocals), Sérgio Britto (keyboards, vocals), Branco Mello (vocals), and Marcelo Frommer (guitar). In 1989 *Cabeça Dinossauro* was chosen as the best Brazilian album of the 1980s by a poll in the Rio daily newspaper *Jornal do Brasil*.

The group's lineup has changed over the years: Frommer died in 2001, and Reis and Antunes left to pursue solo careers, becoming prominent songwriters, their tunes recorded by Marisa Monte, Cassia Eller, and others. Yet Titãs has remained a popular band. Its 1997 *Titãs Acústico MTV*, an "MTV Unplugged" album, was a landmark in the band's career, selling 1.8 million copies, according to its label, Warner.

More of the '80s

Another popular and outspoken band that emerged in the 1980s was Engenheiros do Hawaii (Hawaiian Engineers), whose members came from Porto Alegre, the capital of Brazil's southernmost state, Rio Grande do Sul. An art school band that performed together at college parties, they were influenced by Caetano Veloso, Led Zeppelin, and Pink Floyd and created a style they call "garage MPB." Bassist and bandleader Humberto Gessinger grounded philosophical ideas in long ballads with descriptive lyrics that build to a heavy climax (they sound something like the rock group Rush). In some cities the Engenheiros were invited to give lectures. In Fortaleza, at the end of one particular concert, the crowd chanted, "Philosophy!"

The wide spectrum of Brazilian pop in the 1980s also included blues artists Celso Blues Boy, André Christovam, and Blues Etílicos. Other artists and groups that deserve mention are Lobão, known for bittersweet ballads and a rough, growling voice; guitarist-producer Robertinho de Recife, who mixes frevo and rock; Fausto Fawcett, a bard of Copacabana lowlife; and Eduardo Dusek, a theatrical, satirical crooner who fuses rock, MPB, and brega romantic songs. Vinícius Cantuária, Ritchie, Leo Jaime, Marina, Capital Inicial (Startup Capital), Ultraje a Rigor (Formal Outrage), Ira! (Anger), Camisa de Vênus (Condom, led by Marcelo Nova), and Kid Abelha (Kid Bee), with its ex-integrant, the bassist-songwriter Leoni, were other successful rock and pop-rock artists who established themselves in that era.

THE TURN OF THE MILLENNIUM

Skank is a band from Belo Horizonte that mixes rock, reggae, and ska with *cateretê*, embolada, and calango. The quartet is led by vocalist-guitarist-songwriter Samuel Rosa and includes Henrique Portugal (keyboards), Haroldo Ferretti (drums), and Lelo Zaneti (bass). The unofficial fifth member, saxophonist Chico Amaral, writes many of the group's lyrics, which focus mostly on girls, soccer,

▲ Samuel Rosa, the leader of Skank. *(Courtesy of Coca-Cola and FEMSA Brasil.)*

hawk, topless, or outrageously butch), Eller was very popular in the late '90s. She drew comparisons to Melissa Etheridge because of her musical style and openly lesbian orientation. One of her most popular albums was the "unplugged" *MTV Acústico* (2001), which featured Cassia's stirring rendition of Nando Reis's "O Segundo Sol" (The Second Sun). She caused a great commotion when she died that year of obscure causes, apparently suffering multiple heart attacks.

The '90s and '00s also witnessed the rise of Chico Science and Nação Zumbi (see Chapter Seven), Charlie Brown Jr., with its mix of rock and hip-hop; Jota Quest, a mineiro group with a heavily R&B-influenced sound; Mamonas Assassinas (Killer Castor Beans), whose members died in a plane crash after releasing a successful debut album; the hard-rock band Detonautas; the gaúcho quintet Cachorro Grande (Big Dog); and Los Porongas, a rock band whose founders hail from the state of Acre, in the Amazon. Also in the contemporary pop realm, Pedro Mariano (son of Elis Regina), percussionist Lanlan and her band Moinho, and the bands Pedro Luis e a Parede, Mombojó, Hurtmold, and Manacá are cult acts with loyal followers. Kassin + 2 is a trio that ranges from bossa nova to experimental rock. Vanguart is a five-man band from Cuiabá in Mato Grosso state. Their 2007 debut album had deep roots in American folk and folk-rock from the 1960s and '70s, and hints of Neil Young and Buffalo Springfield. Fino Coletivo fuses samba rock, hip-hop, and traditional Brazilian sounds, and was another critics' favorite for 2007.

Pitty is a female singer-songwriter-guitarist from Bahia who is influenced by punk and alternative rock and became a teen idol early in her career. CSS (Cansei de Ser Sexy) is a band from São Paulo of five women and one man whose eponymous debut album (which means "Tired of Being Sexy") was released in 2006 by Sub Pop Records and soon found an international following. Lead vocalist Lovefoxxx sings in both English and Portuguese (depending on the album version) atop bouncy electro-pop, bubblegum rock, and tongue-in-cheek arty posturing.

and cinema. Occasionally they explore serious themes, as in the song "Sem Terra" (Without Land). Skank hit its artistic stride in 1994 with its second album, *Calango*, which achieved an appealing blend of Jamaican pop with regional *mineiro* styles. Two years later the band launched the multiplatinum-selling *O Samba Poconé*, which united pulsing rhythms with upbeat melodies and Rosa's ebullient vocals, and included the hit single "Garota Nacional" (National Girl). Skank moved toward a more rock-oriented sound, influenced by the Beatles and alternative rock, with the albums *Siderado* (1998) and *Maquinarama* (2000). They remain one of Brazil's most popular bands and won a Latin Grammy in 2004 with *Cosmotron*.

Also coming to the forefront in the 1990s was Cassia Eller (1962–2001). Cassia had a deep, husky voice and intense, passionate singing style. With her interpretative talent, rock-and-roll attitude, and irreverent image (sometimes with a Mo-

Los Hermanos is a group from Rio with a style that fuses alternative rock with influences from samba, bossa, MPB, and the Beatles. Their eponymous 1999 debut album yielded their greatest hit to date, *Anna Júlia*, composed by the band's guitarist-vocalist Marcelo Camelo. The song was covered by Jim Capaldi on his 2001 album *Living on the Outside*, with George Harrison on guitar and Paul Weller singing. Los Hermanos consolidated their cult status with *Bloco do Eu Sozinho* (The Me Alone Bloco), which included Camelo's "Veja Bem Meu Bem" (See Here, My Dear). That song and two others by Camelo ("Santa Chuva" and "Cara Valente") were recorded by MPB singer Maria Rita on her 2003 debut album.

The group's third effort, *Ventura* (2003), was full of low-key, highly melodic tunes and added to Los Hermanos' cachet as an indie-rock band and Camelo's and flutist-guitarist-vocalist Rodrigo Amarante's growing reputation as composers. The album included Camelo's "Samba a Dois" (Samba for Two), recorded by Fernanda Porto, and Amarante's "Deixa o Verão" (Let the Summer Go), covered by Adriana Calcanhotto. In 2007 Los Hermanos decided to take an indefinite break from performing and left behind a legion of musical followers: Mombojó, Ludov, and Eletro are bands whose sound is invariably associated with them.

Hailing from Minas Gerais, Pato Fu has influences as diverse as Devo, the Cure, Bjork, and Nara Leão, and creates playful, intellectualized pop. Music critic Bruce Gilman describes the band's members as "voracious devourers of diverse influences—punk, heavy metal, brega, caipira music—cradled in an orgy of languages and digital information." He adds, "They have been critiqued as too underground, too pop, too comical, even too hard rock."[17] Sometimes likened to Os Mutantes, Pato Fu was named one of the best bands in the world by *Time* magazine[18] and won accolades for *Ruído Rosa* in 2001. They also were praised for *Daqui Pro Futuro* in 2007, a year in which lead singer Fernanda Takai also released the well-received solo album *Onde Brilham os Olhos Seus*, which consisted of bossa nova and MPB songs from the repertoire of bossa muse Nara Leão.

Though rock is a genre that was imported from elsewhere, in Brazil it has gained many interesting new elements. It may be a different kind of percussion, a blend with Brazilian rhythms, or an original way of placing words in the melody. In the hands of artists like Os Mutantes, Raul Seixas, and the Paralamas, rock has assumed a distinctly Brazilian character.

By the turn of the millennium, the growth in popularity of música sertaneja and Brazilian funk, electronic, rap, and Christian music had taken Brazilian music in new directions. Here is a look at those styles, and at other genres we
have not explored elsewhere in the book.

Música Sertaneja and Música Caipira

Música sertaneja, a type of Brazilian country music, is especially popular in Brazil's south, southeast, and central regions, in the states of São Paulo, Minas Gerais,
Mato Grosso, Mato Grosso do Sul, Goiás, and Paraná.[1] It surged in national popularity and became the single largest category in terms of Brazilian record sales in
the 1990s. Its popularity in Brazil can be compared to that of country music in the
United States, often appealing to those who have, came from, or desire a rural lifestyle and its traditional values.

Sertaneja is a pop-music version of *música caipira*, the rural folk music that includes idioms like toada, moda de viola, *cana-verde*, and *catira*. The word *caipira*
literally means "country hick." The style was commercialized in the 1920s and '30s
by artists such as Cornélio Pires (1884–1958), who is credited as being the first
person to bring authentic rural caipira musicians into the recording studio.[2] Later,
Jararaca e Ratinho, Alvarenga e Ranchinho, and Tonico e Tinoco were duos

formed in that era who continued the development of the music. They and Torres e Florêncio, Tião Carreiro e Pardinho, and Zico e Zeca (duos that appeared in the 1940s and '50s) helped establish an acoustic sertaneja sound. Duos (generally tenors) harmonized plaintively in thirds and sixths, frequently using falsetto, as they crooned about romance and rural life, to the accompaniment of strummed guitars and ten-string violas. The term *música sertaneja* replaced the more pejorative *música caipira* in the 1950s, according to Suzel Ana Reily, in much the same way that *country* replaced *hillbilly* in the United States.[3]

Nowadays the two terms are generally used to denote somewhat distinct categories. Música caipira commonly refers to the rural folk music that is the roots music for sertaneja. Sertaneja can be a generic term for all rural music from the South and Center-West, but generally it refers to the commercialized popular music that grew out of música caipira. The distinction is similar to that between bluegrass and country in North America, and there is just as much crossover between the two areas.

From the 1960s on, música sertaneja became more urbanized, as rural migrants moved to big cities, and performances began to include fuller ensemble accompaniments and solo vocal sections.[4] Sertaneja musicians started to incorporate musical influences from Bolivia, Paraguay, Mexico, and Nashville. Sérgio Reis (born in 1940), an ex–Jovem Guarda rocker in the '60s, Léo Canhoto e Robertinho (who debuted in 1969), and the duo Milionário e José Rico (started in 1970) are artists who reached mass audiences with the genre in the '70s.

Brothers Chitãozinho e Xororó are sertaneja trendsetters who were born in Astorga, a small town in the southern state of Paraná; they started their recording career in 1970, when both were teenagers. In 1982 their first big hit, "Fio de Cabelo," sold 1.5 million copies, a landmark in sertaneja music, and boosted the sales of their eighth album, *Somos Apaixonados.* Previously the genre had been heard almost exclusively on AM radio. After "Fio de Cabelo," sertaneja began to invade the FM airwaves and increase its popularity

▲ Sertaneja stars Chitãozinho and Xororó. *(Photo by Renato Aguiar. Courtesy of EMI.)*

among the new middle classes of the countryside and big cities of southern and central Brazil. Chitãozinho e Xororó achieved their success by mixing their caipira roots with American folk and the naive rock of the Jovem Guarda movement, and by introducing electric instruments in their arrangements to accompany lyrics suffused with sentimental lyrics.

And what I found today made me even
   sadder
A little piece of her that's still there
A strand of hair on my jacket
It reminded me of everything we lived
   together

Marciano and Darci Rossi,
"Fio de Cabelo" (Strand of Hair)

Chitãozinho e Xororó's success was paralleled by two other brother duos in the late 1980s and early 1990s. Both were from central Brazil and the state of Goiás: Leandro e Leonardo and Zezé di Camargo e Luciano.

Before forming a duo in 1983, Leandro e Leonardo made a living working in tomato plantations while Leandro acquired some experience singing Roberto Carlos and Beatles songs with a pop band in the late '70s. But sertaneja was the duo's favorite style, and after a long struggle and a couple of flops, they found a large audience in 1989 with the release of their third album, which featured the hit "Entre Tapas e Beijos," written by Nilton Lamas and Antonio Bueno. Their next album included the hits "Pense em Mim" and "Desculpe, Mas Eu Vou Chorar," songs that told of romance and unrequited love and were delivered with intensely emotional interpretations by the duo. Their fourth album sold 2.5 million copies, and Leandro e Leonardo began to accumulate gold and platinum records. Their career was tragically interrupted by the death of Leandro, from a rare type of cancer, in 1998. His brother Leonardo embarked on a solo career that made him one of the most popular singers in Brazil in the first decade of the twenty-first century.

Zezé di Camargo e Luciano's first album, in 1991, featured "É o Amor" (That's Love), a smash hit that crossed every genre border and was heard throughout Brazil all year long. Even MPB icons like Maria Bethânia recorded it.

That's love
It came like a straight shot
Into my heart . . .
And made me understand that my life
Is nothing without you

In 2005 Zezé di Camargo e Luciano had their lives turned into a blockbuster movie, *2 Filhos de Francisco*, more evidence of their enormous popularity.

Bruno e Marrone is another popular duo from Goiás. They won the Latin Grammy award for best sertaneja album in 2002, for *Acústico ao Vivo*.

Their song "Por Te Amar Demais," from the album *Meu Presente é Você*, was the most played tune in Brazil in March 2006 and they led the Top 40 charts in January 2008 with "Pra Não Morrer de Amor."[5] Bruno e Marrone are more eclectic than typical sertaneja artists, recording songs from different music styles, yet their lyrics are just as dramatic as those of the average sertaneja song:

I slept in the square
Thinking of her
Be my friend, Mr. Officer
Hit me, arrest me
Do whatever you want to me
But don't let me stay
Without her
"Dormi na Praça" (I Slept in the Square)

Not all of the category's stars are in duos. Roberta Miranda, Sérgio Reis, and Daniel (José Daniel Camillo) are among the most well known solo singers in sertaneja, along with Leonardo.

Guitarist Almir Sater (born in 1956) is a noteworthy guitarist and vocalist from the city of Campo Grande, in Mato Grosso do Sul. The Pantanal, a huge wetlands area with rich flora and fauna, is located nearby and seems to have inspired Sater's delicate, emotional, sophisticated guitar playing. "The music made here is different from everything else. It was influenced by American folk, by Paraguayan music, by Andean music, and the result is really good. . . . I call it Brazilian folk."[6]

Roberto Corrêa, a mineiro born in 1957, reinvented the most traditional sertaneja and caipira accompaniment: the viola, a type of folk guitar that usually has five pairs of steel strings. It has ancient origins and was brought to Brazil from Portugal, and is a popular instrument in rural Brazil (including in the Northeast). Corrêa's virtuoso playing produces a hypnotizing sound that arouses intense emotion and displays a delicate edge of exoticism. Corrêa already knew how to play the guitar when he picked up his first viola, and he was so fascinated by its primeval sonority that he wanted to learn everything about it. But he was then living in Brasília and nobody knew much about violas, so he had to travel to rural areas to meet old violeiros and absorb everything he could about the instrument. He eventually got a scholarship for his research and became one of Brazil's top viola experts. After four years of painstaking study, he launched his book *Viola Caipira* in 1983. His knowledge of the instrument enabled him to create original tunings, which contribute to his distinctive sound, on display in albums such as *Extremosa Rosa* (2002). With his freshly creative music, Roberto Corrêa is helping to develop, and at the same time preserve, the viola caipira and the musical traditions of central Brazil.

Helena Meirelles (1924–2005), a singer, songwriter, and instrumentalist, was also renowned for her mastery of the viola caipira. Born on a farm in the Pantanal region of Mato Grosso do Sul, she learned to play at age eight, but had a hard life that kept her from gaining recognition until her later years. She was relatively unknown until 1993, when the U.S. magazine *Guitar Player* featured Helena in its "Spotlight" section in its November issue. The resulting international attention led to the release of her first album, *Helena Meirelles*, the following year, when she was seventy, and to long overdue recognition in Brazil. Meirelles was the subject of the documentary *Helena Meirelles, a Dama da Viola*, in 2004.

Renato Teixeira is a singer-songwriter who is equally appreciated by modern sertaneja lovers, traditional caipira music conservationists, and MPB fans. Teixeira is a Paulista born in 1945 who spent his youth in the interior, in Taubaté, where he had his first contact with caipira music. At home, he also listened to the protest folk music of Bob Dylan and Joan Baez, as well as samba greats like Cartola and Noel Rosa. But, as was the case for so many other Brazilian musicians, it was bossa nova that made Renato decide to make music. Every Brazilian knows his biggest hit, "Romaria," recorded by Elis Regina in 1977.

I'm a caipira pirapora.
Our Lady of Aparecida please
Illuminate the dark deep mine,
The train of my life.

Modern sertaneja lovers identify with him because of the American folk influences they hear in his sound. Traditionalists see his music immersed in rural idioms like toada and moda de viola. And urban MPB people like his well-crafted melodies and subtle lyrics, which talk about the simple things of life without the excessive drama of sertanejos. Teixeira's live show *No Auditório Ibirapuera*, released on CD and DVD in 2007, is one of his most popular works. Renato explains his success, saying, "My music has a lot of modulation. It vibrates and grabs the audience."[7]

The highly regarded Pena Branca e Xavantinho were a duo until 1999 and exemplified sertaneja's música caipira roots (see Chapter Five). Edson e Hudson and Rick e Renner are duos who established their careers in the '90s. And Victor e Leo, César Menotti e Fabiano, João Bosco e Vinícius, and Jorge e Mateus are contemporary sertaneja artists who released their first albums in the new millennium.

MUSIC OF THE SOUTH

Brazil's two southernmost states, Santa Catarina and Rio Grande do Sul, feature their own regional rhythms—vanerão, rancheira, milonga, and chula, for instance. *Música gaúcha* (music from Rio Grande do Sul) tends to celebrate the culture and

▼ Renato Borghetti, from Rio Grande do Sul, the southernmost state of Brazil. *(Courtesy of BMG.)*

rural values of the pampa region, which borders Argentina and Uruguay. Leonardo (Jader Moreci Teixeira) was born in Bagé, Rio Grande do Sul, and is a songwriter whose work represents the traditionalist side of the music. More than eight hundred recordings of his songs have been made, by himself and others, and he has released more than forty albums.[8] Renato Borghetti, a virtuoso on the button accordion (called *gaita* in the South and *sanfona* in the Northeast), has fused música gaúcha with forró, samba, and other styles in imaginative blends. Gaúcho da Fronteira is another noteworthy accordion player from Rio Grande do Sul. Kleiton and Kledir, Vitor Ramil, and Nei Lisboa have brought influences of the South into Brazilian popular music.

INDIGENOUS MUSIC OF THE AMAZON

The music of the indigenous peoples of the Amazon rainforest is explored in Marlui Miranda's 1995 *Ihu: Todos os Sons*, on which Miranda sings and plays guitar and *kukuta* (an Indian bamboo flute), as she interprets the music of the Yanomâmi, Kayapó, Jaboti, and other Indian peoples. Excerpts of native Amazonian music can also be heard on Milton Nascimento's *Txai*. Albums of it by the tribes themselves have been released on CD by Smithsonian/Folkways, Unesco, Ocora, and other international labels.

ROMANTIC AND BREGA MUSIC

Amado Batista, Wando, Sula Miranda, José Augusto, Odair José, Waldick Soriano, and Reginaldo Rossi have been among the most popular singers of romantic ballads and boleros in Brazil from the 1960s on, appealing mostly to working-class audiences. Their slow, sentimental, tear-jerking tunes were pejoratively nicknamed brega (tacky) by journalists, and the term stuck as a label for the genre.

Although artists like Roberto Carlos, Fabio Jr., Rosana, and Joana are also very popular for their romantic songs, they're not labeled brega because the production of their albums and shows is much more sophisticated and expensive, and they appeal to the middle class as well. Roberto Carlos has been the king of romantic music since he gave up rock and roll at the end of the '60s (see Chapter Nine); he is the country's best-selling recording artist of all time.

CHILDREN'S MUSIC

Children's music is also a big part of Brazil's music business, and Xuxa (Maria da Graça Meneghel) has been its most successful figure. Hailing from Rio Grande do Sul, Xuxa is a former model who hosts a hugely successful TV Globo children's show, much of which is devoted to musical numbers. In 1986 Xuxa began releasing her own albums. Featuring catchy songs written by top pop songwriters, they were slickly produced and heavily promoted by Globo on her show and elsewhere.[9] Over the next several years she sold millions of albums, and her success had a major impact on the Brazilian music industry, which increased its supply of albums for children with followers like Angélica, Eliana, and Mara Maravilha.

CHRISTIAN MUSIC IN BRAZIL

Christian music's share of the national music market has grown considerably since the late 1990s. In 1998 Catholic priest Marcelo Rossi sold 3.2 million copies of his album *Músicas para Louvar ao Senhor*,[10] and his *Minha Benção* was Brazil's best-selling album in 2006, according to the Brazilian Association of Record Manufacturers.[11] Padre Zezinho is another Catholic priest who has recorded popular albums. Following the growth of Protestant sects in Brazil, evangelical artists were extremely successful in the first decade of the twenty-first century. Aline Barros, Sergio Lopes, Cristina Mel, Fernanda Brum, Cassiane, Oficina G3, Cleber Lucas, and others have recorded ballads, pop, rock, and even rap with religious lyrics, collectively selling millions of albums every year.

BRAZILIAN REGGAE

Reggae widely infiltrated Brazilian music beginning in the 1980s and can be heard in a straightforward form in the music of Cidade Negra, Natiruts, Nadegueto, and Ras Bernardo.

O Rappa is a popular act that infuses reggae with rock, samba, drum 'n' bass, and hip-hop (the name is slang for the police who harass illegal street vendors and confiscate their wares). Its 2001 double live album *Instinto Coletivo* captures the electrifying atmosphere that vocalist Marcelo Falcão and his sidemen create in their live show, one of the best among Brazilian pop bands. One of O Rappa's most accomplished albums is *O Silêncio Q Precede o Esporro* (2003), which applies the band's usual drive and energy to innovative blends of reggae and electronica with bossa nova and samba (Zeca Pagodinho is a guest), and adds arrangements with violins and cellos. The lyrics are cinematographic, full of intense images and oblique social criticism.

The space is small, almost like a corral
My meal stuffed in my worn-out backpack
I have very little money, almost nothing
   "Rodo Cotidiano" (The Daily Rat Race)

BRAZILIAN FUNK

Funk music has long been popular in Brazil. *Bailes funk* (funk dances) have been around since the 1970s and have attracted big crowds to large clubs and gymnasiums on the outskirts of major cities. The *funkeiros* are typically poor blacks and mulattos from the suburbs. Security is heavy as *galeras* (groups from different neighborhoods) compete on the dance floor, exchange taunts, and sometimes start huge brawls. From the mid-1990s on, Rio de Janeiro's *funk carioca*, a.k.a. *batidão* (big beat) or *funk de favela*, conquered the middle classes and became popular all over the country. Overseas, *baile funk* is an alternative name for funk carioca. Singer Fernanda Abreu explains the genre's rise in Rio: "Funk music is fun and it fits very well with the carioca spirit. The city's geogra-

phy and its expansive people make it easier for the different social classes to exchange information."[12]

As funk grew more popular, funk lyrics addressed themes other than just crime and urban violence and reduced their social commentary. Yet funk carioca is still controversial. Renowned literary critic and cultural theorist Heloisa Buarque de Hollanda attributes great social importance to the genre: "It's the favelas claiming their space."[13] Contrary to most scholars, she enthusiastically advocates the inclusion of funk as an expression of carioca culture. Caetano Veloso agrees with her, saying that "funk has guaranteed its place in the history of Brazilian music."[14] Samba songwriter Nei Lopes, a respected researcher of Afro-Brazilian culture, has a different opinion: "the music made in the favelas and ghettos today comes from abroad. It's a product of the transnational cultural industry . . . and, with its aggressiveness and vulgarity, stimulates more and more the anti-black racism in Brazilian big cities."[15]

Historian and researcher Micael Herschmann, the author of two books that analyze the phenomenon (*O funk e o hip-hop invadem a cena* and *Abalando os anos 90*), thinks that what's going on is just part of a cycle. "Funk music has had its moments of popularity before, just like axé and sertaneja. It's all part of the dynamics of mass culture, which has close links with the consumer market," Herschmann told journalist Rodrigues Alves in a *Jornal do Brasil* article that featured a debate about funk's merits.[16] DJ Marlboro, one of the most accomplished funk music stars, considered criticism of the genre a form of prejudice, "Whatever comes from the people and begins to grow is discriminated against."[17] But anthropologist Alba Zaluar didn't see funk as a positive manifestation. "It creates a big gap between sexes and emphasizes sexuality as a form of male affirmation. And besides, it's not rooted in the Brazilian people. It won't stay for many generations like samba did, unless it changes," he commented in Alves's piece, published in 2001.[18] As the decade progressed, funk carioca become extremely popular in Brazil and crossed the Atlantic to fire up raves and nightclubs across Europe, thanks to its contagious heavy beat. As funkeiros Amilcka e Chocolate put it:

It's the sound of blacks
The sound of favela dwellers
But if you hear it
You won't stand still
"Som de Preto" (Black's Song)

DJ Marlboro, Soul Grand Prix, and Furacão 2000 are among the most successful of those who have released remixes for funk dances. DJ Marlboro (Fernando Luiz Mattos da Matta, born in Rio in 1963) is one of the creators of funk carioca and is partially responsible for its boom in the 1990s. Through Big Mix, his production company and label, he puts on about thirty dances a week, each of which attracts some five thousand funkeiros. These fans read *Big Mix*, Marlboro's magazine, listen to his radio show, visit his Web site, and buy his CDs, which have cumulatively sold in the millions. Beginning in 2004, Marlboro became an international act, playing in a series of electronic music events in Europe. In his opinion, "funk doesn't need to be fashionable to exist. In fact, I like it better when the media don't advertise the dances. Then we have more freedom to play."[19]

Tati Quebra-Barraco, MC Serginho, Mr. Catra, MC Sapão, and Bonde do Tigrão are among the more popular funk carioca artists. They fill up dances in Rio every weekend, singing repetitive lyrics dripping with sexual innuendo on top of heavy Miami bass beats spiced up with electronica and, sometimes, candomblé percussion. A milder version of Rio's funk, labeled *funk melody*, made it even more palatable to the middle classes. Featuring melodic, romantic tunes on top of a lively beat, funk melody acts like Buchecha, Perlla, MC Leozinho, and MC Marcinho have sold millions of copies collectively.

Buchecha (Claucirlei Jovêncio de Souza) pioneered the style and has been a regular on the pop charts since the late 1990s, when he was part of a duo with Claudinho. The latter died in a car crash in 2002, but Buchecha moved on as a solo artist.

Some of his hits are "Quero Te Encontrar," "Só Love" and "Xereta." Perlla is an evangelical born in 1999 whose lyrics are miles away from the crudeness of Tati Quebra-Barraco, for instance (both are female singers). In hits like "Tremendo Vacilão" Perlla sings about love and broken hearts. In 2008 she was so popular among youngsters that Rio de Janeiro state officials used her image in a campaign to prevent teenage pregnancy. MC Leozinho (Leonardo de Freitas) is the author of the light, catchy "Ela Só Pensa em Beijar" (She Only Thinks About Kissing), one of 2006's top hits and one of the favorite ring tones of the year, with more than fifty thousand downloads.[20]

An officially "unsanctioned" style of funk is called *proibidão* (highly forbidden). It was created in the favelas in the mid-1990s and is outlawed by the government—you can't buy it in the legal market. Proibidão lyrics depict the violent daily life in the ghetto, glorifying drug dealers and criminals in general, and typically feature sexually explicit content.

Funk has been incorporated into the hybrid sound of many Brazilian artists. Fernanda Abreu took funk music and mixed it with samba and disco to create original dance music in her 1995 album *Da Lata*. Mangueira sambista Ivo Meirelles, a longtime collaborator with rocker Lobão, created a percussion-loaded group called Funk'n Lata that combines funk, rock, and samba (they can be heard in the documentary *Moro no Brasil*). Bonde do Rolê is a lighthearted group from Curitiba that blends funk carioca with hip-hop, techno, punk, rock, and satirical and comically dirty lyrics. Their MySpace page described them as "DJ Marlboro on acid." After being discovered there by DJ Diplo (Wesley Pentz), an American, the tongue-in-cheek band released its first album in 2006 and toured internationally with CSS (Cansei de Ser Sexy), introducing Brazilian funk to many foreign listeners.

BRAZILIAN SOUL AND R&B

Brazilian soul music is best represented by Tim Maia (1942–1998). Singing with a deep voice and ebullient charm, Maia infused a lot of swing into

▲ Tim Maia. *(Courtesy of Continental.)*

▲ Ed Motta. *(Photo by Lidio Parente. Courtesy of WEA.)*

▲ Max de Castro. *(Courtesy of Trama Records.)*

his highly danceable songs, always accompanied by the incendiary horns of the Vitória Régia band. One of his many hits was "Do Leme ao Pontal," an infectious number in which he sings of the beautiful beaches along Rio's coastline. Tim's intense personality and long history of drug abuse turned him into an unpredictable character. He often simply failed to show up for his gigs, or spent the whole show complaining about the sound. Nevertheless, he managed to retain his enormous popularity. In the '90s he enlarged his repertoire, recording romantic songs and even bossa nova. He was a larger-than-life character whose life and career were documented by friend and colleague Nelson Motta in a 2007 biography.[21] Toni Tornado, Hyldon, Banda Black Rio, and Gerson King Combo were prominent contemporaries of Maia in the 1970s in Brazilian soul.

Tim Maia's nephew, Ed Motta, is a sophisticated singer-songwriter with a voice that rivals the best American soul singers. His jazzy renditions often include perfect imitations of several instruments as he winds smoothly through the melody. Motta is a notorious perfectionist, capable of re-recording the same song for hours in search of the right sound. He can be heard as a guest artist on many MPB albums. Cassiano, Sandra de Sá, and Claudio Zoli are also well regarded in the realms of Brazilian soul and funk.

In the late 1990s artists in São Paulo started a new trend, adding elements of R&B, hip-hop, and electronic dance music to their samba and MPB; among the most notable was Max de Castro (the son of the late singer Wilson Simonal). Max's albums *Samba Raro* and *Orchestra Klaxon* are soulful, technologically adept, and full of swing. His brother, Wilson Simoninha, runs on the same track as their father, singing samba and soul music with a warm voice and clear influences of the '70s. Another famous offspring, Jair Oliveira (son of Jair Rodrigues and brother of Luciana Mello), dresses his sophisticated ballads, bossa nova, and samba with drum 'n' bass, electronic touches, and delicate arrangements to enhance his sweet, cool voice.

BRAZILIAN RAP AND HIP-HOP

Brazilian rap artists, more than musicians in any other style, address some of the country's worst social injustices in their lyrics. Many rappers sing about crime, drugs, violence, police brutality, corruption, discrimination, poverty, and the lack of opportunity for the poor. Artists like MV Bill, Marcelo D2, and Racionais MC's depict the harsh realities of life in the urban slums of cities like Rio de Janeiro and São Paulo. "They recenter the periphery as a site of consciousness raising—giving voice to hundreds of favelas and [poor] suburbs which often remain unnamed on maps and in the Brazilian political agenda," according to anthropologist Jennifer Roth Gordon.[22]

Brazilian rap music was being recorded in the 1980s but became widely popular only in the next decade with the arrival of Gabriel o Pensador (Gabriel the Thinker), a carioca rapper. In 1992, at the age of nineteen, he garnered instant fame with the song "Tô Feliz (Matei o Presidente)" (I'm Happy [I Killed the President]), which was directed at the corrupt and soon-to-be-impeached Brazilian president, Fernando Collor de Mello. Gabriel developed a steady career with a long string of hits like "Lôraburra," "Retrato de um Playboy," "Cachimbo da Paz," and "Festa da Música." His 2005 album *Cavaleiro Andante* expanded his musical references and connected his clever and agile rhymes to cultural streams as diverse as the noble poetry of Carlos Drummond de Andrade, the sophisticated bossa nova of Tom Jobim and Vinicius de Moraes, the avant-garde pop of Adriana Calcanhotto, and the messianic spirit of rock star

Renato Russo. Sometimes Gabriel opts for simple, wry commentary, as in "Cachimbo da Paz."

Criminals rule the city
Society blames the authorities
The Indian chief traveled to the Pantanal
Because violence here was just too much

Some other leading Brazilian rap acts from Rio are MV Bill, B Negão, Black Alien, and the biggest name in contemporary Brazilian rap, Marcelo D2. Born in 1967, Marcelo Maldonado Gomes Peixoto mixes rap and samba, creating original beats that he fills with words attacking social hypocrisy, corruption, and bigotry. D2 considers himself a perpetual outsider: a white among blacks and a black among whites. His 2003 album *À Procura da Batida Perfeita* (In Search of the Perfect Beat) includes guest appearances by samba stars Martinho da Vila and Beth Carvalho. The title track was a propulsive "bossa rap" (our phrase) in which D2 rapped atop Luiz Bonfá's sublime "Bonfa Nova" and Mix Mastermike's scratches, creating a lyrical hip-hop fusion. The following album, *Meu Samba É Assim*, runs on the same track, with rhymes on top of themes by João Donato and, again, the participation of two samba greats, Zeca Pagodinho and Arlindo Cruz. This CD consolidated the samba-rap fusion Marcelo had been looking for since his days as a vocalist for Planet Hemp, a successful hip-hop band that had run into trouble with the law because of their support for marijuana use.

A bag full of money doesn't make me happy
But the power of samba and the power of
*   rap do*
The MC who sings partido alto
And the surdo that becomes a scratch
    "À Procura da Batida Perfeita"
    (In Search of the Perfect Beat)

Gustavo Black Alien and B Negão, two other ex–Planet Hemp members, have created their own fusions. Black Alien's first solo album, *Babylon by Gus, Volume 1—Ano do Macaco*, features rap infused with jazz, reggae, and rock beats, topped by surreal psychedelic lyrics. He weaves it all together effortlessly, from mellow sensual beats to fast, aggressive, tongue-twisting rhymes. B Negão and his band Seletores de Freqüência rap out sharp, aggressive rhymes on top of ragga, dub, samba, soul, funk carioca, and rock.

MV Bill (Alexandre Barreto) is better known for his ideological activism than for his music (his sound is similar to that of Public Enemy). He comes from Rio's rough Cidade de Deus (City of God) neighborhood, made famous by the 2002 Fernando Meirelles film of the same name. MV stands for "Mensageiro da Verdade" (Messenger of the Truth), and Bill says that he's an activist, not an artist. For him, hip-hop is a political movement and rap is just one of its manifestations. "Hip-hop culture changed my life. If it weren't for rap, I'd be a criminal or I'd be dead today."[23] He is famous for the shocking crudeness of some of his video clips, which often depict violent scenes of drug dealing, shootouts, and death. "My clips aren't meant to be understood by the police or justice department. I think politicians are the ones to blame for criminality and urban violence because they're the ones that can't stop the arms traffic in Brazil," he told Adilson Pereira.[24]

MV Bill's lyrics address political, socioeconomic, and racial issues and also daily life and even romance, always with a critical approach. Most of all, he gives voice to the often ignored residents of Brazil's ghettos. As he likes to say, "We may be marginalized, but we are not marginal."[25] The rapper has worked for positive change: he founded an NGO called CUFA (United Favelas Central) that aims at giving young favela dwellers all over Brazil the means to express themselves through cultural productions. He also produced an acclaimed documentary movie called *Falcão—Meninos do Tráfico*, which shows the life of teenage drug dealers. He wrote a book with the same title with his manager Celso Athayde, and the two co-authored *Falcão—Mulheres e o Tráfico*, which addresses the role of women in drug trafficking.

The United Nations named MV Bill a Citizen

of the World in 2004, and his NGO work has been officially recognized by the Brazilian government and by UNICEF.

Although Rio is home to stars like MV Bill and D2, the capital of Brazilian rap is arguably São Paulo. The biggest, wealthiest city in the country, São Paulo is a vast metropolis that also has Brazil's highest concentration of poverty. The main difference between the rap made in São Paulo and that made in Rio is attitude. Metaphorically speaking, one can say that rappers from Rio smile. Paulistanos don't. Rappers from Rio are frequently more laid back, more ironic, even when they talk about grave subjects. The approach in São Paulo is more politically oriented and angrier, and the production quality there is generally higher. Some noteworthy names from Paulistano rap are Racionais MC's, Rappin' Hood, Xis, and Negra Li.

São Paulo's quintessential rap group is the "gangsta rap" band Racionais MC's.[26] They stand alone among successful artists in the Brazilian music scene in that they refuse to appear on TV, they never give interviews, and their records are released without marketing campaigns. *Sobrevivendo no Inferno* (Surviving in Hell, 1997) sold more than a million copies. The 2002 double CD *Nada Como um Dia Após Outro Dia* sold a hundred thousand copies in three days. Racionais MC's have garnered admiration from ghetto and middle-class kids alike. Poor kids adore the quartet because of the raw, intense lyrics that depict daily life in the slums and because of the band's defiant attitude, which conveys the message that it's possible to be a winner without surrendering to the system. For middle-class youngsters, listening to Racionais MC's is an easy, comfortable way of showing rebelliousness.

The Racionais have hit a national nerve by openly and aggressively critiquing racial inequality in Brazil.

> *60% of the youth in the periphery without*
> *criminal records have suffered police*
> *violence*
> *Of every four persons killed by the police,*
> *three are black*

In Brazilian universities, only 2% of the
students are black
Every four hours, a young black dies
violently in Sao Paulo
Speaking here is Cousin Black, another
survivor

"Capítulo 4, Versículo 3"
(Chapter 4, Verse 3)

In the beginning of its career, it was clear that the group's gangsta-rap songs were chronicles of hard life in the ghetto, but Mano Brown, Ice Blue, Edi Rock, and KL Jay later seemed to be moving closer and closer to a rationalization of violence and sexism. It wasn't easy to tell whether they were depicting reality the way they saw it or advocating a criminal lifestyle—or both. This is a question asked of some of their North American "gangsta" antecedents as well.

Don't look at me, forget me,
Even when I'm asleep, I'm ready for war,
I wasn't like that, but I feel so much hate,
I know that that's bad for me,
But what can I do

Mano Brown, "Vida Loka" (Parte II)

Rappin' Hood (Antonio Luiz Junior), like Marcelo D2 and B Negão, appears to be searching for a truly Brazilian rap language. His goal is to give rap made in Brazil the same status and sophistication as MPB and samba. That's why he adds traditional Brazilian styles to his rhythmic beat, and his second album, *Sujeito Homem 2* (2005) included Caetano Veloso, Gilberto Gil, Dudu Nobre, Arlindo Cruz, and Zelia Duncan as guests. His renditions of standards like "Odara" (Caetano Veloso) and "Andar com Fé" (Gilberto Gil) were perfect examples of Rappin' Hood's quest. "I want to make rap more musical . . . cross the borders between the rap from the ghettos and rootsy MPB," he told journalist João Bernardo Caldeira.[27]

The heirs, the new warriors
New descendents, Afro-Brazilians

From the ghettos fight night and day
They're in the rat race like most people
"Us Guerreiro" (The Warriors)

Xis, a young rap veteran born in 1972, made his debut in 1992 with a song on the collective album *Consciência Black Vol. 2*. When Xis released his first solo CD, *Seja Como For* (1999), he had already polished his personal style, with lyrics about hope, love, and fun, an unaggressive but still sharp political message on top of original beats.

Another important character in the rap scene is singer-actress Negra Li (Liliane de Carvalho), who has released one solo album and another in a duo with Helião, a Brazilian rap veteran who started his career in the 1980s. Negra Li uses her soulful contralto voice on top of lively beats full of swing, and sings rap with a pop finish. She says of her lyrics, "Our protest is soft. There's no use in talking about crimes if we're peaceful. We have no reason to be rebellious when our life is good."[28] As an actress, Negra Li has appeared in *Antonia*, a TV series and feature film, where she played the part of one of the members of a vocal quartet.

Perhaps Brazilian rap will continue to stir controversy in the future, but the genre may be looked upon rather differently. Heloísa Buarque de Hollanda comments, "Favelas have always produced poetry, and today they're creating a kind of poetry that comes from rap music. A rebellious kind of music that builds a bridge between culture and politics."[29]

ELECTRONICA IN BRAZIL

In the area of electronic dance music, DJ Marky, DJ Dolores, DJ Patife, and Fernanda Porto have achieved international fame playing drum 'n' bass tinged with Brazilian rhythms. Gui Boratto was a critic's favorite for his 2007 album *Chromophobia*, which showed off a variegated sonic palette that ranged from minimal to neotrance to synth pop.

DJ Marky (Marco Antonio da Silva), born in São Paulo in 1975, is the most accomplished Brazilian DJ and enjoys a busy international career. In 2001 the U.K. magazine *Knowledge* named him Best International DJ in its annual drum 'n' bass awards. Marky says that his mission is "to bring Brazilian music classics to the surface."[30] He does this by remixing them in such a way, with so many different interlocking rhythms, that they become irresistibly danceable. A good example is the remix he made with DJ Xerxes, one of Brazil's top electronica producers, for Jorge Benjor and Toquinho's "Carolina Carol Bela." Besides his swing, DJ Marky is also known for his lively performance onstage: he jumps and dances nonstop, keeping the energy level high at his gigs.

Helder Aragão, a northeasterner from the small state of Sergipe, born in 1966, is known in the music world as DJ Dolores. A veteran of the mangue beat movement, Dolores is an exception in the DJ scene: he's also a musician and leads his own band, Orquestra Santa Massa. DJ Dolores translates urban northeastern music into the electronica language, filtering emboladas, cocos, and incidental sounds captured in the streets of Recife through state-of-the-art technology, samples, and heavy beats. DJ Dolores has toured Europe and the United States, and his albums, including *Contraditório?* (2002) and *Aparelhagem* (2005), have achieved public and critical acclaim. Wagner Ribeiro de Souza, a paulistano born in 1977, goes by the name of DJ Patife and is one of the mainstays of the MPB-electronica bridge. His sound runs on the same track as Marky's: powerful drum 'n' bass on top of Brazilian beats. He began his career at age thirteen, spinning discs for dances in São Paulo where he had to play everything from samba to rock, forró to funk. "Playing everything, you learn to like everything," he says. "Electronica came together with that."[31] Some have nicknamed his music drum 'n' bass MPB. His second album, *Cool Steps: Drum 'n' Bass Grooves* (2001), features one of Patife's biggest hits: a remix of Tom Jobim and Aloysio de Oliveira's "Só Tinha Que Ser Com Você." He recorded this song in collaboration with singer-songwriter Fernanda Porto, the voice of Brazilian drum 'n' bass. Prior to that he had achieved success with his remix of Porto's "Samb-

assim." Fernanda is also an important figure in Brazilian electronic music (for more about her, see Chapters Three and Four).

Rio de Janeiro native Marcelinho da Lua is considered significant in modern bossa nova because of his exuberant bossa-electronica fusion in *Bossacucanova* (1997). Produced with Marcio Menescal, the son of bossa nova pioneer Roberto Menescal, and Alexandre Moreira, *Bossacucanova* features bossa standards augmented by drum 'n' bass. The album started a boom of modern bossa nova in Europe and the United States and had sequels with *Brasilidade* (with Roberto Menescal, 2001) and *Uma Batida Diferente* (2004). The talent and success of Marcelinho da Lua, Fernanda Porto, and the DJs mentioned above brought electronic music into the mainstream in Brazil. In the early years of the twenty-first century, the style became popular among youngsters, attracting thousands of fans to raves all over the country, every weekend.

THE FUTURE

As ever, Brazil is absorbing foreign musical styles, rediscovering its own traditions, and using them both to create something new. A century ago this process resulted in the creation of choro and maxixe. Later it produced bossa nova and Tropicália. In more recent decades it gave birth to samba-reggae, guitarrada and mangue beat. The paraense group Cravo Carbono defines itself in terms of this ongoing Brazilian fusion. In singer Lázaro Magalhães's words, the band strives to "apply to Brazilian music the very matrix of the Brazilian people: to be mestizo, mixed, crossed by diverse cultural influences. It's as [anthropologist] Darcy Ribeiro said: we are a nation in formation." To be genuinely Brazilian, the group's music "must be open to all and see in all directions, including past and future, without musical prejudices."[32]

In the twenty-first century, Brazilian music is still as playful, open, vibrant, imaginative, and self-renewing as ever.

INTRODUCTION

1. Herbie Mann, interview by Chris McGowan, 1989.

CHAPTER ONE

1. E. Bradford Burns, *A History of Brazil*, 2d ed. (New York: Columbia University Press, 1980), 44.

2. For more information, see ibid., and James Rawley, *The Transatlantic Slave Trade* (New York: W. W. Norton, 1981).

3. Burns, *History of Brazil*; José Jorge de Carvalho, "Music of African Origin in Brazil," in Carvalho, *Africa in Latin America* (New York: Holmes and Meier, 1984), 227.

4. Diana DeG. Brown, *Umbanda: Religion and Politics in Urban Brazil* (New York: Columbia University Press, 1994), 27–28.

5. Burns, *History of Brazil*, 54.

6. G. Reginald Daniel, "Multiethnic Populations in the United States and Brazil," *UCLA ISOP Intercom* 14, no. 7 (January 15, 1992): 1–5.

7. See Jennifer Roth Gordon, "Hip-Hop Brasileiro: Brazilian Youth and Alternative Black Consciousness Movements" (paper presented at American Anthropology Association meeting, November 18, 1999), http://brown.edu/Departments/Race_Ethnicity/roth-gordon/JenRothGordonAAA1999.pdf, 3.

8. João Gabriel de Lima and Silvania Dal Bosco, "O brasileiro Everardo," *Veja*, August 14, 1996, 113.

9. Migene González-Wippler, *Santería: The Religion* (New York: Harmony Books, 1989), 7.

10. Brown, *Umbanda: Religion and Politics in Urban Brazil*, 29. Also see Paul Christopher Brown, *Secrets, Gossip and Gods* (Oxford: Oxford University Press, 2002).

11. Estimates of Brazil's indigenous population vary widely. To learn more, visit the Web sites of FUNAI (http://www.funai.gov.br/), IBGE (http://www.ibge.gov.br/), and Instituto Socioambiental (http://www.socioambiental.org/).

12. As of January 2008.

13. See Rita Cáurio, *Brasil musical* (Rio de Janeiro: Art Bureau, 1988), 60; Ricardo Cravo Albin, ed. *Dicionário Houaiss ilustrado: Música popular brasileira* (Rio de Janeiro: Paracatu Editora, 2006), 59–60; and Marco Antonio Marcondes, ed., *Enciclopédia da música brasileira: Erudita, folclórica e popular*, 2d ed. (São Paulo: Art Editora, 1998), 59–61.

CHAPTER TWO

1. Rita Cáurio, *Brasil musical* (Rio de Janeiro: Art Bureau, 1988), 126.

2. Ibid., 126; Ricardo Cravo Albin, ed. *Dicionário Houaiss ilustrado: Música popular brasileira* (Rio de Janeiro: Paracatu Editora, 2006), 663; Marco Anto-

nio Marcondes, ed., *Enciclopédia da música brasileira: Erudita, folclórica e popular*, 2d ed. (São Paulo: Art Editora, 1998), 616; Vasco Mariz, *A canção brasileira*, 5th ed. (Rio de Janeiro: Editora Nova Fronteira, 1985), 54; Sérgio Cabral, *As escolas de samba do Rio de Janeiro: O que, quem, como, quando e por que* (Rio de Janeiro: Fontana, 1974), 32; Hermano Vianna, *The Mystery of Samba: Popular Music and National Identity in Brazil* (Chapel Hill: University of North Carolina Press, 1999), 79; and André Diniz, *Almanaque do samba* (Rio de Janeiro: Jorge Zahar Editora, 2006), 34.

3. Cáurio, *Brasil musical*, 129.

4. For a visual and historical journey through Rio's important neighborhoods for samba, see Luiz Fernando Vianna, *Geografia carioca do samba* (Rio de Janeiro: Casa da Palavra, 2004).

5. For a fascinating study of this development, see Vianna, *Mystery of Samba*.

6. Quoted in Jesse Navarro Jr., ed., *Nova história da música popular brasileira*, 2d ed. (São Paulo: Abril Cultural, 1977), "Dorival Caymmi," 1.

7. For more on Brazil's radio era, see Bryan McCann's *Hello, Hello Brazil: Popular Music in the Making of Modern Brazil* (Durham: Duke University Press, 2004).

8. Quoted in Pedro Tinoco, "A raiz e a flor," *Veja Rio*, February 9, 2000, 10.

9. Quoted in Luis Pimentel, "Wilson Moreira festeja seus 70 anos," *Jornal do Brasil*, June 2, 2006, B1.

10. Quoted in Paulo Celso Pereira, "Sargento que está virando general," *Jornal do Brasil*, May 25, 2004, B8.

11. Paulo Cordeiro de Oliveira Neto, interview by Ricardo Pessanha, 2007. Paulo's online journal is at http://www.habitus.ifcs.ufrj.br/vol1num2.htm.

12. Lobão, interview by Ricardo Pessanha and Chris McGowan, 1989.

13. Caetano Veloso, *Tropical Truth: A Story of Music and Revolution in Brazil* (New York: Knopf, 2002), 23.

14. Paulinho da Viola, interview by Ricardo Pessanha, 1989.

15. "Todo mundo na rua," *Revista Programa*, February 24, 2006, 18.

16. Cabral, *As escolas de samba*, 9.

17. Quoted in Navarro, *Nova história da música popular brasileira* (São Paulo: Abril Cultural, 1977), "Paulinho da Viola," 11.

18. Quoted in Ana Cecilia Martins, "Nova aurora de Elton," *Jornal do Brasil*, July 12, 2007, B1.

19. Vladimir Cunha, "Estrelas de Belém," *Rolling Stone Brasil*, January 2008, 44.

20. Quoted in Nelson Gobbi, "Nobreza do samba," *Jornal do Brasil*, December 1, 2005, B6.

21. Quoted in Tárik de Souza, Ziraldo Alves Pinto, et al., "Da Grécia a Marte, via Gamboa," *Jornal do Brasil*, January 15, 2006, B6.

22. Rildo Hora, interview by Chris McGowan, 2007.

23. Nei Lopes, *Partido-Alto: Samba de bamba* (Rio de Janeiro: Pallas Editora, 2005), 10.

24. Hora, interview.

25. Ibid.

26. Quoted in Silvio Essinger, "Vida nova com talento antigo," *Jornal do Brasil*, March 3, 2002, B8.

27. Quoted in Helena Aragão, "Ele dispensa o rótulo de 'raiz,'" *Jornal do Brasil*, February 6, 2004, B1.

28. Tárik de Souza, "A prova de fogo do moleque," *Jornal do Brasil*, May 25, 2001, B6.

29. Bezerra da Silva, interview by Chris McGowan, 1987.

30. Quoted in Gobbi, "Nobreza do samba."

31. See also Tárik de Souza, *Tem mais samba: Das raízes à eletrônica* (São Paulo: Editora 34, 2003).

32. Hora, interview.

CHAPTER THREE

1. Tom Jobim, interview by Ricardo Pessanha and Chris McGowan, 1989.

2. Quoted in José Eduardo Homem de Mello, *Música popular brasileira* (São Paulo: Editora da Universidade de São Paulo, 1976).

3. Marcelo Câmara, Jorge Melo, and Rogério Guimarães, *Caminhos cruzados: A vida e a música de Newton Mendonça* (Rio de Janeiro: Mauad Editora, 2001).

4. Oscar Castro-Neves, interview by Chris McGowan, 1989.

5. Jobim, interview.

6. Ibid.

7. Vinícius de Moraes, liner notes for Paul Winter's *Rio* album (Columbia, 1965).

8. Jobim, interview.

9. Quoted in Mello, *Música popular brasileira*.

10. Zuza Homem de Mello, interview by Chris McGowan, 1989.

11. Castro-Neves, interview.

12. Ibid.

13. Quoted in Neil Tesser's liner notes for *Stan Getz: The Girl from Ipanema, the Bossa Nova Years* (Verve, 1989).

14. Quoted in Augusto de Campos, *Balanço da bossa e outras bossas* (São Paulo: Editora Perspectiva, 1978).

15. Castro-Neves, interview.

16. Quoted in Mello, *Música popular brasileira*..

17. Charlie Byrd, interview by Chris McGowan, 1989.

18. Ibid.

19. Ibid.

20. Paul Winter, interview by Chris McGowan, 1989.

21. Herbie Mann, interview by Chris McGowan, 1989.

22. Ibid.

23. Ruy Castro, *Chega de saudade* (São Paulo: Companhia das Letras, 1990), 336.

24. Tesser, liner notes for *Stan Getz: The Girl from Ipanema*.

25. Caetano Veloso, *Tropical Truth: A Story of Music and Revolution in Brazil* (New York: Knopf, 2002), 43.

26. Castro-Neves, interview.

27. Jobim, interview.

28. Sérgio Cabral, *Antônio Carlos Jobim* (Rio de Janeiro: Lumiar Editora, 1997), 299.

29. Arthur Nestrovski, Lorenzo Mammi, and Luiz Tatit, *Três canções de Tom Jobim* (São Paulo: Cosac Naify, 2004), 49.

30. Quoted in Cabral, *Antônio Carlos Jobim*, 301.

31. Ibid., 309–10.

32. Fernanda Porto, interview by Chris McGowan, 2008.

33. Ibid.

CHAPTER FOUR

1. Charles A. Perrone, *Masters of Contemporary Brazilian Song: MPB, 1965–1985* (Austin: University of Texas Press, 1989), 32–34.

2. Don Grusin, interview by Chris McGowan, 1989.

3. Dori Caymmi, interview by Chris McGowan, 1987.

4. Gilberto Gil, interview by Chris McGowan, 1989.

5. Tárik de Souza, liner notes for *Grandes nomes: Caetano* (PolyGram, 1995).

6. José Emilio Rondeau, interview by Chris McGowan, 2007.

7. Christopher Dunn, *Brutality Garden: Tropicália and the Emergence of a Brazilian Counterculture* (Chapel Hill: University of North Carolina Press, 2001), 3.

8. Tom Zé, liner notes for *The Hips of Tradition* (Luaka Bop, 1992).

9. Dunn, *Brutality Garden*, 95.

10. Ibid., 133.

11. Caetano Veloso, *Tropical Truth: A Story of Music and Revolution in Brazil* (New York: Knopf, 2002), 188.

12. Ibid., 190.

13. Quoted in Jesse Navarro Jr., ed., *Nova história da música popular brasileira*, 2d ed. (São Paulo: Abril Cultural, 1977), "Caetano Veloso," 4.

14. Gil, interview.

15. Ibid.

16. Jon Pareles and Stephen Holden, "Rock's Own Generation Gap," *New York Times*, December 24, 1989, Arts and Leisure section, 29.

17. Ibid.

18. Veloso, *Tropical Truth*, 43.

19. Quoted in Navarro, *Nova história da música popular*, "Jorge Ben," 4.

20. Herbie Mann, interview by Chris McGowan, 1989.

21. George Duke, interview by Chris McGowan, 1989.

22. Ivan Lins, interview by Chris McGowan, 1989.

23. Quoted in Navarro, *Nova história da música popular*, "João Bosco and Aldir Blanc," 5.

24. Djavan, interview by Chris McGowan, 1987.

25. Grusin, interview.

26. Gil, interview.

27. Geraldo Azevedo, interview by Chris McGowan, 1989.

28. André Midani, interview by Chris McGowan, 1987.

CHAPTER FIVE

1. Zuza Homem de Mello, interview by Chris McGowan, 1989.

2. Quoted in Vasco Mariz, *A canção brasileira*, 5th ed. (Rio de Janeiro: Editora Nova Fronteira, 1985), 170, 168.

3. Milton Nascimento, interview by Chris McGowan and Ricardo Pessanha, 1989.

4. Ibid.

5. For more on the folias de reis, see Suzel Ana Reily, *Voices of the Magic: Enchanted Journeys in Southeast Brazil* (Chicago: University of Chicago Press, 2002).

6. This and the quotations in the following paragraphs are from our 1989 interview with Nascimento.

7. Charles A. Perrone, *Masters of Contemporary Brazilian Song: MPB, 1965–1985* (Austin: University of Texas Press, 1989), 151.

8. Lyle Mays, interview by Chris McGowan, 1989.

9. Ibid.

10. Caixas de folia (translated in the album's liner notes as "folia boxes") are played by the folia de reis groups in Minas.

11. Nascimento, interview.

12. Robert Palmer, "Eastern Brazil Exports Influential Pop to the World," *New York Times*, May 4, 1986.

CHAPTER SIX

1. C. Daniel Dawson, "Capoeira: An Exercise of the Soul," *Icarus* 13 (1994): 16.

2. Bira Almeida, *Capoeira: A Brazilian Art Form* (Berkeley, Calif.: North Atlantic Books, 1986), 29.

3. Greg Downey, liner notes of *Grupo de capoeira Angola pelourinho* (Smithsonian Folkways, 1996).

4. Ibid.

5. Raul Giovanni Lody, *Cadernos de folclore: Afoxé* (Rio de Janeiro: FUNARTE, 1976), 4–5. Also see: Larry Crook, *Brazilian Music: Northeastern Traditions and the Heritage of a Modern Nation* (Santa Barbara: ABC Clio, 2005), 128–133, and Raymundo Nina Rodrigues, *Os Africanos no Brasil* (São Paulo: Companhia Editora Nacional, 1932).

6. Jorge Amado, *Tent of Miracles* (New York: Knopf, 1971), 85–86.

7. Ibid., 81.

8. Quoted in Linda K. Yudin, "Filhos de Gandhi Afoxé: Afro-Bahian Dance Traditions in the Carnaval of Salvador da Bahia, Brazil" (master's thesis, University of California at Los Angeles, 1988).

9. Antonio Risério, *Carnaval ijexá: Notas sobre a re-africanização do carnaval baiano* (Salvador: Editora Corrupio, 1982), 47.

10. Ibid., 38.

11. Ibid., 41.

12. Raimundo Santa Rosa, interview by Ricardo Pessanha, 1991.

13. Linda Yudin, interview by Chris McGowan, 1997.

14. Daniel J. Crowley, *African Myth and Black Reality in Bahian Carnaval*, Monograph Series no. 25 (Los Angeles: UCLA Museum of Cultural History, 1984).

15. Linda Yudin, interview by Chris McGowan, 2007.

16. Risério, *Carnaval ijexá*, 53.

17. Larry Crook, "Black Consciousness, Samba Reggae, and the Re-Africanization of Bahian Carnival Music in Brazil," *World of Music* 35, no. 2 (1993): 102.

18. Two music videos were shot in 1996 for the song. One features Olodum and was filmed in Salvador and Rio.

19. Quoted in Jesse Navarro Jr., ed., *Nova história da música popular brasileira*, 2d ed. (São Paulo: Abril Cultural, 1977), "Dorival Caymmi," 10.

20. Risério, *Carnaval ijexá*, 116.

21. Yudin, interview, 1997.

22. Ironically, Daniela Mercury was supplanted as axé music's most popular performer by Ivete Sangalo, another white singer.

23. Bruce Gilman, "And Now, the World," *Brazzil*, January 1997, 40–43.

24. Lauro Jardim, "Ivete é campeã mas a crise continua," *Veja*, January 16, 2008, 39.

25. Carlinhos Brown, interview by Ricardo Pessanha, 1992. The statements by Brown quoted in the following paragraphs are from this interview.

CHAPTER SEVEN

1. Quoted in Jesse Navarro Jr., *Nova história da música popular brasileira*, 2d ed. (São Paulo: Abril Cultural, 1977), "Luiz Gonzaga," 4.

2. Ibid., 1.

3. Ibid., 8.

4. Luis da Câmara Cascudo, *Dicionário do folclore brasileiro*, 5th ed. (Belo Horizonte: Editora Itatiaia Limitada, 1984), 345. See also Marco Antonio Marcondes. ed., *Enciclopédia da música brasileira: Erudita, folclórica e popular*, 2d ed. (São Paulo: Art Editora, 1998), 159; and Mário de Andrade, *Dicionário musical brasileiro*, 2d ed. (São Paulo: Editora da Universidade de São Paulo, 1989), 115.

5. Quoted in João Máximo, "O Quixote do chapéu de couro," *Jornal do Brasil*, August 3, 1989, B1.

6. Navarro, *Nova história da música popular*, "Jackson do Pandeiro," 2.

7. For a recent biography, see Fernando Moura and Antônio Vicente, *Jackson do Pandeiro: O rei do ritmo* (São Paulo: Grupo Pão de Açucar/Editora 34, 2001).

8. Cascudo, *Dicionário do folclore brasileiro*, 670.

9. John P. Murphy, *Music in Brazil* (New York: Oxford University Press, 2006), 86–87.

10. Ibid.

11. Adryana BB, interview by Ricardo Pessanha, 2007.

12. Cascudo, *Dicionário do folclore brasileiro*, 150.

13. Kazadi Wa Mukuna, *An Interdisciplinary Study of the Ox and the Slave (Bumba-Meu-Boi), a Satirical Music Drama in Brazil* (Lewiston, N.Y.: Edwin Mellen Press, 2003), is an excellent resource for information on bumba-meu-boi.

14. Ibid., 82.

15. Sonia Goldfeder, "Farra européia: Grupo amazonense é a febre do Verão Francês," *Veja*, August 14, 1996, 134.

16. Rita Cáurio, *Brasil musical* (Rio de Janeiro: Art Bureau, 1988), 120. See also Larry Crook, *Brazilian Music: Northeastern Traditions and the Heritage of a Modern Nation* (Santa Barbara, Calif.: ABC Clio, 2005), 191; and Marcondes, *Enciclopédia da música brasileira*, 306.

17. Crook, *Brazilian Music*, 190–94.

18. Alceu Valença, interview by Chris McGowan, 1989.

19. Marcondes, *Enciclopédia da música brasileira*, 306.

20. Geraldo Azevedo, interview by Chris McGowan, 1989.

21. Valença, interview. The statements by Valença quoted in the following paragraphs are from this interview.

22. Azevedo, interview.

23. Ibid.

24. Crook, *Brazilian Music*, 311.

25. Ibid., 313.

26. Bruce Gilman, "And Now, the World," *Brazzil*, January 1997.

27. Crook, *Brazilian Music*, 315.

28. More information about mangue beat can be found in José Teles, *Do frevo ao manguebeat* (São Paulo: Art Editora 34, 2000).

29. Paulo Amaral cites a reference to carimbó in 1906 (Paulo Murilio Guerreiro do Amaral, "Tradicão e modernidade no carimbó urbano de Belém," *Overmundo*, January 9, 2007), while Morton Marks cites an 1880 newspaper article mentioning carimbó in his essay for the album *Music of Pará, Brazil: Carimbó, Pajelança, Batuque and Umbanda* (Folkways FE 4346, 1982).

30. Cascudo, *Dicionário do folclore brasileiro*, 196.

31. Cravo Carbono (Pio Lobato, Bruno Rabelo, and Lázaro Magalhães), interview by Chris McGowan, 2008.

32. Ibid.

33. Luis Antônio Giron, "Carnaval de 90 promete lambadear," *Folha de São Paulo*, February 11, 1990, E1.

34. Gilka Wara Céspedes, "Huayño, Saya, and Chuntun-qui: Bolivian Identity in the Music of 'Los Kjarkas,'" *Latin American Music Review* 14, no. 1 (1993): 93.

35. Alan Riding, "Brazilian Wonder Turns Out Bolivian," *New York Times*, July 4, 1990, 16L.

36. Ibid.

37. Cravo Carbono, interview.

38. Ibid.

39. Hermano Vianna, "Isso é calypso: Ou a lua nao me traiu," *Overmundo*, July 17, 2007, http://www.overmundo.com.br/overblog/isso-e-calypso-ou-a-lua-nao-me-traiu, 1.

40. Cravo Carbono, interview.

41. Ibid.

42. Vianna, "Isso e calypso," 1–2.

43. Cravo Carbono, interview.

44. Ibid.

45. Ibid.

46. Vladimir Cunha, "Estrelas de Belém," *Rolling Stone Brasil*, January 2008, 43.

47. Quoted in ibid.

48. See Associated Press, "Brega Sound Turning Industry on Its Ear," October 19, 2007, http://edition.cnn.com/2007/TECH/10/19/brazil.tecnobrega.ap/index.html.

49. Cravo Carbono, interview.

50. Ibid.

CHAPTER EIGHT

1. David P. Appleby, *The Music of Brazil* (Austin: University of Texas Press, 1983), 72.

2. José Ramos Tinhorão, *Pequena história da música popular: Da modinha ao Tropicalismo*, 5th ed. (São Paulo: Art Editora, 1986), 103.

3. Appleby, *Music of Brazil*, 76.

4. Tinhorão, *Pequena história da música popular*, 105.

5. For more information on the history of choro, we recommend Tamara Elena Livingston-Isenhour and Thomas George Caracas Garcia, *Choro: A Social History of a Brazilian Popular Music* (Bloomington: Indiana University Press, 2005). Mário Sève's *Vocabulário do choro: Choro Vocabulary* (Rio de Janeiro: Lumiar Editora, 1999) is a bilingual Portuguese/English book of choro studies and compositions for musicians.

6. Livingston-Isenhour and Garcia, *Choro*, 161.

7. Luciana Ribeiro and Bruno Agostini, "Rio bom de choro," *Jornal do Brasil*, *Revista Programa*, April 19, 2002, 26.

8. Quoted in Tárik de Souza, "Latinidade instrumental," *Jornal do Brasil*, June 21, 2004, B3.

9. Lyle Mays, interview by Chris McGowan, 1989.

10. Bruce Gilman, "EG=mc2," *Brazzil*, June 1998, 41–44.

11. Quoted in Nelson Gobbi and Wagner Tiso, "A música tem que servir à alma," *Jornal do Brasil*, May 8, 2006, B8.

12. Airto Moreira, interview by Chris McGowan, 1989.

13. Jovino Santos Neto, interview by Chris Mc-Gowan, 2007.

14. Moreira, interview.

15. Mays, interview.

16. Santos Neto, interview. The statements by Santos Neto quoted in the following paragraphs are from this interview.

17. Bruce Gilman, "Extramusical Phenomena," *Brazzil*, May–June 2000.

18. Moreira, interview. The statements by Moreira quoted in the following paragraphs are from this interview.

19. George Duke, interview by Chris McGowan, 1989.

20. Moreira, interview.

21. Ibid.

22. John Storm Roberts, *The Latin Tinge* (Oxford: Oxford University Press, 1979), 204.

23. Duke, interview.

24. Moreira, interview.

25. Mays, interview.

26. Quoted in Beatriz Velloso, "Muito além da batucada," *Época*, August 22, 2005, 127.

27. Duke, interview.

28. Quoted in Daniela Canedo, "Nossa diva do jazz," *Jornal do Brasil, Revista de Domingo*, December 22, 2002, 31.

29. Sérgio Mendes, interview by Chris McGowan, 1987.

30. Herbie Mann, interview by Chris McGowan, 1989.

31. Duke, interview.

32. Mays, interview.

33. Ibid.

34. Don Grusin, interview by Chris McGowan, 1989.

35. Duke, interview.

36. Ibid.

37. Quoted in *Dicionário Cravo Albin de música popular brasileira*, http://www.dicionariompb.com.br/.

38. Terry Gilliam, interview by Chris McGowan, 1992.

39. Ben Ratliff, *New York Times Essential Library: Jazz, A Critic's Guide to the 100 Most Important Recordings* (New York: Henry Holt, 2002).

40. Mann, interview.

CHAPTER NINE

1. Paulo Ricardo, interview by Chris McGowan, 1989.

2. ABPD Web site, http://www.abpd.org.br/ (accessed June 2007).

3. Jovem Guarda helped spawn "brega" music in Brazil in the 1970s and 1980s, performed by artists like Reginaldo Rossi, which in turn inspired the "nova brega" and "calipso" sounds of Pará (see Chapter Seven).

4. Rita Lee, interview by Chris McGowan, 1987.

5. Rob Chapman, "Nutters from Brazil," *Times* (London), August 26, 2005, http://entertainment.timesonline.co.uk/tol/arts_and_entertainment/article558910.ece.

6. José Emilio Rondeau, interview by Chris McGowan, 2007.

7. Dana Goodyear, "The Magus," *New Yorker*, May 7, 2007, 41.

8. Quoted in ibid., 42.

9. Marcelo Nova essay for *Raul* boxed set, issued by PolyGram Brazil in 1995.

10. Lulu Santos, interview by Ricardo Pessanha, 1989.

11. André Midani, interview by Chris McGowan, 1989.

12. Herbert Vianna, interview by Chris McGowan, 1989.

13. Ibid.

14. José Emilio Rondeau, interview by Chris McGowan, 1997.

15. Titãs, interview by Ricardo Pessanha, 1989.

16. Willis Guerra Filho to Chris McGowan, 1989.

17. Bruce Gilman, "Cracking MTV's Cliché," *Brazzil*, March 2003, 45–47.

18. Rhett Butler, "Music Goes Global: Best Bands in the World," *Time* magazine, September 15, 2001, http://www.time.com/time/musicgoesglobal/na/mbest.html.

CHAPTER TEN

1. At the beginning of the twentieth century, *música sertaneja* was a generic term for music from rural Brazil, including the Northeast.

2. Larry Crook, *Brazilian Music: Northeastern Traditions and the Heritage of a Modern Nation* (Santa Barbara, Calif.: ABC Clio, 2005), 247.

3. Suzel Ana Reily, quoted in John P. Murphy, *Music in Brazil* (New York: Oxford University Press, 2006), 118.

4. Ibid.

5. Nopem Institute, http://www.nopem.com.br/.

6. Quoted in Rodrigo Teixeira, "Almir sater: Não sou sertanejo, eu sou roqueiro," *Overmundo*, August 27, 2007, http://www.overmundo.com.br/overblog/almir-sater-nao-sou-sertanejo-eu-sou-roqueiro.

7. Quoted in *Veja*, September 26, 2007, 120.

8. Murphy, *Music in Brazil*, 123.

9. Amelia Simpson's *Xuxa: The Mega-Marketing of Gender, Race, and Modernity* (Philadelphia: Temple University Press, 1993), is a great study of the singer and her cultural impact.

10. Adilson Pereira, "Traficando informação," *Jornal do Brasil*, December 22, 2000, B2.

11. See http://www.abpd.org.br/.

12. Quoted in Fabiola Brisolla, Fátima Sá, and Gustavo Autran, "Zona Sul embarca no funk," *Veja Rio*, January 31, 2001, 17.

13. Quoted in Rafael Sento Sé, "Mestra da polêmica," *Jornal do Brasil, Revista de Domingo*, November 21, 2004, 22.

14. Quoted in Luís Pimentel, "Batidão nas livrarias," *Jornal do Brasil*, March 27, 2005, B1.

15. Ibid.

16. Quoted in Rodrigues Alves, "Funk é cultura?" *Jornal do Brasil*, March 24, 2001, *Idéias* section, 1.

17. Ibid.

18. Ibid.

19. Quoted in Gilberto de Abreu, "O rei do pancadão," *Jornal do Brasil*, August 8, 2004, B1.

20. Gustavo Autran, "Ele só pensa em cantar," *Veja Rio*, May 10, 2006, 30.

21. Nelson Motta, *Vale tudo: O som e a fúria de Tim Maia* (Rio de Janeiro: Editora Objetiva, 2007).

22. Jennifer Roth Gordon, "Hip-Hop Brasileiro: Brazilian Youth and Alternative Black Consciousness Movements" (paper presented at American Anthropology Association meeting, November 18, 1999), http://brown.edu/Departments/Race_Ethnicity/roth-gordon/JenRothGordonAAA1999.pdf, 2.

23. Israel Tabak, "Hip-hop: A 'revolução silenciosa' que mobiliza as favelas," *Jornal do Brasil*, June 17, 2001, 24.

24. Adilson Pereira, "Traficando informação," *Jornal do Brasil*, December 22, 2000, B1.

25. Ibid., B2.

26. *Racionais* means "rationals."

27. João Bernardo Caldeira, "Rap também é música," *Jornal do Brasil*, April 11, 2005, B3.

28. Quoted in Tárik de Souza, "Rap com reggae, R&B e jazz," *Jornal do Brasil*, October 21, 2004, B5.

29. Quoted in Sé, "Mestra da polêmica," 22.

30. Quoted in Adilson Pereira, "O mundo dos DJs," *Jornal do Brasil*, December 27, 2001, B1.

31. Ibid.

32. Cravo Carbono, interview by Chris McGowan, 2008.

aboio: wordless song used by cowboys of the sertão to call cattle.

acalanto: lullaby (from Portugal).

afoxé: Carnaval group that performs music and dance derived from candomblé ritual music; the music an afoxé performs.

afoxê: a gourd with beads strung on cords or on wire wrapped around it.

afro-samba: samba mixed with additional candomblé musical elements.

agogô: double bell (each bell is a different size) struck by a wooden stick.

ala: one of the units into which an escola de samba is divided during its Carnaval parade.

alfaia: large, double-headed bass drum used in maracatu.

ao vivo: live performance.

apito: any whistle; whistle used by the bateria's director in an escola de samba.

arame: steel wire attached to the verga of a berimbau; any wire.

atabaque: generic name for conical single-headed drums played with the hands, similar to Cuban conga drum.

auto: dramatic form (often processional) that includes dances, songs, and allegorical characters. Autos are performed during December and January, and came to Brazil from Portugal, where they date to medieval times. Examples include bumba-meu-boi and chegança.

axé: Yoruba word for positive energy or life force.

axé music: general term for Afro-Bahian pop styles, such as samba-reggae.

Bahia: state in northeastern Brazil; common nickname for Salvador, the capital of Bahia state.

baiano (baiana): someone or something from Bahia state; northeastern rhythm related to baião and used in cavalo marinho; old Afro-Brazilian circle dance.

baião: northeastern song style with syncopated melody and instrumental refrains in short arpeggios, typically with raised fourths and flattened sevenths.

baile funk: a dance where Brazilian funk is played; international term for funk carioca.

baixo: bass.

balanço: swing.

banda: group of people who celebrate Carnaval together, especially with marchas, attempting to bring the atmosphere of club festivities out onto the street; any musical group.

bandolim: mandolin.

baqueta: drum stick.

bateria: drums; drum-and-percussion section of an escola de samba.

batidão: big beat, referring to funk carioca.

batucada: samba drumming or percussion playing involving different instruments.

batuque: archaic Afro-Brazilian music and dance observed as early as the eighteenth century; generic name for Afro-Brazilian drumming and dances; type of Afro-Brazilian religion; type of drum used in jongo.

berimbau: wooden bow with metal string and gourd resonator used especially to accompany capoeira.

bloco: group of people who parade together during Carnaval.

bloco afro: Afro-Brazilian Carnaval group, primarily in Salvador.

bloco de empolgação: Carnaval group whose members wear the same costume and parade to samba music.

bloco de enredo: Carnaval group structured like a small escola de samba.

boi-bumbá: variation of bumba-meu-boi in the Amazonian region.

boi-de-mamão: variation of bumba-meu-boi in Santa Catarina.

bolero: Cuban song form that has become a slow, sentimental international style for romantic ballads.

bombo (or bumbo): the largest Brazilian bass drum.

bossa nova: genre of music developed in Rio de Janeiro in the late 1950s that includes rhythmic elements of samba, a highly syncopated style of guitar playing, a generally subdued vocal style (when sung), and harmonic influences from cool jazz and classical music.

brega: pejorative word for sentimental, commercial romantic songs performed from the 1960s on.

brega paraense: brega style of Pará state, also called calipso or calypso (not to be confused with Trinidad's calypso).

bumba-meu-boi: folk drama and processional dance of Portuguese origin with added Brazilian elements. It celebrates the death and resurrection of a magical ox and involves elaborate costumes and choreography.

cabaça: hollow gourd that is part of a berimbau.

caboclinho: northeastern Carnaval group that parades in stylized Indian costumes and plays flutes and pífanos.

cachaça: Brazilian sugarcane liquor.

caixa: snare drum.

calango: popular partner dance in Minas Gerais and Rio de Janeiro states, characterized by simple steps and 2/4 meter.

calunga: fetishistic doll carried by dama de passo in a maracatu procession.

calypso (or calipso): popular musical genre from Trinidad; in Brazil, another name for the brega paraense style performed by artists like Banda Calypso.

canção praieira: fisherman's song.

candomblé: Afro-Brazilian religion primarily of Gege-Nagô derivation. Its ritual music uses three different atabaques (the rum, rumpi, and lê) and pentatonic and hexatonic scales.

cantador: troubador of northeastern and central Brazil who sings improvised or memorized songs.

cantiga: generic term for ballad or popular song.

canto: song.

cantoria: singing; act of performing a desafio.

capoeira: Afro-Brazilian martial art brought to Brazil by Bantu slaves from Angola, practiced and performed publicly to singing and the playing of berimbaus, pandeiros, and other instruments.

capoerista: someone who performs or practices capoeira.

carimbó: Afro-Brazilian song and dance from Pará that dates from at least the nineteenth century. The song has a 2/4 rhythm, fast tempo, and heavy percussion dominated by the carimbó drum (a hollow tree-trunk section covered with deer skin).

carioca: someone or something from the city of Rio de Janeiro.

Carnaval: Carnival, four days of celebration before Ash Wednesday, observed primarily in Roman Catholic countries. Mardi Gras is the U.S. version.

cateretê: rural dance of probable Amerindian origin, performed by couples who are accompanied by a singer and two violas.

catimbó: a type of umbanda in northeastern Brazil.

catira: common alternate name for cateretê.

cavalo-marinho: musical folk drama of Pernambuco and neighboring states, related to bumba-meu-boi.

cavaquinho: a four-stringed instrument similar to a ukulele.

caxambu: Afro-Brazilian song and dance accompanied by drums and handclapping; type of drum used in it.

caxixi: small, closed wicker basket filled with seeds, used as a shaker in capoeira.

cearense: someone or something from Ceará state.

chegança: popular dramatic procession (an auto) about the Christians fighting the Moors; lascivious and sensual Portuguese dance from the eighteenth century. Variations include chegança-de-mouros and cristãos-e-mouros.

chocalho: wooden or metal shaker.

chorão: choro musician.

choro: instrumental genre of music that features rapid modulations, melodic leaps, and improvisation, developed in the late nineteenth century in Rio.

chula: dance of Portuguese origin dating from at least the eighteenth century in Brazil, and accompanying rhythm, most common in Rio Grande do Sul; one of three sections in a capoeira song.

cinema novo: Brazilian film movement of the 1950s and 1960s that sought to create an authentically Brazilian cinema.

ciranda: children's circle dance of Portuguese origin; rural samba in Rio de Janeiro state; folkloric song and dance from Pernambuco.

coco: Afro-Brazilian song/dance in 2/4 from northeastern littoral.

congada (or congo): processional dances that incorporate both African traditions and Iberian elements and often include characters who represent African royalty. Congada is found in southern and central Brazil, while congo is generally found in northern and northeastern Brazil.

conjunto: musical group.

cordão (cordões): originally an all-male group that danced and celebrated Carnaval to the accompaniment of batucada and first appeared in the late nineteenth century.

cozinha: bass, drums, and assorted percussion; rhythmic mix; kitchen.

cuíca: small friction drum with a thin stick inside attached to the drum skin. The drummer rubs the stick with a moistened cloth and with one hand applies pressure to the drum skin, producing grunting, groaning, and squeaking noises.

cumbia: popular dance music from Colombia.

dama de passo: the woman who carries the calunga doll in a maracatu procession.

dança: dance.

desafio: poetic improvisational contests between two vocalists. The question-and-answer exchanges are sung, usually without accompaniment, and are interrupted by short instrumental passages.

desfile: Carnaval parade; any parade.

dobrão: large coin, used by musicians to change the pitch of a berimbau.

drum 'n' bass: type of electronic dance music characterized by fast-tempo broken-beat drums over heavy, sometimes complex bass lines at a slower tempo.

dupla: duo.

embolada: poetic musical form from northeastern littoral with stanza-and-refrain structure, 2/4 meter, fast tempo, declamatory melody, short note values, small musical intervals, and stanzas that are often improvised.

enredo: theme.

entrudo: rude, chaotic style of celebrating Carnaval that originated in Portugal and was popular in Brazil until the late nineteenth century.

escola de samba: samba school, an organization that plans and puts on samba parades during Carnaval. It typically has many other social functions and may serve as the community center in its neighborhood (usually a poorer area of the city).

fado: melancholy, guitar-accompanied Portuguese ballad that derived from lundu. Some scholars believe it actually originated in Brazil but was fully developed in Portugal.

fandango: generic name in southern Brazil for circle dances and accompanying music; also refers to gathering at which these dances are performed.

favela: slum, shantytown.

fluminense: someone or something from Rio de Janeiro state.

fofa: voluptuous Portuguese dance of the eighteenth century.

folia de reis: groups that perform religious music in the streets in December and January; another name for reisado.

forró: generic name for dance-oriented northeastern styles or dance at which they are played; also used by some to signify a certain variation of the baião.

frevo: fast, syncopated marcha that originated in Recife.

fricote: song form that mixes ijexá and reggae.

frigideira: percussion instrument shaped like a frying pan and played with a stick.

funk carioca: Brazilian funk style created in Rio de Janeiro.

funk de favela: funk from the favela neighborhoods; funk carioca.

funkeiro: funk fan; one who attends bailes funk (funk dances).

galope: six-verse martelo (same as agalopado or martelo-agalopado).

ganzá: single, double, or triple tubular metal shaker; wooden or metal square with cymbals.

gaúcho (gaúcha): someone or something from Rio Grande do Sul state.

Gege (or Jeje): Brazilian word for Ewe people who came from Dahomey, now the Republic of Benin.

Gege-Nagô: combined cultural systems of Gege and Nagô peoples in Brazil.

gonguê: metal bell used in maracatu.

guitarra: electric guitar.

guitarrada: instrumental lambada style from Pará created by Mestre Vieira that features electric-guitar soloing over a mixture of carimbó, merengue, and cumbia rhythms.

habanera: slow Cuban song and dance in duple time.

ijexá: rhythm of afoxé song form; also a subgroup of the Yoruba people.

Jeje: see *Gege*.

jogo: game; the playing of capoeira.

jongo: type of rural samba from southeastern Brazil.

Ketu: subgroup of Yoruba people.

lambada: musical style from Pará created by Mestre Vieira (see *guitarrada*) that evolved into an eclectic, popular song form of the 1980s and '90s; a close, sexy dance for two partners that incorporates elements of merengue, maxixe, and forró dances.

lundu (or lundum): song and dance of Angolan origin brought to Brazil by Bantu slaves; ancestor of many urban Brazilian song forms.

maculelê: Afro-Brazilian stick-fighting war dance.

macumba: generic name for various Afro-Brazilian religions (candomblé, umbanda, Xangô, catimbó, batuque, etc.).

malandro: man who makes his living by exploiting women, gambling, or playing small confidence tricks; scoundrel, vagabond, loafer.

maltas: urban lower-class gangs in pre-abolition Brazil.

mangue (or mangue beat): fusion of hard rock and hip-hop with northeastern styles such as maracatu, popularized in Recife in the 1990s.

maraca: hollow gourd with dried seeds or pebbles inside, commonly used musically by Brazilian Indians.

maracatu: slow, heavy Afro-Brazilian processional music and accompanying dance from northeastern Brazil, featuring many characters, including a king, a queen, a dama de passo, and other characters. Types of maracatu include maracatu de baque solto (also called maracatu rural) and maracatu de baque virado (also called maracatu de nação).

marcha: merry Afro-Brazilian form with strong accent on downbeat, influenced in the 1920s by one-step and ragtime.

marcha-rancho: slower and more melodically developed variations of the marcha.

martelo: northeastern poetic form with ten syllables to a line and six to ten lines to a stanza.

marujada: popular dramatic procession (an auto) with maritime themes and men dressed as sailors.

maxixe: song and dance that was a fusion of lundu with polka, habanera, and (later) tango. It was created in the late nineteenth century and was the first original Brazilian urban dance.

merengue: Caribbean song/dance that originated in the Dominican Republic in the early nineteenth century.

mestre-sala: master of ceremonies who symbolically protects the porta-bandeira in an escola de samba parade.

micaretas: off-season Carnaval celebrations.

mineiro (mineira): someone or something from Minas Gerais state.

moda: sentimental song from Portugal.

moda de viola: rural folk song with simple melody, often performed by two vocalists harmonizing in thirds and playing guitars or violas, found in central and southeastern Brazil.

modinha: sentimental Brazilian song style derived from moda and lundu.

morro: in Rio used to mean one of the hills around the city upon which are located poor neighborhoods (the favelas); any hill.

MPB: acronym for música popular brasileira (Brazilian popular music); common term for post-bossa Brazilian urban popular music that combined many different musical elements and whose artists did not fall into individual categories such as samba, forró, jazz, or rock.

mulato (mulata): mulatto.

música caipira: folk music from rural southern, southeastern and central Brazil.

música gaúcha: generic name for music from Rio Grande do Sul.

música gauchesca: rural music from Rio Grande do Sul.

música sertaneja: popular "country" music from southern, southeastern, and central Brazil that derives from música caipira.

Nagô: name for Yoruba descendents in Brazil.

nordestino (nordestina): someone or something from northeastern Brazil.

nueva canción: folk music style that emerged in the 1960s in Chile and Argentina, incorporating indigenous regional song forms and instruments and lyrics that protest poverty and injustice; called nueva trova in Cuba.

one-step: American dance in simple duple time.

orixá: deity in Afro-Brazilian religions.

pagode: party or gathering where samba is played; type of samba popularized in 1980s by composers who gathered in Ramos, a neighborhood in Rio's Zona Norte.

pandeiro: Brazilian tambourine, with tunable skin and inverted jingles.

paraense: someone or something from Pará state.

partido alto: type of samba with short, light refrains that the singers must follow with improvised verses.

passista: person who masters samba steps.

paulista: someone or something from São Paulo state.

paulistano (paulistana): someone or something from city of São Paulo.

pífano (or pífe or pífaro): fife.

polka: a round dance and musical form in up-tempo 2/4 time that originated in Bohemia around 1830.

pontos de candomblé: invocation song for deities in candomblé religion.

pontos de umbanda: invocation songs for deities in umbanda religion.

porta-bandeira: standard-bearer (always a woman) in escola de samba parade.

pratos: cymbals.

preto: black; a black person.

proibidão: illegal Brazilian funk music that glorifies drug dealing and criminality.

quadrilha: quadrille, a square dance popular in France in the early nineteenth century. Danced in Brazil during Saint John's celebrations in June.

quilombo: settlements established by runaway slaves in colonial Brazil.

rabeca: Brazilian fiddle.

rancho: Carnaval group that parades to marcha-ranchos. Heavily influenced early escolas de samba.

reco-reco: a notched instrument (often made of bamboo or metal) that is scraped with a stick and produces a crisp sound.

rei: king.

reisado: popular dramatic processions that celebrate Epiphany; the songs sung by those participating.

repente: improvised stanza sung by a repentista.

repentista: a troubador, generally of northeastern Brazil, who sings improvised stanzas as he tells stories or performs in a desafio.

repique (or repinique): two-headed tenor drum in samba.

rock tupiniquim: nickname, often pejorative, for Brazilian rock.

roda: circle; a ring of musicians or bystanders in a music gathering; the ring of musicians or bystanders surrounding capoeira participants.

rojão: synonym for baião; sometimes refers to a faster-tempo baião.

roqueiro: a rock-and-roll musician or fan.

samba: the most famous Brazilian song and dance, musically characterized by 2/4 meter and interlocking, syncopated lines in melody and accompaniment.

samba-canção: slower, softer type of samba in which melody and lyrics are emphasized more than the rhythm.

samba de breque: type of samba with a "break" during which singer dramatizes situation or improvises dialogues.

samba de gafieira: a dance-hall style of samba, generally instrumental and with horn arrangements influenced by American big-band jazz.

samba de morro: name used by Brazilian media in 1940s and 1950s to characterize samba that kept essential characteristics of the style developed by Estácio composers such as Ismael Silva and Bide, and to differentiate this style from samba-canção, sambolero, etc.

samba de partido alto: see *partido alto.*

samba de roda: circle-dance samba accompanied by hand-clapping and batucada.

samba-enredo (or samba de enredo): theme samba, performed by an escola de samba and written for Carnaval.

samba-reggae: mixture of samba and reggae developed in Salvador in the 1980s.

sambista: someone who sings, writes, plays, or dances samba almost exclusively.

sanfona: accordion; button-accordion.

saudade: longing or yearning for someone or something.

schottische: ballroom dance similar to polka introduced to England in the mid-nineteenth century, also called "German polka."

seresta: serenade.

sertaneja: música sertaneja.

sertanejo: someone or something from sertão; someone who performs música sertaneja.

sertão: general name for remote interior regions of Brazil; arid backlands of northeastern Brazil.

sétima nordestina: the northeastern flattened seventh note.

siriá: folkloric music from Cametá region of Pará; a partner dance with elements of maxixe and forró.

soca: dance-oriented mixture of soul, funk, and calypso introduced by musicians from Trinidad in the 1970s.

som: sound; tone.

surdo: drum in samba played with a wooden stick that has a velvet-covered wooden head, it comes in three sizes and functions as the bass in the bateria of an escola de samba.

tambor: any drum.

tamborim: small tambourine without jingles played with single or double stick.

tango: dance and song form that developed in Argentina at the start of the twentieth century and derived its rhythm from the Cuban habanera and Argentinean milonga.

tan-tan: deep drum similar to an atabaque, substitutes for the surdo in pagode.

tarol: shallow two-headed drum with strings across skin played with two wooden sticks.

technobrega: fusion of electronic music and brega parense.

teclados: keyboards.

terreiro: place of worship in candomblé or umbanda.

toada: generic term for a stanza-and-refrain song with a simple, often melancholy melody and short romantic or comical lyrics.

toque: rhythm or tempo; refers especially to rhythms played on the berimbau during capoeira.

triângulo: triangle.

trio elétrico: musicians playing electrified instruments; the decorated truck atop which they play during Carnaval in Bahia.

Tropicália: art movement of the late 1960s, led in the musical area by Gilberto Gil, Caetano Veloso, and others.

Tropicalismo: see *Tropicália*.

umbanda: Afro-Brazilian religion developed in the twentieth century that has considerable influence from Spiritist beliefs.

umbigada: movement in lundu and other Afro-Brazilian dances in which dancer touches navels with another as an invitation to the dance.

vanerão (vaneirão): accordion-accompanied musical style from southern Brazil.

verga: wooden bow that is part of a berimbau.

viola: type of folk guitar, usually a ten-stringed instrument with five pairs of metal strings. The number of strings (five, seven, eight, ten, twelve, or fourteen) varies according to the region.

violão: six-string guitar.

violeiro: someone who plays a viola, especially a troubador of rural Brazil who plays viola and performs improvised or memorized songs.

violino: violin.

virada: change in percussion pattern.

Xangô: orixá of fire, thunder, and justice; Afro-Brazilian religion most widely practiced in Pernambuco state.

xaxado: northeastern song and dance.

xerém: song and dance from northeastern Brazil, similar to polka and xote, generally accompanied by accordion.

xique-xique: a type of cactus; a type of chocalho.

xote: a northeastern dance in 2/4 derived from the schottische.

Yoruba: an African people from Nigeria; also their language.

zabumba: large double-headed bass drum in northeastern music, especially in forró trios and bandas de pífanos.

Zona Norte: northern zone of Rio that includes neighborhoods such as Estácio, Tijuca, Vila Isabel, and Ramos.

Zona Sul: southern zone of Rio close to the beaches, includes neighborhoods such as Flamengo, Botafogo, Copacabana, Ipanema, Leblon, Jardim Botânico, and Gávea.

zouk: dance music from the French Antilles, with funk, African, and Caribbean influences.

SELECT BIBLIOGRAPHY

Abreu, Gilberto de. "O rei do pancadão." *Jornal do Brasil*, August 8, 2004, B1.

Albin, Ricardo Cravo, ed. *Dicionário Houaiss ilustrado: Música popular brasileira*. Rio de Janeiro: Paracatu Editora, 2006.

Almeida, Bira. *Capoeira: A Brazilian Art Form*. Berkeley, Calif.: North Atlantic Books, 1986.

Almeida, Laurindo. *Latin Percussion Instruments and Rhythms*. Sherman Oaks, Calif.: Gwyn, 1972.

Alvarenga, Oneyda. *Música popular brasileira*. Rio de Janeiro: Editora Globo, 1950.

Alves, Rodrigues. "Funk é cultura?" *Jornal do Brasil*, March 24, 2001, *Idéias* section, 1.

Amado, Jorge. *Tent of Miracles*. New York: Knopf, 1971.

Amaral, Paulo Murilio Guerreiro do. "Tradição e modernidade no carimbó urbano de Belém." *Overmundo*, January 9, 2007. http://www.overmundo.com.br/overblog/tradicaomodernidade-no-carimbo-de-belem.

Andrade, Mário de. *Danças dramáticas do Brasil*. São Paulo: Livraria Martins Editora, 1959.

——. *Dicionário musical brasileiro*. 2d ed. São Paulo: Editora da Universidade de São Paulo, 1989.

Appleby, David P. *The Music of Brazil*. Austin: University of Texas Press, 1983.

Aragão, Helena. "Ele dispensa o rótulo de 'raiz.'" *Jornal do Brasil*, February 6, 2004, B1.

Assumpção, José Teixeira de. *Curso de folclore musical brasileiro*. Rio de Janeiro: Livraria Freitas Bastos, 1967.

Autran, Gustavo. "Ele só pensa em cantar." *Veja Rio*, May 10, 2006, 30.

Bahiana, Ana Maria. *Nada será como antes*. Rio de Janeiro: Editora Civilização Brasileira, 1980.

Barsante, Cassio Emmanuel. *Carmen Miranda*. Rio de Janeiro: Editora Europa, 1985.

Bello, José Maria. *A History of Modern Brazil: 1889–1964*. Stanford: Stanford University Press, 1968.

Bramly, Serge. *Macumba*. New York: St. Martin's Press, 1977.

Brisolla, Fabiola, Fátima Sá, and Gustavo Autran. "Zona Sul embarca no funk." *Veja Rio*, January 31, 2001, 17.

Brown, Diana DeG. *Umbanda: Religion and Politics in Urban Brazil*. New York: Columbia University Press, 1994.

Browning, Barbara. *Samba: Resistance in Motion*. Bloomington: Indiana University Press, 1995.

Burns, E. Bradford. *A History of Brazil*. 2d ed. New York: Columbia University Press, 1980.

Butler, Rhett. "Music Goes Global: Best Bands in the World." *Time* magazine, September 15, 2001. http://www.time.com/time/musicgoesglobal/na/mbest.html.

Cabral, Sérgio. *Antônio Carlos Jobim*. Rio de Janeiro: Lumiar Editora, 1997.

——. *As escolas de samba: O que, quem, como, quando e por que*. Rio de Janeiro: Fontana, 1974.

Calado, Carlos. "Lambada vai dividir com 'negões' a

folia baiana." *Folha de São Paulo*, February 11, 1990, E4.

Caldeira, João Bernardo. "Rap também é música." *Jornal do Brasil*, April 11, 2005, B3.

Calmon, Joana. "O Rei do tum tchi tum tchi tum tchi." *Veja*, June 6, 2001, 85.

Campos, Augusto de. *Balanço da bossa e outras bossas*. São Paulo: Editora Perspectiva, 1978.

Canedo, Daniela. "Nossa diva do jazz." *Jornal do Brasil, Revista de Domingo*, December 22, 2002, 31.

Carvalho, José Jorge de. "Aesthetics of Opacity and Transparence: Myth, Music and Ritual in the Xangô Cult and in the Western Art Tradition." *Latin American Music Review* 14, no. 2 (1993): 202–31.

———. "Music of African Origin in Brazil." In José Jorge de Carvalho, *Africa in Latin America*, 227–248. New York: Holmes and Meier, 1984.

Cascudo, Luis da Câmara. *Dicionário do folclore brasileiro*. 5th ed. Belo Horizonte: Editora Itatiaia Limitada, 1984.

Castro, Ruy. "Bossa fora da cápsula." *Veja*, May 30, 1990, 48–54.

———. *Chega de saudade*. São Paulo: Companhia das Letras, 1990.

Cáurio, Rita, ed. *Brasil musical*. Rio de Janeiro: Art Bureau, 1988.

Caymmi, Dorival. *Cancioneiro da Bahia*. 5th ed. Rio de Janeiro: Editora Record, 1978.

Céspedes, Gilka Wara. "Huayño, Saya, and Chuntun-qui: Bolivian Identity in the Music of 'Los Kjarkas.'" *Latin American Music Review* 14, no. 1 (1993): 52–101.

Chapman, Rob. "Nutters from Brazil." *Times* (London), August 26, 2005. http://entertainment.time sonlineco.uk/tol/arts_and_entertainment/arti cle558910.ece.

Civita, Victor. *Nosso século*. São Paulo: Abril Cultural, 1980.

Crook, Larry. "Black Consciousness, Samba Reggae, and the Re-Africanization of Bahian Carnival Music in Brazil." *World of Music* 35, no. 2 (1993): 90–107.

———. *Brazilian Music: Northeastern Traditions and the Heritage of a Modern Nation*. Santa Barbara, Calif.: ABC Clio, 2005.

Crowley, Daniel J. *African Myth and Black Reality in Bahian Carnaval*. Monograph Series no. 25. Los Angeles: UCLA Museum of Cultural History, 1984.

Cunha, Vladimir. "Estrelas de Belém." *Rolling Stone Brasil*, January 2008, 43–46.

Daniel, G. Reginald. "Multiethnic Populations in the United States and Brazil." *UCLA ISOP Intercom* 14, no. 7 (1992): 1–5.

Dawson, C. Daniel. "Capoeira: An Exercise of the Soul." *Icarus* 13 (1994): 13–28.

Diniz, André. *Almanaque do samba*. Rio de Janeiro: Jorge Zahar Editora, 2006.

Domingues, André. *Os 100 melhores CDs da MPB*. Barueri: SP Editora, 2004.

Draeger, Alain, and Jorge Amado. *Bahia Mystery Land*. Paris: Editions d'Art Yvon, 1984.

Dunn, Christopher. "Afro-Bahian Carnival: A Stage for Protest." *Afro-Hispanic Review* 11, nos. 1–3 (1992): 11–20.

———. *Brutality Garden: Tropicália and the Emergence of a Brazilian Counterculture*. Chapel Hill: University of North Carolina Press, 2001.

Essinger, Silvio. "Vida nova com talento antigo." *Jornal do Brasil*, March 3, 2002, B8.

Feather, Leonard. *The Encyclopedia of Jazz in the Sixties*. New York: Horizon, 1966.

Feather, Leonard, and Ira Gitler. *The Encyclopedia of Jazz in the Seventies*. New York: Bonanza, 1976.

Fonseca, Heber. *Caetano: Esse cara*. Rio de Janeiro: Editora Revan, 1993.

Frade, Cascia. *Folclore brasileiro: Rio de Janeiro*. Rio de Janeiro: FUNARTE, 1979.

Freyre, Gilberto. *The Mansions and the Shanties*. 2d ed. Westport, Conn.: Greenwood Press, 1980.

Galemba, Phyllis. *Divine Inspiration: From Benin to Bahia*. Albuquerque: University of New Mexico Press, 1991.

Gilman, Bruce. "And Now, the World." *Brazzil*, January 1997, 40–43.

———. "Cracking MTV's Cliché." *Brazzil*, March 2003, 45–47.

———. "EG=mc2." *Brazzil*, June 1998, 41–44.

———. "Extramusical Phenomena." *Brazzil*, May–June 2000. http://www.brazzil.com/pages/mus may00.htm.

———. "Planetary Minstrel." *Brazzil*, September 1996, 41–44.

———. "Shut Up and Dance." *Brazzil*, April 1997, 40–44.

———. "Snapshots of Sound." *Brazzil*, February 2002, 44–48.

———. "Sorcerer's Apprentice." *Brazzil*, December 1996. http://www.brazzil.com/musdec96.htm.

Giron, Luis Antônio. "Carnaval de 90 promete lambadear." *Folha de São Paulo*, February 11, 1990, E1.

———. "Obra de Câmara Cascudo omitiu ritmos do Pará." *Folha de São Paulo*, February 11, 1990, E3.

Gobbi, Nelson. "Nobreza do samba." *Jornal do Brasil*, December 1, 2005, B6.

Gobbi, Nelson, and Wagner Tiso. "A música tem que servir à alma." *Jornal do Brasil*, May 8, 2006, B8.

Goes, Fred de. *O país do carnaval elétrico*. Salvador: Editora Corrupio, 1982.

Goldfeder, Sonia. "Farra européia: Grupo amazonense é a febre do verão francês." *Veja*, August 14, 1996, 134.

Gontijo, Ricardo. "Oi . . . Milton." *Canja*, October 1, 1980.

Gonzalez, Lelia. *Festas populares no Brasil*. 2d ed. Rio de Janeiro: Editora Index, 1989.

González-Wippler, Migene. *Santería: The Religion*. New York: Harmony Books, 1989.

Goodyear, Dana. "The Magus." *New Yorker*, May 7, 2007, 38–45.

Gordon, Jennifer Roth. "Hip-Hop Brasileiro: Brazilian Youth and Alternative Black Consciousness Movements." Paper presented at American Anthropology Association meeting, November 18, 1999. http://brown.edu/Departments/Race_Ethnicity/roth-gordon/JenRothGordonAAA1999.pdf.

Graham, Richard. "Technology and Culture Change: The Development of the Berimbau in Colonial Brazil." *Latin American Music Review* 12, no. 1 (1991): 1–19.

Graham, Ronnie. *The Da Capo Guide to Contemporary African Music*. New York: Da Capo Press, 1988.

Hess, David J. *Samba in the Night: Spiritism in Brazil*. New York: Columbia University Press, 1994.

Jardim, Lauro. "Ivete é campeã mas a crise continua." *Veja*, January 16, 2008, 39.

Kernfeld, Barry, ed. *The New Grove Dictionary of Jazz*. New York: Macmillan, 1988.

Levinson, Bruno. *Vamos Fazer Barulho—Uma radiografia de Marcelo D2*. Rio de Janeiro: Ediouro, 2007.

Lewis, J. Lowell. *Ring of Liberation: Deceptive Discourse in Brazilian Capoeira*. Chicago: University of Chicago Press, 1992.

Ligiero, Zeca, and Phyllis Galembo. "Iemanjá, the Sea Queen Mother." *Icarus* 13 (1994): 13–28.

Lima, João Gabriel de, and Silvania dal Bosco. "O brasileiro Everardo." *Veja*, August 14, 1996, 110–14.

Livingston-Isenhour, Tamara Elena, and Thomas George Caracas Garcia. *Choro: A Social History of a Brazilian Popular Music*. Bloomington: Indiana University Press, 2005.

Lockhart, James, and Stuart B. Schwartz. *Early Latin America: A History of Colonial Spanish America and Brazil*. Cambridge: Cambridge University Press, 1984.

Lody, Raul Giovanni. *Cademos de folclore: Afoxé*. Rio de Janeiro: FUNARTE, 1976.

Lopes, Nei. *Partido-Alto: Samba de bamba*. Rio de Janeiro: Pallas Editora, 2005.

Marcondes, Marco Antonio, ed. *Enciclopédia da música brasileira: Erudita, folclórica e popular*. 2d ed. São Paulo: Art Editora, 1998.

Mariz, Vasco. *A canção brasileira*. 5th ed. Rio de Janeiro: Editora Nova Fronteira, 1985.

Martins, Ana Cecilia. "Nova aurora de Elton." *Jornal do Brasil*, July 12, 2007, B1.

Martins, Sergio. "Irracionais MC's?" *Veja*, July 24, 2002, 111.

Máximo, João. "O Quixote do chapéu de couro." *Jornal do Brasil*, August 3, 1989, B1.

Máximo, João, and Carlos Didier. *Noel Rosa: Uma biografia*. Brasília: Editora Universidade de Brasília, 1990.

McCann, Bryan. *Hello, Hello Brazil: Popular Music in the Making of Modern Brazil*. Durham: Duke University Press, 2004.

McGowan, Chris. "Fourteen Acts Ready to 'Rock in Rio.'" *Billboard*, September 29, 1984, 36.

———. "Gilberto Gil: Cultivator of the Spirit." *The Beat* 10, no. 2 (1991): 48.

———. "Industry Struggles Uphill Against Four-Year Recession, Aided by Strong Musical Heritage." *Billboard*, January 26, 1985, VL-22.

———. "The Latest Brazilian Wave." *Pulse*, February 1992, 92.

———. "Monte's Ante." *Billboard*, September 7, 1991.

———. "Música Brasileira: Spirit and Soul." *The Beat* 10, no. 2 (1991): 26.

———. "A Nation of Cannibals." *The Beat* 10, no. 4 (1991): 24.

———. "Olodum: Bahian Powerhouse." *Pulse*, August 1991, 43.

———. "Rhythms of Resistance." *Pulse*, December 1990, 112.

———. "The Road to Rio." *The Beat* 10, no. 6 (1991): 25.

———. "Viva Brazil." *Billboard*, special supplement, November 7, 1987, B1–B32.

Mello, José Eduardo Homem de. *Música popular brasileira*. São Paulo: Editora da Universidade de São Paulo, 1976.

Mesquita, André. "A nova linguagem da viola universal." *Cover Guitar—Acústico*, June 1999. http://www.robertocorrea.com.br/na_imprensa/imprensa_3.htm.

Moffett, Matt. "A Racial 'Democracy' Begins Painful

Debate on Affirmative Action." *Wall Street Journal*, August 6, 1996, Al.

Moore, Zelbert. "Reflections on Blacks in Contemporary Brazilian Popular Culture in the 1980s." *Studies in Latin American Popular Culture* 1 (1988): 213–25.

Moraes Filho, Mello. *Festas e tradições populares do Brasil*. São Paulo: Livraria Itatiaia Editora, 1979.

Motta, Nelson. *Música, humana música*. Rio de Janeiro: Salamandra, 1980.

———. *Vale tudo: O som e a fúria de Tim Maia*. Rio de Janeiro: Editora Objetiva, 2007.

Moura, Fernando, and Antônio Vicente. *Jackson do Pandeiro: O rei do ritmo*. São Paulo: Grupo Pão de Açucar/Editora 34, 2001.

Moura, Roberto M. *Carnaval: Da redentora à praça do apocalipse*. Rio de Janeiro: Jorge Zahar, 1986.

Mukuna, Kazadi Wa. *An Interdisciplinary Study of the Ox and the Slave (Bumba-Meu-Boi), a Satirical Music Drama in Brazil*. Lewiston, N.Y.: Edwin Mellen Press, 2003.

Murphy, John P. *Music in Brazil*. New York: Oxford University Press, 2006.

Navarro, Jesse, Jr., ed. *Nova história da música popular brasileira*. 2d ed. São Paulo: Abril Cultural, 1977–78.

Nestrovski, Arthur, Lorenzo Mammi, and Luiz Tatit. *Três canções de Tom Jobim*. São Paulo: Cosac Naify, 2004.

Nettl, Bruno. *Folk and Traditional Music of the Western Continents*. Englewood Cliffs, N.J.: Prentice-Hall, 1973.

Nkctia, J. H. Kwabena. *The Music of Africa*. New York: W. W. Norton, 1974.

Omari, Mikelle Smith. *The Art and Ritual of Bahian Candomblé*. Monograph Series no. 24. Los Angeles: UCLA Museum of Cultural History, 1984.

Palmer, Robert. "Eastern Brazil Exports Influential Pop to the World." *New York Times*, May 4, 1986.

Pareles, Jon, and Stephen Holden. "Rock's Own Generation Gap." *New York Times*, December 24, 1989, Arts and Leisure section, 29.

Pereira, Adilson. "O mundo dos DJs." *Jornal do Brasil*, December 27, 2001, Bl.

———. "Traficando informação." *Jornal do Brasil*, December 22, 2000, Bl–B2.

Pereira, Paulo Celso. "Sargento que está virando general." *Jornal do Brasil*, May 25, 2004, B8.

Perrone, Charles A. "Axé, Ijexá, Olodum: The Rise of Afro- and African Currents in Brazilian Popular Music." *Afro-Hispanic Review* 11, nos. 1–3 (1992): 42–48.

———. *Letras e letras da música popular brasileira*. Rio de Janeiro: Elo Editora, 1988.

———. *Masters of Contemporary Brazilian Song: MPB, 1965–1985*. Austin: University of Texas Press, 1989.

———. "Os outros rômanticos." *Los Ensayistas: Brazil in the Eighties* 28–29 (1990): 79–97.

Perrone, Charles A., and Christopher Dunn, eds. *Brazilian Popular Music and Globalization*. Gainesville: University Press of Florida, 2001.

Pessanha, Ricardo. "Margareth Menezes: She's Not the Girl from Ipanema." *The Beat* 10, no. 2 (1991): 46.

———. "Street Urchins of São Paulo." *The Beat* 11, no. 4 (1992): 28.

Pessanha, Ricardo, and Carla Cinta Conteiro. *Caetano Veloso: L'âme brésilienne*. Paris: Éditions Demi-Lune, 2008.

Pessanha, Ricardo, and Ana Paula Macedo. "The New Afro Beat of Rio." *The Beat* 11, no. 6 (1992): 26.

Pimentel, Luis. "Batidão nas livrarias." *Jornal do Brasil*, March 27, 2005, Bl.

———. "Wilson Moreira festeja seus 70 anos." *Jornal do Brasil*, June 2, 2006, Bl.

Pinto, Tiago de Oliveira. "Making Ritual Drama: Dance, Music, and Representation in Brazilian Candomblé and Umbanda." *World of Music* 33, no. 1 (1991): 70–88.

Popovic, Pedro Paulo, ed. *Rock, a música do seculo XX*. Consultores Editoriais Ltda. Rio de Janeiro: Rio Grafica, 1983.

Poppino, Rollie E. *Brazil—the Land and People*. 2d ed. New York: Oxford University Press, 1973.

Ratliff, Ben. *New York Times Essential Library: Jazz, A Critic's Guide to the 100 Most Important Recordings*. New York: Henry Holt, 2002.

Rawley, James. *The Transatlantic Slave Trade*. New York: W. W. Norton, 1981.

Reily, Suzel Ana. *Voices of the Magic: Enchanted Journeys in Southeast Brazil*. Chicago: University of Chicago Press, 2002.

Ribeiro, Luciana, and Bruno Agostini. "Rio bom de choro." *Jornal do Brasil, Revista Programa*, April 19, 2002, 26.

Ribeiro, Maria de Lourdes Borges. *Cadernos de folclore: O jongo*. Rio de Janeiro: FUNARTE, 1984.

Riding, Alan. "Brazilian Wonder Turns Out Bolivian." *New York Times*, July 4, 1990, 16L.

Risério, Antonio. *Carnaval ijexá: Notas sobre a re-africanização do Carnaval baiano*. Salvador: Editora Corrupio, 1982.

Roberts, John Storm. *Black Music of Two Worlds*. New York: William Morrow, 1974.

———. *The Latin Tinge*. Oxford: Oxford University Press, 1979.

Rocca, Edgard. *Ritmos brasileiros e seus instrumentos de percussão*. Rio de Janeiro: Europa Editora, 1986.

Rodrigues, Raymundo Nina. *Os Africanos no Brasil* (São Paulo: Companhia Editora Nacional, 1932).

Rohter, Larry. "Ignored for Decades, Os Mutantes Is Now a Hot Band." *New York Times*, April 23, 2001.

Rotella, Sebastian. "Singer Finds Race Issue No Laughing Matter in Brazil." *Los Angeles Times*, September 5, 1996, A1.

Santos Neto, Jovino, ed. *Tudo é som*. Vienna: Universal Edition, 2001.

Sé, Rafael Sento. "Mestra da polêmica." *Jornal do Brasil, Revista de Domingo*, November 21, 2004, 22.

Seraine, Florival. *Folclore brasileiro: Ceará*. Rio de Janeiro: FUNARTE, 1978.

Sève, Mário. *Vocabulário do choro: Choro Vocabulary*. Rio de Janeiro: Lumiar Editora, 1999.

Severiano, Jairo, and Zuza Homem de Mello. *A canção no tempo: 85 anos de músicas brasileiras*. Vol. 1, *1958–1985*. São Paulo: Editora 34, 1998.

Simpson, Amelia. *Xuxa: The Mega-Marketing of Gender, Race, and Modernity*. Philadelphia: Temple University Press, 1993.

Sousa, José Geraldo de, Padre. *Cadernos de folclore: Características da música folclórica brasileira*. Rio de Janeiro: FUNARTE, 1969.

Souza, Tárik de. "A prova de fogo do moleque." *Jornal do Brasil*, May 25, 2001, B6.

———. "Latinidade instrumental." *Jornal do Brasil*, June 21, 2004, B3.

———. "Rap com reggae, R&B e jazz." *Jornal do Brasil*, October 21, 2004, B5.

———. *O som nosso de cada dia*. Porto Alegre: L&PM, 1983.

———. *Tem mais samba: Das raízes à eletrônica*. São Paulo: Editora 34, 2003.

Souza, Tárik de, and Elifas Andreato. *Rostos e gostos da música popular brasileira*. Porto Alegre: L&PM, 1979.

Souza, Tárik de, Ziraldo Alves Pinto, et al. "Da Grécia a Marte, via Gamboa." *Jornal do Brasil*, January 15, 2006, B6.

Tabak, Israel. "Hip-hop: A 'revolução silenciosa' que mobiliza as favelas." *Jornal do Brasil*, June 17, 2001, 24.

Teixeira, Rodrigo. "Almir Sater: Não sou sertanejo, eu sou roqueiro." *Overmundo*, August 27, 2007. http://www.overmundo.com.br/overblog/almir-sater-nao-sou-sertanejo-eu-sou-roqueiro.

Teles, José. *Do frevo ao manguebeat*. São Paulo: Art Editora 34, 2000.

Tenenbaum, Barbara, ed. *Encyclopedia of Latin American History and Culture*. New York: Charles Scribner's Sons, 1996.

Tereza, Irany. "Os deuses do Olimpo." *Revista da Mangueira*, 1997, 20–23.

Tinhorão, José Ramos. *Pequena história da música popular: Da modinha ao Tropicalismo*. 5th ed. São Paulo: Art Editora, 1986.

Tinoco, Pedro. "A raiz e a flor." *Veja Rio*, February 9, 2000, 10.

Vasconcelos, Ary. *Raízes da música popular brasileira*. Rio de Janeiro: Rio Fundo Editora, 1991.

Velloso, Beatriz. "Muito além da batucada." *Época*, August 22, 2005, 127.

Veloso, Caetano. *Tropical Truth: A Story of Music and Revolution in Brazil*. New York: Knopf, 2002.

Ventura, Zuenir. *1968, o ano que não terminou*. Rio de Janeiro: Nova Fronteira, 1988.

Verger, Pierre Fatumbi. *Orixás*. Salvador: Corrupio, 1981.

Vianna, Hermano. "Atravessando o córtex com o Cravo Carbono." *Overmundo*, August 11, 2007. http://www.overmundo.com.br/overblog/atravessando-o-cortex-com-o-cravo-carbono.

———. "Isso é calypso: Ou a lua nao me traiu." *Overmundo*, July 17, 2007. http://www.overmundo.com.br/overblog/isso-e-calypso-ou-a-lua-nao-me-traiu

———. *The Mystery of Samba: Popular Music and National Identity in Brazil*. Chapel Hill: University of North Carolina Press, 1999.

———. "Technoguitarradas do Pio." *Overmundo*, July 18, 2007. http://www.overmundo.com.br/overblog/tecnoguitarradas-do-pio.

Vianna, Luiz Fernando. *Geografia carioca do samba*. Rio de Janeiro: Casa da Palavra, 2004.

Vieira, Marceu. "É nota 1000." *Revista da Mangueira*, 1997, 20–23.

Wafer, Jim. *The Taste of Blood: Spirit Possession in Brazilian Candomblé*. Philadelphia: University of Pennsylvania Press, 1991.

Yudin, Linda K. "Filhos de Gandhi Afoxé: Afro-Bahian Dance Traditions in the Carnaval of Salvador da Bahia, Brazil." Master's thesis, University of California at Los Angeles, 1988.

SELECT DISCOGRAPHY
AND RESOURCES

The following albums are collections of Brazilian music that are readily available in North America. They offer the opportunity to sample a wide variety of artists and styles, and complement the many albums mentioned in the book. Visit our website, http://www. thebraziliansound.com, for an expanded discography and listings by category of Brazilian music CDs and downloads. (BR = Brazilian release.)

COLLECTIONS WITH VARIOUS ARTISTS

Acoustic Brazil. Putumayo, 2005.
Axé Bahia 2005. BR Universal, 2005.
Beginner's Guide to Brazil. Nascente, 2005.
Bossa Nova. Verve, 2006.
Bossa Nova Brasil. Polygram, 1992.
Brazil: The Essential Album. Manteca, 2000.
Brazil: Forró—Music for Maids and Taxi Drivers. Rounder, 1989.
The Brazilian Funk Experience: Rare Grooves from EMI Odeon Vaults (1968–1980). Nascente, 2006.
Brazilian Groove. Putumayo, 2003.
Brazil-Roots-Samba. Rounder, 1989.
Café Brasil. Teldec, 2001.
Candomblé: Afro-Brazilian Music. Buda Musique, 1995.
Canta Brasil: The Great Brazilian Songbook. Polygram, 1990.

Cartografia Musical Brasileira (10-CD series). BR/Itaú Cultural, 2000.
Chill Brazil (multi-CD series). Warner, 2002–8.
Clássicos do Choro. BR/EMI, 1990.
Favela Chic Postonove 3. Milan, 2004.
Forró Total. BR/Sony, 2004.
The Gringo Guide to Bossa Nova. Universal, 2006.
The Gringo Guide to Rio Carnaval. Universal, 2007.
The Now Sound of Brazil. Six Degrees, 2003.
The Now Sound of Brazil, Vol. 2. Six Degrees, 2005.
Pure Brazil (multi-CD series). Universal, 2004–8.
The Rough Guide to Brazilian Electronica. World Music Network, 2003.
The Rough Guide to the Music of Brazil (multi-CD series). World Music Network, 2004–7.
Samba Bossa Nova. Putumayo, 2002.
Samba Soul 70! Six Degrees, 2001.
Sambas de Enredo do Carnaval 2007. Planet Rhythm, 2007.
Soul of Brazil: Funk, Soul & Bossa Grooves: 65–77. EMI, 2005.
Tropicália: A Brazilian Revolution in Sound. Soul Jazz, 2006.
Tudo Azul: Velha Guarda da Portela. BR/EMI, 1999
Verve Jazz Masters 53: Bossa Nova. Verve, 1996.
The Very Best of Brazil. Nascente, 2004.
Yelé Brazil. Blue Note, 1994.

ADDITIONAL REFERENCE CDS

Black Orpheus (soundtrack). Verve, 1959.

Brown, Carlinhos. *Alfagamabetízado*. BR/EMI, 1996.

Carrilho, Altamiro, and Chiquinho et al. *Noites Cariocas*. BR/Kuarup, 1988.

Carvalho, Beth. *De Pé no Chão*. BR/RCA, 1978.

Elomar, and Geraldo Azevedo, Vital Farias, Xangai. *Cantoria*. BR/Kuarup, 1984.

Getz, Stan, and João Gilberto. *Getz/Gilberto*. Verve, 1964.

Gilberto, João. *Chega de Saudade*. BR/Odeon, 1959.

Grupo de Capoeira Angola Pelourinho. *Capoeira Angola from Salvador, Brazil*. Smithsonian/Folkways, 1996.

Nascimento, Milton. *Clube da Esquina 2*. BR/EMI, 1978

Nóbrega, Antônio. *9 de Frevereiro*. BR/Trama, 2006.

Quinteto Armorial. *Do Romance ao Galope Nordestino*. BR/Marcus Pereira, 1975.

Regina, Elis, and Antonio Carlos Jobim. *Elis & Tom*. Verve, 1974.

Veloso, Caetano, Gilberto Gil, Os Mutantes, Gal Costa, Tom Zé, et al. *Tropicália ou Panis et Circensis*. BR/Philips, 1968.

SELECT DVDS

The following titles are currently available through Amazon.com in North America.

Airto Moreira & Flora Purim: The Latin Jazz All-Stars. VIEW Video, 2006. A 1980 concert.

Antonio Carlos Jobim: An All-Star Tribute. VIEW Video, 1995. Jobim, Gal Costa, Shirley Horn, Gonzalo Rubalcaba, Joe Henderson, Jon Hendricks, Herbie Hancock, Ron Carter, Alex Acuna, and Harvey Mason perform Jobim standards.

Axé Bahia. Umvd, 2001. Popular artists from Salvador perform festive, dance-oriented axé music hits.

Baiana da Gema. EMI Brazil, 2005. Simone, Ivan Lins, and samba guest stars.

Black Orpheus (Orfeu Negro). Criterion Collection, 1959. The film, with its Jobim and Bonfá soundtrack, that helped popularize bossa nova worldwide.

Carnaval 2008. Som Livre, 2008. The escola de samba parades in Rio.

Danado de Bom. Sony/BMG Brazil, 2003. With Luiz Gonzaga.

Djavan Ao Vivo. Sony/BMG Brazil, 1999.

Elis Regina Carvalho Costa. Trama, 2005.

Eletrodoméstico. Sony Int., 2003. Bahian singer Daniela Mercury.

Estação Derradeira. EMI Int., 2006. Chico Buarque and the Velha Guarda da Mangueira.

Fundo de Quintal Ao Vivo. BMG Int., 2002. The pagode samba group.

Gal Canta Jobim. BMG Int., 2001. Gal Costa sings Antonio Carlos Jobim songs.

Ivete Sangalo MTV Ao Vivo. Universal Int., 2004. The Bahian axé music star.

Jorge Benjor Acustico. Umvd, 2003. An "unplugged" performance.

Lunário Perpétuo. Trama, 2003. A journey through northeastern music and culture with singer-fiddler-actor-dancer Antônio Nóbrega.

Maria Bethânia-Maricotinha Ao Vivo. Ans Records, 2004.

Maria Rita. Warner Music Latina, 2004.

Moro no Brasil. Milan Records, 2006. Performances by the Mangueira samba school, Walter Alfaiate and Seu Jorge, Antônio Nóbrega, Margareth Menezes, and Ivo Meirelles.

Muito Mais. Umvd, 2004. MPB singer-songwriter Caetano Veloso.

Nova Música Brasileira. Trama/Som Livre, 2004. Twenty music videos with contemporary artists.

Para Caymmi. WEA International, 2004. Dori, Nana, and Danilo Caymmi.

À Procura Da Batida Perfeita. Sony/BMG Brazil, 2007. With Marcelo D2.

Saudades da Casa. WEA Brazil, 2008. With Ivan Lins.

Saudade do Futuro. Laterit, 2004. Northeastern immigrants in São Paulo perform embolada and repente, and recount their life experiences.

A Sede do Peixe. BR/EMI, 2003. Documentary about Milton Nascimento.

The Sound of Brazil: Brasileirinho. Milan Records, 2007. A documentary about choro.

The Spirit of Brazil: Black Music of Brazil. Shanachie, 1982. Includes performances by Gilberto Gil, Milton Nascimento, Chico Buarque, and Leci Brandão.

Tim Maia in Concert. Sony/BMG Europe, 2007.

Tribalistas. Blue Note, 2003. Marisa Monte, Arnaldo Antunes, Carlinhos Brown.

Vinícius de Moraes. BR/Paramount, 2007. Documentary about the poet-lyricist-singer.

Zeca Pagodinho: Acústico MTV. Umvd, 2003. The pagode samba singer-songwriter.

THE BRAZILIAN SOUND: INTERNET RESOURCES

The Brazilian Sound (blog). http://thebraziliansound.blogspot.com/

The Brazilian Sound (Discography, Links, Resources). http://www.thebraziliansound.com/

The Brazilian Sound (Facebook group). http://www.facebook.com/group.php?gid=17585853795

The Brazilian Sound (MySpace). http://myspace.com/thebraziliansound/

INTERNET RESOURCES (IN ENGLISH)

All Brazilian Music. http://www.allbrazilianmusic.com/

The Brazil Music Shop. http://astore.amazon.com/brazilmusic-20

Brazzil magazine. http://www.brazzil.com/

Latin American Network Information Center (University of Texas at Austin), Brazil Links. http://www1.lanic.utexas.edu/la/brazil/

Maria-Brazil (Brazilian music and culture). http://www.maria-brazil.org/

Slipcue.com: Brazilian Music Reviews. http://www.slipcue.com/music/brazil/brazillist.html

INTERNET RESOURCES (IN PORTUGUESE)

Agenda do Samba & Choro. http://www.samba-choro.com.br/

Associação Brasileira de Produtores de Discos. http://www.abpd.org.br/

CliqueMusic. http://cliquemusic.uol.com.br/

Dicionário Cravo Albin da Música Popular Brasileira. http://www.dicionariompb.com.br/

FUNARTE (Fundação Nacional de Arte). http://www.funarte.gov.br/

Instituto Antonio Carlos Jobim. http://www.antonio-carlosjobim.org/

Itaú Cultural. http://www.itaucultural.org.br/

Letras de Músicas. http://letras.terra.com.br/

Museu da Imagem e do Som. http://www.mis.rj.gov.br/

Overmundo. http://www.overmundo.com.br/

MUSIC LABELS IN BRAZIL

Biscoito Fino. http://www.biscoitofino.com.br/

EMI Music Brazil. http://www.emimusic.com.br/

Kuarup Records. http://www.kuarup.com.br/

Lumiar Discos and Editora. http://www.lumiar.com.br/

Sony/BMG Brazil. http://www.sonybmg.com.br/

Trama Records. http://trama.uol.com.br/

Universal Music Brazil. http://www.universalmusic.com.br/

Visom Digital. http://www.visomdiscos.com.br/

Warner Music Brazil. http://www.warnermusicstore.com.br/

INDEX

Chris McGowan has written about Brazilian music for *Billboard*, *Musician*, *Pulse!*, *The Beat*, and other publications, and contributed to *The Encyclopedia of Latin American History and Culture*. He blogs for the *Huffington Post* about Brazil and other subjects.

Ricardo Pessanha has worked as a Brazilian music consultant for foreign journalists, music producers, and filmmakers and as a music lecturer for academic programs. He has been a translator and publicity writer for recording companies in Brazil and is co-author of the musical biography *Caetano Veloso: L'âme brésilienne*, in French.